The Development of Economics in Western Europe since 1945

Are there distinct European traditions in economics? Is modern economics homogenous and American?

This volume explores the development of economics in Western Europe since the war. It goes beyond conventional history of economics in its emphasis on the historical and institutional context, economic policy, and the development of economics as a profession.

The volume includes case studies of the UK, Sweden, the Netherlands, Belgium, Germany, France, Italy, Portugal, Spain and Greece. Each of these examines the conditions relating to the supply of, and demand for, economists. These include: the growth of higher education; the development of postgraduate training in economics; international linkages, both within Europe and outside it; economic ideas and professionalization; and involvement in economics in the context of the postwar movement towards European integration.

A. W. Bob Coats has played a major role in the development of the history of economics, and in the emergence of the study of the Sociology and Professionalization of Economics. As well as publishing numerous articles, many in leading journals, he has edited fourteen books and two collections of his own articles.

Routledge Studies in the History of Economics

The Development of Economics in Western Europe since 1945

Edited by A. W. Bob Coats

London and New York

First published 2000
by Routledge
11 New Fetter Lane, London EC4P 4EE

Simultaneously published in the USA and Canada
by Routledge
29 West 35th Street, New York, NY 10001

Routledge is an imprint of the Taylor & Francis Group

© 2000 editorial and selection A. W. Coats

Typeset in Times New Roman by Stephen Wright-Bouvier
of the Rainwater Consultancy, Faringdon, Oxfordshire
Printed and bound in Great Britain by
Biddles Ltd, Guildford and King's Lynn

British Library Cataloguing in Publication Data
A catalogue record for this book is available
from the British Library

Library of Congress Cataloging in Publication Data

The development of economics in Western Europe since
    1945 / edited by A.W. Bob Coats.
        p.   cm.
    1. Economics–Europe, Western–History–20th century.
I. Coats, A. W. (Alfred William), 1924– .
    HB87.D44   1999
    330' .094' 09045–dc21   98–43368
                        CIP

ISBN 0–415–20291–4

Contents

Illustrations

Figures

Tables

Contributors

Salvador Almenar is Professor of the History of Economic Thought in the Economic Analysis Department of the University of Valencia. He has recently completed several monographs on the diffusion and influence of classical, marginal and Keynesian economics in Spain.

Roger E. Backhouse is Professor of the History and Philosophy of Economics at the University of Birmingham in England. He has published numerous books and articles on the history of modern economic analysis, methodology, and economic thought and policy. He is book review editor of *The Economic Journal*.

Carlos Bastien is Associate Professor at the Higher Institute of Economics and Business Administration in Lisbon, and a researcher at the Economic and Social History Bureau. He has written studies of the history of economics in nineteenth- and twentieth-century Portugal, Portuguese corporative economics, and the reception of modern economics.

Muriël Bouchet is an economist in the research department of the National Bank of Belgium. He has a Master of Sciences degree in economics from the University of Namur.

Erik Buyst is Professor of Economics and History at the University of Leuven. He has published several studies of the economic, social and political history of Belgium, and on the history of European integration.

A. W. Bob Coats is Emeritus Professor of Economic and Social History at the University of Nottingham, and formerly Research Professor of Economics at Duke University, and an Associate Editor of *History of Political Economy*. He is a Distinguished Fellow and past President of the History of Economics Society, and has published widely on the history, sociology and professionalization of economics. Two volumes of his collected essays have appeared (1992, 1993), and a third is in progress.

Harald Hagemann is Professor of Economic Theory at the University of Hohenheim, Stuttgart. He has been a Visiting Professor at universities in several countries and researches on macro-economic theory and policy, and technological change and employment, as well as the history of economics. He is an Editorial Board member of the *European Journal for the History of Economic Thought*, and is Treasurer and an Executive Committee member of the European Society for the History of Economic Thought.

Ivo Maes is an economist in the research department of the National Bank of Belgium and a Professor at the University of Leuven. He has been an administrator at the Commission of the European Communities and a Visiting Professor at Duke University. He has written extensively on recent economic policy and the history of economics.

Henk W. Plasmeijer is an Associate Professor in the Economics Faculty of the University of Groningen. His main research has been in political economy, and he has published books on the theory of unproductive labour (in Dutch) and edited several books, including histories of Dutch and Continental Economic thought. He is managing editor of *Tijdschrift voor Politieke Ekonomie*.

Pier Luigi Porta is Professor of Economics and Director of the Institute of Political Economy at the University of Milan. He has worked extensively on the Cambridge School and has edited several volumes of Sraffa's *Ricardo*, in Italian. He is currently working on the definition and implications of the classical canon in political economy and on issues in the history of Italian economic thought.

Michalis Psalidopoulos is Associate Professor in the Department of Sociology in the Panteion University of Political and Social Sciences, Athens. He has written three books, edited three volumes of essays, and published numerous articles in Greek, German and English, mainly on aspects of the history of economic thought in Greece.

Bo Sandelin is in the Department of Economics at the University of Gothenberg, where he took his doctorate in 1977. He has written extensively on housing economics and the economics of crime, and *The History of Swedish Economic Thought* (1991). He has published numerous journal articles and book chapters, and has edited *Economist Debatt*.

Nikias Sarafoglou is Associate Professor of Economics at Mid-Sweden University. He received his PhD in economics from Umea University in 1988. His current research interests include public sector efficiency, diffusion of research on production efficiency and complexity theory.

Christian Schmidt is Professor of Economics at the University Paris-Dauphine (France). His works include the history of economic thought, the epistemology of economics, game theory and the economics of defence. Among many publications he is editor of *Uncertainty in Economic Thought*, and co-editor with K. Arrow of *Rational Foundations and Economic Behaviour*.

Evert Schoorl is Director of Graduate Studies at the Research School of Economics, Management and Organization at the University of Groningen. He has published on Dutch economic thought and policy, is an associate editor of the *Oeuvres Complètes de Jean-Baptiste Say*, and has recently written *Working for the World Economy* (1998) with the former OECD secretary-general, Emile van Lennvys.

Ann Veiderpass is Assistant Professor of Economics at the University of Gothenberg. Her main research interest is production theory – non-parametric analyses of industry efficiency and productivity.

Preface

The essays in this volume embody the results of a preliminary collaborative effort to serve two distinct but interrelated purposes, namely: (1) to make a significant addition to the available knowledge of the development of economics as a discipline, science and policy profession in Western Europe since World War II; and (2) to place that development within the broader historical context of the postwar movement towards European integration. In both cases the term 'preliminary' is used advisedly with no disrespect to the authors (or, indeed, to the editor!), for this is pioneering work.

International comparative research on the post-1945 history of European economics is still a virgin field, though it is to be hoped that the recent founding of two scholarly organizations (the Annual European Conference on the History of Economics, and the European Society for the History of Economic Thought) and the launching of a new journal (The European Journal of the History of Economic Thought) may soon transform the situation. The country studies included herein have been written with the above-mentioned purposes in mind, and constitute original contributions to their respective areas. The list of European countries covered is incomplete, as attempts to extend the range of countries beyond Western Europe proved abortive. However, the concluding chapter incorporates some tentative intra-European East–West comparisons drawing on the work of Hans-Jurgen Wagener and his colleagues (*infra*, pp. 247–248). It seems unlikely that the addition of the nations omitted would require a substantial modification of the comparative observations made in the first and last chapters of this volume, written by the editor. In the introductory chapter there are examples of the impact of the European integration movement on the demand for economists, and supply-side influences, such as the growth of higher education; the development of postgraduate training in economics; international linkages, both intra- and extra-European; economic ideas and professionalization and involvement in economic policy-making and public affairs. The chapter ends with a brief review of some distinctive features of the country studies. In the Concluding Reflections some common themes and trends are outlined; the ten countries are subdivided (no doubt somewhat arbitrarily) into three groups; and there is a more extended consideration of the distinctive features of the policy process in the

European institutions. Finally, there is a brief comment on the question, is there a European economics? This has been the subject of discussion in recent years.

One feature of this study is that it goes beyond the conventional treatment of the history of economics in terms of the history of ideas, theories, analysis, doctrines and so on, to include relevant aspects of the historical and institutional context and the work of economists in the policy process. In this respect it follows on from earlier comparative studies of the role of economists in national governments and international agencies and, more broadly still, the internationalization of economics. (A list of these studies is provided below, in the first note to the Introduction.) Like the first and third of these projects, the present study transcends the limits of the Anglo-Saxon tradition, which has hitherto dominated the history of economics.

This project has had an unusually protracted period of gestation. The initial scheme was announced at the Second Annual European Conference of the History of Economics held in Lisbon, in February 1996, when early versions of three country studies were presented. The full team of contributors met for a workshop at International Hall, the University of London, in December 1996, to consider the entire undertaking and to discuss draft papers and plan this volume. Invited guests on that occasion were Professor Bruno Frey and Dr Reiner Eichenberger of the University of Zurich, and Dr Roger Middleton of the University of Bristol, England. Professor Frey acted as a general commentator on the papers. During 1997 and 1998 the publication process was delayed owing to the inordinately slow delivery of final versions of some papers, some of which went through several drafts, and to the editor's periods of ill health.

The organizer of an undertaking of this kind inevitably becomes indebted to various individuals and institutions. Some of the participants in the project have been unfailingly helpful, and it is a pleasure to acknowledge the essential funding provided by the Nuffield Foundation's Small Grants Scheme, which was used primarily to cover the costs of the London Workshop and the provision of secretarial and administrative assistance. Additional aid and support was provided by Professor Rob Castle and the staff of the Department of Economics at the University of Wollongong, New South Wales, while I was a Visiting Professor from April to July 1997. Also I wish to express my warm thanks to Professor Chris Milner and the staff of the Department of Economics at the University of Nottingham, my home base, who provided encouragement and various forms of practical assistance. Without the Department's imprimatur, this project would have been impossible.

Above all, I wish to thank my wife, Sonia E. Coats, who, at considerable personal cost provided all the indispensable secretarial and administrative needs, and the psychological support required to bring this project to fruition.

1   Introduction

A. W. Bob Coats

This international comparative study of the post-World War II development of economics in Western Europe forms part of a long-term effort to go beyond the conventional treatment of the history of economics in terms of the history of ideas, theory, analysis, doctrines and so on (useful and important though that is). It includes consideration of the relevant features of the historical and institutional context, economic policy, and the development of economics as a profession.[1] Another objective is to transcend the limits of the Anglo-Saxon historiographical tradition, which has hitherto dominated the subject.

Although the history of European economic ideas has not been entirely neglected by scholars, most of the relevant literature has been written from the standpoint of a particular country or region. Those scholars bold or foolhardy enough to treat Europe as a whole encounter formidable difficulties owing to the continent's diversity: the number of countries involved, each with its distinctive language and culture, historical experiences, political, administrative and educational system, level of economic development, and methods of economic management. These difficulties can be at least partly overcome, as in the present case, by enlisting the expertise of a team of authors each writing on certain common themes from a particular national perspective. This enterprise is more feasible than it might otherwise appear since it is confined to the post-1945 period, during which time there has been remarkable and unprecedented progress towards European economic and political interdependence, cooperation and integration,[2] perhaps eventually leading to unification. This historical situation has given economists unprecedented opportunities to make intellectual and technical contributions to the European movement, and to shape (and be shaped by) the course of events.

The historical context of post-1945 economics in Europe: a brief outline

During the past half-century there has been a remarkable growth and widening range of employment opportunities for trained economists throughout the world, not only in the rapidly expanding higher education sector, but also in a bewildering array of public and private institutions, including national and local governments; parastatal and quasi-public bodies; private businesses – banking industrial and commercial; and international agencies such as the IMF, World Bank, and other United Nations bodies.[3] In early postwar Europe economists became directly involved in the reconstruction and recovery processes, and in subsequent years the development of the mixed economy, the welfare state and other forms of state intervention ensured the continuing public demand for their services. Of particular interest to the present study is the growth of the European Community economic, social and political institutions, a complex process which can only be briefly sketched here.[4]

The antecedents of the European integration movement can be traced back well before World War II, but the postwar phase dates from the later1940s with the United Nations Economic Commission for Europe (1946), the Marshall Plan (1947; i.e. the European Recovery Programme), the creation of the Organization for European Economic Cooperation (OEEC, 1948), the Council of Europe (1949), and – of crucial importance to subsequent economic affairs – the European Coal and Steel Community (ECSC, 1951). Later developments were distinctly uneven, and the process is usually considered to fall into four broad phases:

1   the so-called Euro-optimism phase, 1958–72, based on the Treaty of Rome (1957) and the European Community institutions – the ECSC, the European Economic Community (EEC, 1958) and the European Atomic Energy Commission (EAEC, 1958);
2   a period of stagnation or Euro-pessimism, 1972–84, influenced (among other factors) by the external shocks of the first and second oil crises, the breakdown of the Bretton Woods system and, internally, the bitter budgetary crisis (in which Britain was especially intransigent), and problems associated with the enlargement of the Community's membership;
3   a phase of renewed dynamism and relevance from 1984 to the early 1990s, centering on the Single European Act (1986), further Community enlargement, the Maastricht Treaty (1991), and the movement towards a common currency and monetary system – deriving from the Economic and Monetary Union (EMU, 1969) and the Economic and Monetary System (EMS, 1979).
4   The1990s to the present when attention has focused on the movement towards monetary union, the discussion of common fiscal measures, and the addition of new member states both from inside and outside Western Europe.

This 'rich tapestry of organizations'[5] and agreements is far too intricate to be unravelled here, but its evolution is directly relevant to this project, since the Community organizations provided abundant opportunities for economists to utilize their skills and exert their influence, domestically, transnationally and even internationally.

Politics has undoubtedly played a major, indeed predominant, role in determining the pace and extent of post-1945 European integration, and it will therefore be helpful to recall briefly the highly divergent experiences of the countries included in this project. Sweden and Britain have obviously enjoyed the greatest measure of political continuity over the pre- and post-war periods, for Sweden was neutral during World War II and the British did not suffer under Nazi (or Fascist) rule – unlike Belgium, France, Greece, Italy, the Netherlands, Portugal and Spain. Germany is of course a special case given her comprehensive defeat in 1945, the Nazi legacy, and the subsequent division into the territories of the West and East, each with its own government. Moreover, the influence of Nazism did not disappear in 1945 in West Germany.

The variety of dates on which the various countries joined or were admitted to the EEC (later the European Union; EU) further illustrates the heterogeneity of European political conditions. The timing of these moves was in no way directly correlated with the political experiences referred to in the preceding paragraph. For example, France and Germany, opponents in three major nineteenth- and twentieth-century conflicts, combined in taking the initiative in establishing the Coal and Steel Community which led, six years later, in 1957, to the Treaty of Rome. From the start of this process they were joined by Belgium, Italy, Luxembourg and the Netherlands to form what became known as 'the inner six'. Britain refused to participate on the grounds that membership would entail a loss of national sovereignty. However, subsequently, after two unsuccessful applications for entry, in 1961 and 1967, both of which were vetoed by de Gaulle, Britain was finally admitted in 1973, together with Denmark and Eire. Before that, however, as a counterweight to the EEC Common Market, Britain had joined with other non-EEC members (Austria, Denmark, Norway, Portugal, Sweden and Switzerland) to form the European Free Trade Area (EFTA), in 1960. This group of nations became known as 'the outer seven'.

Acceptance as a full member of the EC has become dependent on the establishment (or restoration) of democratic government. Thus Greece, having experienced totalitarian rule under the Colonels' military regime from 1967 to 1974, did not obtain entry until 1981, despite a long period of preparation. Both Portugal and Spain, having emerged from long periods of dictatorship in 1974 and 1975 respectively, applied for full membership in 1977 and were admitted in 1986. In this piecemeal fashion the European Union has comprised a changing and discontinuously expanding complement of member states, and it will undoubtedly continue to do so in the future, for some time probably at an increasing pace. (At the time of writing the present number of members is fifteen, and eleven further countries are seeking membership in an enlarged EU.)

The demand for economists

How have these developments affected the demand for economists? Four diverse but striking examples from the process of European integration must suffice.[6] First, in 1948, when the OEEC was established to distribute resources under the European Recovery Programme (Marshall Plan) prospective recipient countries were required to submit detailed estimates of how the Marshall funds were to be spent, as well as projections of economic growth, the national budget and foreign trade. These calculations necessarily created an urgent demand for economists, and it is said that the shortage of economic expertise in the Italian government was so great that most of the work had to be farmed out to universities or to private research institutions.[7] This may be viewed, roughly speaking, as the beginning of a demand for economists that has continued to grow as the tapestry of European institutions has become larger and more intricate.

Second, when a non-member country applies to join the European Community a tremendous amount of time and effort must necessarily be expended, both in the applicant country and in the Community's institutions, in the preparation of a persuasive case, examining its compatibility with existing laws, treaties and practices, and in negotiating the terms of entry. In some instances this has proved to be a very prolonged process – for example, twenty-two years in the case of Greece, and twenty-five years in the Spanish case – starting with an application for 'association' and eventually leading to final acceptance.[8] The demands of the Community's mechanisms and bureaucracy have been described as 'awesome', for although a remarkably small number of persons may be directly involved in the actual negotiations there is a vast amount of necessary background preparation involving groups of experts – for example, lawyers, economists and statisticians. In a small country this can put a heavy strain on the available supply of trained personnel. A considerable number of overlapping issues are involved, which are often being negotiated at different speeds and times,[9] and proposals initially based on strictly economic criteria may often be subsequently modified in compromises involving *ad hoc* solutions. Although political considerations generally take priority over economic considerations, it is often the economic and technical issues that dominate the actual negotiations. In these circumstances economists can play a significant role, although they are necessarily subordinate to the politicians and diplomats, and of course the ministers, involved.[10]

Third, consideration of possible membership in the European institutions can obviously generate a demand for economists, even if the idea is rejected. Thus in the Swedish case the proposal to join the European Monetary Union led to the appointment of a government commission to examine the pros and cons. The commission consisted of seven leading Swedish economists and political scientists; and twenty-six Swedish and international social scientists, most of them economists, contributed twenty-one separately published appendices to the main report. The commission's conclusion was that despite political arguments in favour of joining, the economic case was inadequate. Hence on balance the report opposed participation, at least not before 1999.[11] No doubt the proposal will be reconsidered in the future.

Fourth, the role of economists within the various European institutions has so far attracted little scholarly attention, a state of affairs that enhances the value of Ivo Maes's careful study of their position and activities in the European Commission (in Coats 1997). Maes has examined in detail the respective functions of the Secretariat-General and the twenty-two Directorates-General, with special reference to DGII, Economic and Financial Affairs, which is essentially the Commission's research department. He has also examined the nationality and academic background of the 'professional economists' employed in the Commission, and concludes that in terms of methodology and world-view, they seem more heterogeneous than those employed in the IMF or the World Bank. This heterogeneity reflects the diversity among European universities, so that as a general rule, British economists are more free market orientated and Frenchmen more activist; Germans are typically more concerned with questions of economic order and policies necessary for the functioning of a free market (e.g. competition policy). Belgian economists are especially well represented in the Commission partly because of its location in Brussels; but there is also a sizeable number from Italy, Spain and Greece, possibly because of the comparative lack of good positions for well-qualified persons with advanced economics education in these countries.[12]

Economists in the European Community institutions have been primarily concerned with problems of economic organization and integration of the various member countries' economies and policies. This can be a delicate and controversial matter, as for example, in dealing with tax harmonization. The differences between the various countries' objectives concern not only the liberalization of economic policy, but also such sensitive issues as the transfer of sovereignty. Maes denies that the interdependence of economic and political considerations was such that the Commission's economists are essentially functioning as technicians, trying to persuade people or countries to adopt policies that are set up for them for political reasons. They are engaged in genuine economic analysis; but it was said, jokingly, that to identify oneself as an economist in the organization could entail a loss of political influence.[13]

In the discussions within the Commission of the path towards European monetary integration there have been two basic approaches: that of the 'monetarist' and the 'economist' – terms used in the organization in an unusual way. According to the monetarists, monetary integration would stimulate the integration process generally and contribute to a convergence of the various countries' economic policies and performance via the stabilization of exchange rates. These views were held particularly in France, Belgium, Luxembourg and Italy, as well as in the Commission, whose officials on monetary matters were usually French or Italian. The 'economists',[14] on the other hand, emphasized the country differences in inflation, productivity and government finances, arguing that a convergence of economic performances and economic policy was a necessary precondition of monetary integration. Without sufficient convergence the fixing of the exchange rate could break down or lead to major regional problems. These ideas were most prominent in Germany, especially at the Bundesbank, and to a lesser extent in the Netherlands.

The supply of economists

Turning to the supply side, the remarkable post-1945 world-wide expansion in the number of trained economists is by now so familiar a phenomenon that it is usually taken for granted, and has therefore not been studied systematically. For the present purpose it is convenient to view European developments under five headings, which will provide a framework for the country studies that follow. They are:

1   the post-World War II growth of higher education;
2   the development of postgraduate education in economics;
3   international linkages;
4   economic ideas in Europe; and
5   professionalization and involvement in economic policy-making and public affairs

The postwar growth of higher education

The pace, extent and timing of this process has, of course, varied between countries, and there have been marked discontinuities. The state's willingness to fund institutions has been the determining factor, as private provision has been comparatively insignificant – although in rare cases the state has subsidized certain private institutions. Until recently the British situation was unique in Western Europe since the universities were public institutions, almost entirely financed by the state, yet enjoying effective autonomy in academic affairs. Lately, however, there has been a dramatic growth of government intervention and control.

The net effect of these developments has been to increase the heterogeneity of European higher educational institutions and, on balance, to reduce academic standards – e.g. via increased student/staff ratios, overstraining library and research facilities, and heavier reliance on textbooks and other simplifying and time-saving teaching aids. On the other hand, the changes have provided opportunities for innovative pedagogical and organizational methods, especially where state control has been relaxed.[15] Inevitably there has been resistance to change, and generation conflicts, but the general effect has been to undermine the influence of the older universities and the hegemony of the national elite intellectual, cultural and occupational establishment. In economics, for example, the newer or reformed Continental universities have flatly rejected the traditional Continental European system – in which political economy constituted an integral part of a broad law-school curriculum – and facilitated the spread of an Anglo-American type of specialization (see *infra*, p. 7, on graduate education).

Expansion has been achieved in one or more of the following ways:

1   increasing the size of existing universities;

2   creating new universities, ostensibly of comparable standards and usually, but not invariably, of similar organization and structure;

3   conferring university status on existing high-quality non-university institutions – for example, in the case of economics, transforming vocationally orientated business schools into economics departments or faculties;

4   deliberate upgrading of institutions recognized as being initially of lower academic quality than the older-established universities;

5   reducing the length of the undergraduate degree course – however, proposals of this kind were controversial and were implemented, if at all, only after considerable delay.

Of course, the growth of higher education has been fuelled by the general growth of population, the ever-rising public demand for undergraduate degrees, and by government financial aid to undergraduates in the form of grants and scholarships. The extent of this support has, of course, been very different in different countries.

Graduate education in economics

Organized graduate education in economics was non-existent in Europe immediately after 1945, and it has subsequently developed slowly and very unevenly. As in prewar years, an advanced degree could be obtained without formal instruction, and for those studying abroad Germany was still the preferred country until the later 1930s, followed by France. After the war the USA became the principal magnet owing to its superior educational facilities and the availability of generous scholarships and fellowships supplemented by Fulbright travel grants. The outflow of students from Britain to the United States especially benefited from these resources, and the countries' common language was a significant enabling factor. In Sweden, one of the most outwardly orientated European countries, the number of doctoral degrees in economics increased from one in 1945 to a peak of thirty in 1993, and at one point a leading Swedish economist even suggested (perhaps only half seriously) that graduate education should be abandoned at home and the funds thereby saved used to finance scholarships abroad. This proposal was not welcomed, however, for graduate students enrich the local and national academic environment, and also provide a substantial cadre of teaching and research assistants and other academic underlabourers. There is also the fear of encouraging a substantial brain drain. Countries like Portugal, Spain and Greece, with less well-developed educational facilities, have naturally been more dependent on foreign resources and have periodically employed Americans and other foreigners on temporary contracts.

Cultural conditions have significantly influenced the degree of internationalization of economics education. The Dutch, Belgians and Scandinavians, for example, have been more cosmopolitan than the French, although the latter's language has been much more widely accessible. In France the traditional division between the law faculty economists and the economist engineers in the

Grandes Ecoles has meant that the latter have been more hospitable to theoretical analysis, mathematics and econometrics. Despite some evidence of confluence between the two streams in recent years the distinction still persists, and graduate work in economics is more flourishing in the Ecoles. Even so, relatively few French students who take a doctorate go abroad to obtain their degrees.

Like the Scandinavians, the Dutch have been more outwardly orientated than the French, and they have developed a powerful tradition of quantitative economics that has sometimes been described as the Tinbergenization of post-1945 Dutch economics (and, indeed, of Anglo-Saxon economics as a whole). There is a well-developed system of advanced training in economics, and economists have been prominent in the Central Planning Bureau, the Central Bureau of Statistics and other major policy-making institutions.

Belgium is more complex, for while the development of graduate education has more closely resembled the Dutch than the French model, the existence of two distinct, and sometimes hostile, language communities has been the source of recurrent difficulties in academic as in political life. There is no equivalent elsewhere in Europe to the extraordinary division of the long-established University of Leuven into a Flemish and francophone university, with the francophone institution moving to a newly created town, Louvain la Neuve.

International linkages

Although the internationalization of economists, economic ideas and practices obviously did not begin after 1945, the subsequent transformation of global communication has been such as to make this era different in kind, as well as in scale, from earlier periods.

Internationalization can be defined in various ways. At the limit it means that economists throughout many countries come to use similar analytical concepts, techniques, methodology, language and theories and that distinctively national schools of thought techniques and practices tend to disappear (De Vries 1997: 350; Williamson 1997: 357–8). It also involves the training of indigenous economists, whether at home or abroad, in a particular foreign approach or body of ideas. (A neglected concomitant is the development of more uniform statistical concepts and data, without which international comparisons of aggregate data – such as national income, inflation rates, trade balances and so on – would be seriously misleading.)

Internationalization is, at least potentially, a two- or a multiple-way process. It is not the same as Americanization, which implies a single source of influences. In the present study intra-European processes need to be emphasized, as well as transatlantic interactions. European *émigrés* made outstanding contributions to the development of 'American'-style economics, and distinguished European econometricians (e.g. Frisch and Tinbergen) were leading early contributors to the highly internationalized Econometric Society.

The internationalization of economics has involved the movement of vast numbers of individuals, including, for example, students seeking credentials and new experiences; qualified economists seeking lucrative and stimulating foreign employment – both academic and non-academic; those who believe that experience abroad will subsequently enhance their career prospects at home; academic economists undertaking teaching or research abroad – whether in universities, governments, or the innumerable private and public research organizations; government and other officials; economic advisers or consultants; and employees in international banks, industrial and commercial enterprises. The list is endless, and our selected countries provide examples of all these types. However, there are no comprehensive international statistics from which gross and net flows of economists can be constructed.

Indices of the internationalization of economics include: the percentage of students at all levels who have studied or are studying abroad; the percentage of faculty members with foreign degrees; the percentage of foreign nationals holding university teaching or research posts; the content, language and authors' affiliations of articles in economic journals; citations of foreign articles, books – especially textbooks (whether in their original form, or adapted for students in other countries), monographs and research materials. In many instances books are published simultaneously in several countries, so that it is not always easy to identify their national origin; and in some cases journals are printed abroad and even edited from a third country. Some well-established indigenous journals have switched to English to extend their readership and enhance their status in the international community of economists, while some new periodicals are published in the lingua franca, rather than in the language of origin. In Sweden, one of the most internationalized countries in Europe, the percentage of doctoral dissertations in economics written in English has been rising in the long term, reaching 100 per cent in the 1990s – most of the officially appointed 'opponents' have been foreign. The Swedish evidence suggests that internationalization has proceeded in waves, rather than continuously.

Chance plays a major role in the international experience of individual economists. In the French case, for example, Malinvaud and Debreu both went to the USA early in their careers; the former returned home, the latter (later a Nobel Prize winner) did not. By contrast, Maurice Allais, an engineer economist who won the Nobel Prize, and claimed that he was virtually self-taught as an economist, made his entire career in France. Many other examples could be cited, including other Nobel laureates.

In numerous instances a series of graduate students from a given country study abroad at a particular foreign university with which close relationships have been established: for example, the Greek–Yale group of economists who were said to constitute a kind of professional 'mafia' in the Bank of Greece and the Ministry of Planning. They were resented by some of those Greek economists who had lacked the opportunity to be trained abroad, and whose careers had consequently been adversely affected. In Greece, Spain and Portugal during the early postwar decades there were intra-continental connections dating back to prewar days, and it was not until the later 1970s that more 'modern' links with the UK and the USA became dominant.[16]

One clear indication of internationalization is the authorship and citation of articles in leading journals, and references to foreign books. Detailed analysis of some of this material is provided in the British, Dutch, Belgian and Swedish chapters in this volume. Yet another, quite different, indication of internationalization is the establishment of the so-called European Doctoral Programme in Quantitative Economics, introduced by the francophone University of Leuven, in collaboration with the London School of Economics and the Rheinische Friedrichs-Wilhelms-Universität, Bonn. This could well represent a wave of the future.

The extent of internationalization (or Anglicization?) in Sweden is such that it has been claimed that there has been no distinctively Swedish economics since the early 1950s, despite that country's veritable galaxy of native economists in the 1930s and after.[17] However, our Swedish participant acknowledged that there were in fact specific (though not necessarily unique) Swedish economic problems not of interest to foreign economists, which continued to engage his countrymen's economists.

Economic ideas in Europe

Economic ideas in our selected countries have not, of course, been insulated from world-wide trends and movements, although the internationalization process has exerted a greater influence on economic policy than on economic ideas, theories or models. Economic liberalism, Marxism, German historical economics, various varieties of Keynesianism, and monetarism, can all be found in certain situations and times.[18] In Portugal and Italy corporatist ideas[19] were a concomitant and/or legacy of fascist dictatorial regimes. But while this approach seriously inhibited the development of more modern ideas in both countries, in Italy the strong tradition of economic liberalism survived throughout the interwar years and after. Generally speaking, the less developed lands – for example, Greece and Spain (but Portugal less so) were more receptive to German historical economics, which survived the war in various eclectic combinations, for the political climate was less congenial to Anglo-Saxon economics, especially in the early postwar decades. During the 1980s and 1990s, however, the Americanization of Spanish economic literature virtually eliminated Marxist, Post-Keynesian, institutionalist and evolutionist economic ideas.

In the Netherlands, the Austrian economic ideas that had been prominent before the war continued to wane thereafter, but the subsequent prevalence of Keynesian economics was due more to its policy relevance than to its theoretical content. Tinbergen's work at the Central Planning Bureau constituted a species of proto-Keynesian socialism that was central to the creation of a 'bargaining economy', with a social partnership rather than a countervailing power relationship between government, employers and trade unions. The emphasis on econometrics, quantitative economics and macro-economic model building was probably greater in the Netherlands than elsewhere, and in Sweden too the early postwar Keynesianism later gave way to a more technocratic approach to quantitative research and economic policy-making. As in some other countries, the

1980s witnessed a decline in the support for interventionism, the rise of monetarism, and the demand for deregulation. While there was no doctrinaire opposition to economic interventionism in Sweden, there was no strong planning movement, unlike the situation in Norway and the Netherlands. In the latter country ethical economics and social economics continued to be taught at the Catholic University of Tilburg and at the Free University of Amsterdam. In later decades heterodox economics was gradually marginalized, despite a wave of radicalism from the later 1960s.

In Belgium, Marshall was still used as a textbook in the 1950s, but here too the postwar climate of opinion was primarily Keynesian. Links with the OEEC (and later the European Commission) were important in the development of Belgian economics, and there was a significant monetarist group at the Flemish Catholic University of Leuven.

Professionalization and involvement in economic policy making and public affairs

On the European continent, by contrast with Britain, professors of economics have customarily been prominent and active in public affairs, even while continuing to hold their academic chairs. Indeed, public service has often been regarded as an inescapable concomitant of their professorial responsibilities, and this is generally compatible with the higher cultural status of the professoriat on the European continent than in the United States. European economists have occasionally served as national Heads of State (e.g. Einaudi in Italy) or Prime Minister (e.g. Eyskens in Belgium, Erhard in Germany, Einaudi and Prodi in Italy, Papandreou in Greece, Salazar in Portugal).[20] Much more frequent, however, have been the appointments of economists as cabinet ministers (usually Minister of Finance, and/or Treasury and/or Economic Affairs); official or unofficial advisers to government, or to particular ministers; heads or members of public commissions or regulatory bodies, or as Director of the Central Bank, Central Planning Bureau, Statistical Office, or some such body.

It is difficult to gauge in which countries economists have been most active and influential (a term lacking a precise and unambiguous meaning), but Sweden, the Netherlands and Belgium would surely rate highly in our sample. However, such a general assessment can be misleading, for an individual economist may be disproportionately influential, even if few economists occupy high public office, especially if the profession as a whole is weak or poorly organized. In addition to influence on policy decisions, the economists' impact on public discourse and the political agenda should also be considered.

There are times and circumstances enhancing the economists' public role – e.g. when the country is in an economic crisis or in the process of applying for entry into the European Community; and the concomitant increase in demand for their services may be disproportionately great in the case of small countries, like Eire. An authoritarian regime (as in Portugal) or a military dictatorship (as with the Greek junta in the 1970s) may empower economists if they are viewed as technocrats capable of improving economic performance and thereby further-ing the regime's goals. Nevertheless, in Portugal economists have been most influential since the mid-l980s and are still influential in quantitative terms and in the political discourse and agenda.

Needless to say, the economists' collective reputation is difficult to gauge, but in certain obvious cases (e.g. Britain and the Netherlands) the profession's high prestige of the early postwar (Keynesian) years has not been maintained in more recent decades. However, the level of economic development, and the country's importance in international affairs, do not seem to have been determining factors (e.g. Greece, Portugal and perhaps Italy). Obviously, doctrinal and ideological divisions and conflicts within the community of economists are damaging to the profession's scientific status.

There is, of course, much more to professionalization than prominence in public affairs, but it is difficult to find reliable indices of effective professional organization and cohesion. The formation of a national association of economists – as in Greece (in 1951) and Portugal (in l976) – is probably an unreliable guide.[21] Despite their relatively weak professionalization, individual French economists played a prominent role in the formation of the International Economic Association in the early postwar years. The Belgian initiative in launching the European Economic Association in the early 1980s is a more convincing example, for Belgian economists had already founded *The Euro-pean Economic Review,* in l969. Like the Dutch and Scandinavians, they were decidedly 'outward orientated'.[22]

The growth in the number of transnational intra-European societies and journals has contributed to the trend towards a more homogenous European economics.

A brief review of the country studies

The following paragraphs are designed to highlight some of the distinctive features of the individual countries. Similarities and more general themes will be treated in the Concluding Reflections (pp. 245–257).

Britain

Despite Britain's long and intellectually distinguished tradition in economics, the discipline was poorly organized and institutionally weak in the early post-1945 years. The subsequent university expansion, especially from the late 1960s, brought a shift of power and influence away from the prewar centres – Cambridge, London and Oxford – towards the more flexible and innovative new universities. As elsewhere, economics became more specialized, mathematical, quantitative and professional – although recently the academic community has been 'proletarianized', largely owing to central government controls and financial pressures. Undergraduate teaching has declined in importance relative to postgraduate training and research, a change both directly and indirectly influenced by American aims and methods. Nevertheless, the indigenous academic culture was resistant to change, especially in the older elite universities – hence its mid-Atlantic or hybrid character.

Sweden

Economics in Sweden has gradually been transformed since 1945, despite the constraints on academic life imposed by central government. The small, but outstandingly gifted leading members of the prewar generation of economists inevitably passed away, but their successors have continued to be heavily involved in public affairs, at least until recently. Swedish economic policy-making has tended to be economist-intensive and economists have served as ministers, Members of Parliament and as public officials. The seven-fold increase in the number of university chairs in economics has been accompanied by increasing specialization and subject differentiation, but the expansion of postgraduate training and research has been slow. There has been a striking increase in the use of English in doctoral theses, journals and books – so that Swedish economics has been denationalized – internationalized as much as, if not more than, Americanized.

The Netherlands

Although World War II did not represent a complete break with the past in Dutch economics, either intellectually or organizationally, it accelerated the decline of the law-school tradition, the growth of the link between academic economics and business education, and facilitated the progress of modernization and internationalization. Like their Swedish counterparts, Dutch economists have played an important part in public policy-making, through the Central Planning Bureau, the Netherlands Bank and other major public institutions. Jan Tinbergen exercised so great an influence on the discipline that the development of postwar economics in the Netherlands (and indeed, it has been claimed, throughout the Anglo-Saxon world) has been characterized as Tinbergenization. This has involved, for example: belief in the natural science ideal of economic knowledge; the conception of economic theory (including Keynesianism) in instrumentalist terms; a heavy emphasis on quantification; the preoccupation with macro-economics; the persistence of a strong tradition in monetary economics; and a great interest in European integration. Despite a tendency towards homogenization in economics training and research, American influence has been limited.

Belgium

Belgium has been inhibited by the coexistence and rivalry between the French- and Flemish-speaking intellectual, educational and political communities. There were few universities, and the discipline was dominated by a small number of professors (mandarins) with differing academic preoccupations and interests. With the rapid educational expansion of the 1960s, however, new research and career opportunities were opened up. Research seminars and institutions – notably the Centre for Operations Research and Econometrics at Leuven (later at Louvain la Neuve) – led to advances in mathematical economics, game theory and macro-economic modelling. Communications and exchanges between Belgian and foreign economists increased markedly; and collaborative doctoral programmes involving three or more countries have been launched. The widening geographical sources and institutional affiliations of authors in Belgian economic journals constitute further evidence of growing internationalization. The location of the European Community institutions in Brussels has encouraged research on economic integration, and provided abundant employment and educational opportunities for Belgian economists.

France

In France the traditional division between the prestigious university law-school professors of political economy and the so-called 'economic engineers' of the Grandes Ecoles has persisted. The latter species has led the modernization of economics in the country, often becoming high-level civil servants with influential positions in public administration. In recent decades there has been some convergence between the two categories, but government control of the universities has inhibited structural change, despite the rapid expansion in higher education. The centralized appointments system has inhibited academic mobility. Although there have long been national (often sectarian) organizations of economists, and individual French economists took a leading part in establishing the International Economic Association, the professionalization of economics has been generally late and weak. Collectively speaking, French economists have been somewhat insular, and innovative movements like the regulation and convention schools have not aroused much interest among other European economists. Language seems to have been a greater barrier to internationalization in France than in the smaller European countries, whose national languages are more inaccessible to English speakers.

Germany

Economics in the German-speaking countries was severely crippled by the effects of the Nazi period, wartime, and the large emigration of many of its leading practitioners. In the early postwar years the Allied powers, in an effort to restore academic freedom and autonomy, ceded effective power in the academic community to an older generation of (non-Nazi) professors, many of whom lacked the capacity or the desire to produce distinguished research. In the subsequent post-1945 university expansion economics was usually closely associated with business studies, not to its advantage. Economic ideas were prominent in the development of Ordoliberalism and the emergence of the social market economy policy, which was directly influenced by party political considerations. Keynesian ideas exerted a limited impact except in the early postwar years, yet a distinctive blend of Keynesianism and the neo-classical synthesis persisted. The strong emphasis on monetary stability meant that the mark was often undervalued in the Bretton Woods system, so that even before monetarism exerted a growing influence from the 1970s, Germany's economic growth (miracle) was largely export-led. There were significant developments in mathematical economics and game theory, with one Nobel Prize awarded to a German (Reinhard Selten). Economics became more technical and Anglicized, for example in professional journals, and European integration figured prominently in postgraduate work.

Italy

Economics in Italy has long been internationally orientated, yet the influence of Americanization has been limited partly owing to the country's educational system. Despite the rapid postwar expansion of higher education the progress of political economy in the university curriculum has been very slow, especially at the postgraduate level. Even the dramatic 'reform' of 1969 did not bring about significant structural change in the system. Young, would-be academic career economists often had to go abroad to obtain the requisite advanced professional training. Doctrinal divisions within the Italian economics community have been marked, most noticeably between the long-established liberal/*laissez-faire* approach to economic policy and the quasi-corporatist predominance in industrial policy and in economic planning. There was also a vigorous Marxist stream of thought with strong links to Cambridge, England. Many leading economists have been prominent in the country's economic and political affairs, but the professional organization of economics has been limited.

Portugal

After 1945 economics became an integral part of Portugal's modernization process. Even under the dictatorship, the dominant corporatism was neither stagnant nor inflexible, but it failed to provide a *via media* between socialism and capitalism. The rapid expansion of higher education from the 1960s freed economics from its subordinate position in the engineering and law faculties, facilitating increased specialization and disciplinary autonomy. Amid the considerable doctrinal pluralism there was limited support for Keynesianism either in theory or policy. The growth of research institutes and professional journals in economics revealed the economists' late but increasing involvement in the international scientific community, while domestically economists enjoyed enhanced public recognition and increased employment opportunities, in both the public and private sectors.

Spain

Prior to the 1960s, the development of economics in Spain was inhibited by the country's cultural isolation and the restrictive government controls over the academic community and public life. Thereafter, during the dictatorship, economists became heavily involved in the development and stabilization plans of the 1960s and 1970s, and some even obtained employment in international agencies. From the mid-1970s there was rapid growth and significant structural change in the universities, and economists penetrated more deeply into Spanish society as experts, ideologists and politicians: for example, as ministers. They were actively involved in negotiations for entry into the EEC. Interest in economic policy was greater than in economic theory, and although foreign textbooks had long been used in teaching, Spanish economic literature did not become internationalized until the 1980s. The development of economics in Spain has been very similar to that in Portugal, except for the absence of corporatist economics in Spain.

Greece

The junta's fall in 1974 marked the real beginning of the modernization of Greek economics. By this time most economists had studied abroad, either prewar in Germany or France, or later in the UK or USA. Greek academic life changed little from 1945 to 1970, and economics was still dominated by an older generation of professors. Doctoral pluralism flourished, with prominent schools of liberal-dirigiste, structuralist and Marxist proponents. Neither French economic liberalism nor Keynesianism was widely accepted, and the need for strong government was recognized. Economic growth and membership of the EEC were major policy objectives. After 1975 rapid expansion transformed the university system and facilitated the introduction of international ideas and practices.

Notes

1 This project is the fourth in a series organized and edited by the author. It includes: (1) *Economists in Government: An International Comparative Study* (1981). Focusing on the post-1945 period, the volume covers Australia, Brazil, India, Israel, Italy, Japan, the Netherlands, Norway, the UK and the USA; (2) *Economists in International Agencies: An Exploratory Study* (1986); (3) *The Post-1945 Internationalization of Economics* (1997), which includes eight country studies: Australia, Brazil, India, Italy, Japan, Korea, Sweden and the UK, also chapters on the European Community, the IMF, the World Bank, the role of economists in Latin America (two essays), a survey of post-1945 economic development doctrines, and a review of recent literature on the political economy of economic policy reform.
2 Unless otherwise stated these terms will be treated as interchangeable.
3 Cf. Coats (ed.) (1986).
4 There is, of course, an abundant secondary literature. I have found Tsoukalis (1992) and Laffan (1992) especially helpful.
5 Laffan 1992: 22ff.

6 The domestic demand for and employment of economists is considered in the country studies in Part II.

7 There were similar shortages in other countries (e.g. Belgium) because of the inadequacy of the national accounts. In Portugal the difficulty of finding qualified economists to participate in international discussion was one reason for the reform of economics teaching in l949. (It is said that when the figures were totted up the OEEC countries proposed to export to each other more than twice as much as they proposed to import from each other!)

8 This paragraph is based on Tsalicoglou (l995). By contrast, in Portugal no special economic studies were undertaken in support of the country's EEC application, probably because the issue was regarded primarily as a political matter. (I owe this reference to Carlos Bastien.)

9 For example, transport; environment and consumer protection; taxation; social affairs (including social security for migrant workers); institutional, budgetary, and staff regulation matters; agriculture; economic and financial affairs; right of establishment and freedom to provide services; rules of competition; Euratom Acts and EEC and ECSC Acts in the areas of research and energy; customs legislation; 'informatics' and statistics (Tsalicoglou 1995: 38). In the Greek case, agriculture was of critical importance to the applicant nation.

10 See the Concluding Reflections (pp. 248–50) for further discussion of this point.

11 I am indebted to Bo Sandelin for this example.

12 Important posts in the Commission's administration (e.g. Director-General) are allocated according to a quota system by nationality, and there is remarkable continuity in the occupation of senior positions by nationality. The higher the position, the greater the likelihood that a vacancy will be filled by somebody from outside the Commission with the appropriate nationality. Even at junior positions there is very great concern for 'equilibria', so that the different EC countries are represented.

13 Cf. Maes (1997: 366). Some writers on the economics of integration raise general questions about the proper role of economic research in situations where the objective of economic policy is non-economic – for example, Krauss (1993: 16–17). In many instances there is no clear-cut distinction between the two categories. For comments on the interactions of economics and politics in the European context see below (Concluding Reflections, p. 253).

14 Of course this does not mean that all the proponents of this view were professional economists, or that their opponents were monetarists in the narrower, doctrinal sense of the term. As Rosenthal observes, the 'differences of opinion about the correct method of instituting an economic and monetary union sprang both from different economic traditions and from deep-seated differences in political aims' (1975: 102), also Maes (1997: 263–5). Rosenthal provides a fascinating blow-by-blow account of the protracted negotiations over the proposals for monetary union in the period from December 1969 to February 1971 (1975: 102–25).

15 Such control prevailed early in our period in Spain and Portugal. In Greece, prior to the mid-1970s, strict control over curricular and appointment matters was maintained by senior professors backed by government regulations. While state control in Sweden has not prevented considerable adaptation and innovation, in Italy the major university 'reform' of 1969 was badly designed and ineffectively implemented. For example, the curriculum was radically changed from complete rigidity to complete flexibility. The requisite expansion of academic staff was achieved by appointing substantial numbers of annual appointees, but structural change was limited. The British situation has already been referred to (*supra*, p. 12). It is currently deeply depressing to one who has lived through the postwar golden age.

16 There are, of course, innumerable examples of international linkages, some quite exotic, like the training of African economists to PhD level at the WIDER development

institute in Helsinki. American links with India and Latin America are, however, more significant – for example, the notorious case of the Chicago Boys in Chile.

17 For example, Akerman, Hammarskjold, Heckscher, Lindahl, Lundberg, Myrdal, Ohlin, Palander.

18 Peter Hall's stimulating collection, *The Political Power of Economic Ideas: Keynesianism across Nations* (Princeton, 1989), gives a clear idea of the potentialities of international comparative studies of the dissemination of economic ideas.

19 Corporatism is difficult to define because it was not a coherent economic theory or doctrine, but rather a body of social and political ideas designed to resist modernization, industrialization and social change. It involved active collaboration between wealthy landowners, non-entrepreneurial industrialists and commercial bankers. Corporatist regimes opposed economic liberalism, socialism and Marxism, which were suppressed by government control of universities and political groups. The Portuguese version of corporatism was greatly influenced by the Italian example. It should, however, be noted that the term 'corporatist' has been applied to a wide variety of contexts. For example, Henk Plasmeijer and Evert Schoorl refer to the 'almost corporatistic fabric of organs linking government, employers and labour unions' in the post-1945 Netherlands (in a private letter to the editor).

Nevertheless, corporatism was not entirely negative. In certain cases a kind of corporatist-liberal synthesis emerged as a foundation for subsequent modernization.

For a suggestive interpretation of the economic, political, social and cultural relationships between economic ideas and policies in Spain, Portugal and Greece, see Holman (1996, especially chapters 1 and 2).

20 Some would include Harold Wilson in this list. However, like Keynes, he was never a professor. His degree was the non-specialist Oxford PPE, and in his brief period of service in British government he was officially a statistician, not an economist. (There were very few of the latter in the early postwar decades.)

21 For example, the Portuguese Association of Economists was already active in the early postwar years, and in the 1950s. Once again Britain was an odd case, for the prestigious Royal Economic Society, originally founded in the 1890s, did little to promote professional solidarity or influence until the 1980s, and even then only to a limited extent.

22 The role of economists in policy-making will be considered in the Concluding Reflections (p. 248), with special reference to the distinctive features of the European Community (Union) institutions. The question whether there is in fact a European economics will also be discussed.

References

Coats, A. W. (ed.) (1981) *Economists in Government, An International Comparative Study,* Durham, NC: Duke University Press.
—— (ed.) (1986) *Economists in International Agencies, An Exploratory Study*, New York: Praeger Scientific.
—— (ed.) (1997) *The Post-1945 Internationalization of Economics*, Durham, NC: Duke University Press.
De Vries, M. (1997) 'Comment', in A. W. Coats (ed.) *The Post-1945 Internationalization of Economics*, Durham, NC: Duke University Press, pp. 357–63.
Hall, Peter (1989) *The Political Power of Economic Ideas: Keynesianism across Nations*, Princeton: Princeton University Press.
Holman, Otto (1996) *Integrating Southern Europe: EC Expansion and the Transnationalization of Spain*, London: Routledge.
Krauss, M. B. (ed.) (1993) *The Economics of Integration*, London: Allen & Unwin.

Laffan, Brigid (1992) *Integration and Cooperation in Europe*, London: Routledge.

Maes, Ivo (1997) 'The Development of Economic Thought at the European Community Institutions', in Coats (ed.) *The Post-1945 Internationalization of Economics*, Durham, NC: Duke University Press, pp. 244–76.

Rosenthal, G. G. (1975) *The Men Behind the Decisions: Cases in European Policy-making*, Lexington, MA.: D. C. Heath.

Tsalicoglou, Iacovos S. (1995) *Negotiations for Entry: The Accession of Greece to the Economic Community*, Aldershot: Dartmouth Publishing Co.

Tsoukalis, Loukas (1992) *The New European Economy: The Politics and Economics of Integration*, Oxford: Oxford University Press.

Williamson, J. (1997) 'Comments', in Coats (ed.) *The Post-1945 Internationalization of Economics*, Durham, NC: Duke University Press, pp. 364–8.

2 Economics in mid-Atlantic

British economics, 1945–95

Roger E. Backhouse

Britain, continental Europe and the USA

From the numerous Europe–USA comparisons that have been made recently, several contrasts emerge. American economics, compared with that of Europe, is characterized by:

1 greater proneness to fashions and intolerance of heterodox ideas (Baumol 1995);
2 greater homogeneity across departments (Forte 1995), at least in research-orientated universities (Niehans 1995);
3 more competitive labour markets and higher mobility (Frech 1995; Tabellini 1995);
4 greater emphasis on technique and less emphasis on applied theory (Frey and Eichenberger 1992, 1993; Portes 1987; Eggertson 1995);
5 less hierarchical organization of departments, with individuals free to pursue independent research at a much earlier age (Frech 1995);
6 less involvement in public policy debates and (Frey and Eichenberger 1992, 1993);
7 lower social status of academics (Klamer 1995); and
8 more highly developed graduate programmes (Niehans 1995).

Regarding all of these factors, Britain has been argued to lie somewhere in the middle. Thus Baumol, in making a comparison between economics in Europe and the United States, avoided citing British examples on the grounds that Britain constituted 'a home halfway, culturally, between the European and North American continents' (1995: 187).

On top of this, British economics is close to American economics in that British academics are much more familiar with work by American economists than with work by many economists from Continental Europe, with visits to the USA being very frequent.

Some of the reasons for this are obvious and have little to do specifically with the economics profession. Firstly, language barriers make communication with the USA much easier than with much of Europe. Second, air transport – the organization of the airline industry – means that the cost difference between fly-ing from Britain to Europe and to the USA is much less than the ratio of their physical distances would suggest. The cost per mile of transatlantic travel is so much lower than that of travel within Europe that, in terms of travel cost, Britain is much closer to being mid-way between Europe and the USA than its geo-graphical position would suggest.

Although there have always been differences between Britain and the rest of Europe, they became accentuated in the period after 1945 because what may best be termed American-style professional economics spread much more rap-idly in Britain than on the Continent. The background to this is the profound social and economic changes that affected the university system as a whole dur-ing this period.

Universities and society in Britain

In 1945 the English higher education system was small, and available only to an elite, mostly drawn from the wealthier groups in society, though with a few opportunities, provided by scholarships, for very bright working-class children. Scotland was different, with a much higher participation rate and greater diver-sity in students' social origins. Oxford and Cambridge were perceived as the dominant institutions to such an extent that one writer could describe England as having 'two large residential universities for those who are either well-to-do or brilliant, and nine smaller universities, mainly non-residential, for those who are neither' (Truscott, quoted in Halsey 1992: 79). The 'redbrick' universities (such as Birmingham, Bristol, Manchester and Leeds), the fruit of the late Victorian expansion of higher education, were regarded as distinctly inferior throughout the interwar period. After 1945, however this changed in several ways.

The first change was the rapid expansion of numbers in higher education. The proportion of the relevant age group going to university rose from 3 per cent just before World War II to 7.2 per cent in 1962/63 and to 16.9 per cent by 1988/89. This was brought about in the 1950s and 1960s through the creation of new uni-versities, and through the granting of independent charters to colleges that previously offered London University degrees, the creation of new universities from scratch, and the 'upgrading' of colleges of advanced technology and, later, polytechnics, to university status. The number of universities in Britain rose as shown in Table 2.1. In 1992, when the polytechnics' status changed, the number of universities increased to approximately 100.

The structure of Oxford and Cambridge universities, where the key position was the college fellowship, with its traditions of collegiate responsibility, not that of the professor, made for a less hierarchical academic structure than in Europe. Keynes, for example, was never a professor, simply a Fellow of Kings College, Cambridge. Colleges were more important than departments. The result was a system that was less hierarchical than the Continental one, but at the same time very different from the competitive US system. It was elitist, but non-competitive. Universities other than Oxford and Cambridge, on the other hand,

Table 2.1 Number of British universities

Year	Number
1945	18
1955	20
1965	33
1975	49

were organized in departments, and had a more professional ethos. University expansion, involving universities other than Oxford and Cambridge, therefore involved change. Students were inevitably drawn from a wider cross-section of society, but university teachers' role in society changed. Dons ceased to be 'gentlemen', a status group, and became a profession.

One indication of the changing social status of academics is the decline in relative salaries. Before World War II, the average university teacher's salary was 3.3 times average earnings in manufacturing. By 1951/52 this ratio had fallen to 2.4, and by 1988/89 to 1.54. In short, relative to manufacturing earnings, university teachers' income more than halved in fifty years. At the same time workloads rose. The number of full-time-equivalent students per staff member rose from 8.1 in 1971/72, to 11.2 in 1989/90, and 14.0 in 1993/94. Class sizes have risen, and teaching methods have had to change. These changes in the role of university teachers are reflected in their attitudes towards the Association of University Teachers (AUT), a situation which came to a head in the 1970s with the issue of whether the AUT should affiliate to the Trades Union Congress (TUC). In the traditional collegiate view of universities, as communities of equals, there was no place for a trade union, and so many opposed joining the TUC – opposed becoming a 'proper' trade union. Academics were gentlemen, who received remuneration, not pay. Furthermore, in the period of expansion up to the 1970s, there was no major role for a union to play. By the 1970s, however, this view was becoming out of date, academics clearly having become employees of the institutions for which they worked. During the 1980s and 1990s, with budgetary cuts and sharply declining real earnings, the AUT organized strikes and other forms of 'industrial' action, something that would have been unheard of a generation earlier.

Alongside such changes has been a change in academics' political allegiance. In 1964, support for the three main parties (Conservative, Labour, Liberal) was divided approximately 38:40:15. By 1976 this had changed to 31:36:25, and by 1989 to 17:38:35.[1] For polytechnics the equivalent figures were 25:44:22 in 1976, and 18:44:25 in 1989. Interestingly, in 1976, university staff were more likely than polytechnic staff to vote Conservative, and less likely to vote Labour, as one would expect if there were a class divide between the two sets of institutions. By 1989, support for the Conservatives had fallen to comparable levels in both groups, though university staff showed significantly more support for the Liberals, and less for Labour than polytechnic staff. Again, this could be taken as reflecting differences in the social composition of these two groups. The major change, however, is that support for the Conservative Party is substantially lower among university staff than in the electorate as a whole.[2]

Though the Conservative government, in the 1980s and 1990s, sought to make universities more market-orientated, competitive institutions, salaries remained less unequal than in the US in the sense that, for most positions, the same salary scale applied to all institutions.[3]

An aspect of this process whereby universities moved away from a small elite system to a more professional one, in which academics have, to use Halsey's phrase, become 'proletarianized', is that formal criteria for assessment became much more widespread, with the result that the pressure to publish was greater. The number of academics with no publications fell from 12 per cent in 1976 to 3 per cent in 1989; the number who had published more than twenty papers rose from 26 per cent to 53 per cent during the same period; and the average number of publications per member of staff rose from 3.5 to 6.3 (Halsey 1992: 187).

These changes in the university system were associated with changes in the character of the system. In 1945 the British university system was small, which meant that Cambridge, the London School of Economics and Oxford (in that order) could dominate the economics profession numerically as well as in the production of important work. Other universities, such as Manchester, which supplied many members of the Economic Section and Central Statistical Office, were significant, but were hardly competitors for Cambridge, the London School of Economics and Oxford. The small scale of the profession meant that reputations were built as much on personal contacts as on publications. Graduate education was underdeveloped, few academics had doctorates, and there was little pressure to publish. The contrast with the situation in the USA could hardly have been greater. This began to change in the 1950s, with 'Americanization' proceeding apace during the 1960s and thereafter, with the result that by the 1990s, in contrast, the system had developed into one much closer to that found in the USA.

The spread of American-style professional economics in British universities[4]

Many of the changes that have taken place in British academic economics reflect more general changes in higher education: the move away from an elite system towards one that provides higher education to a much broader spectrum of the population; the proletarianization of university teachers; and the resulting stress on formal qualifications and research output. Three particularly significant developments were: (1) the growth of new universities, organized very differently from the collegiate structure of Oxford and Cambridge; (2) the imposition, in the 1980s, of formal research assessment (RAE), which forced academics to focus on the number and 'quality' of their publications;[5] and (3) a dramatic expansion of student numbers as well as reduced resources in the 1980s and 1990s.

Economics has, however, gone faster and further towards an American-style system than many other disciplines, even in the social sciences, or than economics in much of the rest of Europe.[6] One of the reasons for this is that for success many economists needed to follow the US model for graduate training and organization of research, at least part of the way, if only because the rising technical demands of the subject have necessitated more advanced technical training. Economists have, therefore, been ahead of those in Europe and of their colleagues in other social sciences in pushing towards graduate education that is closer to that found in the US and in seeing publication in leading international (predominantly American) journals as the criterion by which to judge research. The type of economics undertaken in leading universities has increasingly been very similar to that undertaken in the USA.

An important indicator of this change is the role of the doctorate. In 1945, a doctorate was not essential for an academic career. It was normal for those with a good first degree to go straight into a teaching position, and to study for a doctorate was unusual. For example, at Cambridge as late as 1970 the professors included Brian Reddaway, Joan Robinson, Richard Kahn and Nicholas Kaldor, none of whom had doctorates. Richard Stone was the only professor in economics with a doctorate. At Oxford, Jim Mirrlees had a doctorate, but Robin Matthews did not. At the LSE, professors without doctorates included Peter Bauer, Terence Gorman, Michio Morishima, Denis Sargan, Alan Walters, Peter Wiles and Basil Yamey; those with doctorates were Frank Hahn, Harry Johnson, Hla Myint and Alan Prest. By the 1990s, on the other hand, the situation had changed to such an extent that league tables published in the press, designed to rank universities, were using the proportion of staff with doctorates as an indicator of quality. By the 1990s, a doctorate had almost become required for new university staff. This is reflected in Figure 2.1, which shows the proportion of university staff in a sample of economics departments with a doctorate.[7] This rose from 20 per cent in 1945 to 56 per cent in 1995. The clear departure from the longer-term trend in the 1960s can probably be explained by the rapid expansion of the university system (see above, Table 2.1), which greatly increased the number of openings for teaching staff. Variations across groups of institutions are shown in Figure 2.2.

At the same time, there has been a distinct move away from the traditional model for the doctorate, which involves writing a thesis over a period of three years, with no requirement to do coursework or written examinations, and where the expectation is that the thesis is publishable as a book, to a model involving at least a year's coursework, followed by a shorter thesis, which in many universities can comprise three potential journal articles in the same field. This process started in the 1950s. By the 1980s and 1990s, those departments that had not changed were forced to do so by pressure from the Economic and Social Research Council (ESRC), which laid down conditions that had to be met if programmes were to be eligible for recognition (and funding). In moving towards this model, the goal of either emulating the US model, or seeking a 'mid-

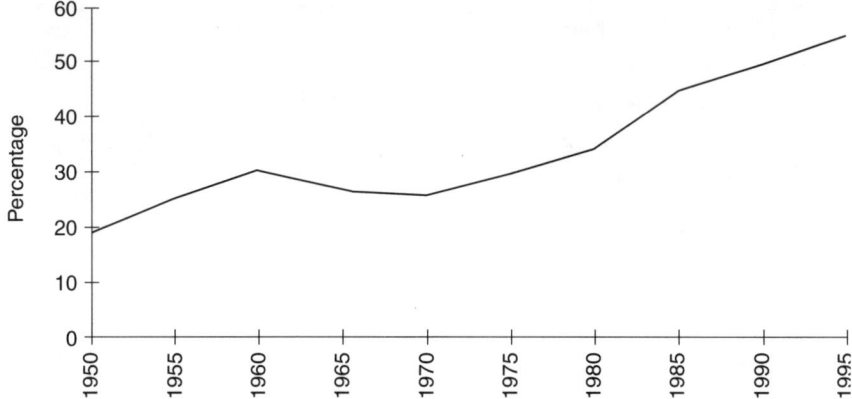

Figure 2.1 Proportion of university staff with a doctorate in a sample of economics departments

Source: *Commonwealth Universities Yearbook*

Note
The sample includes Oxford, Cambridge, LSE, Bristol, Birmingham, Manchester, St Andrews, Edinburgh, Essex and Warwick.

Atlantic' model, combining what was thought to be the best of both worlds, was frequently an explicit objective.[8]

This process has been uneven, as is illustrated by the methods of graduate training. Some universities made the change in the 1950s and 1960s, whereas others changed only in the 1990s, under pressure from the ESRC. There was also unevenness across institutions. The desire to move towards an American-style professional economics was strongest at some of the new universities, established in the 1960s and at the LSE, where there was a large proportion of US-trained staff. In the 1950s, technical economics (one aspect of this process) was very strong in the provincial universities (Jack Johnston at Manchester; Frank Hahn and Terence Gorman at Birmingham; Denis Sargan at Leeds), but in the 1960s the lead undoubtedly passed to the LSE, especially after Harry Johnson's arrival there. Hahn and Sargan both moved to the LSE in the 1960s. In the 1970s there was a strong group at Manchester, centred on David Laidler and Michael Parkin, working on monetarist theories, but with their departure to Canada in 1974 British monetarism was seriously weakened. The London Business School was an important centre for monetarist thinking, but in most universities Keynesian ideas remained stronger than was the case in the USA.

The international connections of British academic economists

Figure 2.3 shows the rise in the proportion of staff with doctorates from outside the UK. The large majority of doctorates were from British universities, but a

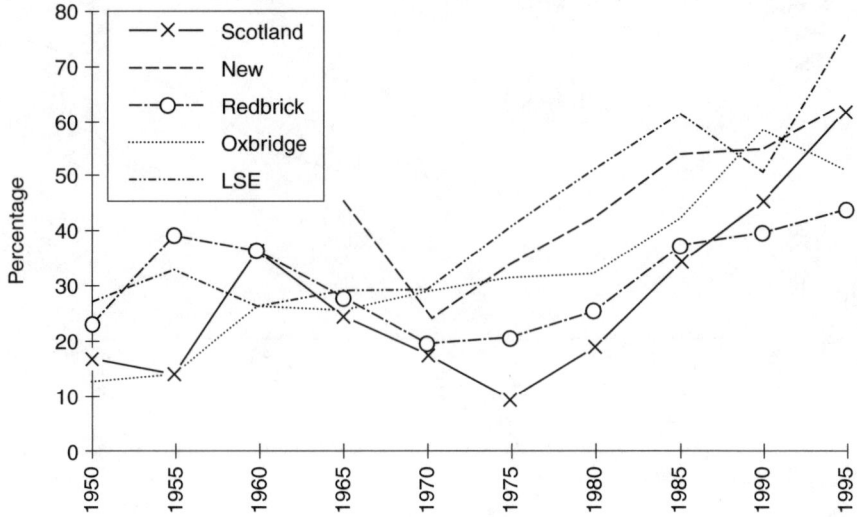

Figure 2.2 Proportion of staff with a doctorate in different types of university

Source: *Commonwealth Universities Yearbook*

Note
Scotland = St Andrews, Edinburgh. New = Essex, Warwick. Redbrick = Birmingham, Bristol, Manchester. Oxbridge = Oxford, Cambridge. Averages are unweighted averages of ratios for individual universities.

substantial number (typically 20–30 per cent) were from abroad. The low point is the 1960s, which suggests that the explanation does not lie simply in a shortage of supply of British doctorates, for if it were so, this is the period when one would expect to see a rise: expansion of universities went beyond the supply of new British doctorates, so if universities turned abroad to fill the gap, one would expect the proportion of overseas doctorates to rise, not fall. On the other hand, the fall in 1985 could be explained by such factors: the university system was no longer growing, and the availability of British doctorates combined with unattractive salaries would explain the fall. In the 1990s, the rise may reflect the extreme scarcity of British doctorates, and poor conditions in the US job market.

Figure 2.4 shows where these doctorates came from. Subject to the qualification that numbers in the early period are very small indeed, there is a clear picture. In the 1950s and 1960s, doctorates were more likely to come from Europe than from the USA, whereas from 1970 onwards the USA dominated. There was even a rise in doctorates from the rest of the world. Table 2.2 shows that these came from a wide variety of US universities, Harvard and California being particularly important. It is notable that Chicago was important in the 1970s, declining since then.

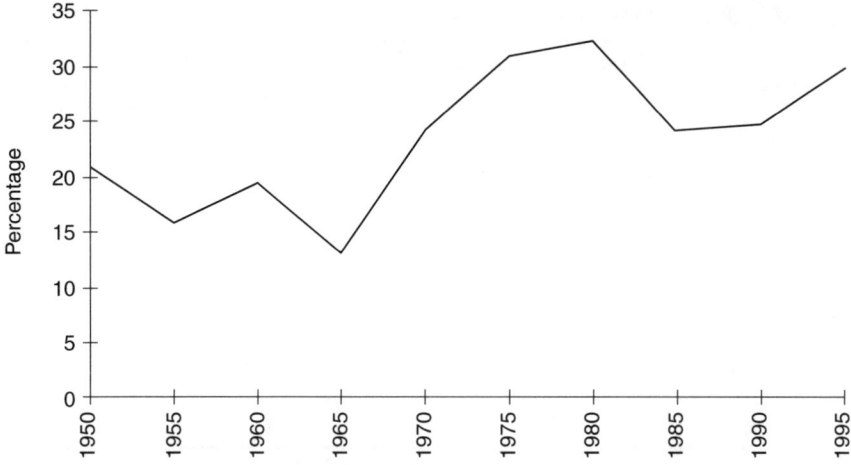

Figure 2.3 Proportion of overseas doctorates in a sample of British universities

Source: *Commonwealth Universities Yearbook*

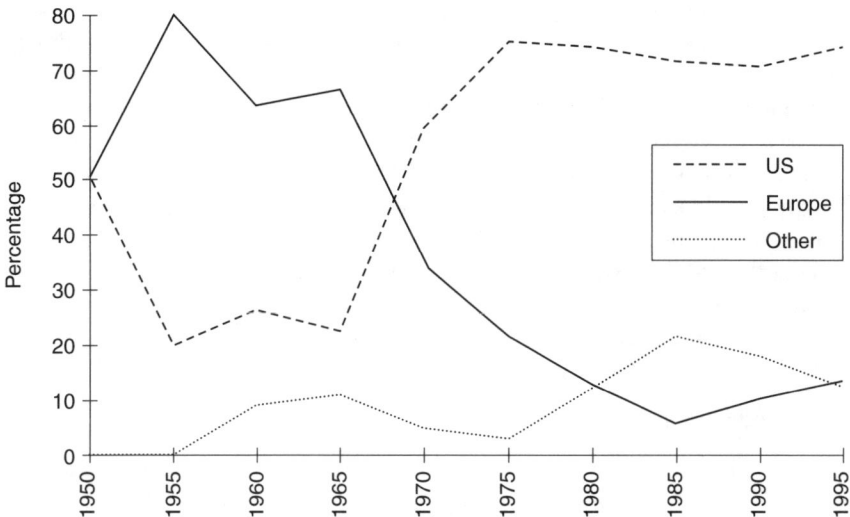

Figure 2.4 Source of overseas doctorates in a sample of British universities

Source: *Commonwealth Universities Yearbook*

Note
'Other' includes, in order of importance, India, Australia, Canada, Israel and Japan. Note that these figures refer to the *stock*. Individuals who came and stayed in Britain will thus be counted for several years.

Table 2.2 Origins of US doctorates in a sample of British universities

	1950	1955	1960	1965	1970	1975	1980	1985	1990	1995
Harvard			1	1	3	3	3	2	4	8
California			1	1	4	4	5	7		
Cornell	1		1	1		1	1	3		
Yale					2	4	2	3		
MIT				2	2	5	4	3	3	
Penn		1	3	2	2	1	2			
Princeton			2	1	2	1	2			
Chicago		1	1	2	5	3	2	2	2	
Stanford					2	2	4	2		
Elsewhere[2]	0	1	0	2	7	6	3	4		11

Source: *Commonwealth Universities Yearbook*

Figure 2.5 shows the uneven spread of US doctorates across the sample of departments. There is a clear distinction between the LSE and the new universities (Essex and Warwick, founded in the early 1960s), which, since the mid-1970s, have had a larger proportion of staff with US doctorates than have other universities. Scotland and the redbrick universities have fewest, with Oxford and Cambridge close behind.

Notable is the presence of US-trained staff, including not only those with US doctorates but also many with US Master's degrees, and some with first degrees from the USA (presumably the majority of these were Americans). Harry Johnson was enormously important, both at the LSE and elsewhere during his comparatively brief period in Britain. At Manchester, David Laidler was one of the driving forces in British monetarism in the 1970s. It is probably significant that around a third of the economists with American doctorates in the sample were at the LSE.[9] Looked at another way, by 1995, the LSE's thirty-seven doctorates included only seventeen from the UK, fifteen from the USA and five from the rest of the world.

Economists in government[10]

Britain, unlike many countries in Continental Europe, had for a long time a very small civil service. The tradition of employing experts in specific fields was weaker than in the USA and though, from the late nineteenth century, the government did employ experts in several fields (such as health and factory safety), economists had little to offer that was not available within established policy networks. The cult of the amateur was strong. Prior to 1924, when an economist was employed in the Department of Agriculture, economic advice was sought not from professional economists but from civil servants' extensive links with the City of London. A significant permanent staff developed only from World

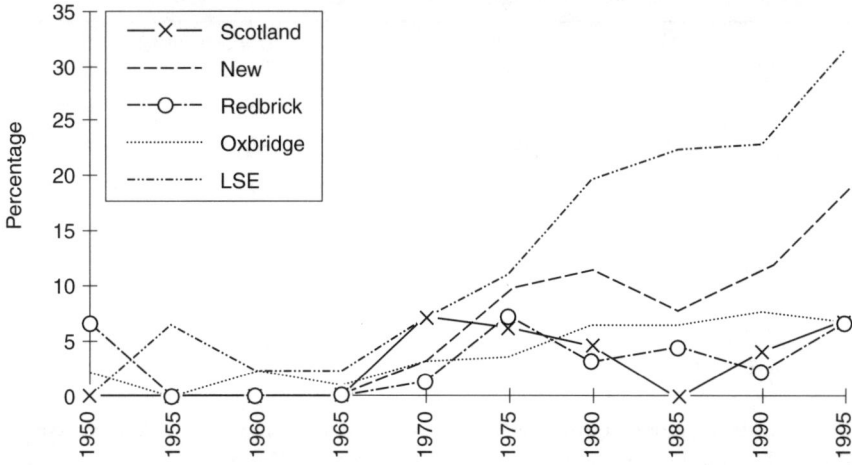

Figure 2.5 Proportion of staff with US doctorates in types of university

Source: *Commonwealth Universities Yearbook*

War II, when it was recognized that good economic advice could make an important contribution to the war effort. The Economic Section and the Central Statistical Office were established in 1941, fifty academic economists (many of them eminent figures in postwar economics) being employed in the Economic Section at some stage during the war. After the war, however, the Economic Section, and the Government Economic Service which succeeded it, remained very small, with economists scattered among a small number of departments. Most of the economists who joined the Economic Section during the war returned to academia within a few months of its ending. Total numbers of economists in the government are shown in Table 2.3. Statisticians are also included, partly for comparison, and partly because there was overlap between the functions performed by them and by economists.

The 1950s saw virtually no change in the number of economists employed in the government, with the few that there were being confined to the Board of Trade and the Treasury. Not only was demand low, with influential civil servants doubting the need for the Economic Section, but supply was also low, in part due to low salaries and poor conditions of service. It was, for example, difficult to keep up-to-date while working in government. The dramatic change came with the Labour government of 1964–70, during which the number of economists (excluding agricultural economists) rose tenfold. It is worth noting that the Prime Minister, Harold Wilson, had been an academic economist, as had his predecessor as leader of the Labour Party, Hugh Gaitskell.[11] Of the ministers in Wilson's government, Douglas Jay was also an economist.

Not only did the number of economists increase dramatically during the first Wilson administration, but a number of academic economists adopted a high public profile, notably Nicholas Kaldor and Thomas Balogh. The major reason for this

Table 2.3 Economists and statisticians in the British government, 1950–80

	Economists	Statisticians
1950	17(37)	104
1964	21.5 (46.5)	128
1970	208.5 (242.5)	266
1975	365	477
1980	379	538

Source: Coats (1981b): 523

Note
Numbers in parentheses include agricultural economists, not part of the Government Economic Service until 1974.

high profile was that, starting with the 1964 election campaign, economic issues dominated politics during this period as never before. The government came into office aiming to transform the British economy. Motivated by the view that economic policy-making had always been excessively dominated by the Treasury, the interests of which did not necessarily coincide with those of the economy as a whole, the government set up a separate Department of Economic Affairs (DEA), which took on the task of creating a National Plan, designed to raise the growth rate. This task was in itself controversial, but was made more so in that the DEA was set up explicitly to provide a counter-weight to the Treasury – to promote the interests of the real economy rather than the financial. Conflict was thus built in from the start.[12] Cooperation was not helped by the tension that existed between the leading political figures: the Prime Minister, the head of the DEA, George Brown (a close runner-up to Wilson in the Labour leadership contest), and the Chancellor of the Exchequer, James Callaghan (who had come third).

The involvement of economists in government during this period had a damaging effect on the reputation of the profession, from which it has perhaps never recovered. Within government, the influence of economists on major decisions was limited. Most economists were employed providing economic and statistical information, not as part of the policy-making process. Even when economic advisers did offer a clear message, they were on important occasions ignored. For example, on the first weekend of the Wilson administration, four of the government's top five economists advised, correctly, that without a devaluation of sterling, its economic programme would be impossible to carry out. This advice was ignored. The DEA, set up in part to provide a suitable job for George Brown, achieved little. It ended up being more involved with administrative machinery for controlling prices and wages (the National Board for Prices and Incomes) than with enhancing industrial performance. Above all, the choice of Kaldor and Balogh as the government's main economic advisers served to politicize the giving of economic advice. Thus when planning failed, and economic policy became dominated by a series of measures which did no more than postpone devaluation, the reputation of the economics profession as a whole suffered. Neither did it help that economists were seen to disagree over the need for devaluation.[13]

After the (surprise) defeat of the Labour government in 1970, the growth in numbers of government economists continued, though at a diminishing rate. The emphasis was increasingly on technical skills – notably, econometric modelling and forecasting – with the running of the Treasury model of the UK economy (a large forecasting model with upwards of 1,000 equations) taking a substantial share of the government's economic expertise. Despite the resources invested in it, the Treasury model was widely seen as being no better at forecasting than its major rivals, or even than the forecasts that an increasing number of stockbrokers and financial institutions produced. The failure to produce an adequate response to the shocks of 1973–74 until monetary and fiscal restraint was imposed by the International Monetary Fund after the 1976 sterling crisis further diminished the reputation of economists. Behind all these short-run problems, there was the underlying issue of European union, on which economists were completely divided.[14]

Perhaps as bad as forecasting errors for the reputation of economists were frequent errors in crucial economic statistics, such as the balance of payments or the public sector borrowing requirement (fiscal deficit). In both the years 1964–67 and 1976, policies were based on beliefs that there was a serious balance of payments problem that turned out after the event not to have existed. Denis Healey, widely regarded as one of the most acute Chancellors of the Exchequer since the war (for the entire Wilson–Callaghan government, 1974–79), like many of his predecessors was sceptical about both forecasting and formal economics (Healey 1990: 381).[15] Referring to the impossibility of applying Keynesian policies because the relevant statistics were too unreliable, or of applying monetarist policies because 'no one has yet found an adequate definition of money, no one knows how to control it, and no one except Friedman himself is certain exactly how the control of money supply will influence inflation', Healey developed 'a deep scepticism about all systematic economic theories' and 'an innate curiosity about how the economy actually worked in practice' (1990: 382), to satisfy which he turned not to economists, but to financial institutions, business leaders, trade unions and members of his local constituency party.

The reputation of economists was further tarnished in government circles in 1981 when a letter strongly critical of the government's deflationary policies was published in *The Times*, signed by 364 economists, either current or retired academics. Its central point was that there was no basis for the claim that deflation of demand would bring inflation permanently under control, thereby stimulating recovery. To the contrary, it argued, 'Present policies will deepen the depression, erode the industrial base of our economy and threaten its social and political stability' (*The Times*, 30 March 1981). The government was unmoved, and ministers were subsequently able to point to this letter as indicating that economists were out of touch. Thus Lawson, in his memoirs, wrote of this letter, 'Its timing was exquisite. The economy embarked on a prolonged phase of vigorous growth almost from the moment the letter was published. . . . the Budget was a prelude to eight years of uninterrupted growth and left our economic critics bewildered and discredited' (Lawson 1993: 98).

Though the DEA was abolished in 1970 by the incoming Conservative government, it was not till the 1980s, under Margaret Thatcher, that the Treasury regained its pre-eminent position among government departments. An important reason for this was the government's decision to implement a medium-term financial strategy (MTFS), to which all spending plans would be subordinated. Terry Burns, from the London Business School, was appointed Chief Economic Adviser, the MTFS having been an idea proposed by economists at the LBS before the government took office.

Under the Conservatives, members of the government took advice not only from civil servants, but also from economists outside Whitehall. Most prominent among these was Alan Walters, by then at Johns Hopkins University, who was appointed economic adviser to the Prime Minister in 1981. After leaving for a while, he returned to advise the Prime Minister in 1989, his public disagreements with Lawson over the European Monetary System causing the government great problems (and doing the reputation of economists little good either).[16] From 1986, Lawson made sure that the government got independent economic advice. This took the form of informal private meetings with a group of outside independent economists. Though excluding economists involved in advising the Labour Party, the aim was to cover a range of opinions, those involved including Walter Eltis, Geoffrey Maynard, Harold Rose, Patrick Minford, Samuel Brittan, Gordon Pepper, Mervyn King and John Muellbauer. Lawson commented, however, that it was only after he started to take outside advice in this way that problems developed with macro-economic policy, and that his independent advisers failed to anticipate the problems which eventually arose. In 1993, a more public consultative process was instituted, involving the appointment of seven outsiders (popularly known as the 'Wise men', even though they have subsequently included two women) who made public statements of their views on policy (Lawson 1993: 389).[17]

In addition to those employed within government proper, economists are also involved in other ways. The most important is the Bank of England, which has a substantial research department, over 200 strong, which, in addition to providing advice within the Bank, makes a significant published contribution to economic research, including many articles published in the *Bank of England Quarterly Bulletin*, most of the articles in which are written by members of the Bank's staff.

A number of economists were also brought into the machinery of government, yet remaining outside the Civil Service, with the privatization of public utilities such as electricity, water and gas. When these industries were privatized, regulatory authorities were established, as quasi-autonomous bodies responsible to ministers. Given the nature of their role (for example, balancing the pressure for lower costs to consumers against the need to provide incentives to invest and innovate) it was natural for economists to be involved. Stephen Littlechild, who had proposed the RPI − x rule for utility pricing, became head of the Office of

Electricity Regulation. Ian Byatt, another economist, became head of the Office of Water Regulation.

Economic societies

The society that represents British economists as a whole is the Royal Economic Society (RES). This dates back to 1890 and publishes the *Economic Journal*.[18] By the 1990s, its membership exceeded 3,000 and the *Economic Journal*'s circulation was over 7,000. For most of its history, however, the RES did relatively little. Annual conferences were organized not by the RES but by the Association of University Teachers of Economics (AUTE), established for this purpose in the 1920s.[19] Alongside this the Association of Polytechnic Teachers of Economics (APTE) organized a separate conference and journal, the *British Review of Economic Issues*, echoing the divide between the two sectors in higher education.

It was only in the 1980s that the role of the RES expanded. The society became more democratic, electing the President and members of the governing body by a postal ballot of all members.[20] The annual conference came to be jointly organized by the RES and AUTE, and eventually the AUTE disappeared altogether. Conference papers were published as an issue of the *Economic Journal*. Later, there was a further merger, with the APTE conference. When higher education came under pressure in the 1980s, the RES was instrumental in defending the interests of the subject, convening a regular meeting of heads of all university economics departments for this purpose.[21]

From the beginning the membership of the RES included more than just academic economists, and the *Economic Journal* contained material aimed at a wide readership. However, like comparable US journals, it soon became a purely academic journal,[22] and the role of non-academics in the RES declined.[23] Some of the needs of economists in business were met instead by the Society of Business Economists, which organizes seminars and a journal. Parallel developments took place in Scotland, for although the RES covered Scotland, a Scottish Economic Society was formed in the 1950s, with its own journal, the *Scottish Journal of Political Economy*, in 1954. Prior to this there had been a Society of Scottish Economists, founded in 1897, but after 1914 this had become moribund. At its inception, the *Scottish Journal of Political Economy* was to focus on Scottish problems and to be interdisciplinary, but from the 1970s neither of these goals was achieved. The journal became exclusively economic and the proportion of articles on Scotland became very small.

Research institutes and policy forums

The research institute with the longest history is the National Institute for Economic and Social Research (NIESR), founded in 1938.[24] Though half the initial finance came from the Rockefeller Foundation, one of the aims was to establish an institute that could carry out research independent of the US foundations. The last Rockefeller grant ended in 1959, though Ford Foundation finance was important from 1957 to 1962. After 1962 the NIESR received support from the Treasury, but this ended in 1980. Since then it has received support from the ESRC and various foundations, including Leverhulme, Nuffield, Volkswagen and the Anglo-German Foundation. The NIESR was to have its own staff, who would undertake research; it would assist university economists in carrying out research, raise funds and publicize economic research; and it would collaborate with other institutes. By 1950 its research staff numbered ten; by 1956, sixteen; and by 1960, twenty-two.

The NIESR sponsored research which led to the publication of monographs in a variety of applied, policy-related areas. Perhaps the most distinctive feature of its work has been fundamental research on various aspects of productivity and growth. From 1955 it began to develop as a source of information on the business cycle (a *Konjunctur Institut*) and from 1960 its assessment of the current outlook was published regularly in the *National Institute Economic Review*. One reason for Treasury support in the 1960s and 1970s was the NIESR model, which provided the basis for its forecasts. During the 1970s, however, the London Business School's *Economic Outlook* and the *Cambridge Economic Review* also appeared, and the NIESR ceased to be the only source of such economic commentary. In addition, many financial institutions, notably stockbrokers, started to provide assessments of the current situation.

Very different in emphasis, though similar to the NIESR in having full-time research staff, was the Institute for Fiscal Studies (IFS), established in 1969, funded primarily by a group of large financial institutions.[25] Its aim was to ensure that tax changes would not be introduced without there having been a thorough analysis of their effects. The IFS has, therefore, concentrated on making proposals for tax reform and on regular analysis of budget proposals, focusing primarily on their micro-economic implications. From 1989 it published a journal, *Fiscal Studies*, and in 1991 it successfully bid to become a research centre supported by the ESRC. By the mid-1990s the IFS employed twenty-seven economists itself, and had a further thirty-three affiliated researchers based in universities in the UK, the rest of Europe and the USA.

In contrast with the NIESR and the IFS, the Centre for Economic Policy Research (CEPR), established in 1983 with support from the Bank of England, the ESRC and the Esmée Fairburn foundation, and directed by Richard Portes, is entirely a networking and support organization. By 1997 it was employing twenty-three people, but these were entirely in a support role, all research being done by an international team of more than 300 economists, most of whom were based in European universities. Of the 240 Research Fellows associated with the CEPR in 1996, 29 per cent were based in the UK, 55 per cent in the rest of Europe, 13 per cent in the USA.[26] Though a small number of these were in central banks and international organizations (the World Bank, IMF and WTO), most were based in universities. It publishes both monographs and a journal, *Economic Policy*, as well as digests of its research aimed at journalists and government economists.

Policy-orientated, applied research was published in the *Bank of England Quarterly Bulletin* and, from 1960, in the *National Institute Economic Review*.

A major forum for policy discussions, however, was provided by the reviews published by the major banks: Barclays, Lloyds, Midland, NatWest and the Royal Bank of Scotland. These bank reviews were the location for some important discussions of policy, such as over monetarism in the early 1970s. They attracted articles by leading academic economists, as well as others by economists from government and financial institutions. Financial pressures, however, resulted in all the major bank reviews being discontinued between 1987 and 1993. Given the appearance of *Economic Policy* and, from 1985, the *Oxford Review of Economic Policy*, and the creation of a policy section in the *Economic Journal*, there were, by this time, significantly more alternative outlets for policy discussions.

Economic journalism and think-tanks[27]

Britain has a long tradition in financial journalism, going well back into the nineteenth century, when *The Economist* was a major voice in the cause of free trade. In the interwar period, Keynes's journalistic and political activities were arguably as important as any purely academic work – some of his books were first published as newspaper articles (for example, the *Tract on Monetary Reform* in *The Manchester Guardian*). Keynes, however, was not typical of university economists, who generally focused much more on writing for their peers. This pattern continued into the postwar period with the result that, whereas in the USA leading university economists (Samuelson, Friedman, Galbraith, Tobin, Klein) contributed regularly to newspapers and popular magazines, there was no comparable tradition in Britain. Some academic economists have contributed regularly to the press and written books aimed at a wide audience (John Kay, Paul Ormerod) but most have not. The leading role in public discussion of economic ideas has been taken by journalists, some of whose ideas have proved more influential in changing public opinion than have ideas originating in the universities. Indeed, if Keynes is seen primarily as a journalist, this could be seen as following his example: exploring and developing ideas in the press, after which they are taken up by academia.

The postwar generation of economic journalists had, unlike their American counterparts, close political ties, and produced what has been described as 'a kind of politically informed economic writing which had, for all intents and purposes, died out in the nineteenth century' (Parsons 1989: 101). The first such writer was Andrew Shonfield, with the *Financial Times* from 1947 to 1957, and then economics editor of the *Observer* till 1961. He had close links with the Labour Party, and made frequent appearances on radio and television. His book, *Modern Capitalism* (1965), was widely read, and argued a case (influenced by what had proved successful elsewhere in Europe) for reforming the institutional apparatus of the British economy so as to improve its growth performance. In 1961 he left journalism, moving towards academia, becoming at various times Chairman of the Social Science Research Council, Director of the Royal Institute of International Affairs, and Professor at the European University Institute in Florence.

Two other major figures who illustrate the close links between economic journalism, public service and politics in Britain are Samuel Brittan and Peter Jay. Samuel Brittan, seen by some as the leading economic journalist of his generation, succeeded Shonfield as economics editor of the *Observer* from 1961 to 1964, after which he spent two years in the DEA. Brittan then returned to journalism, joining the *Financial Times*, much more sanguine about the prospects for planning and interventionist policies. In addition to his newspaper columns, he wrote books that were widely read, his best-selling being *The Treasury under the Tories* (1964). During the 1970s, when policy-makers were at a loss as to what policies to pursue, it was Brittan who, along with Jay (another journalist who had close links with the Labour Party), took up and publicized Friedman's ideas. Jay was in the Treasury till 1967, when he left to become the first Economics Editor of *The Times*. During the 1970s and early 1980s he worked as a television presenter, and had a brief spell as British Ambassador in Washington. Brittan and Jay provide a major channel between academic ideas (originating in the USA) and politics. For both of them, it was the first Wilson administration, in the mid-1960s, that resulted in their disillusion with conventional policies, and led to their search for an alternative.

On the left, the most prominent economic journalist in recent years has been Will Hutton, economics correspondent of *The Guardian* from 1990 to 1996, and since then Economics Editor of the *Observer*. His ideas have been publicized not only in the *The Guardian* and *The Observer*, but also in a best-selling book, *The State We're In* (1995) and an accompanying television series. For the 1997 general election, he argued the need for change in another book, *The State to Come* (1997). Drawing on the work of academic economists and historians, and observing the social consequences of more than a decade of free-market policies, Hutton has challenged the efficacy of such policies, arguing for example, that rising inequality can have adverse effects on economic performance, and challenging the notion that Thatcherite policies represent a radical break with British traditions. They are, he has argued, policies that are consistent with what some historians have seen as the long-standing dominance of the City of London over the interests of manufacturing industry, a dominance that goes back to the eighteenth century if not before.[28] It is noteworthy that, like the IEA and the Adam Smith Institute which were inspired by Hayek as much as by any more orthodox economist, Hutton draws freely on non-mainstream economists and social and political thinkers.

The process whereby monetarism and free-market ideas displaced the Keynesian orthodoxy of the 1960s was given increased impetus by a number of think-tanks committed to the propagation and application of free-market ideas. Pre-eminent amongst these was the Institute of Economic Affairs, founded in 1955, the first director of which was Ralph Harris. Its origin lay in a meeting between Anthony Fisher, a businessman who made a fortune introducing battery-farming methods to the poultry industry, and Friedrich Hayek.[29] He was attracted by the ideas of Hayek's *The Road to Serfdom* (1945), and after being dissuaded by Hayek from a political career, worked to set up the IEA. The IEA was a pressure group seeking to influence university economists and, through them, students of economics, with the long-term goal of producing a change in the way economic policy-making was organized. In doing this, they went much further than the Mont Pèlerin Society, formed several years earlier, and with which many supporters of the IEA, including Hayek, were closely involved. Their model was the Fabian Society, founded in 1883,[30] which sought to advance socialist ideas through similar methods.[31] Its successes had been in influencing the Liberal government's policies after 1906, and in the establishment of the Labour Party, with its socialist agenda. In the post-1945 period, the Fabian Society's influence was minor: it played a role in the thinking that underlay the setting up of the DEA in 1964, but this came to nothing. In the postwar period, it was free-market ideas that were setting the agenda.

The IEA was important in bringing several leading members of the Conservative Party round to a committed free-market position, notably Keith Joseph and Margaret Thatcher. To encourage the spread of such ideas within the Conservative Party, these two founded, in 1974, the Centre for Policy Studies (CPS). Its role, however, as an organization closely bound up with the Conservative Party, was very different from that of the IEA which, in party-political terms, was non-partisan.[32] It was followed, in 1976, by the bicentennial of Adam Smith's *Wealth of Nations*, with the Adam Smith Institute, which proved an important source of free-market ideas during the 1980s, when the existence of a government committed to free-market policies created problems for the IEA and the CPS in knowing what role they should be playing. The CPS, for example, found a role defending the government's social policies, but this was hardly the radical role for which it had originally been set up. There were close links between economists working for the IEA, the Adam Smith Institute and equivalent organizations in the USA. For example, Friedman and Hayek were influential figures both in the USA and Britain. The success of the IEA and similar groups led to the founding of the Institute for Public Policy Research by Labour Party supporters and trade unionists in 1988.[33]

Conclusions

The British economics profession has become much larger, both inside and outside the universities, and as a result has changed dramatically over the past half-century. American-style professional economics has spread within academic economics, though in the past decade this has been given a distinctive twist by Britain's centralized funding system and the effects of the research assessment exercise. Outside academia, the main development is the growth in the number of economists, in both government and business – the giving of economic advice has been professionalized in the sense that it has increasingly been provided by specialists. British economics has, however, remained distinct from both American and Continental European economics.

It is no longer possible to sustain any illusion that Britain dominates world economics in the sense that might have been possible in the era of John Stuart

Mill, Alfred Marshall and John Maynard Keynes.[34] As the Nobel Prize indicates, the discipline is now dominated by the United States. However, it is arguable that economics is now, to a much greater extent than in 1945, a single market, in which the nationality of economic ideas (and in a sense of economists) is much harder to define. In this larger, more integrated market, British economists, whether domestically produced or imported, have played an important role, especially in particular areas of the subject. It could, therefore, be argued that British economics can legitimately be described as 'mid-Atlantic'. In this sense the aims of those economists who sought to modernize the subject in the 1960s have been achieved. Whether the outcome, in terms of testable and successfully tested theories, is being achieved is perhaps more controversial.

Acknowledgements

I am indebted to Roger Middleton for pointing out how to rectify some faults in the first draft of this chapter, and for making available draft chapters of his forthcoming book, on which I have drawn extensively.

Notes

1 These figures are averages of those for Oxbridge and 'All other universities' in Halsey (1992: 237). Note that no allowance is made for gender. Women are more likely than men to vote Conservative. Given that the proportion of academics who are female has risen (admittedly very slowly), it may be that these figures understate the shift away from the Conservatives.

2 Coats and Coats (1973) have analysed the social status of Royal Economic Society members (using father's occupation as an indicator), but because of the small sample size it is difficult to draw conclusions about changes during the postwar period.

3 Lorenz curves for US and UK salaries in 1964 were virtually identical, suggesting that there was no difference in inequality. However, salaries vary much more with age in the UK, where the median salary for academics aged between 61 and 64 was three times the median for those under 26. The equivalent figure for the USA is 2.2, which is substantially less. Given that the overall degree of inequality is the same, inequality due to factors other than age must be higher in the USA. In addition, earnings in excess of salaries are more significant in the USA, where ten-month contracts are common. Such earnings will be less equally distributed than basic salaries (AEA 1968: Appendix III, Table H; AUT 1965: Table 8).

4 Though much material has been added, this section and the following one draw extensively on Backhouse (1997).

5 'Quality' is placed in quotation marks, for universities are concerned with quality as they expect it to be perceived by the RAE panels. Though panel members have denied this, there is a widespread concern that quality will be judged simply by the status of the journal in which material is published, with non-journal publications counting for little.

6 For contrasts between Britain and the USA in an earlier period, see Perlman (1977) and Coats (1980).

7 Normally, but not always, a PhD or D. Phil.

8 See Backhouse (1997) for evidence on this point. For additional evidence, see the interview with Richard Lipsey in Tribe (1997).

9 The exact figures are as follows:

	1950	1955	1960	1965	1970	1975	1980	1985	1990	1995
No. of US doctorates	0	1	1	1	4	6	10	10	11	15
Percentage of US doctorates in sample	0	100	33	50	33	25	36	38	41	35

The sample is likely to be biased in favour of those departments to which US-trained economists were likely to move.

10 This section is heavily influenced by Middleton (forthcoming), especially chapter 3.

11 He was the author of a paper on the theory of capital. Attlee's government of 1945–51 contained, in addition to Wilson and Jay, economists in H. Marquand, Hugh Dalton (Chancellor of the Exchequer) and Hugh Gaitskell.

12 There was a precedent for this, in that during the war responsibility for financial matters lay with the Chancellor of the Exchequer, and responsibility for resource allocation with the Lord President of the Council, an arrangement that lasted until Stafford Cripps became Chancellor in 1947.

13 It has been suggested that economists were agreed over the merits of devaluation. That they were not is documented in Hutchison (1977), chapter 5 (entitled 'Economic knowledge and ignorance in action: economists on devaluation and Europe, 1964–74)'.

14 Britain joined the EEC in 1973, under Edward Heath. After the 1974 elections, Wilson renegotiated terms, and then held a referendum in 1976.

15 'After only eight months in the Treasury, I decided to do for forecasters what the Boston Strangler did for door-to-door salesmen – to make them distrusted for ever' (Healey 1990: 381). He thus gave a speech in which he said of forecasts that 'their origin lies in extrapolation from a partially known past, through an unknown present, to an unknowable future according to theories about the causal relationships which are hotly disputed by academic economists, and may in fact change from country to country or from decade to decade' (ibid.) Nigel Lawson (1993: 50–1) expressed great sympathy with this view.

16 It is important to note the contrast between Burns's position, as a senior Treasury official, and that of Walters, simply an adviser to the PM, with no departmental responsibilities.

17 Though hers was the most well-known, Thatcher was not the only minister to have an economic adviser. For example, Eltis was adviser to Michael Heseltine.

18 It was originally the British Economic Society, becoming the Royal Economic Society in 1902. For discussion of its history, see Hey and Winch (1990) and Coats and Coats (1973).

19 Not to be confused with the AUT, the trade union.

20 Prior to this, elections had simply been at the Annual General Meeting, often very poorly attended.

21 For example, the RES carried out an analysis of the RAE assessment, and sought to mitigate changes in research council policy that were perceived as damaging to the profession.

22 See Coats (1993), Hey and Winch (1990), Tribe (1992) and Backhouse (1997).

23 See Coats and Coats (1973).

24 This discussion of the NIESR is based primarily on Jones (1988).

25 See Robinson (1970) and 'IFS grows up' at http://www1.ifs.org.uk/ifsinfo/IFSGrow.htm.

26 In addition to its Research Fellows, it had more than seventy Research Affiliates, young economists within three years of completing their PhD, and more than thirty Research Associates, linked to the CEPR through specific research projects.

27 This section owes much to Parsons (1989).

28 For example, Cain and Hopkins (1993), from whom Hutton takes the term 'Gentlemanly capitalism'.
29 This account of the IEA is based primarily on Cockett (1994). See also Seldon (1981).
30 Its original title was 'The Fellowship of the New Life'.
31 Those involved even referred to the IEA as the 'anti-Fabian' society.
32 As a registered charity, the IEA is obliged to adopt a non-partisan stance.
33 This is not a comprehensive list of such organizations, either on the left or the right. See Cockett (1994).
34 I leave open the question of whether it was ever reasonable to speak of such British dominance.

References

American Economic Association (AEA) (1968) 'Studies of the structure of economists' salaries and income', *American Economic Review* 58(5), part 2: xxxv, 1–153.
Association of University Teachers (AUT) (1965) *The Remuneration of University Teachers, 1964–5: A Study of the Annual Rates of Remuneration and Promotion Prospects of University Teachers at October 1964*. London: Association of University Teachers.
Backhouse, Roger E. (1997) 'The changing character of British economics', in A. W. Coats (ed.) *The Post-1945 Internationalization of Economics*, Annual Supplement to *History of Political Economy* 28: 33–60.
Baumol, William J. (1995) 'What's different about European economics?', *Kyklos* 48(2): 187–92.
Brittan, Samuel (1964) *The Treasury under the Tories*. Harmondsworth: Penguin.
Cain, P. J. and Hopkins, A. (1993) *British Imperialism*. London: Longman.
Campbell, R. H. (1997) 'The Scottish Society of Economists: The Scottish Economic Society – 1897–1997', *Scottish Journal of Political Economy* 44(4): 359–67.
Coats, A. W. (1980) 'The culture and the economists: some reflections on Anglo-American differences', *History of Political Economy* 12(4): 588–609; reprinted in Coats (1993), pp. 134–54.
——(1981a) *Economists in Government: An International Comparative Study*. Durham, NC: Duke University Press.
——(1981b) 'Britain: the rise of the specialists', *History of Political Economy*, 13(3): 365–404; reprinted in Coats (1981a) and Coats (1993), pp. 519–55.
——(1993) *The Sociology and Professionalization of Economics: British and American Economic Essays,* vol. II. London and New York: Routledge.
Coats, A. W. and Coats, Sonia (1973) 'The changing social composition of the Royal Economic Society 1890–1960 and the professionalization of British economics', *British Journal of Sociology* 24(2): 165–87; reprinted in Coats (1993), pp. 338–60.
Cockett, Richard (1994) *Thinking the Unthinkable: Think Tanks and the Economic Counter-Revolution, 1931–1983*. London: HarperCollins.
Eggertson, Thrainn (1995) 'On the economics of economics', *Kyklos* 48(2): 201–10.
Forte, Francesco (1995) 'European economics: a tiny creature under tutorship', *Kyklos* 48(2): 211–18.
Frech, H. E., III (1995) 'European versus American economics, artificial intelligence and scientific content', *Kyklos* 48(2): pp. 219–30.
Frey, Bruno S. and Eichenberger, Reiner (1992) 'Economics and economists: a European perspective', *American Economic Review* 82(2): 216–20.
——(1993) 'American and European economics and economists', *Journal of Economic Perspectives* 7(4): 185–94.
Halsey, A. H. (1992) *The Decline of Donnish Dominion: British Academic Professions in the Twentieth Century*. Oxford: Clarendon Press.

Healey, Denis (1990) *The Time of My Life*. London: Penguin Books.
Hey, John D. and Winch, Donald (1990) *A Century of Economics: 100 Years of the Royal Economic Society and the Economic Journal*. Oxford and Cambridge, MA: Basil Blackwell.
Hutchison, Terence W. (1977) *Knowledge and Ignorance in Economics*. Oxford: Basil Blackwell.
Hutton, Will (1995) *The State We're In*. London: Jonathan Cape.
——(1997) *The State to Come*. London: Vintage.
Jones, Kit (1988) 'Fifty years of economic research: a brief history of the National Institute of Economic and Social Research 1938–88', *National Institute Economic Review* (May): 36–59.
Klamer, Arjo (1995) 'A rhetorical perspective on differences between European and American economists', *Kyklos* 48(2): 231–40.
Lawson, Nigel (1993) *The View from No. 11: Memoirs of a Tory Radical*. London: Corgi Books.
Middleton, Roger (1998) *Charlatans or Saviours: Economists and the British Economy from Marshall to Meade*. London: Macmillan.
Niehans, Jürg (1995):'Transatlantic perspectives', *Kyklos* 48(2): 257–66.
Parsons, Wayne (1989) *The Power of the Financial Press: Journalism and Economic Opinion in Britain and America*. Cheltenham: Edward Elgar.
Perlman, Mark (1977) 'Orthodoxy and heterodoxy in economics: a retrospective view of experiences in Britain and the USA', *Zeitschrift für Nationalökonomie* 37: 163–4.
Portes, Richard (1987) 'Economics in Europe', *European Economic Review* 31(6): 1329–40.
Robinson, Bill (1990) 'The early days of the IFS', *Fiscal Studies* 11(3) (August): 1–11.
Selden, Arthur (ed.) (1981) *The Emerging Consensus?* London: Institute of Economic Affairs.
Shonfield, Andrew (1965) *Modern Capitalism*. Oxford: Oxford University Press.
Tabellini, Guido (1995) 'The organization of economic research: why Europe is still behind', *Kyklos* 48(2): 297–302.
Tribe, Keith (1992) '*The Economic Journal* and British economics, 1891–1940', *History of the Human Sciences* 5(4): 33–58.
——(1997) *Economic Careers: Economics and Economists in Britain, 1930–1970*. London and New York: Routledge.

3 The post-1945 development of economics and economists in Sweden

*Bo Sandelin, Nikias Sarafoglou
and Ann Veiderpass*[1]

The post-1945 era in Sweden, as well as in many other countries, has witnessed the success and decline of Keynesianism and other kinds of interventionism, the rise of the welfare state and the ideological attack on it, and a huge growth together with continuous internationalization of economics as a university discipline.

In this chapter we shall treat some aspects of these issues. Firstly, we shall discuss the changes in the university system, including a growth from eight extensively defined chairs in economics in 1945 to fifty-seven more narrowly defined chairs in 1996.[2] After that we shall take up some aspects of the internationalization of Swedish economics. Internationalization is not a new process; the introducers of neoclassicism in Sweden a century ago were also highly internationalized.

We shall devote considerable space to the role of Swedish economists in policy-making. As the country is small and the required amount of economic expertise in government is not proportional to the size of a country, Swedish economists tend to spend much effort in public affairs; they tend to be *policy-intensive*. Furthermore, during most of the postwar period, Sweden has had a Social Democratic government inclined to intervene in economic affairs. This has left room for economists; policy-making has tended to become *economist-intensive*. We shall discuss the contributions by economists in commissions, in the Parliament and as ministers, and in public discussions. European integration implies that economic policy decisions are to a larger extent taken on a European level, instead of in each individual country, especially if the monetary union is created. This will probably lead to less involvement in public affairs by Swedish economists, although a few of them may be absorbed in Brussels.

The growth of higher education

The growth of higher education during the post-1945 era is an almost universal phenomenon, standing in a mutually dependent relationship to technological progress, income growth, changing attitudes towards studies and so on. Since it is not a specifically Swedish or Scandinavian phenomenon, we shall not undertake a deeper study of the general causes but focus on some aspects of the outcome in Sweden.

In 1945 undergraduate economics was taught at six places in Sweden: the universities at Uppsala, Lund, Stockholm and Gothenburg, and the business schools at Stockholm and Gothenburg.[3] In 1996 undergraduate economics was offered at six universities, two formally private business schools (Stockholm and Jönköping) and eighteen university colleges.

There has, of course, also been growth in postgraduate training, manifesting itself, for instance, in a growth in the number of annual doctoral degrees in economics, from one in 1945 to seventeen in 1995 with a peak of thirty in 1993; see Figure 3.1.[4] That growth has not, however, been connected with a similar increase in the number of institutions giving post-graduate degrees. In 1945 a doctoral degree in economics could be taken at the four universities at Uppsala, Lund, Stockholm and Gothenburg. At the beginning of 1996, a doctoral degree in economics could be taken at the six universities at Uppsala, Lund, Stockholm, Gothenburg, Umeå and Linköping, at Luleå University College and Institute of Technology, and at the business schools in Stockholm and Jönköping.[5] However, in 1996 the government decided that Luleå University College and Institute of Technology should be granted university status in 1997. In addition, a number of other university colleges were to get government means for research and create professorships.

Outside the universities, business schools were established in Stockholm in 1909 and in Gothenburg in 1923. They were originally organized mainly according to the German model. Undergraduate teaching was originally their sole task; they had not the right to give doctoral degrees until 1946 at Stockholm and 1950

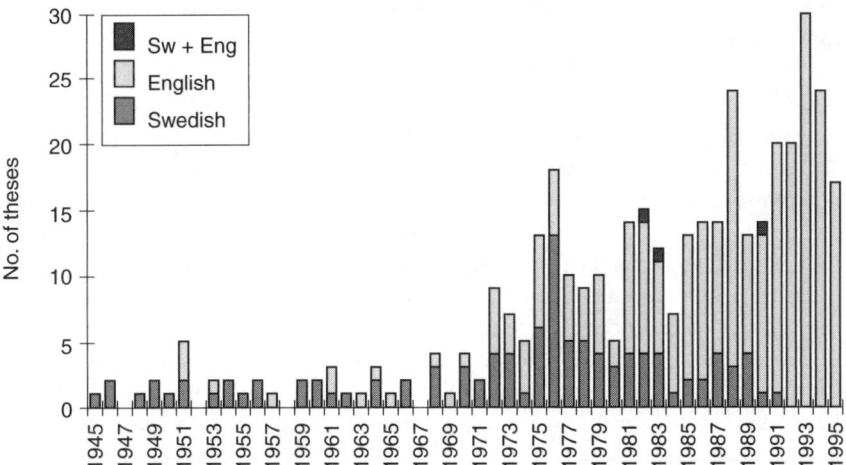

Figure 3.1 Language and number of theses (Swedish and English)

Source: Data compiled by the authors from research by Wadensjö and Engwall

at Gothenburg. Especially at Stockholm, economics obtained a strong position due to influential professors on the faculty such as Eli Heckscher and Bertil Ohlin. The business school at Gothenburg was dissolved, and incorporated in the university in 1971.

The Swedish term for business school, *handelshögskola,* is prestigious among students aiming at a business career, as well as among teachers in the departments of business administration at the universities. Consequently, during the 1980s the term reappeared as a designation for part of the Faculty of Social Sciences at Gothenburg University, and for 'an organization for cooperation between five departments at Umeå University'. In the tables below, only the original, independent business schools are treated as separate units.

Universities, university branches and university colleges

A large increase in the number of students in the 1960s was neither unforeseen nor unplanned. In 1955, the government appointed a commission to 'make a comprehensive and unprejudiced inquiry into the objectives and needs of universities in modern society'. One reason for the investigation was that for demographic and other reasons 'the number of students during the period 1955–1965 will increase strongly at the same time as the need for a university trained labour force will increase continuously' (SOU 1957:24, p. 9). The commission produced seven reports, permeated by the ideology of social engineering and filled by tables of the historical, actual and forecast number of, as well as the 'need' for, people with a certain kind of university education.

How should growth be organized? One possible solution might have been the establishment of new universities. However, when the question became acute at the beginning of the 1960s, a committee[6] put forward a quite different proposal: branch universities *(universitetsfilialer)*. Uppsala University became the mother university of a branch university at Örebro; Lund University of a branch university at Växjö; Stockholm University of a branch university at Linköping; and Gothenburg University of a branch university at Karlstad, all of which taught undergraduate economics. In connection with university reform in 1977, the four branch universities became independent university colleges *(högskolor)*, and a number of new university colleges were also established.

The university colleges have lacked the highest prestige, basically because they were designed only for undergraduate teaching, and were not guaranteed public research funding. Many of them have so few teachers within a discipline that the risk of isolation is evident. It is often difficult for the university colleges to engage and retain good teachers and researchers. As a consequence, according to statistics from the university teachers' trade union, the university colleges have been forced to offer higher salaries than the larger universities for the same kind of position.

As a rule, the university colleges strive to obtain full university status; i.e. to replace *högskola* in their Swedish title with *universitet.*[7] One can discern a difference between the political parties concerning the attitude towards the old, larger universities and the university colleges. The present Social Democratic government favours the university colleges. Recently, the government has decided to increase considerably the dimensions of undergraduate teaching at the university colleges, and many of them will get permanent government funding for research. This is in line with the egalitarian ideology of the Social Democratic Party that forms the government. It has an aspect of regional policy as well; this is especially appealing to the Centre Party (the old Farmers' Party), which is at present closely collaborating with the government.

From 'Economics and . . .' to sub-fields

Specialization is a phenomenon that is partly caused and facilitated by the growth of higher education and research. In 1958 the first lectureships were created in order to meet the expected growth in the number of students. They were designed exclusively for undergraduate teaching, and represented a first step towards the separation of teaching and research. Full professors, on the other hand, became specialized in post-graduate teaching and research. Another step was taken in 1977, when different governing bodies were created for under-graduate teaching and post-graduate teaching and research. At the same time the appropriations to undergraduate teaching were separated from the appropria-tions to post-graduate teaching and research. In spite of declarations about the desirability of a closer relationship between undergraduate teaching and research, the separation has essentially remained.

Another kind of specialization is the introduction of chairs within sub-fields of economics. This can be considered a consequence of several factors. Firstly, the growth of the teaching staff of a department makes specialization possible; it is no longer necessary that one person teaches within the whole area of econom-ics. Second, the growth of knowledge within a discipline makes it more and more difficult for one person to master the whole discipline; part of a discipline can form a sufficient basis for a chair.

The evolution is illustrated in Tables 3.1 and 3.2. In 1945 most Swedish universities had only one professor of economics (Table 3.1).[8] In the whole country, there were only eight chairs (of which three were in a faculty of law); at the beginning of 1996 there were fifty-seven (of which one was in a law faculty).

The chairs were defined very extensively in 1945. They usually encompassed economics and something more (Table 3.2). Thus, Erik Lindahl at Uppsala and Johan Åkerman at Lund were Professors in 'Economics and Financial Law' *(nationalekonomi med finansrätt)*, Gunnar Myrdal at Stockholm in 'Econom-ics and Finance', Gösta Bagge at Stockholm in 'Economics and Social Policy', Gustaf Åkerman at Gothenburg in 'Economics and Sociology', Sven Brisman at the business school in Stockholm in 'Economics and Banking', and Tord Palan-der at the business school in Gothenburg in 'Economics and Statistics'. Only Bertil Ohlin's chair at the business school in Stockholm was just in 'Economics' *(nationalekonomi)*.

Table 3.1 Number of chairs in economics at Swedish universities and business schools

Year	1945	1980	1996
Uppsala	1	2	12
Lund	1	4	6
Stockholm Univ.	2	5	14
Gothenburg Univ.	1	2	8
Umeå	–	2	5
Stockholm Bus.	2	4	11
Gothenburg Bus.	1	–	–
Jönköping	–	–	1
Total	8	19	57

Source: *Sveriges Statskalender*

The tendency towards narrowing and specialization is evident if we look at the year 1980 and 1996. In 1980 most of the chairs were just in 'economics'. Furthermore, there were two chairs in 'economics, especially . . .' (*national-ekonomi, särskilt . . .*), where the latter word refers to 'economic policy' and 'business cycle research', respectively. Chairs had also been established in sub-fields – three in 'international economics' (held by Assar Lindbeck, Staffan Burenstam Linder and Bo Södersten), and one in regional economics (held by Åke Andersson).

The specialization process is confirmed if we look at the situation at the beginning of 1996. The number of chairs has trebled since 1980, and the whole increase is located to the categories 'economics, especially . . .' and 'sub-field'. This evolution can be ascribed not only to the growth of knowledge and the increased number of teachers and students in the discipline: since 1980 it has been easier to appoint professors, and since 1993 the establishment and appoint-ment procedure is left to the universities themselves (before that the government made the final decision). The increased freedom has evidently fostered a narrower delimitation of some chairs than would have been the case if the will of external donors or individual departments to tailor a chair for a certain individual or a certain interest group had not been realized. (One can, however, also find examples where a special delimitation is initiated 'from above' but not

Table 3.2 Scope of chairs in economics at Swedish universities and business schools

Year	1945	1980	1996
Economics and . . .	7	1	1
Economics	1	12	11
Economics, especially . . .	0	2	24
Sub-field	0	4	21
Total	8	19	57

Source: *Sveriges Statskalender*

supported by the profession, and, therefore, is more or less neglected during the appointment process.)

The internationalization of Swedish economics

The existence of an international community of economists and other scientists is not a new phenomenon; nor is the participation of Swedish economists in this community new. A century ago, David Davidson, Knut Wicksell, Gustav Cassel and Gustaf Steffen spent long periods of time at foreign universities, they read foreign literature, and they corresponded with foreign scholars, all of which was reflected in their writings. The same applies to the Stockholm School generation.

Nevertheless, there are indications that Swedish economics (as well as economics in most other countries) as a whole is internationalized to a much higher degree now than it was some decades ago. In two earlier articles (Sandelin and Veiderpass 1996; Sandelin and Ranki 1997) we presented a number of proxy variables for the internationalization process and for the degree to which Swedish economics has become international.[9] We pointed at the decline of the proportion of references to domestic sources. We pointed at the growth of the use of the English language by Swedish economists, and at the same time the diminished use (at least proportionally) of Swedish and German. (An example of this is found in Figure 3.1, which shows that after 1991 all doctoral theses in economics have been written in English, while about 50 per cent were in Swedish during the 1970s.) We pointed at the fact that while about 50 per cent of the foreign books on economics acquired by Swedish university libraries in 1903–7 were from Germany or Austria, the share had declined to 15 per cent in 1954–5. We also pointed out that in 1969 the post-graduate system was replaced by one inspired by the North American system. In sum, we established a denationalization of Swedish economics, and a shift from German and Austrian to American influences in a century-long perspective.

However, the interpretation of proxy variables is not always simple. Some outward signs of the process of internationalization give a more drastic picture of recent changes than a scrutiny of the content of economics texts would give. Let us look at one example.

A Swedish doctoral thesis has to be defended in public at a ceremony where an official opponent puts forward his or her criticism.[10] Figure 3.2 shows the home country of the opponents. We see that in the 1930s and 1940s the opponent always came from Sweden. In the 1990s, only 18 per cent of the opponents have been Swedish, which is less than the share of American opponents.[11]

Of course, this does not mean that the international influence on Swedish economics was zero in the 1930s and 1940s. The figure is to a large extent a reflection of the improvement in the transport system and in the supervisor's contacts. This is *one* aspect of internationalization; it may be correlated with, but is not the same as, internationalization of the content of economics.

What about influences in the opposite direction – from Swedish to foreign economists? One might maintain that those influences have increased, too, in the process

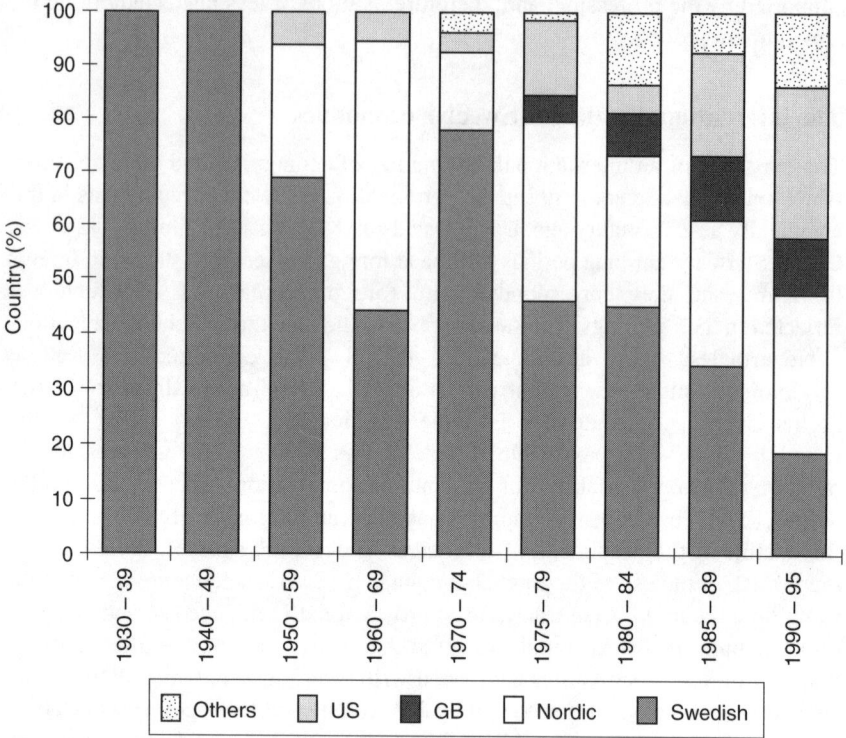

Figure 3.2 Country of residence of appointed thesis opponent

Source: Data compiled by the authors from research by Wadensjö and Engwall

of internationalization, and one might find evidence in an increased tendency to publish in English in international journals rather than in domestic forums.

However, the picture is not quite clear. Older generations – Wicksell and others in the first Swedish neoclassical generation as well as the Stockholm School generation with Ohlin, Myrdal, Lindahl and others – were not, and still are not, neglected abroad.

Table 3.3 gives an interesting picture. It shows citation statistics according to the Social Science Citation Index data set for the period January 1995 to August 1996.

The first neoclassics in Sweden include Wicksell, Cassel and Heckscher. We find that this group, as well as the group defined by the professors in 1945, compare favourably even today with the 1996 professors, in spite of the fact that, unlike the present professors, they cannot be supported by self-citations in 1995–96. The high mean value for the eight 1945 professors (Myrdal, Ohlin, Lindahl, Palander, J. Åkerman, G. Åkerman, Bagge and Brisman) is to a large extent a consequence of Myrdal's high citation rate – 209 of the 246 citations, which is almost twice as many as for any of the now active professors.[12] The large difference between the mean and the median, as well as the positive

Table 3.3 Citations in journals of four vintages of Swedish professors of economics, January 1995–August 1996*

	First neoclassics	*1945 prof.*	*1980 prof.*	*1996 prof.*
Mean	27	31	14	16
Median	29	2	4	10
Standard dev.	14	68	25	22
Skewness	−0.6	2.7	3.2	3.1
Total number of citations	80	246	272	768
No. of professors	3	8	19	47

Sources: *Social Science Citation Index* and *Sveriges Statskalender*[†]

Notes
* The quotient between the third moment and the standard deviation raised to the third power.
† The reason why the number of professors in this table is 10 less than the number in Tables 3.1 and 3.2 is that those tables include vacant chairs while Table 3.3 does not, as it is based on individuals.

skewness, indicates that one or a few professors got many citations while most professors got only a few.

One might argue that the most evident characteristic of economists of the new generation is that to a larger extent they *strive* to write for an international audience. There are Swedish economists who hardly write anything in Swedish. Myrdal's description of the contrary attitudes of the Stockholm School economists represented by himself, and the evolution of his own opinion, is illustrative. In an interview not long before his death, he answered the question, why he did not in his early career try to publish in foreign languages, in the following way:

> I was very peculiar. I was not interested in propagating my opinions abroad. When the *International Labour Review* wished to publish a translation of my supplement to the Government budget in 1933, I answered that I had no time for that. Therefore, the supplement did not get translated. It was my unemployed friend at Halle, Mackenroth, who began to translate me into German. He was an honorary *docent* and earned his living by translating me. Later on, I changed my mind and have written almost only in English.
> (Jonung 1987).[13]

A tendency nowadays to focus on publishing for an international audience is, of course, not unique to Sweden, or to economics. In Table 3.4, we see the number of articles published per million inhabitants in 130 economic journals[14] and in all the Social Science Citation Index journals in 1995 by authors from the different OECD countries. However, this method of calculating publication activity creates problems of interpretation. At the top we find five of the six Anglo-Saxon countries, and after that countries with fairly minor domestic languages but close relations to Anglo-Saxon culture. Non-Anglo-Saxon countries with widely known domestic languages like France, Germany, Luxembourg, Italy,

Table 3.4 Number of articles in economics and social science
journals in 1995 per million inhabitants by authors'
OECD country of residence

Country	Economics	Total social sciences
UK	2	236
USA	1	232
Australia	1	194
Canada	1	239
Ireland	1	80
Norway	1	142
Netherlands	1	129
Iceland	1	186
Denmark	1	90
New Zealand	1	177
Sweden	7	109
Switzerland	7	86
Belgium	7	57
Czech Republic	7	24
Austria	5	47
Finland	4	90
France	4	32
Germany	3	42
Luxembourg	3	37
Greece	2	19
Italy	2	16
Spain	2	16
Hungary	1	14
Japan	1	8
Portugal	1	7
South Korea	1	4
Poland	0	4
Mexico	0	3
Turkey	0	1

Sources: *Social Science Citation Index* and *Statistisk Årsbok 1996*

Spain, Japan and Portugal and others are in the lower part of the table, in spite of the glorious scholarly tradition some of them can present.[15]

To what extent can these differences be explained as real differences in publication activity? Can part of the differences be explained by a tendency to publish more in journals and less in books in the Anglo-Saxon countries as compared with other countries? Can some of them be explained by a bias in the set of journals, such that an English-language journal of modest significance is included more easily than a journal of the same significance but in another language? If the latter is the case, would it, nevertheless, be correct to interpret the table as a measure of differences in international publication with the argument that non-English articles are usually read only domestically and should be excluded completely (which they are not) if we wish to measure international publication? Is it a question of international publication when Americans publish in American journals and the British publish in British journals? We shall not try to answer all those questions but will elaborate on the third.

We find that the USA does not have an outstanding position at the top. This is, of course, a consequence of the fact that we have divided the number of published articles by the number of inhabitants. The much discussed leading position of the USA in economics is dependent not only on the good quality of the economists but also on their quantity.

If we exclude the English-language countries at the top of the table, there is a tendency towards a negative relationship between the global extent of the largest language of a country and the number of articles published per million inhabitants. This applies both to economics and to the total social sciences (cf. the estimated regression equations in note 15. This observation is consistent with, *inter alia,* the following hypothesis: English-language journals are over-represented in the *Social Science Citation Index* (SSCI). Scholars in English-speaking countries publish only in English. Scholars in countries with minor domestic languages frequently publish in English, too, because they would only get a small audience in their domestic languages. However, the larger the domestic (non-English) language is, the larger is the potential audience in the same language, and the larger, therefore, is the inclination to publish in that language. This keeps down the publication rate according to the SSCI, as non-English journals are under-represented in this database.

Although this hypothesis is consistent with our data, our questions above indicate that other hypotheses may also be relevant. The interpretation of comparisons based on SSCI data deserves special research which, however, would be a task beyond the bounds of this chapter.

Swedish economists in policy-making

It is commonly believed that Swedish economists have had, and still have, a greater influence on public policy than economists in most other countries – cf. Jonung 1992: 39–45; Bergström 1977: 116. As far as we know, nobody has tried to 'measure' whether this belief is correct or not, but our impression is that it is correct, at any rate if we compare it with the situation in the US and other larger Western countries. In our neighbour country Norway, economists seem to have played an even larger role during most of the post-1945 era, and have strived to implement more far-reaching elements of planning than what is usually ascribed to Keynesianism (cf. Hanisch and Søilen 1996).

Here, we should make two distinctions. Firstly, economists (however an economist is defined) may be influencing a smaller or greater proportion of the economic (and, perhaps even other) questions on the political agenda. Similarly, each single question can be influenced to a lesser or greater degree by the economists. We may summarize this aspect by the term 'economist-intensity'. Policy-making may be more or less *economist-intensive.*

Second, a larger or a smaller proportion of the professional economist community may influence policy, and each economist may be more or less involved. The corps of economists, as well as an individual economist, may be more or less *policy-intensive.*

The influence may take place through at least four kinds of channels. Firstly, an economist may be engaged in a government commission of inquiry on a certain question; this is very common. Second, economists may be directly involved in policy-making if he or she is a member of the government or Parliament. Third, an economist may work in the administration. Fourth, an economist may take part in the public debate in newspapers, magazines, books, television and radio. Let us assume that the standard of comparison is with the large Western countries, especially the USA. What could explain a comparatively high policy-intensity among Swedish economists, or a high economist-intensity in Swedish policy-making?

The most apparent reason for a high policy-intensity is evidently the smallness of the country. A country has one currency and one income-tax system, and if, for instance, a certain change in the monetary system requires an investigation by x economists, those x economists constitute a larger proportion of the economists in a small country than they would do in a large country. The fact that Knut Wicksell, David Davidson and Sven Brisman were members of a government committee on the regulation of money at the same time, meant that 50 per cent of the Swedish professors in economics were involved. When Dixit *et al.* (1992: 179 and *passim*) criticize the involvement of good Swedish economists in public affairs – academics should not spend their time on 'routine studies' – we get the impression that they disregard that the absolute need for top economic expertise in government is almost as great in small countries as in large, which implies that a larger proportion of the economists tends to be involved in small countries. The *policy-intensity* among economists tends to be larger in small countries even if the *economist-intensity* in policy-making is not.

However, for most of the twentieth century the Social Democratic Party has formed or led the government. That has been the case for different periods in the 1920s, and more permanently in 1932–1976, 1982–1991 and since 1994.[16] Until the middle or even the end of the 1980s, the Social Democratic Party was quite interventionist, and this resulted not only in an active short-term economic policy but also in a very large public sector. Economists were involved on different levels in this process which, thus, tended to be an economist-intensive element in Swedish postwar development. Consequently, Sweden seems to have been characterized not only by *policy-intensive* economists, but also by *economist-intensive* policy-making.[17]

Thus the smallness of the country can explain a large part of the first phenomenon, while the interventionism of the dominant political party seems to have contributed to the second, too. However, other factors may also have played a role. In the introduction to a book about the role of economists in public discussions, Jonung (1996: 9–12) draws attention to several factors that he thinks have contributed to the strong position of the economists. Some of them are relevant to this discussion.

Firstly, he says, Sweden has been spared war and severe ethnic and religious conflicts. Therefore, the large political questions have been economic in character: unemployment, currency policy, socialization, pensions, employee funds, income policy, taxes, income distribution and so on. Furthermore, some Swedish economists – for instance Wicksell, Cassel, Heckscher, Ohlin, Myrdal and Lundberg – were well known not only on a national level, but also internationally. They gave prestige in Sweden both to economics and the economists' message. Moreover, Swedish economic policy and the 'Swedish model' seemed for a long time to be successful, and economists had played a significant role in its creation.

After these introductory speculations about possible reasons for a high policy-intensity among Swedish economists as well as a high economist-intensity in Swedish policy-making, we shall discuss in which concrete ways the economists have exerted their influence.

Work in commissions

Two commissions, and the documents they produced, can be considered the basis of the first decades of postwar economic policy. In 1944 the Social Democratic Party and the Confederation of Trade Unions presented a common programme for postwar policy *(Arbetarrörelsens efterkrigsprogram)*. The commission behind the programme was led by the Minister of Finance, Ernst Wigforss, and Gunnar Myrdal was one of its members. The programme consisted of twenty-seven items, and was intended to prevent the economic crisis and mass unemployment that was expected as a consequence of the peace. Even though Sweden had not been directly involved in the war, a large part of its manpower had been in military service, and would now glut the labour market. The economy should, according to the programme, be coordinated and led by the government; the welfare state should expand; nationalization was required where private enterprise entailed mismanagement or monopoly (Gustafsson 1989).[18]

The second commission forming the platform was the governmental Commission for Economic Postwar Planning, established in 1944 and led by Gunnar Myrdal. It was a large commission which engaged many experts; in order to facilitate the work it was split up into twelve delegations. As a consequence of its magnitude and organization, the commission did not deliver a common, coherent report but a large number of separate proposals on an investment council, control of monopolistic organizations, higher unemployment benefits in recessions than in booms, subsidizing of durable consumption goods and so on. The question of socialization was handed over to the Ministry of Commerce when the commission was dissolved in 1945.

The proposals of the two commissions were not realized to the extent that was expected when the commissions were established. Especially, the ambitions of central economic planning were moderated. One reason was that the economy developed in a quite different direction compared with what was expected; overheating became the problem rather than a postwar depression. However, the commissions corroborated and legitimated an interventionist economic policy that lasted with full intensity until the end of the 1980s, as a way of building the welfare state and promoting the primary goal of full employment.[19] Economists could interpret the documents of the commissions as something that gave hope of a bright future labour market for economists in government.

Commissions designed to solve expected postwar problems were not unique to Sweden. For instance, in Denmark a committee of professors presented a number of reports; in Britain the White Paper on Economic Policy approached the same kind of problems (Welinder 1948).

The economist-intensity of the above-mentioned two commissions was moderate; politicians played a heavy role. This was not so in the regular economic 'long-range investigations' *(långtidsutredningarna);* here economists outside and inside the universities played the leading role. Those investigations appeared during the postwar period, usually at intervals of 3–5 years. The first one was set up in 1948 as a consequence of a request from the OEEC. Karin Kock, then Minister without Portfolio and previously one of the Stockholm School of economists, commissioned Professor Ingvar Svennilsson to lead the investigation. Svennilsson is also usually classified among the Stockholm School economists because of his 1938 doctoral thesis 'Ekonomisk Planering' (economic planning), and he continued to play a leading role in the long-range investigations until the end of the 1960s.

What has been the main purpose of the long-range investigations: to analyse the past, to make forecasts or to elaborate plans for the future? From the beginning, one can discern a conflict between these objectives. The titles of the first main reports in the series were *Svenskt Långtidsprogram 1947–1952/53* (Swedish long-range programme 1947–1952/53) and *Svenskt Långtidsprogram 1951–1955.* The word 'programme' indicates that the planning aspect prevails. Furthermore, in the instructions to the commission in 1950, the Minister of Finance used the word 'plan' several times:

> The multi-year plans mentioned above[20] have been an important help for economic policy in recent years. In addition to their significance as a general guideline for the national economy on how to attain equilibrium and provide better living, those plans have made up the basis for co-ordination of the economic policy. In the latter respect, they have provided a basis for the detailed plans that have constituted part of the basic material for the economic outlook which now is drawn up each year. In connection

with this, the long-range plans have served as guidance in the administration of the regulations in different parts of economic life.

(SOU 1951:30, p. 7)

On the other hand, the commission itself 'wishes to stress emphatically that the
alternatives and guidelines that it has discussed must not be interpreted as a true
plan or a rigorously fixed schedule, but only as general aims of principle based
on the assumptions shown in different contexts. It is even less a matter of
forecast' (SOU 1951:30, p. 6). We may add that the figures in the long-range
investigations about the future nevertheless have been regarded as some kind of
semi-official forecasts. They have been used in several documents in the public
sector where they have liberated officials from the burden of making forecasts
of their own.

There are, no doubt, clear elements of planning in the early long-range investigations – for instance, concerning aggregate investments. The planning aspect
is, however, not so important as the language might suggest to a reader today.
We think it is safe to say that in Swedish (and many other languages) words like
'plans' and 'programmes' sounded much more pleasurable in the 1950s and
1960s than in the 1980s and early 1990s. They were positively value-laden. This
might explain why they apparently were used more often, and in other connections, than now.

In the long-range investigations of the 1990s it is difficult to find anything
about planning. Both the language and the contents are marked by the anti-interventionist currents among economists and politicians. In the introduction to the
1990 report, we find that 'the evolution during the last decades justifies a new
character for the long-range investigations. The purpose to serve as a tool for
indicative planning does not seem relevant any more.' Instead, the investigation
focuses on 'descriptions and analyses of structural problems in the Swedish
economy' (SOU 1990:14, p. 9).

The 1992 investigation is characterized by three themes, the first of which is
deregulation – the opposite of central planning. 'The investigation pays attention to rules, institutions and other circumstances that hamper an efficient
allocation of labour, capital and natural resources' (SOU 1992:19, p. 9). In 1995,
it was emphasized that the prime purpose of the long-range investigation was to
'constitute a *basis* for economic policy'. Therefore, the report is dominated by
broad surveys of the structures, problems and possibilities of the Swedish
economy' (SOU 1995:4, p. 35).

There is also a difference between the economists involved in the early
decades and those involved in the 1990s. Earlier, the commissions included full
university professors of economics. For instance, the commission of 1959 was
led by Professor Ingvar Svennilsson of Stockholm and included among its seven
members Professor Ragnar Bentzel and Dr Rudolf Meidner. The latter spent
most of his active life as an economist at the Swedish Confederation of Trade
Unions, but was at Stockholm University for five years and obtained his professor's title (without a chair) in 1983.[21] The commission was assisted by a number

of experts, among whom we find four future full professors of economics (Börje Kragh, Bengt Höglund, Karl Jungenfelt and Lars Werin).

In the 1990s, the main reports were prepared by officials in the Ministry of Finance, some of them doctors of economics. No university professor is mentioned among all the names that appear in the prefaces. That does not mean, however, that they are completely excluded from the investigations. A few of them appear as authors of some of the separately published supplements. Furthermore, a number of seminars with different experts were arranged during the work. Here, university economists were involved, too.

To sum up, the long-range investigations have changed character. The planning aspect has become less salient. The guidance and the coordinating work have been transferred from a commission where university professors played a leading role to officials in the Ministry of Finance.

The latter can be seen to be a consequence of at least two factors. Firstly, when different kinds of interventionism – from Keynesianism to socialist central planning– lost ground among economists and politicians, the prestige of the long-range investigations fell.[22] Second, due to the expansion of post-graduate education during the last decades, the stock of competent economists in the Ministry of Finance and other parts of the administration has increased. It has become easier to dispense with university professors. This category remains, however, among specialists writing supplements.

We will finish this section with the media favourite among commissions in the 1990s: the Economic Commission *(Ekonomikommissionen)*, appointed in 1992. On a superficial view, the establishment of this commission might appear paradoxical: in a situation where, according to many commentators, economists were to blame for the severe economic problems the country encountered, the government gives a group of (almost exclusively) economists a far-reaching commission. However, on second thoughts, this is not very surprising. A non-socialist government was in power from 1991 to 1994, and we believe it is safe to say that scepticism towards economists is less general among Swedish non-socialist politicians than among socialists.[23] Furthermore, Ann Wibble, the then Minister of Finance who made the appointments, comes from university economic circles. Her father is Bertil Ohlin; she was a graduate student of Erik Lundberg (and never did take the doctoral degree but settled for a licentiate degree), and she has taught economics at the Stockholm School of Economics.

The Economic Commission consisted of six members (plus a secretary), of whom four were full professors of economics; one of the members was a political scientist. Assar Lindbeck was chairman. In addition to the main report, twenty-seven supplements were published. About a dozen of the authors of the supplements were full professors of economics and most of the others were highly competent individuals.

The commission had three grandiose tasks: firstly, 'to identify basic weaknesses and propose improvements in the working of the Swedish *economic system,* especially with respect to rules and institutions that are politically determined'; second, 'to propose changes in the working of the *political system* in order to improve the possibility of creating stable rules and institutions that can conduce to a good economic environment for firms and households'. Third, they were 'to propose appropriate ways out of today's serious economic situation towards a better situation, and to *restrict the transition problems*' (SOU 1993:16, p. 5).

The commission identified both economic problems (macroeconomic instability, low efficiency and slow economic growth) and deficiencies in the political system. It summarized its proposals in 113 points, including not only traditional economic policy measures but also, for instance, the teacher-intensity in public schools (which should diminish; point 77), pupils' homework and time in school (both of which should increase; point 78), the education of journalists (which should be more advanced; point 113), the legal rights of trade unions (which should be reduced; points 30-31 *et al.*), the right of the Church of Sweden to impose taxes upon its members (which should be abolished; point 107), the number of Members of Parliament (which should be halved; point 100), and so on.

Faced with several of the proposals, it is difficult to avoid the thought that the authors in many cases take the opportunity to express their personal values and political preferences rather than 'scientific' results. The report seems to be an extraordinarily clear example of Myrdal's (1969) thesis that an author's values inevitably tend to permeate their economic writings, perhaps without the author being aware of it.

Institutional changes are in focus. Deregulation is a recurring theme. The grand Economic Commission of the 1990s is an antipole to the grand Commission for Economic Post-War Planning five decades earlier, favouring the market, while the Commission for Economic Post-war Planning favoured the strong and wise state. Both reflect the spirit and conventional wisdom of their times.

To what extent were the proposals of the Economic Commission implemented? A couple of years ago, a business journal investigated this question. It found that an overwhelming majority of the 113 proposals had not been effected. A few had been implemented, but would have been so even without the support of the commission; and only an insignificant number of steps had been taken as a consequence of the commission. In this respect, the result of the Economic Commission was even less successful than that of the Commission for Economic Post-war Planning, and it provides a good illustration of the sluggishness of the political system. However, regarded as a weighty contribution to public debate, it may have legitimated other measures of the same spirit and, thus, have had an indirect effect on the course of events that is difficult to evaluate.

Economists as ministers, Members of Parliament and government officials

The political activity of the founders of modern economics in Sweden – Davidson, Wicksell, Cassel and Heckscher – was extensive, but mainly restricted to work in commissions and intense participation in public political debate. They did not appear in the government or Parliament.[24]

Direct, extensive involvement in political decision-making processes came with the next generation. Thus, in the mid-1940s, 43 per cent of the Swedish professors of economics (i.e. Gunnar Myrdal, Bertil Ohlin and Gösta Bagge) were Members of Parliament. Those three were also ministers in the governments of the 1940s, but not all at the same time.[25]

On the whole, the Stockholm School generation was the most politically active Swedish economist generation ever. That can be ascribed to at least two factors.

Firstly, they had a genuine interest in political questions. Economics and politics were interwoven. This was a natural consequence of the fact that their most decisive common basis was, perhaps, the large Unemployment Commission, working in 1927–35 (cf. Ohlin 1972: 162–4). The Stockholm School economists regarded economics 'as a branch of the science of a statesman or legislator', to cite Adam Smith's well-known words.

It is significant that the subtitle of the first volume of Bertil Ohlin's memoirs, covering the period 1899–1945, is 'Young man becomes politician' *(Ung man blir politiker)*, not 'economist'. Among the Swedish general public, Ohlin is mainly known as the leader of the Liberal Party *(Folkpartiet)* from 1944 to 1967, and as a Member of Parliament from 1938 to 1967. Similarly, Gösta Bagge (who, however, is not usually classified as a member of the Stockholm School) was the leader of the Conservative Party *(Högerpartiet)* from 1935 to 1944, and Member of Parliament from 1932 to 1947.

Second, the Swedish academic appointment system was very rigid, and the number of chairs was low (cf. Sandelin and Veiderpass 1996). This was evidently an important reason why others in the Stockholm School generation ended as high officials, more or less closely connected with a political party (usually the Social Democratic Party). Thus, Dag Hammarskjöld, who was considered a brilliant man although his scientific performance was puzzling,[26] started an official career in his early thirties as an Under-secretary of State in the Ministry of Finance, moved to the Ministry of Foreign Affairs in 1946, was delegate at the OEEC negotiations in 1947–48 and vice-chairman of its executive committee, Minister without Portfolio 1951–53, and Secretary-General of the United Nations 1953–61. Alf Johansson, one of the most gifted but least known of the Stockholm School economists, specialized in housing policy and set his mark on a 'social' Swedish housing policy for several postwar decades. He was a member of a large number of government commissions on housing policy, and was in 1948 appointed director-general of the National Housing Board. In 1960, he was given the title of professor without a chair at Stockholm University. Similarly, Karin Kock made a career mainly in public service. She taught as a professor *pro tempore* 1938–1946, and in 1945 was given a professor's title without a chair. In 1947 she became the first female member of a Swedish government, and in 1950–57 she was director-general of the National Statistics Office of Sweden. To give eminent economists in public service the title of professor but not a chair was a cheap way to introduce a connection with the university, which, however, had to remain quite loose.

What about the situation in recent years? If we concentrate on the full professors, none of the forty-seven professors at the beginning of 1996 was a Member of Parliament or in the government. If we look back, a few stray names have appeared in recent decades. Staffan Burenstam-Linder, Professor of International Economics in Stockholm, was a Member of Parliament (Conservative) from 1969 to 1986 and Minister of Commerce 1976–78 and 1979–81. Bo Södersten, Professor of International Economics at Lund, was a Member of Parliament (Social Democrat) from 1979 to 1988. Hugo Hegeland, professor at Umeå 1965–69, was a Member of Parliament (Conservative) from 1982 to 1994. A few others have had other positions close to the highest positions of power. Lars Jonung, professor at Stockholm School of Economics, was personal economic counsellor for the Conservative Prime Minister Carl Bildt from 1992 to 1994. Ingemar Hansson, professor at Stockholm University, is a high official in the Ministry of Finance. Göran Ohlin, professor at Uppsala 1969–1992 and Bertil Ohlin's nephew, was Deputy Secretary-General of the United Nations 1985–92, and had in the 1960s and 1970s worked for the OECD, the World Bank and the Brandt Commission. In sum, the policy-intensity in the now large group of economics professors has decreased.

Economists in public discussions

The old generation – Wicksell, Cassel and Heckscher – spent considerable time taking part in public discussions in the press during the first part of the twentieth century. Cassel published about 1,500 articles in the daily *Svenska Dagbladet* and Heckscher about 300 in the *Dagens Nyheter* (Carlsson 1994: 3). For them it was an obligation to 'educate' the public. This attitude was taken on by several members of the Stockholm School, and especially Bertil Ohlin wrote a large number of articles for the daily press.

In the present generation, specialization and professionalization seem to have reduced the inclination among academic economists to write for the general public in daily newspapers, although a few authors appear quite often.[27] Other forums have, however, developed. We shall briefly consider the *Ekonomisk Debatt,* the Confederation of Trade Unions, the Economic Council and the SNS Economic Policy Group.

The central journal for Swedish economists from Davidson and Wicksell to the Stockholm School was the *Ekonomisk Tidskrift.* For several decades its contents were a mixture of purely theoretical articles and discussions of practical economic questions; the latter were often presented by public officials or, sometimes, business people. In the 1950s, the journal changed character towards more pure theory and mathematics, and several articles were written in English. The definite step into the group of international academic journals was taken in 1965 when its name was changed to the *Swedish Journal of Econom-*

ics. It was changed once again in 1976 to the *Scandinavian Journal of Economics.*

This left room for a new journal on economics in Swedish, published not solely for economists at university departments. Therefore, in 1973 the first number of *Ekonomisk Debatt* was published, intended to bridge the gap between the academic and the political sphere.

The journal became a success, read and cited in public administration as well as by university teachers and newspapers' editorial writers. Although competition among the growing number of media voices seems to have reduced its impact in recent years, it is still one of the most efficient channels between university economists and political decision-makers.[28]

The connection between the Confederation of Trade Unions and the Social Democratic Party is close, and until recent decades, the ideas of a couple of trade-union economists had a large impact on economic policy. Rudolf Meidner and Gösta Rehn are usually considered as the fathers of a special kind of selective economic policy. Their original theory held that if an acceptable level of employment were to be attained even in the weakest industries by means of a general economic policy, the general level of demand would have to be so high that it would be impossible to avoid an unacceptably high inflation.[29] Therefore, it would be better to pursue a general deflationary economic policy, combined with selective measures directed towards those parts of the economy that would suffer problems.

The general deflationary policy was not pursued to the extent that Meidner and Rehn recommended; only in very recent years, when Meidner and Rehn had been forgotten in the Ministry of Finance and the economic situation was quite different, a sharp deflationary policy was performed. Nevertheless, selective means were used extensively. Mobility has been stimulated, not least during the 1960s. Retraining and subsidizing of moving costs should encourage workers to move from unprofitable companies and industries to expanding industries. The arsenal of means is continuously changing.

An official institution consisting of university economists was set up by the government in 1987: the Economic Council (*Ekonomiska Rådet*). It is to initiate and present research that is relevant to economic policy, and advise the Ministry of Finance and the National Institute of Economic Research (*Konjunkturinstitutet*) in scientific matters (Ysander 1989). The Economic Council is known among Swedish economists for its publications. It has published booklets on current economic issues such as financial markets and the tax reform of 1991. In addition, it published year-books for the years 1988–93.

Subsequent developments are significant. Following a pattern that we recognize from other similar cases, the council decided to replace the year-book with an English-language journal, called *Swedish Economic Policy Review,* from 1994. Part of the domestic economic policy debate became internationalized, at least with respect to the language.

The last institutionalized forum that we shall mention is the SNS Economic Policy Group (*SNS Konjunkturråd*).[30] This group published its first annual report in 1974. Most of the four to five members are exchanged each year; the exception was Erik Lundberg who remained as long as his vigour permitted. Until 1985, the group was intended to include members with different political preferences.

In the early years, the presentation of the annual report was an important media event. Serious newspapers showed photos of the 'wise men' who gave detailed recommendations to the politicians on how to intervene and solve economic problems.

The report of 1985 introduced a new era. The group now consisted of an intellectually homogeneous collection of economists. Its new president, Hans Tson Söderström, had declared that the annual reports should have three *leitmotifs:* an international perspective, a long-range perspective and a public choice perspective (Tson Söderström 1991; cf. Agell and Vredin 1991).

Following a tendency in current mainstream economic thought, economic policy was to be based on stable norms rather than be interventionist. The 'employment norm', which had prevailed since the 1930s, was to be replaced by a 'price stabilization norm'.

Such ideas were taken *ad notam* by the policy-makers. In the words of Tson Söderström: 'Soon, we noticed that many of our proposals appeared quite intact in the Government's Budget Proposal. Sometimes, the proposals from the Ministry of Finance were more far-reaching and radical than our own.'

Conclusions

The behaviour of Swedish economists and Swedish economics is clearly influenced by the smallness of the country, leading to a large amount of policy-orientated economics. This is in line with the opinion that European economists tend to be more inclined to work with policy questions than American economists (cf., for example, Frey and Eichenberger 1993; Van Winden 1995). In Sweden the tendency has been reinforced by interventionist Social Democratic governments for most of the post-war period.

In the course of the last few years, one may discern a gradual change, partly because the economists have become so many that a smaller share of them is needed for practical policy applications, and partly because of new priorities and new values. However, so far this is only a weak tendency. Still several top academic economists are involved in practical questions; the last great manifestation is the work of a commission on Sweden and EMU.

However, the fact that Sweden has joined the European Union may result in less extensive involvement in public affairs by Swedish economists. The more of monetary, fiscal and other questions that are handed over to the EU, the less remains to be investigated, decided and planned in each individual country. Even though some economists may be transferred to the EU, the total amount of economists' manpower required to handle, for example, one common currency policy will quite likely be less than what is required to handle fourteen or more separate policies. Participation in public discussions on policy matters may decrease, too, as the stimulus of being read and influencing the real policy-makers will decrease; the real policy-makers will be too far away, unable to listen to all the inconsistent voices from different corners of the Union.

If one remaining difference between European and American economics is that European economics is more policy-orientated, we think that Frey and Eichenberger (1993) as well as Eggertsson (1995) are right in believing that European integration will wipe out this difference. We think that the drop in the amount of policy analyses demanded in Europe will be at least as important a cause as a possibly more competitive European research market.

Notes

1 University of Gothenburg, Mid-Sweden University College, Sundsvall, and University of Gothenburg respectively. Financial support from the Swedish Council for Research in the Humanities and Social Sciences (HSFR) is gratefully acknowledged.
2 We often focus on professors of economics in this chapter. This is not because it is always the ideal group of economists to study but because it is an easily defined group about which it is quite easy to find information.
3 At that time, the universities at Stockholm and Gothenburg were not called '*universitetet*' but '*högskola*' in Swedish. The present official English translation of the name of the business school *(handelshögskola)* in Stockholm is the Stockholm School of Economics. We shall, nevertheless, in some cases call it 'business school' in this paper in order to emphasize to which category it belongs.
4 The sharp rise in the 1970s can to a large extent be explained by a reform in 1969 aimed at shorter and less time-consuming theses. For details about the reform, see Sandelin and Veiderpass (1996).
5 Post-graduate training at Jönköping and Luleå started recently and has not yet produced any doctor. The theses at Linköping have been restricted to health economics. In addition to the enumerated universities and business schools, the special institutes for technology, agriculture and forestry give doctoral degrees within their special fields of economics.
6 *1963 års universitets- och högskolekommitte.*
7 This can be illustrated with anecdotal examples. For instance, the street leading to the *högskola* may be called Universitetsgatan. Several of them call themselves 'University' in English translations. At the beginning of the 1990s that resulted in a letter from the controlling authority, saying that the official translation according to a certain decree should be used, which meant 'university college'. However, obedience is often not accorded.
8 Vacant chairs are included in Table 3.1. The special institutes for technology, agriculture and forestry have chairs within their special fields of economics. They are not included. Only independent business schools, not parts of the universities, are denoted business schools. For a couple of chairs in 1996, most of the duties are located at a university college although the professor is formally a member of the faculty of a larger university.
9 In the first article we defined the internationalization of Swedish economics as 'a process of integration of Swedish thought, techniques, behavior, and institutional solutions with foreign thought, techniques, behavior, and institutional solutions'; in the second, as 'flows of ideas between countries'.
10 Before the reform in 1969 there were three opponents of different ranks. In Figure 3.2, only the 'first opponent' is taken into account. For more details about the Swedish doctoral degree, see Sandelin and Veiderpass (1996).

11 The sudden increase in the proportion of Swedish opponents in the first half of the 1970s can probably be ascribed to the reform in 1969, including a less demanding thesis.

12 A large share of Myrdal's citations comes from disciplines other than economics; in 1989 that applied to more than two-thirds of his citations (Sarafoglou and Sandelin 1992).

13 Myrdal's next sentence is interesting: 'But now I wish to have my *American Dilemma Revisited* translated into Swedish.' Firstly, it evokes a question that would be interesting to study: is the desire to return to one's native language in one's old age, when one is satisfied with one's international fame, common to most renowned non-Anglo-Saxon scholars, and if that is the case, how should it be explained and how does it manifest itself? Second, the *American Dilemma Revisited* was never published in English but only in a Swedish translation as *Historien om An American Dilemma.* Rumour has it that a member of Myrdal's family stopped the English edition, believing that it would have become disadvantageous to Myrdal's reputation as a scholar.

14 Those 130 journals do not completely cover the list of journals defined as journals of economics in the 1995 version of SSCI. Nikias Sarafoglou can provide a list of included journals.

15 An OLS estimation of a regression equation with the dependent variable, ECART, defined as the economics column in Table 3.4, while LANG refers to the largest language in the country and expresses how many millions of people in the world have that language as their native language – Campbell (1991); Grimes (1984); and *Nationalencyklopedin* – and where ENG is a dummy variable equal to 1 for English-language countries (UK, USA, Australia, Canada, Ireland and New Zealand) and 0 for the rest, yields the following result:

$$\text{ECART} = 6.293 - 0.025\text{LANG} + 18.32\text{ENG} \quad R\text{-square} = 0.66$$
$$(5.96) \quad (2.52) \qquad (5.66)$$

Numbers in parentheses are t-statistics. The significance of the two language variables remains if we also control for former socialist countries, introducing a dummy variable SOC, because those countries during many years worked under a different tradition, and for GDP per capita in 1993 in US dollars, because it is supposed that rich countries spend more money on research than poor countries:

$$\text{ECART} = 3.392 - 0.023\text{LANG} + 17.64\text{ENG} - 8.807\text{SOC} + 0.163\text{GDP} \quad R\text{-square} = 0.73$$
$$(1.61) \quad (2.38) \qquad (5.84) \qquad (0.30) \qquad (2.02)$$

Similar estimations for total social sciences, SOART, yield:

$$\text{SOART} = 71.54 - 0.294\text{LANG} + 223.7\text{ENG} \quad R\text{-square} = 0.63$$
$$(5.26) \quad (2.31) \qquad (5.23)$$

and

$$\text{SOART} = 32.53 - 0.273\text{LANG} + 215.0\text{ENG} - 19.00\text{SOC} + 2.279\text{GDP} \quad R\text{-square} = 0.74$$
$$(6.02) \quad (2.88) \qquad (5.75) \qquad (2.16) \qquad (2.26)$$

16 There was a short interruption for three months in 1936 when the Farmers' Party *(Bondeförbundet)* formed the government. In 1936–39 and 1951–57 there was a coalition with the Farmers' Party, and in 1939–45 there was a large coalition led by a Social Democratic prime minister.

17 Although anti-interventionist currents have influenced the Social Democratic Party in the last years, economic experts remain. Stig Malm, former leader of the Swedish Confederation of Trade Unions, recently complained in a TV programme that there are too many economists in the chancellery.

18 Insurance companies should be nationalized and local authorities should take over building sites and blocks of flats.

19 A moderate stabilization policy had been introduced in 1933. The proposals of the two commissions can be regarded as an extension of prewar Social Democratic economic and social policy.

20 He refers to an inquiry made in 1946, and the long-range programme for 1947–1952/53. (Our note.)

21 Meidner can be considered the father of 'employee funds' *(löntagarfonder)* as a form of collective savings in Sweden. However, when the funds were introduced by a parliamentary resolution in 1983, Meidner's original proposal was changed in several respects. The employee funds got their money from a profit tax and an employment payroll tax. When a non-socialist government was in power 1991-94, one of its first decisions was to dissolve the employee funds. This was effectuated at the turn of the year 1991/92. The assets of the funds then amounted to 22 billion SEK.

22 Maybe, somebody would like to add that the attitude among professors has been 'Americanized' in the way that publishing in scientific journals has become almost the sole thing that counts, while practical applications in, for instance, government commissions neither count nor are considered as a civil duty any more. However, at the same time the total number of professors has increased considerably (cf. Tables 3.1 and 3.2), and their attitudes are not totally homogeneous. Therefore, it would probably not have been very difficult to establish a leading commission of the same kind as in the 1960s. Considering those who have written all the supplements which have been provided during the last decades, the absolute number of top economists involved from the universities is larger in the 1990s than in the 1950s and 1960s. We should notice, however, that this increase is restricted to the authorship of supplements where the author writes within their speciality, whether this speciality be the labour market, monetary policy, environmental policy or something else. This is further evidence of the changed role of economists, from – if we borrow the medical terminology – 'general practitioners' to specialists, also illustrated in Table 3.2.

23 Bergström (1977) discusses tensions between independent economists and the Swedish labour movement (defined as the Social Democratic Party and the Confederation of Trade Unions) in connection with four major political questions since the beginning of the 1930s. Those tensions are ascribed to different basic views of the society. In Bergström's incisive wording, 'an economist is a person with a doctoral degree in "liberalism"' (p. 155) while the labour movement is more inclined to emphasize 'solidarity, unity, the subordination of the individual will to the collective' (p. 117).

24 An exception during that time was Gustaf Steffen, Professor of Economics and Sociology at Gothenburg, who in 1910 was elected a member of the first chamber of Parliament, representing the Social Democratic Party.

Gustav Cassel (1940) says in his memoirs that he was once asked to be a candidate for the Conservative Party, but that he claimed to be allowed 'not to join any party, but in the Parliament be free to take up the position that [he] would find correct on every issue' (p. 67). The party leader could not accept this claim, so the proposal was dropped.

25 Members of Parliament and ministers in the government are not forced to give up their former positions permanently.

26 Ohlin's (1972: 172) characterization is worth quoting:

Already by that time [1934], I appreciated very much Dag Hammarskjöld's high intelligence, firm will, high ambitions, psychological eye, and incredible working capacity – and I have not changed my mind. Therefore, I and many others were surprised when it became apparent that his doctoral thesis *Konjunkturspridningen* hardly could be regarded as a fruitful contribution to the evolution of economic theory. He, who was used to get the highest mark for everything he accomplished, seemed to have difficulties to accept that Gunnar Myrdal appeared as a harsh opponent when he publicly defended his thesis, which conduced to the fact that the faculty did not give a higher mark than the minimum mark that was required for a readership.

A few lines below, Ohlin says:

Once at the beginning of the 1930s, when Hammarskjöld had spent some time at Cambridge and had attended Keynes' seminars, I asked Keynes if he could remember Hammarskjöld, and what he, in that case, thought about his scientific talents, which we in Stockholm appreciated so much. Keynes hesitated a moment, and then answered . . .: 'I remember him quite well. Without any doubt an extremely intelligent young man. But I don't suppose you expect anything scientifically important from him?'

27 Bo Södersten is probably the most diligent one in this genre.
28 Eight numbers are published annually with approximately 2,000 copies. In 1996, *Ekonomisk Debatt* began to publish 'Contents in Brief' and a few other pieces of information in English. The reason given was that this would be a necessary (although not sufficient) step to get the journal registered in databases like the *Social Science Citation Index* and *Econlit*. The latter was believed to stimulate the inflow of manuscripts at a time of stagnation. Earlier, graduate students writing theses often published an article based on their thesis in the journal. A few years ago, at a meeting with the editorial board, Assar Lindbeck characterized the situation in the following way: graduate students are now more technically advanced than the students in the 1970s. But they know less about actual economic problems. Therefore, they are less suited for writing articles for *Ekonomisk Debatt.*
29 One of several documents where this policy is presented is the report from the Confederation of Trade Unions (LO), *Fackföreningsrörelsen och den fulla sysselsättningen.*
30 SNS is short for *Studieförbundet Näringsliv och Samhälle*, which in English is Centre for Business and Policy Studies. It is a private organization with about 4,000 individual members and 200 company members. It carries on research, holds meetings and issues publications, including the annual report of its Economic Policy Group.

References

Agell, Jonas and Vredin, Anders (1991) 'Normer eller diskretion i stabiliseringspolitiken', *Ekonomisk Debatt* 19: 336–50.
Bergström, Villy (1977) 'Nationalekonomerna och arbetarrörelsen', in J. Herin and L. Werin (eds) *Ekonomisk debatt och ekonomisk politik. Nationalekonomiska föreningen 100 år.* Stockholm: P. A. Norstedt & Söners Förlag.
Campbell, George L. (1991) *Compendium of the World's Languages,* vols 1–2. London: Routledge.
Carlsson, Benny (1994) *The State as a Monster. Gustav Cassel and Eli Heckscher on the Role and Growth of the State.* Lanham: University Press of America.
Cassel, Gustav (1940) *I förnuftets tjänst,* vol. 1. Stockholm: Natur och Kultur.
Dixit, Avinish K., Honkapohja, Seppo and Solow, Robert (1992) 'Recommendations', in L. Engwall (ed.) *Economics in Sweden.* London: Routledge.
Eggertsson, Thráinn (1995) 'On the economics of economics', *Kyklos* 48: (2) 201–10.
Engwall, Lars (ed.) (1992) *Economics in Sweden: An Evaluation of Swedish Research in Economics.* London: Routledge.
Frey, Bruno S. and Eichenberger, Reiner (1993) 'American and European economics and economists', *Journal of Economic Perspectives* 7(4): 185–93.
Grimes, Barbara F. (ed.) (1984) *Languages of the World Ethnologue.* 10th edn. Dallas: Wycliffe Bible Translators.

66   *Bo Sandelin, Nikias Sarafoglou and Ann Veiderpass*

Gustafsson, Agne (1989) 'Arbetarrörelsens efterkrigsprogram', *Nationalencyklopedin*, vol. 1.

Hanisch, Tore Jørgen and Søilen, Espen (1996), 'Keynesianisme på norsk', Paper presented at the fourth Scandinavian meeting on the history of economic thought at Turku (August).

Jonung, Lars (1987) 'Intervju med Gunnar Myrdal', *Ekonomisk Debatt* 15(4): 327–8.

——(1992) 'Economics the Swedish way 1889–1989', in L. Engwall (ed.) *Economics in Sweden*. London: Routledge.

——(ed.) (1996) *Ekonomerna i debatten – gör de någon nytta*. Stockholm: Ekerlids Förlag.

Landsorganisationen (1951) *Fackföreningsrörelsen och den fulla sysselsättningen*. Malmö.

Myrdal, Gunnar (1969) *Objectivity in Social Research*. New York: Pantheon.

——(1987) *Historien om An American Dilemma*. Stockholm: SNS Förlag.

Ohlin, Bertil (1972) *Bertil Ohlins memoarer. Ung man blir politiker*. Stockholm: Bonniers.

Sandelin, Bo and Ranki, Sinimaaria (1997) 'Americanization or internationalization of Swedish economics', *European Journal of the History of Economic Thought* 4(2): 284–98.

Sandelin, B. and Veiderpass, A. (1996) 'The dissolution of the Swedish tradition', in A. W. Coats (ed.) *The Post-1945 Internationalization of Economics,* Annual Supplement to vol. 28 of *History of Political Economy,* Durham, NC: Duke University Press.

Sarafoglou, Nikias and Sandelin, Bo (1992) 'Myrdal fortfarande mest citerad', *Ekonomisk Debatt* 20(3): 229–32.

SOU (Statens Offentliga Utredningar) 1951:30. *Ekonomisk långtidsprogram 1951–1955.*

——1957:24. Den akademiska undervisningen.

——1990:14. Långtidsutredningen 1990.

——1992:19. Långtidsutredningen 1992.

——1993:16. Nya villkor för ekonomi och politik.

——1995:4. Långtidsutredningen 1995.

Sveriges Statskalender (different years).

Tson Söderström, Hans (1991) 'Den ekonomiska politikens möjligheter. Svar till Agell och Vredin', *Ekonomisk Debatt* 19(6): 525–30.

Van Winden, Frans (1995) 'On European economics', *Kyklos* 48(2): 303–11.

Wadensjö, Eskil (1992) Appendix D. 'Doctoral theses in economics in Sweden 1895–1989', in Lars Engwall (ed.) *Economics in Sweden: An Evaluation of Swedish Research in Economics*, London: Routledge.

Welinder, Carsten (1948) 'Ekonomisk efterkrigsplanering', *Svensk uppslagsbok,* vol. 8.

Ysander, Bengt-Christer (1989) 'Ekonomiska Rådet – en brygga mellan forskning och förvaltning', *Ekonomiska Rådets Årsbok 1988*.

4 Postwar Dutch economics

Internationalization and homogenization

Henk W. Plasmeijer and Evert Schoorl[1]

> The economic research of present Dutch PhD candidates seems increasingly to be developing in the direction of American research culture, where a high degree of mathematical skills is pursued. This development is a threat to the Dutch research tradition, where the accent is more on empiricism and societal relevance.
>
> (PhD thesis statement of Niels Hermes, Groningen, November 1995)

Introduction: some conceptual problems

From the early beginnings of economics in the Netherlands, Dutch economists have always orientated themselves on the international literature. Moreover, many Dutch citizens, from Grotius and Spinoza onwards, have contributed to international debates about subjects such as economic institutions and the economic order (see Wagener 1994a and b). Was not Bernard de Mandeville born and educated in Leiden? One of the greatest adherents of Petty's political arithmetic was Willem Kersseboom (1690–1771), nowadays internationally recognized as one of the founding fathers of demography, at the time a closely related subject. This international orientation never really changed, although it took the greater part of the nineteenth century before Dutch economists, in the wake of N. G. Pierson, came to participate actively on the international scene.[2]

One basic assumption behind this book is, of course, that postwar economics in Europe is very different from prewar economics. We have little doubt about that, but in the Dutch case this is not a story about internationalization, but one about a mutually reinforcing modernization and institutionalization. Both processes started in the early 1930s.

Since the early nineteenth century, economics had been taught in the faculties of law. When in 1913 the Rotterdam 'Handelshoogeschool' (Higher Commercial School) was founded, and in the following decade the Amsterdam economics faculty (1922) and the Tilburg (Roman Catholic) higher commercial school (1927) came into being, their education was primarily aiming at the education of businessmen. Civil servants with a knowledge of economics and economics teachers in secondary schools continued to be educated at the law faculties as well. Since 1945, most people working as economists have been trained at economic faculties, as the Rotterdam and Tilburg institutions have become universities, while new faculties have been founded in Groningen and at the Free University of Amsterdam in 1948, and in Maastricht in 1984. Yet every faculty of law still has a chair of economics, and most faculties of social sciences have at least one as well. Since the 1970s, the number of graduate mathematicians working as academic economists and econometricians has increased.

Before the war, there was a small but influential group of engineer-economists like Vos, Goudriaan and Van der Schalk, often social democrats concerned about social reform and the battle against unemployment. Tinbergen, who graduated as a physicist, can also be labelled as belonging to this group. This stream did not get a notable follow-up after the war.

To get to our subject, we shall start by listing a number of possible meanings for the word 'internationalization':

1   looking at developments abroad for comparison and inspiration;
2   publishing in international journals, and visiting international conferences;
3   using (original or translated) foreign textbooks in university curricula;
4   exerting an influence on the international development of (branches of) the science;
5   importing and/or exporting scholars – or the development of an international labour market for economists; and
6   the homogenization of methods, techniques and paradigms within the profession.

To a greater or lesser extent, all these developments have taken place in the Netherlands since 1945. We shall try to examine each of them more closely. In doing so, we start from the following hypotheses.

1   Since 1945, Dutch economics has increasingly been standardized in conformity with the international mainstream.
2   The mainstream has come to embrace the larger part of the professionals, and heterodox or fringe schools have increasingly been marginalized.
3   While economics in the Netherlands has undergone a tremendous influence from abroad, there has been a marked Dutch influence upon the development of the discipline (a) through the work of Tinbergen and (b) through the brain drain of economists such as J. J. Polak, Tj. Koopmans, H. Theil and H. S. Houthakker.
4   Starting with the work of Tinbergen at the Central Planning Bureau in 1945, there has been a considerable influence of Dutch scientific economics upon economic policy.

As the case of no other European country can be considered typical or average, we shall plough our own track. In the first section we present some general observations concerning Dutch academia and postwar economics. The second section presents an overview of economic faculties and student numbers. In the third section, we present some figures on the subject matter of articles in academic journals, while in the fourth section we focus on some of the leading professors. The discussion on the theory of economic policy is singled out in the fifth section. The sixth section takes a brief glance at the labour market for economists. Radicalism in the 1970s is the subject of the seventh section, and the institution of graduate schools in the 1980s is sketched in the eighth. In the ninth, we compare our findings to those of Harry van Dalen and Arjo Klamer, and the final section is devoted to a few concluding remarks.

The impact of the war on continental economic thought

Already before the war, a serious debate had taken place in the Netherlands about the modernization and possible Americanization of higher education in general. In 1931, the Utrecht chemistry professor H. R. Kruyt had written a brochure on the relationship between higher education and society. In his opinion, higher education in the Netherlands was fossilized and had failed to respond to the needs of modern society. In particular he criticized the ease with which the education of academic scholars was seen as identical to the training for various kinds of higher civil jobs. He found the American distinction between colleges and graduate schools a much better response (see van Baalen 1995).

Kruyt's brochure elicited various reactions, and although this discussion was carried on with some intensity during the 1930s, there was no pressing need to implement alternative policies, as the employment situation for everyone – including academics – had deteriorated. Only after 1945 did the questions raised by Kruyt and others demand new answers. On the one hand, there were people asking for more specialized training and shorter academic curricula in response to the needs of postwar Dutch society. On the other hand, there was an influential stream stressing the importance of traditional academic ideals and the need to educate all-round intellectuals. Had not the war demonstrated the necessity of an academic elite with a straight backbone? In a manifesto published in 1945 by a group of Groningen professors, one of them being the later Education Minister G. van der Leeuw, the attitude of neutralism and nihilism among many academics and students during the Occupation was explicitly heckled. This latter, more generally formative ideal prevailed, although a revision of the Higher Education Act was only carried through in 1960. Later in this chapter, we will return to this same subject matter and the solutions of the mid-1980s to the twin demands for academic scholars and professional experts in the market for the more highly educated.

It is easy to speculate about the consequences of the blow delivered to Dutch political neutralism in 1940. In a wider perspective, perhaps we may say that both intellectual and political events put an end to a distinctive Continental history of economic thought. We are convinced that intellectual history would have done so anyway. It is inconceivable that the cross-Atlantic intellectual exchange, which had intensified between 1890 and 1932, could have had any other result. But unfortunately, the argument that the political turmoil only speeded up the process of world-wide internationalization is counterfactual, for there can be no doubt that political events had a tremendously disruptive impact on the Continental intellectual climate. The emigration of hundreds of social scientists following the Nazi takeover in Germany (see Hagemann 1997) is perhaps the least shocking example of the dramatic drain on intellectual resources which the European tragedy produced.

Whether it is true or not that in 1933 a distinctive Continental history of economic thought came to an end, there was no such thing as a drastic 'internationalization' of economics in the Netherlands after 1945. Postwar economics shows features of both continuity and discontinuity with respect to prewar economics. On the one hand the long-standing tradition in monetary economics, which was mainly influenced by British and American authors, was in 1945 as strong as ever (see Fase 1992). Extraordinarily promising with respect to both policy and theory development was the new tradition in econometrics, which had been started by Tinbergen in the 1930s. On the other hand, however, there were only a few traces left of the old Austrian school, which reigned supreme in the Netherlands between 1909 and 1933. Equally forgotten were the old controversies about the Austrian theory of capital and income distribution (see Plasmeijer and Haan 1992) or about the mathematical and non-mathematical method (see Plasmeijer 1997). As early as 1946 J. A. Veraart of the (then) Tilburg Higher Economic School wrote:

> It is inconceivable that after the war such a book as the one written by C. A. Verrijn Stuart [the 'dean' of the Austrians] could be reprinted in the Netherlands; the new generation does not accept from the Austrian-American school anything more than a few, fairly unimportant propositions.
>
> (*Maandschrift Economie* 1946 (1) p.27)

Veraart's statement is certainly an exaggeration, for many – and not all that unimportant – of the Austrians' propositions, such as Böhm-Bawerk's roundabout production, led a tenacious life in Dutch economic debates and education, as indeed they did everywhere else.[3] But he was right in concluding that in 1946 there was no longer such a thing as a Dutch Austrian School. In 1952 the former Austrian F. de Vries (1884–1958), professor in Rotterdam and at the time the Nestor of Dutch economists, declared the Austrian School dead:

> The reasonably firm foundation, upon which we believed forty years ago we could build, is in my opinion seriously undermined.
>
> (*Maandschrift Economie* 18(52))

The peculiar point about the decline of the Dutch Austrian School is that many contemporaries may not have experienced this as a break in economic theorizing. And those who did would almost certainly have denied that between 1933 and 1945 the development of economic theory had taken a different course. The postwar generation strongly believed in the virtues of what Thomas Kuhn later came to label 'normal science'. Normal science is what the Austrians had done and what this new generation was doing. When engaged in this practice, one can only improve upon the existing body of knowledge, and never break away.[4]

The postwar generation may not have experienced it as such, but in reality it broke away. The changes in economic theorizing in the period between 1933 and 1955 were, however, far more subtle than a dramatic Kuhnian revolution or a drastic, world-wide internationalization. The practice of economic science changed and so did the tools of analysis and the standards for objectivity. The process of normal science itself was modernized. We will examine this in the next section.

The modernization and further institutionalization of economics

The period directly preceding and following Word War II is fascinating for a Dutch historian of economic thought. Elzas (1992) suggests that 'all of a sudden' the Dutch profession 'grew away from provincialism' with internationally outstanding scientists as Tinbergen, Tj. Koopmans, J. G. Koopmans, J. J. Polak, Theil, Verdoorn, Holtrop, Hennipman, Witteveen, Houthakker and Stuvel.[5] This sounds a bit like a Promethean story, yet in many respects this was precisely what happened.

In this period scientific modernism (as defined by McCloskey) gets a firm grip on economics. In the Netherlands economics used to be a subject for lawyers and 'men of practical affairs'. What mattered for these groups was a general understanding of both human economic behaviour and economic processes and a capability to read statistics. Austrian methodology, in particular the causal-genetic form of explanation and methodological individualism, perfectly fitted in with these needs. Most economists of the prewar generation doubted very strongly, whether a (Walrasian) mathematization could contribute anything to this understanding. Anyway it was of no use in the classroom, where Wieser's tables were already an obstacle. It was believed that value judgements could be avoided by abstraction and deduction: the understanding of economic processes should depend on the understanding of individual behaviour. The interest in statistics was interpretation; by interpreting them one could get an insight into real economic and demographic processes.[6]

In 1913 the Higher Commercial School was founded in Rotterdam, in 1922 the economics department of the University of Amsterdam opened its doors and in 1927 the Catholic Business School in Tilburg followed. In the Netherlands, economic faculties traditionally include what would elsewhere be business schools, and most of its students are business economists. But gradually, general economics became the activity of a specialist with a scientific background, for whom mere understanding or explanation is not enough. For them, scientific economics was also an instrument to deal practically with the economic environment and, at the time, in particular with government's budget, taxes, monetary policy, the institutions of the economic order and, in the 1930s, unemployment. With respect to public finance and monetary theory the students were well served, for their education was founded on the German tradition in *Finanzwissenschaften* and (neo-)classical monetary theory. But with respect to subjects such as economic order, income distribution and unemployment, the toolbox was empty.

The institutionalization of a specialized economic education may have contributed to a change in the outlook on how economics should be practised. A causal-genetic explanation is, as far as the tools are concerned, much too imprecise, and the typical Austrian methodological essentialism was almost irrelevant for the new specialists. Specialized economic education was of course not the only influence – intellectual developments in Great Britain and Sweden no doubt contributed a lot to the change – but we think it is an important one. The fact is that in the period directly preceding and following World War II economics in the Netherlands was rapidly remodelled according to an ideal of 'scientific knowledge', which resembles the ideal in the natural sciences. Economics became 'scientism', as Hayek would have it. The development of precise tools for rigorous analysis, which such an ideal requires, wonderfully took advantage of the needs of the practical economic specialists. Mathematics and empirical[7] testing became the instruments for both the practical specialist (for whom they became indispensable in calculating policy effects), and the economic scientist (for whom they were engines of inquiry as well as the only way to reach objectivity and to come close to the truth).

In 1948 the Free University in Amsterdam and the university in Groningen opened economic faculties, both with an enrollment of about fifty students. In the opinion of some of the founders and of local politicians, the latter faculty should have had an agrarian character in the still agrarian north, but despite some initial efforts in this direction, and some quarrels in the 1950s and 1960s about a more sociological orientation, Groningen was quite a mainstream faculty.

Before the war, a distinct feature of Dutch economics (recognizable, for example, in the Gold Standard debate) had been its normative bias. Since 1945, Robbinsian value-free economics had become the standard approach, but the Roman Catholic business school at Tilburg and the Protestant Free University maintained an ethics examination in the curriculum.

In 1984 an economics faculty was added to the redbrick university of Maastricht. It was innovative in the sense that the traditional boundaries between general and business economics in its departments were largely ignored, and also in its educational system, which was founded upon a tutoring method – unlike any other Dutch university. But in general its orientation was no less mainstream than that of the older economic faculties (due to reasons discussed below), although it must be remarked that here an interest in neo-Austrian and institutional economics was revived.

To indicate the rapid growth in university education in economics, we present the figures for the number of graduates between 1913 and 1952 (see Table 4.1). In 1944, thirty years after Rotterdam had opened up, 1,351 economists had a

Table 4.1 Graduates in economics between 1913 and 1952

	Rotterdam	Amsterdam	Tilburg	Free University	Groningen	Total
Until 1943–44	865	293	193	..	..	1,351
1944–45	0	0	25	..	..	25
1945–46	130	29	28	..	..	187
1946–47	239	27	48	..	..	314
1947–48	68	20	46	..	..	134
1948–49	77	25	56	0	0	158
1949–50	121	32	55	0	0	208
1950-51	135	53	53	1	1	243
1951–52	124	53	88	2	1	268

degree in economics. Eight years later, in 1952, this number had more than doubled.

Economists – like other scientists – cherish the idea that their discipline has grown because independent scholars discovered that they shared a common object of study, to be tackled by common methods and paradigms. In short, they are inclined to overestimate supply causes and underestimate the demand factor. But as the comparative research project The Institutionalization of Political Economy has shown, demand much more than supply determined the growth of economics departments and faculties. The enormous growth of student numbers in economics – which intensified during the 1980s when other social sciences became unfashionable – was for the larger part determined by the numbers of business economics students (often more than 75 per cent of the total).

Continuity and discontinuity in economic theorizing

The process of modernization proceeded very slowly. Between 1943 and 1955 the Dutch literature clearly shows the continuity in economic thought, brought about by 'overlapping' generations. We have taken a look at the subject matter of book reviews and of articles in the two leading professional economists' periodicals between 1943 and 1955. *De Economist* had been founded in 1852.

It was the only Dutch journal to publish a large quantity of book reviews. (It still does.) A first glance at Figure 4.1 confirms the traditional international orientation. The figure also shows that the interest in English and American literature is increasing at the expense of an interest in the Dutch literature.

Much more interesting is perhaps what they were reading. Hardly any book now known as a classic escaped their attention. We find much interest in Keynesian economics (including the biography by Harrod). Hennipman even drew attention twice (in two successive years) to Chamberlin's *Imperfect Competition*. His remark on the publication of the English translation of Walras's *Eléments* is amusing: he had no doubt that Dutch economists would continue to prefer the original French edition.

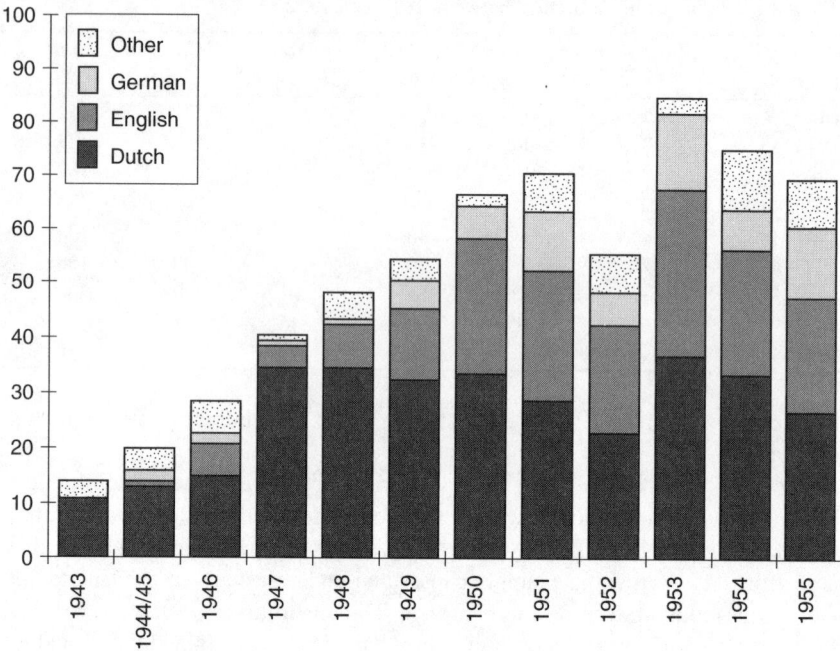

Figure 4.1 Book reviews in *De Economist*, 1943–55

Source: Authors' original research

Maandschrift Economie, a journal which was filled mainly, although not exclusively, by economists from Tilburg, included only a few book reviews. But here we find in 1946 a rather long review of Kalecki's *Studies in Economic Dynamics*. Finally, we were a bit surprised to find in the 1948 volume a review of Stackelberg's contribution to economics.

The quality of the articles lagged a bit behind the quality of the reading. During the first years model presentations are scarce and empirical investigations have a prewar quality. Moreover, the articles show the traditional preoccupations of Dutch economists, such as international economics, the economic order and demography.

In *De Economist* the modernization of economics is unmistakable, considering the increasing number of articles with applied econometrics. This journal was willing to publish articles by H. Theil (on development aid) and Houthakker (on Tinbergen's theory of economic policy).

The distribution of subjects in macro- and micro-economics is even more interesting. Macro-economics clearly shows the Dutch tradition in monetary theory, in which at the end of our period Keynesian economics (Hicks-Hansen modelling) is completely integrated. In micro-economics, Hennipman in 1943 conclusively discussed the difference between Austrian and the 'new' theories of objective value. The debate about imperfect competition, occasioned by the

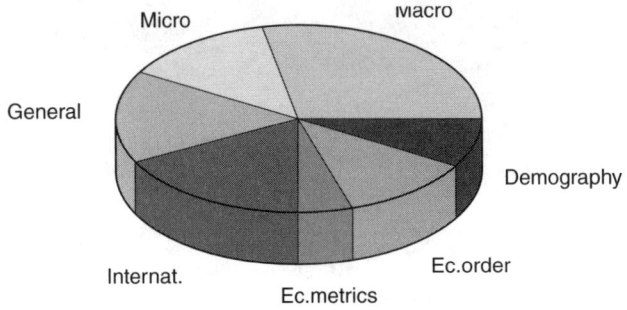

Figure 4.2 Subjects of articles in *De Economist*, 1943–55

Source: Authors' original research

1954 law on economic competition, draws almost exclusively upon the British and American discussions.

Maandschrift Economie was a journal of general economics, business economics and social questions. Its articles show many preoccupations of Roman Catholics, not the least of which was the question how to be a Catholic economist? The debates about the economic order are mainly about corporatistic institutions, for which a law was passed in 1952. In the articles about wage policy child allowances are extensively discussed. The journal's modernization lagged a bit behind that of *De Economist*. The reason for this was probably that the older generation of Catholic economists was in its fifties when the war ended (remember, Tilburg University was founded in 1927). Consequently, the journal's 'scientific' quality lagged also a bit behind. In the early 1950s the quality of the articles improves when the younger generation (D. B. J. Schouten and others) starts to publish. In this early period, no econometric studies are to be found. Again we find macro-economics a bit over-represented. It is our hypothesis that this is the result of both the tradition in monetary theory and the postwar job opportunities for economists.

The distribution of subjects in macro- and micro-economics once again shows the Dutch interest in monetary theory and banking. In micro-economics, the attention paid to theory seems to be peculiar. What is counted as micro-economics here, is the interest of business economists in marginal cost pricing. In

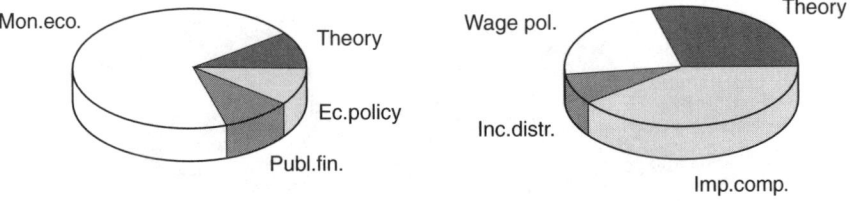

Figure 4.3 Subjects in macro- and micro-economics in *De Economist*, 1943–55

Source: Authors' original research

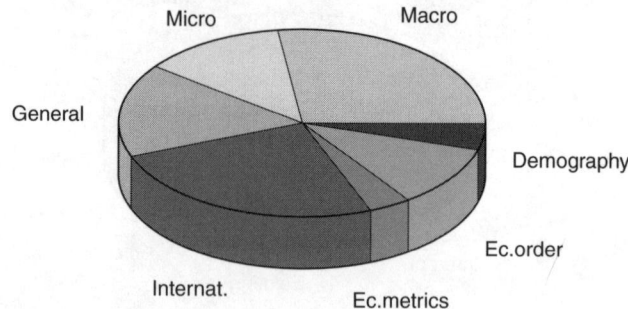

Figure 4.4 Subjects of the articles in *Maandschrift Economie*, 1942–56

Source: Authors' original research

the early 1950s these business economists, and particularly Van Berkum, came up with the mathematical representation of the profit function, which is nowadays taught in micro-economics courses. But of course in those days the true interests of the business economists still were finance and accounting.

In this early period of modernization we find in both journals general and descriptive articles, the style of which one would associate with prewar economics. In the early 1950s the quantity of articles of this kind is rapidly declining when the younger generation takes over, and the method of scientific reasoning is substantially changing. As to policy matters, it seems that the macro-economic toolbox truly was the most important thing. One of those arguing this has been J. E. Andriessen, who between 1955 and 1965 was first an Amsterdam academic and simultaneously a civil servant at the Ministry of Economic Affairs, and later the minister of this department. At the time the ministry employed more than 200 economists. Recalling from this period what these were doing, he records, with some feeling for drama:

> Macro-economics was everything and micro-economics almost nothing. . . .
> In economic policy business life was a somewhat shadowy phenomenon,
> which largely could find its way under its own steam. The former profes-

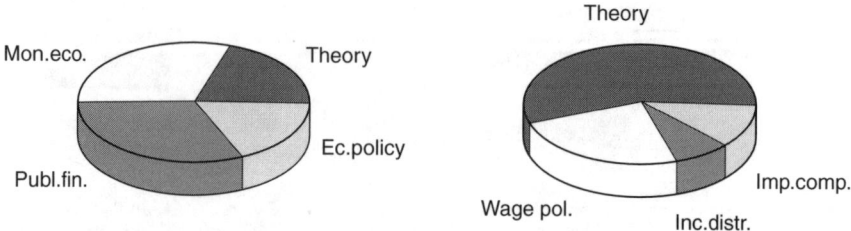

Figure 4.5 Subjects in macro- and micro-economics in *Maandschrift Economie*, 1942–56

Source: Authors' original research

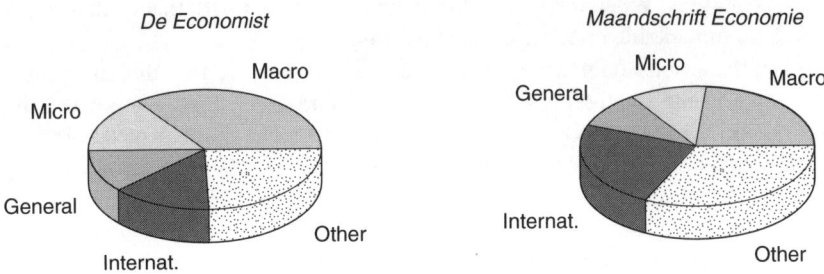

Figure 4.6 Subjects of articles in two scholarly journals between 1960 and 1970

Source: Authors' original research

sors could excel in their strongest point: juggling with macro-economic variables for an economy without serious disturbances.

(Andriessen, 'Het Economisch Eldorado 1955–1965', in Knoester 190)

We are doubtful however, whether this is indeed the whole story for the academic economists. The reason indicated by Andriessen for the predominant preoccupation with macro-economics – i.e. the interests of the former profes sors – seems rather coloured by his own experiences.

For comparison with our figures above, as well as with Andriessen's statement, we continue our story with an analysis of the subject matter of articles in academic journals in the 1960s.

From this we may certainly conclude that the interest in macro-economics was rather strong. What cannot be read from the figures is that the theoretical articles on macro-economics are analytically (mathematically) much more refined than the other ones, except for a few articles in which econometric techniques are used. As expected, we also found a strong interest in international matters. European integration is the subject of many articles. *Maandschrift Economie* published a special issue on the GATT Treaty. Interest in the problems of underdevelopment is increasing. And finally we found many descriptive

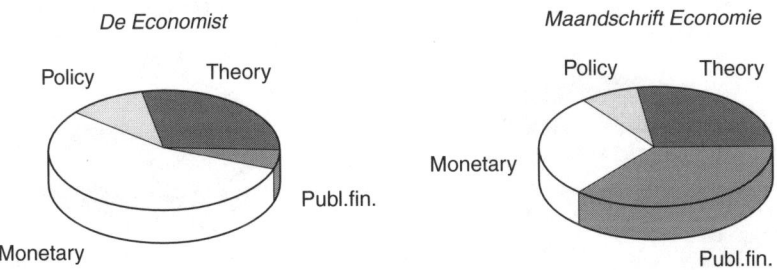

Figure 4.7 Macro-economics in two scholarly journals between 1960 and 1970

Source: Authors' original research

country analyses. When the focus of interest is compared with that of the earlier period, no remarkable differences can be found.[8]

When the articles on macroeconomics are subdivided, we find the same interests as we found for the period between 1945 and 1955. Figure 4.7 gives the subdivision for the period between 1960 and 1970. The number of theoretical articles increased in both journals. The number of articles on macroeconomic policy is rather modest. The enormous amount of articles on monetary theory and policy in *De Economist* reflects the traditional interests of Dutch economists in monetary economics. It should be noted that at the end of our period (1960–70) it becomes customary to discuss monetary theory within a Keynesian-type framework, which makes our subclassification rather arbitrary. The articles on public finance are mainly about the government budget, although at the end of the period public choice makes its entry.

Figure 4.8 gives an impression of the interest in micro-economics. It should be noted that in our period it is not the micro-economics one would expect nowadays. We have, of course, found some jewels in the crown. In most cases however, the use of analytical instruments is highly tentative. Only a few examples of econometric analysis were found. Very often the analyses of imperfect competition, price policy and the economic order are purely descriptive and by present standards would hardly qualify for this category. Most of these are intended to discuss policy matters. It should be noted that our main category, 'other', in Figure 4.6, contains many sector studies, of which quite a few are about the health-care system and agriculture. These are equally descriptive and serve the same purpose. Because by including the articles in this or that category no rational choice was involved (except perhaps for the criterion that the author at least engaged in some discussion of market functioning) we present our Figure 4.8 rather hesitantly.

The most remarkable thing to note about the two journals is the quality change during the period. In macro-economics the use of mathematical techniques seems to have become required to get an article published. What we classified as 'general' in Figure 4.6 were in the period between 1945 and 1955 almost always general accounts (how to be a Catholic economist, and so on).

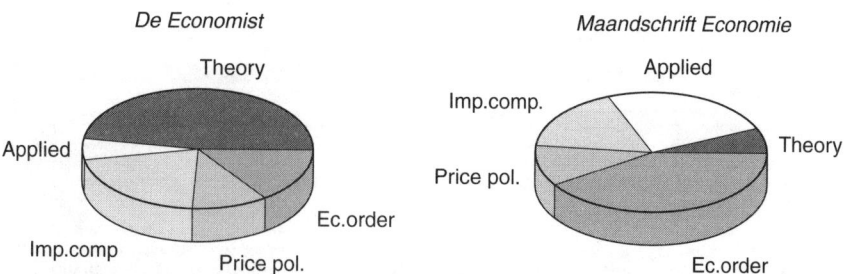

Figure 4.8 Micro-economics in two scholarly journals between 1960 and 1970

Source: Authors' original research

These kinds of accounts can still be found, but between 1960 and 1970 they are gradually substituted by very good essays in methodology, the history of economic thought and economic history. *Maandschrift Economie*, particularly, changed in this respect. It is true, we found at least three stories about the financial problems of the Roman Catholic Church, a most pressing problem in Tilburg of course. But during the decade the parochial character of the journal diminished and the last volumes we examined were quite readable (one single issue even for a Marxist reader). This could be indirectly explained by the growth of the economics departments. For it seems that the supply of articles had reached such a critical mass that the editors could engage, at least more than they did before, in raising their acceptance standards.

What can we make of all this? The interests of the academic economists were certainly very broad. The predominant interest in macro-economics, which ruled the roost in the Ministry of Economic Affairs, is not unambiguously reflected in the scholarly journals. The academic economists went their own way and discussed the topics they considered relevant. But we certainly found an enormous interest in refining the tools of macro-economic and monetary analysis.

Actors, institutions and schools

Clearly, the towering figure in postwar Dutch economics is Jan Tinbergen (1903–95). He had been influential before 1940, both as one of the authors of the proto-Keynesian, socialist Plan van den Arbeid (Labour Plan), which demanded an active role of government as a way out of the crisis, and as a League of Nations expert working on the Statistical Testing of Business Cycles project. Immediately after the war his co-author of the Labour Plan, Hein Vos (whom we mentioned above as one of the Dutch engineer-economists), in his capacity as cabinet minister, asked Tinbergen to lead the newly founded Central Planning Bureau. From 1945 to 1955, he led the CPB in its pioneering efforts at macro-econometric model-building, while at the same time developing his theory of economic policy (*On the Theory of Economic Policy*, 1952; *Economic Policy: Principles and Design*, 1966).

In 1955, deeply concerned with the poverty in Third World nations, he totally switched to development economics. After a year as Visiting Professor of International Economics at Harvard, he held a chair in the subject at Rotterdam (Erasmus) University until his retirement in 1973.

Regarding Tinbergen's influence, it seems appropriate to speak of a worldwide Tinbergenization of economics in the subjects of macro-econometric model-building, economic policy and development economics. His Rotterdam School of Development Planning produced many non-European PhDs who later became university professors and leading politicians in Asian and African countries. Tinbergen was the ideal econometrician of the public and the politicians, combining serious scholarship with politically correct ideas – at least in progressive circles.

In the meantime, the econometrician's econometrician working in Rotterdam was Henri Theil. Both as a scholar and as an organizer, he led the first economic or econometric subdepartment in any Dutch university where internationalization was a serious item on the agenda. Until his departure for America in 1966, he institutionalized regular visits by prominent foreign scholars (Rothenberg and Goldberger, to name a couple) and an American-style PhD programme in an econometrics and operations research department where a broad, internationally orientated mainstream research agenda was pursued.

In the Netherlands, there is the unique situation in which all economics faculties have econometrics departments; until the end of the 1980s they were in so-called 'interfaculties' or joint ventures between mathematics and economics faculties. Of course the econometricians had the advantage over other economists of speaking an international language. This fact, combined with the authority of Tinbergen and Theil, led to a truly international tradition in which many of their successors at other universities (like Cramer in Amsterdam, van Praag in Leyden and Rotterdam, Kapteyn in Tilburg) have continued a tradition of international standards.[9]

It is tempting to start name-dropping with regard to the various faculties. We know that our limited choice is very biased and can be replaced by a dozen other names. But regardless of individual names it is remarkable that many economics professors were recruited from the Central Planning Bureau, and that a majority of the CPB recruits came from the Rotterdam Hogeschool (later Erasmus University), with the (municipal) University of Amsterdam following in second place.

Witteveen in Rotterdam and Schouten in Tilburg – the former more Keynesian than the latter – had both been working at the CPB. Witteveen later became Minister of Finance and IMF president. Zijlstra at the (Protestant) Free University of Amsterdam started as a young Keynesian professor in the 1950s. Later, as Finance Minister, he formulated his so-called 'structural budget norm', and finally as the Dutch Central Bank president he called himself a moderate monetarist.

In Amsterdam, Hennipman was very influential as a teacher and as a *trait d'union* between Austrianism and Keynesianism. He was not a prolific writer and his work has only recently been made available to the English public (Hennipman 1995). His work in welfare economics is connoisseur's reading. Many of his students have been equally influential in economics and in politics, like Hans van den Doel: *Democracy and Welfare Economics*, Cambridge 1979. Hennipman's lectures were an antidote to any narrow, mainstream approach.

In Groningen, F. J. de Jong – who corresponded with D. H. Robertson – claimed to teach Keynesian economics, but of course the true Keynesian there was Jan Pen in the law faculty. He earned his reputation through his work on trade-union power and (jointly with Tinbergen) on income distribution, but his international fame is equally based on his widely translated elementary textbook *Modern Economics* (in Dutch 1958, Pelican 1965).

In the 1940s and 1950s, hardly any distinction was made in the labelling of economics chairs. At most there was a distinction between chairs of general economics and of business economics. In the 1960s and 1970s, an increasing specialization took place. For example, when Hennipman took early retirement in the 1970s, he was succeeded by three professors: one of welfare economics, one of economic systems and one of history and methodology. Of course this expansion was also occasioned by the enormous growth in student numbers, and it was accompanied by a multiplication of the numbers of assistant and associate professors. The growing teaching loads and the reorganization (and democratization) of the universities drew the attention of many away from publishing articles and writing PhD dissertations. Only after 1980 did a catching-up manoeuvre get under way.

The theory of economic policy

In the Netherlands neither Hennipman nor Tinbergen were the first to stress the need for a theory of economic policy. In 1944 W. L. Valk had devoted his contribution to the *Festschrift* for F. de Vries to the subject.[10] In November 1945, however, Hennipman descended from his beloved ivory tower to address the problem of postwar economic recovery in his inaugural lecture on Theoretical Economics and the Postwar Reconstruction. In three sections he manages to discuss the theoretical notion of economic policy, the problem of unemployment and the problem of shaping the economic order. At that time already Hennipman was reputed to have read everything, and apart from Dutch authors he quotes just as many German-language authors as Anglo-Saxon ones. Quite significantly, however, when dealing with unemployment he does not mention Keynes, but Beveridge. And even more significantly, when dealing with the economic order he does not hide his admiration for the theoretical contributions of the German Ordoliberals, such as W. Eucken, W. Röpke and F. Böhm. In his conclusion he raises the competence of economic theorists to evaluate social ideals of the economic order:

> When one wishes to maintain in principle the so-called capitalist or liberal system, it will be necessary to take a whole of finely furcated and differentiated measures in order to remove its deficiencies. Whether one takes as a point of departure the socialist or the liberal ideal, in any case it turns out that one is forced upon the road leading to a synthesis of freedom and restraint, and where the market mechanism is deliberately employed as an instrument of government policy. Only theoretical considerations could point out the road to such a solution.
>
> (1945: 22)

Hennipman left no doubt that, according to him, only a value-free theory is able to produce suggestions for these 'finely furcated and differentiated measures', because only such a theory can impartially evaluate the objective economic consequences of socialist and liberal ideals.

Keynesian theory offered no solution to the fundamental question of the theory of economic policy which Hennipman addressed. The answer it came up with is that economic theory is able to develop policies which benefit everyone. Useful as this may seem, a theory of economic policy which is confined to such policies was soon evaluated as too restrictive. It is our impression that in Amsterdam Keynesianism was only gradually admitted into the curriculum during the 1950s. Nowhere in the Netherlands was there a radical turn to Keynesianism in macroeconomics. Rotterdam may have been one of the first places where Keynesian ideas became firmly rooted, if we can believe Zijlstra's[11] recollections:

> [The General Theory] had an enormous influence and in many respects completely overturned traditional economic theories. During the war, and even more thereafter Keynes's message came to the Rotterdam Hogeschool [Economics Polytechnic, the present Erasmus University] and from the start we, the students were enthusiastic. It meant that an economic crisis no longer was such a thing as pneumonia, where you just had to wait whether or not the patient would recover. No, the economic penicillin had been discovered. Only able and energetic politicians were needed to build a new world, free from want and unemployment. In 1945 after the liberation, that was the gospel. Especially the younger generation of economics students felt an almost missionary zeal to contribute to such a world.
>
> (1992: 13)[12]

Zijlstra's phrasing betrays the social engagement with the real world problems of poverty and unemployment, an engagement he shared with many if not all Dutch economists. Indeed, as Zijlstra notes, the concern with the needs of the day led to a strong belief in the instrumentality of economic theory. It should be noted, however, that the economists' social engagement was fuelled by rather diverging belief systems. It is easily seen that at the time it must have been impossible to reach a consensus about the instrumentality of economic theory on the basis of a mere willingness to 'better the world'. For when it comes to social justice we may expect a confessional economist like Zijlstra to hold a rather different vision of a 'new world' than a socialist colleague like Tinbergen.

Although Tinbergen's *On the Theory of Economic Policy* (1952) is a masterpiece on its own, it hardly addressed Hennipman's fundamental question. It is in fact a superior tract in instrumentalism, which clearly betrays its background in ideas about planning. Tinbergen's argument is sufficiently known: when the goals of economic policy are given, the empirical model enables the economic expert to define 'instrument variables' with which 'target variables' can be influenced. It is, of course, absolutely true that at the time Tinbergen's combination of instrumentalism and a deep personal political engagement and concern with the poor (both in the developed and the less developed world) was – and according to the questionnaires collected by Van Dalen and Klamer (1996a) still is – a shining example to the Dutch economics profession. But, notwithstanding this admiration, it was equally felt at the time that Tinbergen's *On the Theory of Economic Policy* had carried the scientific econometric model beyond scientific purposes. It is also true that Tinbergen repeatedly stressed that the goals of economic policy are a matter for politicians to determine, although he never hid his personal opinion that a fair income distribution ought to be among them. He equally stressed that an economist does not only design an econometric model for isolating 'targets' and developing 'instruments', but also for testing the consistency of the goals of economic policy. We will see that the objection to that was not that when testing the consistency of political aims necessarily social values come in, but that Tinbergen had left the matter inconclusive and perhaps a bit unqualified. Social values come in – and the cherished value-freeness of the economic sciences is lost – when the experts' debates about the consistency of political objectives are not sufficiently distinguished from the social debates about political priorities.

Hennipman fought the battle for a value-free economics mainly on his own ground, which was Paretian welfare economics.[13] Hennipman was more Robbinsian than Keynesian, and for him the real scientific question in economics was the employment of scarce resources which have alternative uses. Economics is, according to him, neither about the ends nor about the origins of individual material and political preferences. This being the case, Paretian welfare economics is by all the criteria of what is called Hume's guillotine (Blaug 1992) a positive science, for a statement that an allocation is economically optimal is quite different from one which says that it is desirable. Quite the contrary, for the optimal allocation depends on the original distribution of resources and may evidently be highly undesirable by criteria of human rights. Hennipman explicitly denied that in welfare economics normative statements are involved. For more than one generation of Dutch economists, Hennipman's essays epitomized the creed of value-free economics, meticulously documented from the entire history of economic thought. In 1992, when criticizing Blaug on the subject, Hennipman referred to the actual agreement among Dutch economists as follows:

> When in 1962 I criticized the ethical conception of welfare economics in a Dutch study I could refer not only to Archibald but also to a number of other like-minded economists. Since then the same view has been briefly voiced by, among others, Buchanan and Ferguson. . . . It has gained wide support in The Netherlands.
>
> (Hennipman 1995: 125)

The Dutch article Hennipman refers to was his tremendously influential intervention in the debate on the theory of economic policy.[14] For a long time it was considered to be the definitive statement on the topic.

The labour market and the Dutch Royal Economics Association (KVS)

From 1945, the reconstruction of the Dutch economy in a fairly regulated and controlled system called for more and more professional economists in business and in government, and, from the end of the 1950s, also for international tasks in the Coal and Steel Community, the EEC, OEEC, OECD and other international organizations.

Between 1945 and 1950, the Dutch government and its agencies like the Central Planning Bureau absorbed a large percentage of academic economists. In the 1950s and early 1960s, the majority of newly graduated economists found a job outside public employment. In the 1960s and 1970s, most ministries and all provincial and local administrations developed branches of economic advisers which absorbed large quantities of policy assistants (*beleidsmedewerkers*). At the same time universities underwent an enormous expansion, accompanied by the creation of many new chairs in economics, as well as new positions for assistant and associate professors. The majority of these got tenure after two or three years, and in most cases even without a PhD degree.

The professional society in which the academic economists and their colleagues working in banking, government and research agencies continued to communicate was the Economics and Statistics Association (1852–1950), subsequently the Dutch Economics Association (titled Royal in 1987). At its annual meetings, policy-orientated topics were discussed, following at first an introduction by one member, and from 1893 following the pre-circulated '*pre-adviezen*' (annual proposals) by two or more academic or other experts. At first repesentatives of various political attitudes were asked to produce these, but by the end of the 1960s it had become customary to ask one or more representatives of academia, the business world and government.

Already in 1959, the economics professor of the newly founded Technical High School of Eindhoven, Wemelsfelder, had asked to include a Flemish representative in the discussions: 'May the board consider in this respect, which are the consequences of the internationalization of society for its policy.' We take this quotation from the official history of the Association. Its author draws attention to the fact that after 1975 many proposals are prepared by more than one author, especially when the first author happens to be a civil servant:

> Perhaps the increased complexity of the questions – in relation with the relatively brief term of preparation – may be the reason behind this development. An additional factor is the treatment from an international perspective, leading to a far greater perusal of the literature. Halfway through the 1960s, the character of the proposals changes. More often, the problem in question is approached in a quantitative way. The postwar generation of economists gets trained in a more mathematical approach of economics, discriminating them from their older colleagues. However, for quite a while only the staff of the Central Planning Bureau have used this method. From the beginning, the proposals using models are the product of cooperation, though seemingly authored by one person. Later this approach spreads rapidly.

> (Mooij 1994: 172)

The Association continues its tradition of having the annual '*preadviezen*' exclusively written by Dutch authors. Proof of the fact that it is still a meeting place for academics and practical economists can be seen in the unsuccessful attempt to hold the annual meeting on a Friday instead of a Saturday. Apparently the economists outside academia were too busy to attend on the Friday.

Radicalism in the 1970s

In 1968 the radical student movement hit the universities, which led to a strong demand for courses in heterodox economics. Since knowledge about Marxian or other currents in radical economics was in short supply, local student groups organized study groups, which were called 'the critical university', in which they discussed among others *Monopoly Capital* by Baran and Sweezy, *Marxist Economic Theory* by Mandel and the literature on the capital controversy. With the help of a few faculty members, these groups also succeeded in organizing talked-about congresses with distinguished keynote speakers such as Joan Robinson (at the Free University in Amsterdam) and Herbert Gintis and Bob Rowthorn (at the Catholic University in Tilburg). During the time that Ernest Mandel was not allowed to enter the United States, he was a regular visitor to the Netherlands, and we suspect that mainstream economists such as Schouten have held unpleasant memories of a few debates with him. The academic profession does not seem to have been very impressed by the students' 'criticism of neoclassical theory'. However, since in the early 1970s 'repressive tolerance' was the talk of the day, most universities raised a few clever clogs from the 'critical university' to the rank of assistant professor and offered courses in Marxian economics. In 1975 the University of Groningen installed a chair in Comparative Systems and Marxian Economics. The university in Tilburg followed in the early 1980s only after the left-wing students had succeeded in intensifying the student revolt once

Table 4.2 The subject matter of the *preadvizen* since 1945

Subject	Number	Year
Economic order	7	1945, 1946, 1947 (twice), 1948, 1960, 1977
Economic and monetary policy	7	1949, 1950, 1955, 1957, 1983, 1986, 1991
Economic development	8	1951, 1954, 1956, 1962, 1967, 1973, 1982, 1987
Public finance	2	1963, 1988
International economics	8	1952, 1959, 1961, 1966, 1970, 1972, 1980, 1993
Social insurance	4	1974, 1981, 1984, 1992
Employment	3	1975, 1978, 1985
Spatial planning & environmental issues	3	1969, 1976, 1990
Other subjects	8	1953, 1958, 1964, 1965, 1968, 1971, 1979, 1989

again. Marxian economics was not to live long at the Dutch universities. In the early 1980s the students' interest declined rapidly, and most universities abolished courses in what was then called 'political economy'. In 1993 the chairs in Groningen and Tilburg were abolished after becoming vacant.

For those who were there from the beginning, the decline of Marxism at the universities came as no surprise. Already in 1977 it was crystal clear that many Dutch radical economists were turning their backs on it, tired of transformation problems and falling profit rates. In 1977 the first issue of the Dutch quarterly for radical economics, *Tijdschrift voor Politieke Ekonomie*, was published. Although the then editors, of whom three out of six had been educated at the Free University in Amsterdam, presented the journal explicitly as 'socialist', the first conflict they fought was with a rather strong group of Marxists at Tilburg University.[15]

The *Tijdschrift* was certainly not parochial. Browsing through the volumes one finds articles by Keynesians, Marxists, Schumpeterians and neoclassicals. Many debates drew the attention of a wider audience, as was the case in 1980 when a group of radical Keynesians at the University of Amsterdam came up with an alternative for government's macro-economic policy. The journal's strength, however, was the critical empirical evaluation of economic policy in subareas such as technology policy and labour-market policy. From 1990 onwards the present editors have strictly applied a peer review procedure. Since then the journal's standing among non-radical economists has grown. The *Tijdschrift voor Politieke Ekonomie* is now looked upon as a somewhat unorthodox platform for discussions on economic theory and policy, in which non-mainstream economics gets a fair chance.

In the mid-1980s a group of graduates from Tilburg founded a society for radical political economists, the *Vereniging voor Politieke Economie*. Originally the society was looked upon as Marxist and the few Marxists at other universities joined. But since Marxism in the Netherlands is not a current of thought to build a flourishing society upon, it soon became clear that at the annual conferences all currents of heterodox thought ought to be represented. The society has about 80 to 100 members, who regularly meet at conferences and in workshops. Only once, in 1987, did it publish the proceedings of the conference. Radical political economy, however, is a very small niche in the Dutch book market, with respect to both supply of papers and demand for books. Both the society and the editors of the *Tijdschrift voor Politieke Ekonomie* realized that competition in the same market will drive average quality down. Since then the members of the society have preferred to have their papers published in the journal.

Catching up in the 1980s

By the end of the 1970s there was growing discontent among younger economists with the provincial climate in Dutch economic research and the lack of stimuli for research on an international level. A ranking of the 'top forty' Dutch economists, published in the economists' weekly *Economisch Statistische Berichten* – by the standard of articles published in prominent international journals – aroused a small sensation, not least because a fair number of young Turks figured prominently on this list. One year later, another ranking was prepared on the basis of the *Social Sciences Citation Index*, which redressed the balance somewhat in favour of the older generation.

In the early 1980s, academic economists at large followed the example given by their econometric colleagues by holding an annual '*Ecozoekdag*', or nationwide economists' research day, organized by the economic branch of the Netherlands Organization for Scientific Research (NWO). This Dutch national science foundation also stimulates research by funding research projects supplementary to the regular university funding.

It must be noted that the impulses from younger researchers to get together and discuss current research came at least as much from 'think-tanks' like the Central Bureau of Statistics, the Central Planning Bureau, the Dutch Central Bank and the more recently founded Social and Cultural Planning Bureau, as from the universities. Already in the early 1970s, the first version of a vintage model for the Dutch economy had been built not in academia but at the CPB.

Around 1980 it had also become clear that with the growing numbers of university students, the old pretension of training all students to become qualified researchers in principle had become vain (and very costly as well). The old five-year curriculum (on average) which took most students longer to complete, was comparable to an MA in other countries. The new '*Tweefasenstelsel*' (two-tier system) shortened the programme of the first degree to four years, and instituted a number of professional and scientific programmes for those who needed (such as medical doctors) or wanted this kind of further education. Also, a new system of assistant and associate professors was introduced, in which research qualifications and publications output carried a much heavier weight. PhD candidates became junior staff members (AIOs, i.e. *Assistenten-in-Opleiding* or research trainees) on a temporary (four-year) contract, and formal requirements for their research training were developed.

Dutch academic economists took up this challenge by instituting local or inter-university graduate schools, like the Tinbergen Institute, and by founding the so-called national networks of subdisciplines for the purpose of the training of AIOs. The most successful of these are the Dutch Network of Economics (which started as the Network of Quantitative Economics but soon came to include general economics), the Network of Business Economics and the Network of Operations Research.

The size of the Netherlands is such that it is fairly easy to bring together all AIOs from various universities and make the best use of economies of scale. Since 1987, the Dutch Network of Economics has been extremely successful in organizing weekly courses by Dutch teachers, concentrating in Utrecht, and having one-week workshops twice a year with reputed American and European professors, such as Joseph Stiglitz, Frank Hahn and James Mirrlees. AIOs taking the full programme earn a diploma which has rapidly developed into an additional qualification for academic positions.

According to some, however, this development has also brought about a high degree of uniformity among AIOs of all Dutch universities, who are well trained in the latest economic and econometric techniques and fashions, but know little of the history and methodology of the subject, let alone of heterodox schools of thought.

These new institutional developments have also led to a kind of 'reverse brain drain'. Economists like Van Wijnbergen, Van der Ploeg and Magnus now hold full-time positions in the Netherlands; Buiter teaches regularly in his native country.

The latest development in the organization of research in Dutch universities is the institution of so-called research schools (*onderzoekscholen*). This is a further development of (post)graduate schools in an Anglo-American fashion, aimed at creating a better working environment for a faculty's best researchers. An *onderzoekschool* can be compared to a two-storey building with the AIOs on the ground floor and three categories of researchers on the top floor: (1) tenured staff who get more time and better facilities for doing research; (2) visiting professors who publish together with the locals while also teaching courses to AIOs and participating in seminars; (3) postdoctoral students – promising young PhDs on a further temporary contract.

Thus the introduction of the AIO system in the mid-1980s, and the institution of research schools in the early 1990s both contribute to a continuing adaptation to the international mainstream in economics. Moreover, a first nation-wide survey of the state of economic research in the 1980s has been followed by regular research assessments of the faculties by internationally composed 'visitation committees'. We share the view of Thráinn Eggertson (*Kyklos* 95–2) that for the time being, this seems to have put a number of faculties on the road leading from a 'good bad' faculty to becoming a 'bad good' one. Or, the loss of colourfulness and heterogeneity is less than compensated by the homogenization and adaptation to an international average.

Tinbergen's progeny?

In 1996, Harry van Dalen and Arjo Klamer published their book *Telgen van Tinbergen*, in which they presented the present generation of Dutch economists as 'Tinbergen's progeny'. It is a 'making-of' as well as a 'conversations-with' Dutch economists survey. In an abbreviated English paperback version of it (1997), the authors have reproduced their main argument of the book, but not their family tree of nineteenth- and twentieth-century Dutch economists (1996). One of the peculiarities of this tree is the virtual impossibility of distinguishing schools of thought in it. For example, the welfare economist Hennipman is put in the same category with the monetary economists Holtrop and J. J. Polak, while the Keynesian Jan Pen is mated with the econometrician Theil.

However, their picture confirms the fact that the typical successful Dutch economics professor in the 1960s would be one with a Central Planning Bureau background, while the typical 1990s professor is one who has worked at a British or American university or with an international organization.

It must be said that Van Dalen and Klamer do not care much about schools: 'Dutch economists . . . do not go in schools as the Americans do' (1997: 9). But we find some apparent contradictions in their picture. On the one hand, they find that 'the Dutch economists, the graduates included, are much less diverse than their American counterparts'. But on the other:

> Characteristic is further the eclecticism to which Dutch economists are prone . . . many Dutch economists continue to embrace eclectic strategies and beat on drums that are out of tune with the American ones. Post-Keynesian economics, which is all but dead in American academia, is still alive and well in Dutch academia.
>
> (1997: 9 and 25)

Their overall verdict on the present state of Dutch economics is quite negative:

> So here we are with a picture of an ambiguous and uncertain economist: he wants to combine economic theory with practice or empirical research but he sticks to his specialization or research programme; he thinks that ideology should not matter in economics and still it does matter; he appreciates in the true spirit of Tinbergen the contributions other disciplines make to economics, still he remains within the walls of his subject.
>
> (1997: 24)

One of their arguments for this conclusion is found in the ratings of the 1995 research assessment, organized by the Dutch Universities Association (VSNU). Only a few of the ninety-two research programmes submitted received a rating of 5 (on a 5-point scale) from the international assessment committee. It is far too easy, however, to compare this exercise with the results of the British research assessments.

In the first place, British universities may decide themselves about the percentage of faculty they wish to submit for assessment, while the Dutch universities were required to account for almost all of the non-teaching hours of the faculty members. Second, in the Netherlands it was possible to display strategic behaviour in determining the size of the various programmes. So in many cases, when the performance of a research group was considered to possibly endanger the rating of a number of their colleagues, programmes were split. Accordingly the number of programmes submitted varied significantly between the economics departments and other departments.

The total of ninety-two programmes embraced economics, econometrics and business economics programmes. In Table 4.3 we represent the division of the forty-five economics programmes, so as to enable a superficial comparison with the subject matter of articles in the first postwar decades, with all the caveats one can imagine – not the least being our own remark about the differences in staff participation between the programmes. It seems that the interest in general subjects (note that this includes history and methodology) has dwindled, while there is a larger number of microeconomic programmes than macroeconomic ones.

Table 4.3 Distribution of economics programmes in the 1995 Dutch Universities Association VSNU research assessment

International	10
General	4
Macro	9
General	12
Other (including spatial and labour economics	10

Moving on to the quality ratings of the programmes, we concentrate on the 3–5 ratings. The results are summarized in Table 4.4. These ratings lead us to conclusions that are altogether different from those of Van Dalen and Klamer. When focusing a little more widely than they have done, the picture that emerges for econometrics and mathematical economics is that no fewer than twelve out of the sixteen programmes are good or excellent, and the remaining four are average. Here we find no scores below average. In economics, seventeen out of forty-five programmes are good or excellent, and another seventeen are average. Just one in four programmes is below average. We do not find this unsatisfactory. For econometrics it might even be difficult to find countries where all the academic research efforts would be equally highly rated.

Only in business economics did half of the total of twenty-eight programmes receive below average scores. Precisely here the specific character of Dutch economics departments, embracing a majority of business economics students, has a negative impact. In the business economics subdepartments, teaching loads are high and a culture of publishing in international journals is often underdeveloped. However, this phenomenon is outside the scope of this chapter.

We may conclude that with respect to economics and econometrics there is no reason for self-deprecating statements. So while agreeing with Van Dalen and Klamer about the image of the Dutch economist as a policy-orientated macro-economist, we have serious doubts about their 'cultural analysis' of the postwar Dutch canon and we strongly disagree with their judgement on the quality and international standing of the profession.

Table 4.4 Quality ratings of all economics and econometrics programmes in the 1995 research assessment

	Total submitted	*4 & 5 rating (good & excellent)*	*3 ratings (average)*	*1 & 2 ratings (poor)*
Econometrics & math. economics	16	12	4	
Business economics	28	7	7	14
Other (2 in computer science and 1 in law)	3			

Concluding remarks

Dutch economics has never been really provincial. But it is true that since 1945 international communication between Dutch and foreign economists was intensified in comparison with the prewar situation. The lead was taken by the econometricians. Keynesian macro-economists soon followed suit.

By all the criteria in our first paragraph, there was an increased internationalization of Dutch economics after 1945. In autonomous and applied research, as well as in the organization of departments and in PhD and publication culture, the econometricians set the pace and exerted an international influence of their own, which we have called the Tinbergenization of international economics. In other subdisciplines, it took longer before an adaptation to international standards and practices was carried through. The reverse of this has been an increasing homogenization, which we regret as much as Van Dalen and Klamer do (but we don't know if their proposed remedy of specializing in comparative advantage is the cure). A continuous thread running through the Dutch economics landscape since prewar years is its policy-orientation. Here also, like everywhere else, there has been a switch in attention from macroeconomic policies to the functioning of markets. We see no indications of radical departures from the international mainstream highway by Dutch economists.

Notes

1 Henk W. Plasmeijer is an Associate Professor in the Economics Faculty, and Evert Schoorl is the director-coordinator of the Graduate School SOM (Systems, Organisations and Management); both at the University of Groningen.

2 The only period in which the Dutch opinions about economic policy differed substantially from international doctrines was in the golden age of Dutch capitalism (the seventeenth century) when mercantilism swept over Europe and the Dutch fought their wars for free trade.

3 Moreover, Verrijn Stuart's textbook was reprinted in 1948.

4 The idea of normal science seems to have been the main reason why the postwar generation rejected the very idea of school formation. It had very little to do with a conviction that there can be only one truth. The new generation, and certainly the social democrats in it, may have felt some uneasiness about the manner in which many Austrians had not lived up to the standards of objectivity that normal science requires. In the middle of the Great Depression and even after Keynes had published the *General Theory*, the leading Dutch Austrian, C. A. Verrijn Stuart (1865–1945), had propagated a rather dogmatic libertarian view on the functioning of a market economy. Verrijn Stuart himself believed that unprejudiced economic theorizing was the firm foundation of his views.

5 In our opinion, Elzas's characterization of 'provincialism' for the period up to 1933 neglects the international reputation of N. G. Pierson (1839–1909) and C. A. Verrijn Stuart (1865–1945).

6 Statistics, however, were generally lacking, and from 1848 onwards Dutch economists have argued for a centralized assembling of statistics. In 1899, C. A. Verrijn Stuart became the first head of the 'Central Bureau for Statistics' (see Mooij 1994).

7 It should be noted that the availability of statistical material facilitated the development of the positivist 'scientific' programme enormously. Indeed, Tinbergen was affiliated with both the 'Central Bureau for Statistics' and the faculty in Rotterdam

when he presented the first econometric model of a national economy in 1936.

8 Here we combine the figures of two papers (Plasmeijer and Schoorl 1997a, 1997b). The paper on the postwar canon of Dutch economics and the research memorandum on the content of the journals go into more detail about the nature of the debates.

9 We are grateful to Tom Wansbeek for suggestions concerning this paragraph.

10 Willem Lodewijk Valk was mainly known for his contributions to Walrasian theory, from which perspective he criticized Austrian theory. In the 1920s and 1930s François de Vries (1884–1958) was a leading member of the Austrian School in the Netherlands. In 1952 he turned his back on Austrian theory; see Plasmeijer (1997) *Early Walrasians*.

11 Jelle Zijlstra (b. 1918) is well known for his work on monetary theory and public finance. In the 1960s and 1970s he was, respectively, Prime Minister and director of the Central Bank. He also was a professor at the Free University in Amsterdam. As Prime Minister he was extremely popular. He is perhaps the only economist in the world about whom a song has been written. The song hit the charts, and at carnival (Mardi Gras) it was sung in the streets: Jelle will take care (*'Jelle zal wel zien'*).

12 Although Zijlstra's recollections are not very different from those expressed by J. Tobin (when interviewed by M. Blaug for a video on Keynes's legacy), in the Netherlands there was no sect of converts of the type described so well in Colander and Landreth's *The Coming of Keynesianism to America*. Perhaps with Jan Pen we meet a true Keynesian.

13 In the Netherlands there probably was not much of a battle. In later studies in the English language, however, Hennipman criticized Mishan (*Welfare Economics, Ten Introductory Essays*) and Blaug (*The Methodology of Economics*), both of whom had argued that Paretian welfare economics are normative. The essays are reprinted in Hennipman (1995).

14 The title was 'The ends and criteria of economic policy' (Doeleinden en criteria der economische politiek', in Andriessen 1962, pp. 1–106). It is partly republished (omitting most references to Dutch literature) as 'On the theory of economic policy' in Hennipman (1995, pp. 1–58).

15 The conflict was about a paper on Marx's falling rate of profit. After the paper had been refused, the representative of Tilburg's radicals left the editorial board.

References

Andriessen, J. E. and van Meerhaeghe, M. A. G. (eds) (1962) *Theorie van de Economische Politiek*, Leiden: Stenfert Kroese.

Baalen, P. J. van (1995) 'Management en Hoger Onderwijs: De geschiedenis van het academisch managementonderwijs in Nederland', PhD thesis, Rotterdam.

Bemelmans-Videc, M. L. (1984) 'Economen in overheidsdienst, 1945–1975', PhD thesis, Rotterdam.

Blaug, M. (1992) *The Methodology of Economics, or How Economists Explain*, Cambridge: Cambridge University Press.

Dalen, H. P. van and Klamer, A. (1996) *Telgen van Tinbergen, het Verhaal van de Nederlandse Economen*, Uitgeverij Balans.

——(1997) 'Blood is thicker than water: economists and the Tinbergen legacy', in P. A. G. van Bergeijk (ed.), *Economic Science and Practice*, Cheltenham: Edward Elgar, pp. 60–91.

Dullaart, M. H. J. (1984) 'Regeling of Vrijheid, Nederlands Economisch Denken tussen de Wereldoorlogen', PhD thesis, Rotterdam.

Elzas, B. D. (1992) '1870–1950: growing away from provincialism', in J. van Daal and A. Heertje (eds) *Economic Thought in the Netherlands*, Aldershot, pp. 75–97.

Fase, M. M. G. (1992) 'A century of monetary thought in the Netherlands', in J. van Daal and A. Heertje (eds) *Economic Thought in the Netherlands*, Aldershot, pp. 154–181.

Haan, M. and Plasmeijer, H. W. (1997) 'On the decline of an intellectual empire, the paradigm shift in the Netherlands', in H. Hagemann (ed.), *Die Deutschsprachige Wirtschaftswissenschaftliche Emigration nach 1933*, Marburg: Metropolis Verlag, pp. 459–78.

Hagemann, H. (ed.) (1997) *Die Deutschsprachige Wirtschaftswissenschaftliche Emigration nach 1933*, Marburg: Metropolis Verlag.

Hennipman, P. (1945) *De Theoretische Economie en de Wederopbouw*, inaugural lecture, University of Amsterdam, Amsterdam: Noord-Hollandse.

——(1995) *Welfare Economics and the Theory of Economic Policy*, edited by D. A. Walker, A. Heertje and H. van den Doel, Avebury.

Kadish, A. and Tribe, K. (eds) (1993) *The Market for Political Economy: The Advent of Economics in British University Culture, 1850-1905*, London: Routledge.

Knoester, A. (ed.) (1987) *Lessen uit het Verleden, 125 Jaar Vereniging voor de Staathuishoudkunde*, Leiden/Antwerp: Stenfert Kroese.

Mooij, J. (1994) *Denken over Welvaart, Koninklijke Vereniging voor de Staathuishoudkunde 1849–1954*, Utrecht.

Passenier, J. (1994) *Van Planning naar Scanning, een Halve Eeuw Planbureau in Nederland*, Groningen: Wolters Noordhoff.

Plasmeijer, H. W. (1997) 'Early Walrasians in the Netherlands', in A. Gronert, J. Glombowski and H. W. Plasmeijer (eds) *Zur Kontinentalen Geschichte des Ökonomischen Denkens*, Marburg.

Plasmeijer, H. W. and Haan, M. (1992) 'Via Von Böhm-Bawerk terug naar de klassieken; over de campagne van Mevr. E. C. van Dorp in de jaren dertig', *Tijdschrift voor Politieke Ekonomie* 14(4): 22–46.

Plasmeijer, H. W. and Schoorl, E. (1997a) 'The postwar canon of Dutch economics', paper presented at the Third European Conference on the History of Economics, Athens, April 1997.

——(1997b) 'Postwar conversations among Dutch economists: figures and observations', Research Memorandum, Groningen.

Sinderen, J. van (ed.) (1990) *Het Sociaal-Economisch Beleid in de Tweede helft van de Twintigste Eeuw*, Groningen: Wolters Noordhoff.

Tinbergen, J. (1952) *On the Theory of Economic Policy*, Amsterdam: Elsevier.

Vermaat, A. J. , Klant, J. J. and Zuidema, J. R. (eds) (1987) *Van Liberalisten tot Instrumentalisten*. Leiden/Antwerp.

Wagener, H-J. (1994a) 'Cupidate et potentia: the political economy of Spinoza', *The European Journal of the History of Economic Thought* (1): 475–93.

Wagener, H-J. (1994b) 'Free seas, free trade, free people: early Dutch institutionalism', *History of Political Economy* 26: 395–422.

Zijlstra, J. (1992) *Per Slot van Rekening: Memoires*, Amsterdam: Contact.

5 The post-1945 development of economics in Belgium

Ivo Maes, Erik Buyst and Muriël Bouchet

The history of Belgian economic thought has not been a very popular topic of research. There have been a few studies on individual authors and also some (auto-)biographical essays. However, we are not aware of any comprehensive study on economic thought in Belgium.

In this chapter an overview of the post-1945 development of economics in Belgium is presented. First, as a background, the changing nature of the university, with the tremendous changes in the 1960s, is analysed. Thereafter attention is given to the evolution of economics, focusing first on the three 'mandarins' who dominated economics in the 1950s: Dupriez with his business cycle analysis; Eyskens and the regional economics of Flanders; and Kirschen, the father of the Belgian national accounts. Thereafter the focus is on the growing professionalization and internationalization of economics, from the 1960s onwards. CORE, the Centre for Operations Research and Econometrics played a crucial role here. In the next sections these phenomena of professionalization and internationalization are further analysed for postgraduate education and the economic journals. Finally, an assessment is given of the international dimensions of Belgian economics.

University expansion in the 1960s

The academic landscape changed profoundly in Belgium in the post-1945 period. Whereas the university in the 1950s was a rather elitist phenomenon, there was a major expansion and democratization in the 1960s and early 1970s. The concomitant increase in university budgets allowed for the professionalization of research and facilitated international contacts.

In the 1950s there were only four universities in Belgium: two state universities: Gent and Liège, and two private universities: Leuven (Catholic) and Brussels (free-thinking).[1] Of these four, Leuven was, by far, the biggest. The two private universities received considerably less state subsidies than the state universities, leading to low salaries at these universities, so that mainly people with a certain income and wealth were attracted to a professorship.[2] In 1950 there were about 20,000 students in Belgium, in 1960 about 30,000.

Lectures in economics were given both at the universities and at 'business schools', with most universities also having a 'business school' (*école supérieure de commerce*). At the universities, economics professors were typically members of the law faculties. Several of the business schools would later become faculties of economics and applied economics, both at existing universities and at newly created ones.

The 1960s saw a massive movement of university expansion and democratization. Several legal and institutional changes contributed to these developments:[3]

- the law of 2 August 1960, which increased considerably state subsidies to the free universities;
- the law of 3 August 1960 provided subsidies for social services to students (restaurants, student housing and so on);
- the Royal Decree of February of 1962 created the 'Foundation for Collective Fundamental Research', which stimulated a re-orientation of research from applied topics, for private or public clients, to more fundamental research;
- the law of 9 April 1965 created new universities and extended existing ones – several 'business schools', especially in Antwerp and Mons, were transformed into departments of applied economic sciences (business schools) in these new universities;[4]
- the law of 7 April 1971 created a new university (in Limburg) and extended the competences of existing ones. The universities of Leuven and Brussels were split into Flemish and francophone universities.

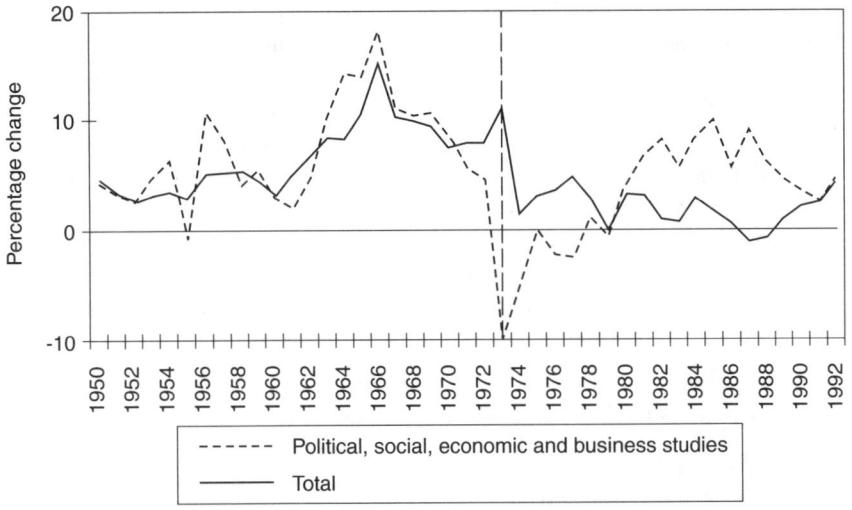

Figure 5.1 Evolution of the number of university students in Belgium 1950–92 (percentage change a year).

Source: Fondation universitaire

Note
* There is a change to the coverage of institutions in 1973, excluding polytechnics

Together with these institutional changes, there was an explosion of the student population: growth rates, both for economics students and for the total, amounted to over 10 per cent in the second half of the 1960s. The student population more than doubled between 1960 and 1970 (see Figure 5.1).

Several socio-economic elements contributed to the growth in student numbers (cf. Lenders 1991: 22), like the entry of the post-war baby-boomers, who reached the age for higher education by the mid-1960s, the increase in income, especially in the 'golden sixties', and changes in mentality, whereby education became more important, also for women.

The expansion and democratization of higher education went together with a considerable increase in the financial means for the universities. This contributed to the professionalization of research and facilitated international contacts.

The data available on the student population do not allow a meaningful breakdown between economics and applied economics. The most reliable classification concerns data on students in political, social, economic and business studies together. These data indicate that the evolution of the number of economics students followed, more or less, the same general pattern as the student population in general: strong expansion in the 1960s, slower thereafter.

The evolution of economic thought

The time of the 'mandarins'

As the financial means of Belgian universities were limited in the 1950s and early 1960s, the number of professors in economics was very small. Three scholars dominated the Belgian scene, each with his own research agenda: Dupriez at the French-speaking part of Leuven University with business-cycle analysis; Eyskens at the Dutch-speaking part of Leuven University with the regional economics of Flanders; and Kirschen at the University of Brussels with the construction of the national accounts. In the next paragraphs an overview is given of the research conducted under the leadership of these three 'mandarins'. One can also note that much of this research was done by volunteers in their leisure time, given the universities' limited budgets. Moreover, studies for private and public institutions were very important for the financial survival of the university research institutes.

The francophone Catholic University of Leuven (UCL)

The *Ecole des sciences politiques et sociales* at Leuven University was founded in 1892. In contrast to the Free University of Brussels (cf. *infra*), the new school in Leuven remained a part of the Faculty of Law. As a result, the study programme focused on legal analyses of institutions and little time was left for training in economics (cf. Lamberts and Roegiers 1986: 266).

By the mid-1920s Leuven University had changed its strategy *vis-à-vis* economics, probably as a response to the post-World War I economic turmoil in

Belgium and the success of the economics programme at the University of Brussels. In October 1928 an *Institut des sciences économiques* was created to organize education and research in economics. Young, dynamic professors were nominated, such as Léon-H. Dupriez. Inspired by foreign research institutes, such as the Harvard Committee on Economic Research, he directed most energy towards business-cycle analysis. His theories had a close resemblance to Hayek's, general equilibrium-orientated business-cycle theories of the late 1920s (cf. Hayek 1928). He was also, like Hayek, free market-orientated, and disapproved of government intervention in the economy. Under his stimulating leadership Leuven economists gained an international reputation in this field of research during the 1930s. On several occasions this research group – later called IRES – obtained grants from the Rockefeller Foundation. In 1947 Dupriez published his *magnum opus Les Mouvements économiques généraux* (Dupriez 1947). This book was very influential in Belgium and France, and to a lesser degree in Germany.

Besides his theoretical research, Dupriez also produced economic forecasts, which were sold to private and (semi-) public corporations and institutions in order to assure the financial situation of IRES.

In the 1950s and early 1960s business-cycle analysis remained a top priority for Dupriez. In the meantime, however, Keynesian ideas had taken over the international economics scene. Dupriez never joined this trend. On the contrary, he rejected the Keynesian approach because it lacked solid microeconomic foundations. Instead, he continued to work in the tradition of the Austrian School (cf. Dupriez 1972). Dupriez's attitude certainly slowed down the penetration of Keynesian ideas at Leuven University, or to put it more precisely, at the French-speaking part of Leuven University.

The Flemish Catholic University of Leuven

The Dutch-speaking (= Flemish) part of the University of Leuven expanded rapidly in the early 1930s. It required the nomination of young Dutch-speaking professors, such as Gaston Eyskens.[5] In the late 1940s Karel Pinxten joined the *Instituut voor economische wetenschappen*, the Dutch-speaking equivalent of the *Institut des sciences économiques*. He introduced Keynesianism at Leuven and managed to convince Gaston Eyskens of the merits of these new ideas. In 1955 the Dutch-speaking economists at Leuven University created their own research institute (Centre for Economic Studies). The focus of their research was on regional problems, especially unemployment in different Flemish districts. They also developed proposals for a more interventionist regional policy for the Flemish economy, something which went squarely against Dupriez's free-market ideas. In 1959 Gaston Eyskens – by then (once again) Prime Minister of Belgium – succeeded in putting these recommendations into law. The strong dependence on external financing also induced the Centre for Economic Studies to undertake several sector studies, the so-called 'bread-and-butter studies'.

The francophone Free University of Brussels (ULB)

In 1897 an independent *Ecole des sciences politiques et sociales* was established at the Free University of Brussels (cf. d'Aviella 1909: 134–6). It consisted of three sections, each with its own study programme:

1   *section des sciences sociales*;
2   *section des sciences politiques et administratives*;
3   *section des sciences économiques*.

In 1950 Etienne Sadi Kirschen became professor at the economics section. In his previous job, as a Belgian representative at the Organization of European Economic Cooperation (OEEC), Kirschen had become familiar with Keynesian economics and, in particular, national income accounting. Kirschen used this knowledge to introduce Keynesianism at the University of Brussels. Moreover, as the Belgian Statistical Office was unable to provide the Belgian national income estimates asked for by the OEEC, Kirschen started a project of his own (cf. Kirschen 1988: 109–17). With the help of several collaborators a first report providing GNP estimates for Belgium was published in 1953. In 1957 Kirschen institutionalized this research group by founding DULBEA and a year later an economics journal was started, the *Cahiers économiques de Bruxelles*. In the early 1960s the Belgian Statistical Office finally took over the task of calculating and publishing national income estimates from DULBEA. It allowed Kirschen and DULBEA to start a new, large-scale research project focusing on the theoretical and empirical analysis of economic policy (cf. Kirschen *et al.* 1964).

A growing professionalization and internationalization

In the course of the 1960s the universities' financial situation improved substantially and the number of economics students soared. Several new young professors were hired, breaking the 'monopoly' of the mandarins on research and education. A major consequence was that the different institutes lost their specialization and developed into more general economics departments, with a wider range of research.

The francophone Catholic University of Leuven (UCL)

In the course of the expansion of the 1960s Dupriez's influence on the economics department declined rapidly – notwithstanding the fact that, still today, business-cycle analysis remains important at the UCL. From the 1960s until today, Keynesianism, in its different varieties (cf. Coddington 1976) has blossomed. Macroeconomic modelling, a typical element of 'hydraulic Keynesianism' gained in importance, especially under the influence of Albert Kervyn, the first secretary-general of the Belgian Planning Bureau (cf. Steinherr 1987: vii). Moreover, 'fundamentalist Keynesianism', and other types of left-wing economics became quite popular, especially after the events of May 1968. Most influential, however, was 'disequilibrium Keynesianism', inspired by Jacques Drèze.

Also other, more microeconomic-orientated research programmes were launched. One of them concerned industrial economics, where Alexis Jacquemain played a leading role. Probably most important, however, was the foundation of CORE.

Jacques Drèze and the Centre for Operations Research and Econometrics (CORE)

In the history of Belgian economics in the 1970s and 1980s, a central role was played by Jacques Drèze and the Centre for Operations Research and Econometrics (CORE). According to the latest ranking of economists according to citations, covering the period 1991–95, Drèze was by far the most quoted Belgian economist, with nearly double the number of citations than the number two (cf. Table 5.1). CORE dominated academic research in the 1970s and 1980s and is still, notwithstanding a certain fallback among the top three research institutions in Belgium, according to the rankings of both publications and citations (cf. Table 5.2).

Drèze, after graduate studies in the United States, became a professor at the University of Leuven. He founded, together with some colleagues, the Centre for Operations Research and Econometrics (CORE) in 1966, at the then still unitary University of Leuven. The purpose was to stimulate research in mathematical economics, econometrics and operations research.

For Drèze this was also an opportunity to attract American economists to Leuven. As he had noticed in the early 1960s, when he was Ford Foundation

Table 5.1 Top ten Belgian economists, 1991–95[a]

According to publications[b]			According to citations		
Name	Institution	Points	Name	Institution	Citations
M. Dewatripont	ULB/ECARE	557	J. Drèze	CORE	300
G. Roland	ULB	384	C. d'Aspremont	UCL	187
P. Bolton	ULB	356	A. Jacquemain	UCL	170
P. Pestiau	ULG	318	Ph. Weil	ULB	160
A. Rustuchini	CORE	255	P. De Grauwe	KUL	140
J. Thisse	CORE	249	A. Barten	KUL	132
C. G. de Vries	KUL	238	R. Anderson	UCL	114
Ph. Mongin	UCL	234	P. Bairoch	ULB	110
P. Sercu	KUL	231	D. Gros	CEPS	106
J. Steenkamp	KUL	186	J. Jaskold-Gabszewicz	UCL	104

Source: *Elewaut*, 1996

Notes
(a) Belgian: working in Belgium
(b) In reputed economic journals

Table 5.2 Top five Belgian faculties and research institutions[a]

According to publications[b]			According to citations		
Name	Institute 1987–91	Points 1991–95	Name	Institute 1990–94	Citations 1991–95
Centre for Operations Research and Econometrics (CORE)	2.507	1.497	CORE	944	724
			UCL	712	864
Catholic University of Leuven (Fr) (UCL)	1.869	1.445	ULB	698	736
Catholic University of Leuven (Fl) (KUL)	1.587	2.683	KUL	629	701
Free University of Brussels (Fr) (ULB)	1.492	1.518	University of Liège (Fr) (ULG)	186	200
University of Antwerp (Fl) (UFSIA)	241	697			

Source: *Elewaut*, 1996

Notes
(a) Fl: Flemish, Fr: Francophone
(b) In reputed economic journals

Professor at the University of Chicago, many American economists wanted to go to Europe, but there was no research centre with the appropriate facilities. CORE decided then to create, instead of two posts of assistants, two fellowships, which would be open for anyone in the world. It enabled CORE to welcome economists like M. Miller, a subsequent Nobel Prize winner, and J. Hirshleifer, as fellows.

CORE received a big impetus in 1968, when Drèze succeeded in obtaining an important grant from the Ford Foundation. Moreover, this grant was matched by the university, which provided CORE with new buildings and six positions of professor (three Flemish and three francophone). A setback for CORE was the division of the university. After a vote, CORE chose to join the francophone side (UCL), and moved to Louvain-la-Neuve in the mid-1970s.

The following characteristics account for the distinctive nature of CORE:

• *Interdisciplinary cooperation* The original founders came from three different disciplines: applied sciences, business administration, and economics. Mathematical and statistical methods formed the common language.

- *Cooperation between specialists in the fundamental sciences and in new applications* Initially CORE concentrated on fundamental research. Gradually more attention has been given to applied research, as awareness of the big gap between theory and applications increased.
- *Inter-university cooperation* The permanent staff of CORE consists of professors of several Belgian universities. While UCL professors, like Drèze, Phlips and Thisse, formed the nucleus of CORE, there were also permanent members of other universities like Barten (KUL), Waelbroeck (ULB) and several others.
- *International cooperation* Openness and hospitality for researchers from all over the world has been a characteristic of CORE from the beginning.

The scientific activities at CORE can be distinguished according to the three weekly seminars (Cornet and Tulkens 1989: xii):

1 *Mathematical economics and game theory* Researchers at CORE made important contributions to the theory of equilibria of a large economy. Arrow and Hahn (1971: vi) refer to a 'Belgian school'. Later, attention shifted to price rigidities, and 'the microeconomic foundations of macroeconomics' was for some time a big theme (Hildenbrand 1989: 66).
2 *Operations research and mathematical programming.*
3 *Econometrics* CORE has made major contributions in, for example, disequilibrium and Bayesian econometrics. However, according to one observer, not so much of this work has 'filtered down' into the economics profession (Pagan 1989: 320). He attributes this to US preferences for the assumption of price-clearing markets (certainly a difference between American and European economics) and the computational burdens that these techniques entail.

CORE has always been a widely international institution. From the beginning, English has been the working language at CORE. The great openness of Belgians, a rather natural consequence of living in a small country, certainly contributed to the emergence of an institution such as CORE. Also the personality of Drèze played an important role: a brilliant economist, in the mainstream of economic thought, and an excellent organizer.

In Belgium, CORE has been criticized for being too 'academic' and 'international' and not producing concrete practical studies on Wallonia. However, Drèze has been concerned about actual economic problems, especially unemployment. His presidential address to the European Economic Association was entitled 'Underemployment equilibria: from theory to econometrics and policy' (Drèze 1987). As with so many Belgian economists, much of his policy work has to be situated in a European framework. So Drèze was a member, and later chairman, of the Macroeconomic Policy Group of the Centre for European Policy Studies (CEPS).

The ULB

During the 1960s and 1970s Jean Waelbroeck acquired more influence in the economics department of the francophone Free University of Brussels (ULB). While also being an applied economist like Kirschen, Waelbroeck was more theoretical and econometrically orientated, partly as a result of his studies in Canada. In order to pursue his own projects, he left DULBEA and founded his own research institute: CEME, the *Centre d'Economie Mathématique et d'Econométrie* (Centre for Mathematical Economics and Econometrics). He was also an active member of CORE.

Waelbroeck was very active in macroeconometric modelling, as a founding member of Project Link with Lawrence Klein, and in applied general equilibrium modelling. He was mainly interested in international economic problems, especially in developing countries and in European integration. He was a special adviser to the research department of the World Bank, and undertook several research projects for the European Commission.

Waelbroeck also contributed to European integration in economics, especially by founding, together with Glejser, the *European Economic Review* in 1969. He remained its chief editor for twenty-one years. In the 'Editor's Introduction', Waelbroeck and Glejser (1969: 3) attacked the narrowness of European economics: 'It has become customary for all universities and research institutes to publish their own journals, addressed usually to a narrow circle of readers.' They notice some changes as 'a few good European journals have been contributing to some "internationalization" of our science by publishing articles in two or more languages.' They want to go further with the *European Economic Review*, 'published entirely in English, the lingua franca of economics'. Their aim is to assemble some of the best research being done throughout Europe and to make it accessible world-wide.

European integration, in the academic community and as a topic of research, was also the motive for the foundation of ECARE, the European Centre for Advanced Research in Economics at the ULB, in 1991. It was a joint initiative of the interdisciplinary Institute of European Studies of the ULB and the London-based Centre for Economic Policy Research (CEPR). Its aim is to encourage high-quality research in economics, with special emphasis on policy issues relevant to Western and Eastern Europe, and to provide a meeting place for academics, professional economists, and civil servants from the EC Commission.

A monetarist counterrevolution in Leuven

Macroeconomic thought in Belgium remained very Keynesian in the 1970s and 1980s. The exception is the Flemish Catholic University of Leuven (KUL), where monetarism gained ground, without however dominating the economics department. Leuven became the Belgian branch of the 'Brunner-Meltzer' or credit market variant of monetarism. One of the most important events was the 'All Saints' Day Manifesto for a Monetary Union' (*The Economist*, 1 November 1975), a proposal for a market-led introduction of a single European currency, wherein the Leuven monetarists played a very important role.

The growth of graduate education in economics

In the late 1940s and early 1950s Marshall's *Principles of Economics* was still the basis for economics lectures. Gradually, Keynesian economics would gain influence.[6] The economics curriculum also displayed a greater emphasis on quantitative techniques. The first econometrics course was taught in the academic year 1957–58, by John van Waterschoot, at the (Flemish) University of Leuven (cf. Drèze 1985: 451). The use of English also increased. We will focus on graduate education, itself a new phenomenon,[7] which most clearly reveals the new tendencies.

Several universities, like the (francophone) Free University of Brussels (ULB), in 1959, and the University of Gent, in 1969, introduced Master's degrees in econometrics.[8] The (Flemish) University of Leuven was the first to introduce an economics Master's degree programme in English in the early 1970s.

Most innovative was probably the introduction of the European Doctoral Programme in Quantitative Economics at the end of the 1970s by the (francophone) University of Leuven (UCL), together with the London School of Economics and the Rheinische Friedrich-Wilhelms-Universität Bonn. Later it was also joined by the Ecole des Hautes Etudes en Sciences Sociales in Paris. This programme, necessitating a minimum of three years of work, comprises a preliminary level, an advanced level and a dissertation, and has to be undertaken at two of the participating institutions.

The preliminary-level course work lasts one year and, in principle, the teaching is in the local language of the chosen university. Students admitted to the advanced level do a further year of course work, in English, at one of the other three institutions. The dissertation, normally in English, may be written at either of the institutions where course work was done.

Journals

We will focus in this section on the *Recherches Economiques de Louvain* and the *Tijdschrift voor Economie en Management*, the leading journals among respectively francophone and Flemish-speaking economists. Furthermore, attention is also given to the *Bulletin of the National Bank of Belgium*, which played an important role in the propagation of foreign ideas in Belgium, especially in the 1950s and 1960s.

Recherches économiques de Louvain[9]

The *Recherches économiques de Louvain* has played a central role at the UCL, as can be seen in particular from the large number of contributions from the 'patriarch' Dupriez, especially during the prewar period, and the articles written

Table 5.3 Recherches économiques de Louvain: classification by origin of the author[a]

	Belgium		Foreign countries					Total number of articles
	UCL	Others	France	UK	Germany	USA–Canada	Others	
1929–33	100	0	0	0	0	0	0	103
1934–39	100	0	0	0	0	0	0	120
1946–50	99	0	0	0	0	0	1	114
1951–55	100	0	0	0	0	0	0	122
1956–60	97	3	0	0	0	0	0	123
1961–65	99	1	0	0	0	0	0	117
1966–70	75	8	1	2	1	12	1	100
1971–75	52	17	1	6	2	13	8	98
1976–80	42	20	7	10	3	10	8	90
1981–85	34	9	9	22	4	12	11	86
1986–90	14	8	23	14	1	14	25	90
1991–96	14	6	36	4	11	10	19	113

(a) Percentage of the total

by important representatives of the Catholic University of Louvain (UCL), such as Rousseaux, Duquesne de la Vinelle, Woitrin, Löwenthal and Drèze.

Among Belgian institutions, UCL is clearly the dominant contributor, with a total of 915 articles since 1929. The other Belgian institutions have published only seventy articles in the *Recherches économiques de Louvain*. France, the United Kingdom and the United States are the most active foreign countries represented, but notwithstanding the notable presence of the two last-mentioned countries, only 20 per cent of the articles were published in English. Literary analyses greatly exceed the number of mathematical or statistical articles as far as methods are concerned.

Too general an examination of the data contained in the Table is, however, misleading because changes, sometimes rather dramatic, have occurred. The end of the 1960s is crucial from this point of view. It goes together with a restructuring of the *Recherches*, diminishing the importance of the diagnoses of the actual business cycle and giving more space to a 'modern, more complete and profound analysis'. Alexis Jacquemain (UCL) became editor in 1968.

The break appears, among other things, from the change in profile of the contributing institutions. While UCL accounted for almost all the articles published between 1929 and the beginning of the 1950s, it represented no more than 75 per cent of the articles published between 1966 and 1970. It declined further in later years, amounting to only 14 per cent from 1991 to 1996.[10]

This considerable decrease did not give rise to a large increase in the number

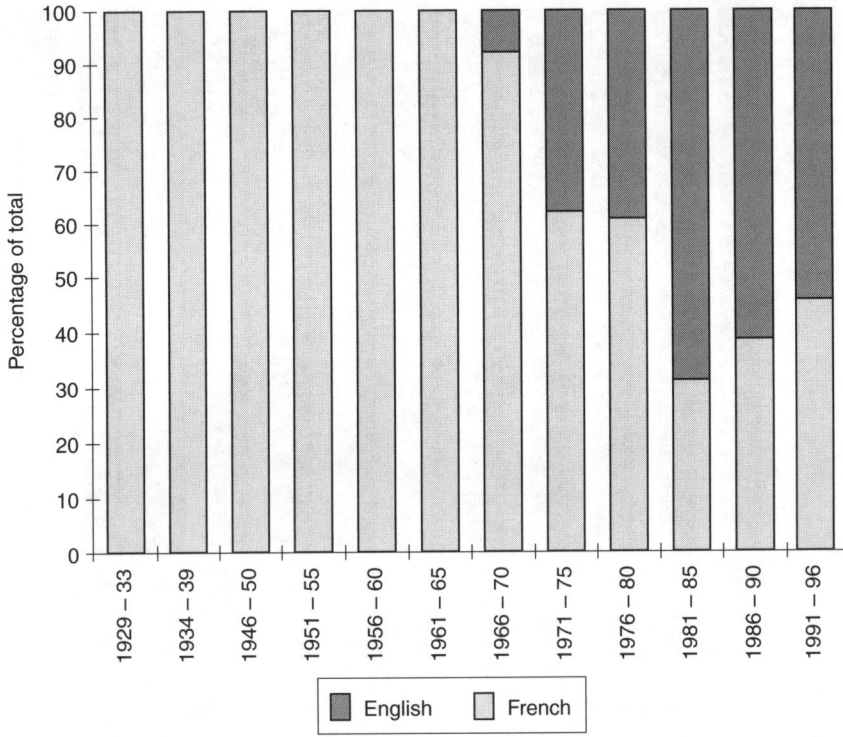

Figure 5.2 Recherches économiques de Louvain: classification by language, 1929–96 (in percentage of the total)

of published articles from the other Belgian institutions. In contrast, foreign contributions expanded enormously. This general movement consisted of three
waves. The first, fed by the United States, developed from 1968 onwards. The
second wave, which started during the first half of the 1970s, mainly concerned
the United Kingdom and Canada. This wave expanded until 1980, and then
declined. The third wave is accounted for exclusively by France, but it has taken
on spectacular dimensions, reaching 36 per cent of the total number of articles in
1991–96. Belgium itself is consequently far surpassed by France as regards the
number of publications. The large share of German authors in 1991–96 is likewise a striking phenomenon, but it remains to be seen whether this will last.

The growing internationalization of the articles is coupled with an increasing
use of English as the drafting language, and a greater recourse to statistical analytical methods and mathematics. As was the case with the institutions to which
the authors belong, these developments started at the end of the 1960s. It would,
however, be risky to deduce from this parallel trend the existence of some
causality among these three phenomena. A close examination of the articles
shows that many UCL researchers had been drafting their articles in English and
applying quantitative methods ever since the 1960s.

106   *Ivo Maes, Erik Buyst and Muriël Bouchet*

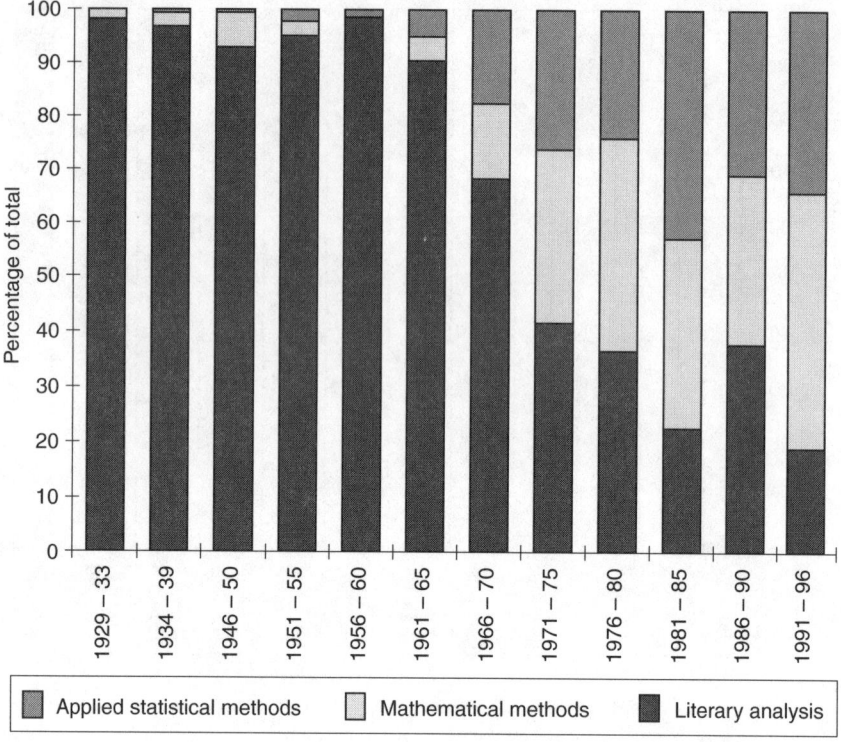

Figure 5.3 Recherches économiques de Louvain: classification by method of analysis, 1929–96 (in percentage of the total)

Tijdschrift voor Economie (en Management)

Several reasons explain the creation of the *Tijdschrift voor Economie* (Journal of Economics) in 1956. Firstly, it was designed to give Dutch-speaking economists an outlet for publications in their own language. Indeed, before 1956 the *Bulletin de l'IRES* (see above) was the only academic economics journal in Belgium, but it did not accept contributions in Dutch. So, Flemish economists were forced to publish in French. Second, the editorial board of the *Bulletin de l'IRES* was not interested in publishing scientific articles analysing the economic problems of Flanders.[11] Under the influence of Dupriez the editorial board of the *Bulletin de l'IRES* remained very much focused on business-cycle analysis.

In these circumstances it is not surprising that during the first decade of the *Tijdschrift voor Economie* almost all articles appeared in Dutch. The late 1960s were an important turning-point as the share of contributions in English jumped to more than 20 per cent. A peak was reached in the first half of the 1970s, when more than 50 per cent of all the published contributions were in English. This high share provoked a call for more Dutch-speaking articles by some readers of the

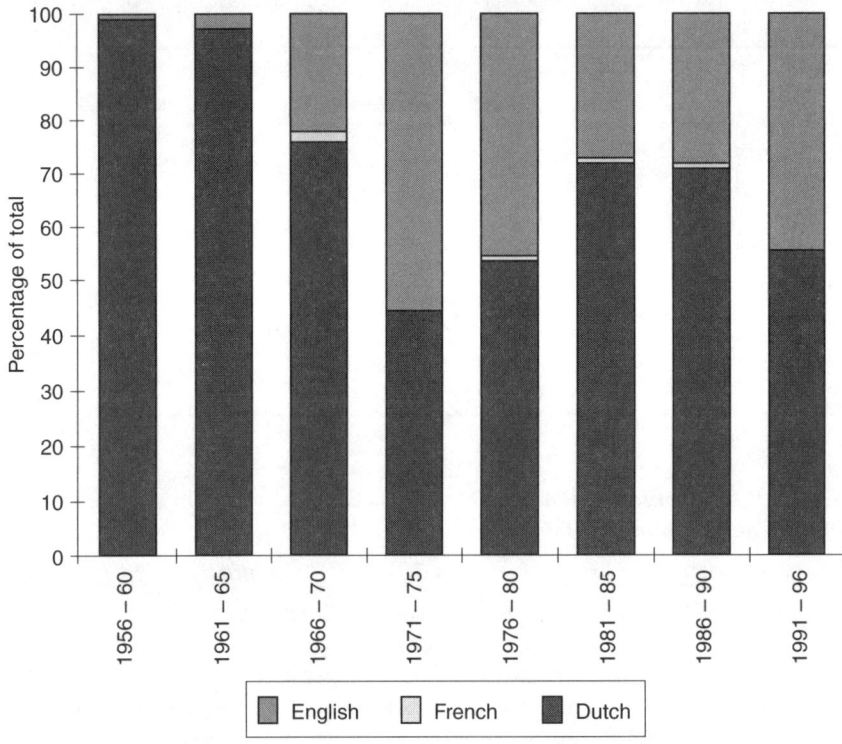

Figure 5.4 Tijdschrift voor Economie (en Management): classification by language (in percentage of the total), 1956–96

Tijdschrift. As a result, the number of contributions in English declined again from the late 1970s. In the early 1990s the continuing internationalization of research in economics led again to a substantial rise in the share of articles in English.

Despite these fluctuations in the use of language, the *Tijdschrift* has remained an important outlet for research by Dutch-speaking Belgian economists. Until the late 1980s their share amounted to more than 80 per cent of the total number of articles. Within this group the Leuven economists played a key role. It is only during the last fifteen years that the other Flemish universities – and especially the University of Antwerp – have increased their share.

The number of publications by scholars affiliated to foreign universities in the *Tijdschrift* has remained fairly limited during the past forty years. For example, American or Canadian researchers published on average one to two articles per year.

The steep increase in the number of contributions by Dutch economists in the early 1990s is remarkable. Only time will tell whether this is a permanent new trend.

Table 5.4 Tijdschrift voor Economie (en Management): classification by origin of the
author:[a]

Years	Belgium		Foreign countries		
	KUL	Others	Netherlands	USA & Canada	Others
1956–60	83	9	8	1	0
1961–65	88	7	3	2	0
1966–70	78	7	7	3	5
1971–75	74	8	1	16	1
1976–80	75	16	2	6	0
1981–85	54	35	2	5	4
1986–90	65	28	1	3	3
1991–95	56	22	14	8	0

(a) Percentage of total

The Bulletin of Information and Documentation
of the National Bank of Belgium

During the decades following the war the *Bulletin of Information and Documentation of the National Bank of Belgium* played an important role in the
propagation of foreign economic ideas in Belgium. It was a monthly publication, containing articles both by Bank economists[12] and outsiders. It was
published both in French and Dutch. It had a very wide circulation, not only in
the academic world but also in other circles, such as banks, ministries and
enterprises.[13]

During the period from 1949 to 1972, ninety-three articles by foreign economists were published in the Bank's *Bulletin*. The peak period was 1953–62,
when, on average, more than six articles a year by foreign economists appeared.
Thereafter only anonymous articles by Bank economists were published, with
the exception of the papers and proceedings of a seminar on the European monetary system in 1979.

Over three-quarters of the ninety-three articles were written by academics,
seventy-five in total. Among these were many distinguished economists, such as
Balassa, Bloomfield, Cooper, Fourastié, Goldsmith, Harrod, Kaldor, Kenen,
Kindleberger, Machlup, Sayers, Stern, Tinbergen and Triffin. Eighteen articles
were from policy-makers, in which category the US Federal Reserve economists
clearly dominated with nine papers.

With respect to the country of residence of the foreign economists, the USA
clearly dominated with thirty-one out of ninety-three articles. These articles came
from both academic economists and policy-makers (Federal Reserve, IMF,
IBRD). They are followed by contributions from the Netherlands, France and the
United Kingdom with, respectively, sixteen, fourteen and thirteen publications.
In the beginning first the Dutch and then the French contributions were relatively more important, while more British contributions appeared at the end of the
period.

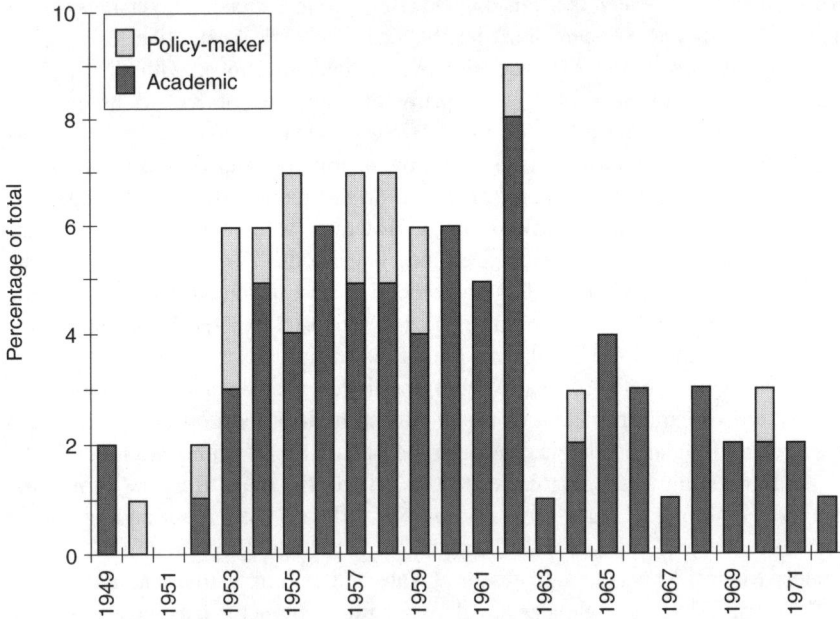

Figure 5.5 Articles by foreign economists* in the *Bulletin of Information and Documentation* of the National Bank of Belgium, 1949–71[†]

Notes
* By country of residence   † Excluding the 1979 EMS conference

Most of the topics treated in these articles by foreign economists concern monetary policy, the financial system and the international economy. However, other areas, such as fiscal policy, economic forecasting and economic development, were also covered. There were even a few articles on economic methodology and philosophy, such as 'Recent critiques of economic science' (Hennipman) and 'Searching for a humanist economy' (Piettre).

The decrease and eventual disappearance of articles by foreign economists in the *Bulletin* can be explained by the development of many other channels of international contacts in the 1960s, which reduced the need for this kind of article, and by the diminishing enthusiasm of academics to publish, for a fee, in the *Bulletin of the National Bank of Belgium*. Academic economists preferred increasingly to publish in professional journals, even if they were not paid for doing so.

The international dimension[14]

In the early 1950s Belgian economics was already relatively open and internationally orientated. Thus it was considered normal for good Belgian students to do graduate studies in the United States.[15] There were also contacts with other European countries, especially between the francophone (Belgian) and French universities. In the 1950s, Dupriez was president of the International Economic Association.

Internationalization clearly accelerated in the late 1960s, with the foundation and expansion of CORE as the prime example (see above). Belgian economics has become more 'professional', 'international' or 'American' (cf. Coats 1992: 5) – research has focused more on abstract issues defined within the academic economics profession, formalization has increased, graduate education has grown, English is increasingly used. However, when considering the internationalization of economics in Belgium one should certainly not forget the European dimensions. Many Belgian academics have undertaken research for the European Commission or have participated in groups of experts. The geographical proximity of most of the European Community institutions and the fact that many Belgians worked there (cf. Maes 1996), facilitated contacts and the obtaining of grants and research projects. Consequently, a high proportion of the (applied) research by Belgian academics has been focused on European integration.

An interesting figure in this respect is Triffin, the only 'Belgian' economist mentioned among Blaug's 'great economists' (Blaug 1985). After undergraduate studies at the UCL and a PhD at Harvard in 1938, he took up a job in the United States, where he became a professor at Yale and acquired American nationality (cf. Triffin 1981). However, he also became Monnet's trusted adviser on European monetary matters (cf. Duchêne 1994: 312, 335).

Belgian economists have also played a leading role in the initiatives concerning European integration in the academic field. Waelbroeck and Glejser founded the *European Economic Review*, of which the first number appeared in the autumn of 1969. Belgian economists were also actively involved in the foundation of the European Economic Association. According to Drèze (1986: 261), the first president, 'the project of organizing a European Economic Association took form in the minds of four Belgians: Gabszewicz, Phlips, Thisse and Waelbroeck'. In 1986 the Belgians were also the largest group in the Association, with 143 members, out of a total of 1,058 (data for 1 June 1986). So one can see that Belgian economics has become both more 'American' and more 'European' during the last five decades.

Conclusion

In the 1950s economics in Belgium was dominated by three 'mandarins': Dupriez at the francophone University of Leuven, Eyskens at the Flemish University of Leuven, and Kirschen at the francophone University of Brussels.

Initially, Keynesianism developed only slowly in Belgium, mainly due to the dominant position of Dupriez, who was strongly in favour of an Austrian type of business-cycle analysis. However, Keynesianism gained ground, initially mainly at the Flemish University of Leuven and the francophone University of Brussels. From the 1960s to today, however, Keynesianism, in its different varieties, has occupied a dominating position in Belgian economic thought.

Economics changed profoundly in the 1960s, becoming more professional and international: formalization increased, microeconomics gained in importance, English became the lingua franca. A typical exponent of this tendency was the establishment and growth of CORE, the Centre for Operations Research and Econometrics. Also the journals of the different Belgian research institutes published more quantitatively orientated articles and attracted more contributions from outside their own university. This professionalization and internationalization was greatly facilitated by the increase in government funding of the universities in the 1960s.

The European dimensions are a notable feature of economics in Belgium. Much research is focused on European integration and Belgian economists have been at the forefront of European academic initiatives, such as in the creation of the European Economic Association.

Notes

1 In the 1950s, at the universities of Leuven and Brussels, courses were given both in Dutch and in French. The universities of Leuven and Brussels would later be split into a francophone and a Flemish university.
2 This was the main reason why Drèze took up a visiting professorship at the University of Chicago in the early 1960s.
3 From 1958 to 1961 Gaston Eyskens, Professor at the University of Leuven and figurehead of the Flemish economics department, was Prime Minister. Together with several other Flemish economists, he played a crucial role in many of these changes.
4 In the Belgian context the term 'department of applied economic sciences' means a business school.
5 Cf. Loeys 1975: 18–19.
6 It is remarkable that people have different perceptions about the relationship between Marshall's economics and Keynesian economics: some stress the differences and the break between the two, while others emphasize the complementarities and the continuity.
7 A greater emphasis on graduate education can be considered as more typical of American than European economics (cf. Frey and Eichenberger 1993: 185).
8 Cf. Salmon (1984: 205). This degree was abolished in Gent in 1978, as it did not attract many students.
9 The (present) *Recherches Economiques de Louvain* changed name a few times. From 1929 to 1939 it was called *Bulletin de l'Institute des Sciences Economiques*, and from 1946 to 1960 *Bulletin de l'Institut de Recherches Economiques et Sociales*.
10 This tendency towards a diversification of contributors is also apparent in the *Cahiers Economiques de Bruxelles* (cf. Praet 1983: 480).
11 See also Drouillon (1982: 62).
12 Usually anonymous.
13 In 1962 the circulation amounted to 1,478 copies in French and 532 in Dutch. About 20% went to foreign countries (source: Archives of the Research Department, National Bank of Belgium).
14 We do not discuss the importance of 'colonial economics' or, later, development economics.
15 The Commission for Relief in Belgium, set up during World War I, and later renamed The Belgian American Educational Foundation, played an important role herein.

References

Arrow, K. and Hahn, F. (1971) *General Competitive Analysis*, San Francisco: Holden Day.
Blaug, M. (1985) *Great Economists since Keynes*, Brighton: Wheatsheaf.

Buyst, E. and Maes I. (1996) 'De impact van veertig jaar centrum voor economische studiën', *Leuvense Economische Standpunten*, no. 83.

Coats, A. W. (1992) *The Post-1945 Global Internationalization (Americanization?) of Economics*, mimeographed.

Coddington, A. (1976) 'Keynesian economics: the search for first principles', *Journal of Economic Literature*: xiv (2): 1258–73.

Cornet, B. and Tulkens H. (eds) (1989) *Contributions to Operations Research and Economics: The Twentieth Anniversary of CORE*, Cambridge, Mass.: MIT Press.

D'Aviella, G. (1909) *L'Université de Bruxelles pendant son Troisième Quart de Siècle, 1884–1909*, Brussels.

Drèze, J. (1985) 'Econometrics in the general economics curriculum: teachers in a quandary', *Tijdschrift voor Economie en Management*: xxx (3–4): 445–52.

——(1986) 'European Economic Association. News and announcements', *European Economic Review* (30): 261–3.

——(1987) 'Underemployment equilibria: from theory to econometrics and policy', *European Economic Review* (31): 9–34.

Drouillon, J. (1982) *Karel Pinxten, Een Bio-bibliografische Proeve*, Brussels.

Duchêne, F. (1994) *Jean Monnet. The First Statesman of Interdependence*, New York: W. W. Norton.

Dupriez, L. H. (1947) *Les Mouvements Economiques Généraux*, I & II, Louvain: IRES.

——(1972) 'Voie large ou voie etroite de l'economie politique', in L. H. Dupriez, *et al.* (eds), *Problèmes Economiques Contemporains*, Louvain: IRES.

Elewaut, G. (1996) 'Belgisch economisch onderzoek in de lift', *De Financieel-Economische Tijd*, 6 July.

Frey, B. and Eichenberger, R. (1993) 'American and European economics and economists', *Journal of Economic Perspectives*, 7(4): 185–93.

Hayek, F. A. (1928) 'Das intertemporale Gleichgewichtssystem der Preise und die Bewegingen des Geldwertes', *Weltwirtschaftliches Archiv*, xxviii: 3–76

Hildenbrand, W. (1989) 'CORE and equilibria of a large economy', in B. Cornet and H. Tulkens (eds) *Contributions to Operations Research and Economics: The Twentieth Anniversary of CORE*, Cambridge, Mass.: MIT Press.

Kirschen, E. S. (1988) *Autobiographie d'un Mandarin*, Brussels: Vander.

Kirschen, E. S. *et al.* (1964) *Economic Policy in our Time,* Amsterdam: North Holland.

Lamberts, E. and Roegiers, J. (1986) *De Universiteit te Leuven, 1925–1985*, Leuven.

Lenders, P. (1991) *Ontstaan en Groei van de Universiteit van Antwerpen*, Leuven: Garant.

Loeys, M. (1975) 'Professor Dr Gaston Eyskens: vierenveertig jaar hoogleraar' in M. Loeys (ed.), *Liber Amicorum Professor Dr. Gaston Eyskens*, Leuven.

Maes, I. (1996) 'The development of economic thought at the European Community institutions', in A. W. Coats (ed.) *The Post–1945 Internationalisation of Economics*, History of Political Economy, Annual Supplement: 245–76.

Pagan, A. (1989) 'Twenty years after: econometrics, 1966–1986', in B. Cornet and H. Tulkens, (eds), *Contributions to Operations Research and Economics: The Twentieth Anniversary of CORE*, Cambridge, Mass.: MIT Press.

Praet, P. (1983) Editorial, *Cahiers Economiques de Bruxelles*, 100: 479–85.

Salmon, P. (1984) 'La faculté des sciences sociales, politiques et economiques', in A. Uyttebrouck and A. Despy-Meyer (eds), *Les Cent Cinquante Ans de l'Université Libre de Bruxelles (1934–1984)*, Brussels: Editions de l'Université de Bruxelles.

Steinherr, A. (1987) 'In honour of Albert Kervijn de Lettenhove', in A. Steinherr and D. Weiserbs (eds), *Employment and Growth: Issues for the 1980s,* Amsterdam: Kluwer.

Triffin, R. (1981) 'An economist's career: What? Why? How?', *Banca Nazionale del Lavoro Quarterly Review*, 138: 239–59.

Waelbroeck, J. and Glejser H. (1969) 'Editor's introduction', *European Economic Review*, 1 (1): 3–6.

6 The post-1945 development of economics in Germany[1]

Harald Hagemann

The post-1945 development of economics in Germany is characterized by important similarities as well as by some marked specialities compared to the development of economics in other European countries. With the professionalization process widely advancing, the postwar era saw a remarkable growth in the number, scale and importance of economists and economic research institutions, particularly in the 1960s and 1970s. Professional economists came to play more significant roles as advisers to policy-makers, as members of the central bank's directory or as politicians themselves. Internationalization for the greater part was related to Americanization, due to the increasing dominance of American economics after World War II.[2] Thus German economics also saw the rise and fall of Keynesianism and the stronger influences of monetarist ideas since the 1970s. The move towards a 'professional *Gleichschaltung*', diagnosed by Peacock (1995) and characterized by a growing importance of mathematics, statistics and econometric techniques and the motivation to satisfy one's peer group, certainly can be observed in Germany. As in most other countries the 1980s saw the development of a far greater preference of students for business studies. In the German system, where business administration and economics normally are taught in one faculty, the enormous growth of student numbers and the dominance of business studies had a negative impact on the demand for pure economic reasoning and fields like the history of economic thought and economic history.

On the other hand, there are some special factors which distinguish the German case from the development of economics elsewhere. In so far as elements of a 'German *Sonderweg*' are identifiable, they are for the greater part caused by political factors. The events in Germany in 1933 marked a significant turning point for the economics profession as well. The Nazi-induced intellectual emigration from Germany and Austria – see the contributions in Hagemann (1997) – had long-term consequences from which German universities never fully recovered.

In East Germany the period from 1945 to 1989, with the worst combination of the old German 'mandarin' university with Stalinism, where economics basically was reduced to orthodox Marxism-Leninism and a narrowly defined socialist business administration, dealt a further blow to economics as a science. East Germany never produced economists of a similar stature as, for example, Kalecki, Lange and some of their students in Poland or Kornai in Hungary.

As is well known, West Germany's economic order – the concept of the social market economy – and economic policy after World War II had been decisively influenced by the theories, doctrines and ideas of the members of the Freiburg School. Christian convictions motivated their resistance against the Nazi regime as much as their scientific work, in which freedom and the rule of law have as important a place as some optimal economic efficiency. Their basic ideas, which also emphasized the requirements for a smooth transformation process from the Nazi war economy to a successfully functioning, market, peace-time economy thus were markedly shaped as early as the period 1938–45 (see Rieter and Schmolz 1993).

The Nazi period and its long-term consequences

It is generally recognized that the post-1945 development of economics is characterized by American leadership. All available data, from the Nobel Prize awards since 1969 to the list of eminent economists based on the *Social Science Citation Index*, confirm American dominance in research and publication output. However, it has to be emphasized that '[t]he triumphant rise of American economics after 1940 was enormously accelerated by importation of scholars from Hitlerian Europe' (Samuelson 1988: 319).[3] Whereas in Europe much was destroyed by fascism and in the eastern part by Stalinism, there can be no doubt that the United States greatly benefited from intellectual immigration. Some of the most innovative contributions of the *émigré* economists are characterized by the crossing of different traditions.

An outstanding example is the work of Richard Musgrave, who was born near Frankfurt in 1910 and emigrated to the United States immediately after finishing his Diploma in Economics at the University of Heidelberg in May 1933. His contributions to public finance are characterized by a fruitful combination of the Anglo-Saxon and German traditions of public finance. The former had developed as part of standard economics, and shared the rigour of its analysis. The German tradition of *Finanzwissenschaft* had a broader perspective, including institutions, history and the theory of the state (see Musgrave 1996 and 1997 for a more detailed analysis).

In contemporary critiques of developments in mainstream economics the process of internationalization is sometimes identified and confused with Americanization, although concepts imported by Europe from North America have been shaped for a greater part by scholars who originally came from Europe. The most important instance is the work of the Cowles Commission in the decade after Jacob Marschak became director in 1943, which laid strong foundations for the mathematization of economics and the development of econometric techniques. With Marschak, Koopmans (who succeeded him as the director in 1948) and Haavelmo, and among the younger scholars Modigliani or

Debreu, there had always been a strong component of economists of European origin.

During the Weimar Republic German economics itself had benefited from hosting *émigré* scholars, particularly from Soviet Russia – like Marschak, who gained his PhD and *Habilitation* at the University of Heidelberg, and Wassily Leontief, whose PhD thesis was entitled 'The economy as a circular flow', which can be regarded as the overture to his later ring of input-output-analysis, with Sombart and Bortkiewicz at the University of Berlin in 1928. Like Marschak, who emigrated to the United Kingdom in 1933 where he became the first director of the Oxford Institute of Statistics in 1935 before he left for the United States at the outbreak of World War II, Leontief worked for some years at the Kiel Institute of World Economics before he went to Harvard in 1932.

The long-term implications of the political developments can also be seen from some statistical figures. Whereas the Soviet Union lost twenty-four of its thirty-six eminent economists and Austro-Hungary thirty-six of its fifty eminent economists due to emigration, the United States, on the other hand, had a net gain of 161 from the mobility of eminent economists, which accounts for about 30 per cent of the share of economists born in the United States (see Frey and Pommerehne 1988: 103). The world share of leading economists living in German-speaking countries has declined from 15 per cent among the dead to 3 per cent among the living.

Thus political events in Germany in 1933 and thereafter played a decisive role in the long-term loss of quality and the international reputation of German economics. German-language journals, for example, lost not only most of the *émigré* economists as authors, but also many foreign economists, who stopped writing in the German language and publishing in German journals. The great increase in the number of articles written by *émigré* German and Austrian economists in the leading American and English journals corresponds to the dwindling importance of foreign and *émigré* economists in German-language journals. What happened to the German journals can best be illustrated by the case of the *Archiv für Sozialwissenschaft und Sozialpolitik*, which became the most eminent scholarly journal in the social sciences after the three new editors, Werner Sombart, Max Weber and Edgar Jaffé, took over responsibility in 1904 (from 1922 to 1933, Emil Lederer in cooperation with Joseph Schumpeter and Alfred Weber). The list of many outstanding contributions still cited in the literature includes Max Weber's classic study on 'The Protestant ethic and the "spirit" of capitalism' (1905), Ladislaus von Bortkiewicz's two famous articles on 'Value and prices in the Marxian system' (1906–7), Ludwig von Mises' 1920 paper which launched the socialist calculation debate, Nikolai Kondratieff's article on 'The long waves in economic life' (1926) which made his statistical investigations known to the Western world, and Leontief's PhD thesis (1928) already mentioned. Whereas most scholarly journals had to substitute editors to survive in 1933 – with Spiethoff who stayed as the editor of *Schmoller's Jahrbuch* as a notable exception – the *Archiv* was the only economics journal which had to terminate publication after the Nazis took power.

With Oskar Morgenstern (1930-38, until 1934 in cooperation with Paul Rosenstein-Rodan) as the managing editor, the Vienna-based *Zeitschrift für Nationalökonomie* became the most important scholarly journal in the German-language area in the 1930s when important contributions to capital theory, business-cycle theory and general equilibrium theory were published. The list of internationally respected authors includes Aftalion, Fanno, Frisch, Hicks, Knight, Lange, Marget, Myrdal, Ohlin, Tinbergen, Zeuthen and many others. After Hitler's invasion of Austria the quality of the journal deteriorated significantly. In the post-1945 era no German language journal ever reached the scholarly reputation of the *Archiv* in the social sciences in the first third of the century or the *Zeitschrift für Nationalökonomie* in economics during the 1930s. For a considerable period they were mainly characterized by papers narrowing the wide margin by which German economics had fallen below international standards during the Hitler years, standards to which *émigré* economists from Austria and Germany themselves had made important contributions.

Economic ideas and policy

The post-1945 development of German economics experienced a further blow with the untimely deaths of August Lösch (1945), Heinrich von Stackelberg (1946) and Walter Eucken (1950).[4] Lösch, a researcher at the Kiel Institute of World Economics who, as a passive opponent of the Nazi regime, did not follow a career as a university professor, was another outstanding representative of location theory where German economics had been dominant since the days of Thünen, later followed by Launhardt, Alfred Weber and Christaller.

Stackelberg was a highbrow theorist who made important contributions to price theory, capital theory and general equilibrium theory. Born into an elitist German-Baltic *Junker* family, and politically an ardent believer in the nationalist right since his early experience with the Bolshevist revolution, he became a member of the Nazi Party in 1931 and even of the SS in 1933. From 1935 onwards Stackelberg started to distance himself from the Nazi regime, and cooperated with the '*Freiburger Kreis*' whose members, like Stackelberg, were in favour of a strong state. In 1943 he went to Spain, where he lectured on economic theory until his death, at the age of only 41.[5]

Eucken, a committed liberal who actively fought against the Nazis, was the intellectual head of the Freiburg School. His *Foundations of Economics* (1940) set the theoretical basis for the economic policy ideas of Ordoliberalism which were practised after the war and became a key ingredient of the concept of the social market economy. The approach of the Freiburg School, with its concern for the legal and institutional order and its emphasis on infrastructural measures to reach a higher market equilibrium, has very much in common with the original ideas of Adam Smith but is strongly at odds with *laissez-faire* views. In the distinctive Freiburg contribution, 'regulative principles' (like monopoly controls, the correction of external effects or social security measures) have to be added to the 'constituent principles' (private property, open markets, a competitive order with a functioning price mechanism, freedom of contracts, regularity and predictability of economic policy) to establish or maintain the permanent economic order of a free society, since a successful market economy can neither develop spontaneously nor survive unaided. The so-called 'Freiburg Imperative' is committed to the model of a strong state, which is in marked contrast to the dominant view of Anglo-American economics. Although Eucken became well known as an opponent of the Historical School, one may identify here stronger influences of that school (see, for example, Hutchison 1979).

Following the traumatic experiences with hyperinflation after World War I and the renewed erosion of the value of the currency after World War II, monetary stability became a prime goal not only of the Freiburg economists. The fear of inflation and political dictatorship led to the creation of a strong and independent central bank. With the Bundesbank as a key player there certainly was no room for easy-money policies to stimulate an upswing of the economy. After the currency reform of 20 June 1948, German economic policy was biased in favour of investment and export-led economic growth, reinforced by the restrictive monetary policies of the Bundesbank which, under the rules of the fixed exchange rates in the Bretton Woods system, led to a major undervaluation of the mark in the late 1960s. Whereas the high growth rates in the 1950s and early 1960s made Keynesian ideas influential and popular in many other countries (see Hall 1989), the impact of Keynesian economics on policy and policy-makers in Germany remained rather limited in this period. The success of the policies of the social market economy contributed to the centre-right government's dominance of the political scene in the Cold War years, and Ludwig Erhard (1897–1977), who was Minister of Economics from 1949 to 1963 when he followed Adenauer as the Chancellor, became famous as the 'father of the *Wirtschaftswunder*'.

The situation changed with the economic recession of 1966–67, when the government lost credibility. Erhard, who was a less successful Chancellor, had to resign; a 'Great Coalition' of Christian and Social Democrats formed the new government, and Karl Schiller (1911–94) became the new Minister of Economics (from 1971 until his resignation in July 1972 also Minister of Finance) whose star was soon rising. In the new 'Godesberg programme' of 1959 the SPD had finally given up Marxist ideas and made a commitment to the market economy (with a stronger emphasis on the adjective 'social') which, in the light of the existing socialism in the eastern part of divided Germany was a precondition for electoral success. With the entry of the SPD into government, Keynesian ideas now came to play a substantially greater role in economic policy.

The changed historical-economical background was another reason for this development. At the beginning of the 1960s the end of the reconstruction period was reached.[6] This implied a shift in the agenda of German economists. In the first ten to fifteen years after the war they had been occupied with topics like the currency reform, *Lastenausgleich* (equalization of burden), the Marshall Plan, the integration of refugees from the East, unemployment and capital shortage. All this is reflected in the conference volumes of the *Verein für Socialpolitik* – the German Economic Association which had been founded in 1872, and which dissolved itself three years after the Nazis came to power, after an attempt for *Gleichschaltung* had failed, and which was refounded after the war[7] – and in the reports of the advisory board to the Ministry of Economics.[8] In about 1960 the major supply-side deficiencies were overcome and full employment was reached.

With the building of the Berlin Wall in August 1961, the migration of Germans coming from the East stopped and until 1973 labour was in chronically short supply. This led to the recruitment of guest workers by West German industry. The number of guest workers went up from 279,000 in 1960 to a maximum of 2,498,000 in 1973. The attention of policy-makers in the years of full employment (1960–73, with the exception of the 1966–67 recession) quite naturally turned away from supply-side problems to issues of demand management – restraining inflationary pressures, avoiding external disequilibria – and to fine-tuning the economy. The stage was set for a charismatic economist.

Karl Schiller had been a Professor of Economics at the University of Hamburg (where the later Chancellor Helmut Schmidt was one of his students) since 1948 but had always been active in the political arena: Senator of Economics in Hamburg 1948–53 and in Berlin after the building of the wall from 1961 to 1965 and a member of the Bundestag since 1965. He became the architect of the 'Stability and Growth' law which the new government launched in June 1967, with the macroeconomic goals of the 'magic polygon' (price-level stability, adequate economic growth, a high level of employment and external equilibrium). The year 1967 saw a swing in the growth rate of the German economy from minus 6 per cent in the first half to plus 6 per cent in the second half, basically an export-led growth as the consequence of an undervalued mark and moderate longer-term wage contracts in the wake of the recession. With Schiller as the charismatic interpreter of his own economic policy and the underlying theoretical ideas, the years from 1967 to the first oil price shock have to be regarded as the heyday of Keynesianism in Germany. Economics became a very popular subject and attracted many new students. For a few years there was a widespread belief in the government's capability in macro policy management in the market economy. '*Globalsteuerung*' was one of Schiller's popular phrases which had earlier played a major role in his highly influential article on economic policy (Schiller 1962). Another popular phrase, which dominated theoretical debates between academic economists as well as public policy discussions, was '*Wettbewerb soweit wie möglich, Planung soweit wie nötig*' (Competition as much as possible, planning – in the sense of Keynesian demand management policies – as much as necessary).

Schiller committed himself to Eucken and Keynes. His public and powerful credo was the 'combination of the Freiburg Imperative with the Keynesian message': the supplementation of *Ordnungspolitik* with process policy (that is, Keynesian demand management, which he regarded as necessary to reach the macroeconomic goals, particularly full employment, but also to safeguard the market economy against more far-reaching Marxist interventions). Naturally Schiller's synthesis between Ordoliberalism and Keynesianism could only be followed in economizing on one side: the ordoliberal one during the few years of the initial success in macroeconomic management, before, in the stagflationary period after 1974 Keynesian 'fine-tuning' lost its appeal.

However, even in the years when Keynesian ideas reached the peak of their influence on economic policy in Germany, there had always been important constraints on their full implementation. The main proponents, the Social Democrats, were only junior partners in government from 1966 to 1969 and later needed the parliamentary backing of the Liberal Party from 1969 to 1982. But even with an absolute majority changes in economic policy would never have been made on such a scale as in the United Kingdom with a change in political power. The independent Bundesbank always followed its own policy to secure price stability. Chancellor Helmut Schmidt experienced this in a very painful way when the restrictive monetary policy, which was followed after the second oil price shock, led to a deficit in the balance of payments on current account and some devaluation pressures on the Mark and raised interest rates to double-digit numbers, thus negatively affecting investment and employment. Since December 1974, when it had announced a target for the growth of the money supply, the Bundesbank had been on an explicitly monetarist track.[9]

There were no insurmountable differences between the economic convictions of the two politically most influential economists in the postwar era, Ludwig Erhard and Karl Schiller, despite the shift in economic policy in a more Keynesian direction after 1966. Both mentioned the 'liberal socialist' Franz Oppenheimer, under whom Erhard had done his PhD in economics at the Goethe University in Frankfurt in 1925, and who had been among their most influential academic teachers. It was Erhard who initiated the foundation of the Council of Economic Experts in August 1963, when the West German Parliament passed a new law. Since 1964 this Council has delivered its annual report on the macroeconomic development in mid-November, to which the government has to give a public response to Parliament in January. Although the independent, five-member Council was explicitly denied the right to make specific policy recommendations, in practice the difference between a lawful evaluation of macroeconomic policy performance with regard to the four goals and specific policy recommendations not authorized by law turned out to be purely academic. The new Council of Economic Experts soon came to play a major role in the economic policy debate, although it is apparent that in the first decade of its existence – when, for example, Schiller was involved in a permanent constructive dialogue with its members – the Council had a stronger political influence than it now does.[10] Under the strong influence of Herbert Giersch, the Council made a powerful plea for a greater flexibility of exchange rates during the final years of the Bretton Woods system. This position was also taken by Schiller, who became one of the architects of the Smithsonian Agreement in December 1971. Schiller also contributed significantly to the electoral success of the Social Democrats in September 1969, when the split in the Grand Coalition came up on the issue of 'freeing' the exchange rate of the mark (which, as expected, would lead to a major revaluation), favoured by the Council and Schiller, but heavily opposed by the Christian Democrats and the German export industry.

Later the Council, whose majority always favoured moderate wage policies and where normally, even in the years with Social Democratic governments, only the one of the five members who had to be appointed in agreement with the trade unions strongly favoured Keynesian positions, came to be entangled in major controversies with the trade unions, particularly after 1976 when the Council explicitly favoured supply-side policies.

Whereas at the beginning Keynesian policies were partly sabotaged by the Bonn administration, which in 1966, even in the Ministries of Finance and Economics, was still dominated by lawyers, Schiller was by no means the only or the first German economist favouring a synthesis of Keynesian macroeconomics with neoclassical microeconomics. Contrary to the position in Italy (see the contribution in Hall, 1989), the neoclassical synthesis had a strong position among academic economists from the beginning of the Federal Republic, although it lacked a greater impact on economic policy until 1966. Samuelson's textbook was very popular and in its German translation one of the few economic successes of the trade unions' publishing company.

An even greater role was played by the textbooks of Erich Schneider (1900–70), a former student of Schumpeter in Bonn, who in 1936 was appointed Professor of Economics at the University of Aarhus in Denmark, where he stayed until 1945 before returning to Germany, where he became Professor at the University of Kiel, and also from 1961 to 1969 the Director of the Institute of World Economics. Schneider's textbooks,[11] heavily influenced by the neoclassical synthesis view with a Scandinavian flavour (for example, Frisch's work on dynamics), dominated German universities until the late 1960s. It is widely recognized that Schneider played a major role in connecting German economics after the war with the major international developments, particularly the contemporary Anglo-Saxon mainstream. In a famous dispute with Röpke, one of the leading liberal economists, he strenuously supported Keynesian economics in the early 1950s (see Schneider 1953).

It might be argued that despite the strong influence of the Ordoliberals, particularly on economic policy in the first two decades and with the new Kohl government after 1982, a rather conservative Keynesianism with a neoclassical blend has been the regression line of German mainstream economics after World War II. Although monetarist ideas have had some influence since the early 1970s, with the annual Konstanz seminar, founded by Karl Brunner, as a kind of theoretical flagship, as in many other European countries, the more radical versions such as the new classical macroeconomics never became as influential as they did in North America.

Growth and the current landscape
of teaching and research

Two indicators of the almost ubiquitous rise of economics after World War II are the growing number of journals and the increased importance of economic research institutes. Additional to the old German journals such as the *Zeitschrift für die gesamte Staatswissenschaft*, the *Jahrbücher für Nationalökonomie und Statistik*, *Schmoller's Jahrbuch* or the *Finanzarchiv*, which normally had been published again since 1948, several new journals were founded: for example *Kyklos* in Switzerland in 1947.[12] The list includes *Ordo* (founded by Eucken in 1948), and the *Jahrbuch für Sozialwissenschaft* and *Kredit und Kapital* (1968), which reflects the growing importance of financial markets.

Other new journals have been founded by the great institutes for economic research, such as *Konjunkturpolitik* (1954), by the German Institute for Economic Research (DIW) in Berlin, or *Ifo-Studien* (1955) by the Ifo Institute in Munich. The well-established and internationally known *Weltwirtschaftliches Archiv*, focusing attention on the world economy, was founded by Bernhard Harms as early as 1913 with the Kiel Institute of Economic Research. Together with the DIW in Berlin, the *Hamburgisches Weltwirtschafts-Archiv* (HWWA) in Hamburg, the *Rheinisch-Westfälisches Institut für Wirtschaftsforschung* (RWI) in Essen, the IFO in Munich, and the more recent institute in Halle (founded after German unification and specializing in the transformation process of the East German economy), Germany today has six major economic research institutes which are on the 'blue list', that is, they are jointly financed by the federal and regional governments. Twice per year the institutes make a joint diagnosis of and forecast on the overall economic development (*Konjunkturdiagnose*). From 1977 they have also reported regularly on structural changes within the German economy at an interval of three to five years (*Strukturberichterstattung*). The division of labour which has developed over decades is that economists at the institutes are primarily involved in empirical studies, whereas researchers at the universities focus on pure theoretical analysis. Although it certainly would be an exaggeration to state that the former do 'measurement without theory' and the latter 'theory without measurement', the cooperation between universities and economic research institutes has been inadequate. The referees of the *Wissenschaftsrat*, which evaluated the research output of the institutes during the previous year in many cases complained of an insufficient consideration of new theoretical developments.

Whereas the RWI had great difficulties in an earlier refereeing process, the critique of the research output of the HWWA and the IFO was particularly severe. With the financial problems in the public sector, the current situation for the institutes in Hamburg and Munich is more dangerous. They run the risk of being eliminated from the blue list and thereby will suffer from a heavy reduction in their budget. Since the IFO Institute is strongly backed by the Bavarian government it probably will survive (with a reduced number of researchers), whereas the Hamburg institute may be reduced to service functions (such as library facilities).

On the other hand, three younger research institutes have been able to build up a high international reputation within a rather short time span. This holds for the *Wissenschaftszentrum Berlin* (WZB), which became well known in the social sciences in the 1980s, and in economics, particularly for their labour-market studies. The ZEW in Mannheim, which focuses on European issues, has a team of young and well-trained econometricians, and very probably will consolidate its position under the new director Wolfgang Franz, who recently succeeded Heinz König. The Max Planck Institute in Jena, founded in 1993, is the first MPI in economics. Whereas it was designed originally to focus on the transformation processes of what had formerly been socialist economies, under the two current directors, Manfred Streit and Ulrich Witt, it restructured its research programme some time ago and is now concentrating on institutional and evolutionary economics. Finally, there are two research institutes with a more partisan approach: the Institute for the German Economy (IW) in Cologne, financed by industry; and the considerably smaller Institute for Economics and Social Sciences (WSI) in Düsseldorf supported by the German trade unions.

The German university system expanded considerably in the 1960s and early 1970s, when many new universities were founded and the number of staff at the old ones was enlarged. Between 1960 (when economics and law were very often still together in one faculty for *Staatswissenschaften*) and 1980, the number of professors of economics and law in (West) German universities went up from 537 to 2,907, and the number of researchers from 629 to 5,344.[13] Since then there has been stagnation in the numbers of members of academic staff, whereas the rapid expansion in student numbers has continued for many years. The total number, as well as the share of students in the areas of economics, law and social sciences, increased over many years, as did the share of women. In 1995 there were 564,719 students in these fields, 372,843 at the universities and 191,876 at the *Fachhochschulen* (a kind of polytechnic). The proportion of female students, which until the 1960s was only about 10 per cent, reached a level of 41.0 per cent (46.6 per cent of the freshmen), slightly differing between universities – 37.8 per cent (freshmen, 44.1 per cent) – and *Fachhochschulen*: 47.1 per cent (freshmen, 49.7 per cent).[14] In the winter term of 1972/73 there had been 98,260 students at the universities; in 1980/81, 168,094; and in 1986/87, 242,146. The proportion of female students in economics among the freshmen had increased from 20.5 per cent in the winter term of 1976/77 to 34.5 per cent in 1986/87.[15]

The number of students who successfully finished their diploma exam in economics rose from 2,892 in 1960 to 7,603 in 1986. Whereas in 1960 only 389 were women, in 1986 the total had expanded to 2,013. The frequency of PhD degrees has not grown in line with the student and diploma figures since the second half of the 1970s, when the expansion phase of the universities largely came to an end. Most of the jobs had been taken over by younger people in the decade before and the prospects for an academic career worsened. In 1986, the number of Germans taking a PhD degree in economics was 501 (among them 58 women) – only slightly higher than in 1975, when 444 PhD degrees were achieved (only 22 by women). In the mid-1980s there were 8.2 PhD exams per 100 diploma exams in economics. On average, the time span between the diploma and the doctoral exam was six years (which does not imply that the candidates needed six years to write the dissertation since many of them had jobs outside the university). In 1986 the average age of graduates in economics was 31.9 years, when they got their doctoral degree, and 35.4 years when finishing the *Habilitation*, compared to a combined average of 39.1 years, ten years older than at the beginning of the century. Between 1981 and 1986, on average there were 36 *Habilitation* theses per year in economics, with 944 full professors (C4 and C3 category) at German universities in 1985, only 14 of them women. The whole academic staff of teachers and researchers in 1985 comprised 3,617 economists, 354 or 9.8 per cent of them women. The share of women has gone up significantly in recent years but is still lagging far behind the student shares.

A significant role in the teaching of economics and business administration has been played in this century by the *Handelshochschulen* (high schools of commerce), such as those in Cologne, Leipzig, Mannheim and Vienna. In 1929, for example, almost one-half of all German students in these fields studied at the new universities of Frankfurt (founded in 1914), which focused on economics and the social sciences, and Cologne (founded in 1919), which until today has retained its high reputation in business studies. The Faculty of Economics and the Social Sciences today has about 10,000 students and is the largest one in Germany.

Among the economics departments at the new universities, none became as outstanding as Essex, Warwick and York in the UK, but Konstanz in economics theory and Bielefeld in mathematical economics and game theory won a certain reputation, whereas Bremen, where many former leaders of the student movement obtained appointments, particularly in the turbulent 1970s, provided hospitality to critical perspectives of the New Left and thus became the equivalent to the New School for Social Research in New York and the University of Massachusetts at Amherst in the United States. In conventional ranking lists the top positions are still held by older economic faculties like Bonn – with the only German Nobel Prize winner hitherto, Reinhard Selten (1994) – Kiel, Mannheim and Munich, (see Kirman and Dahl 1994: 518). The latter two are exceptional in the German system because they have separate faculties for economics and business administration. Since some old faculties like Kiel and Tübingen were 'forced' in about 1980 to add a full course in business studies to their programme, there are now very few universities left where the faculties of economics do not offer full courses in business administration, particularly in the southwest of Germany, as in Freiburg, Heidelberg and Konstanz. Whereas most universities offer a degree in economics (*Diplom-Volkswirt*) and/or business studies (*Diplom-Kaufmann*), some universities – such as Augsburg, Bochum, Bremen, Gießen or Stuttgart-Hohenheim – have a joint examination (*Diplom-Ökonom*). So far there are only very few private universities existing, such as the two smaller ones in Witten-Herdecke with an interesting programme in economics and philosophy, and Koblenz concentrating on management studies.

At the East German universities after 1990 most members of the old academic staff were dismissed and new faculties of economics (such as in law and the social sciences) were built up, recruiting most of their professors from West Germany. The frictions and controversies caused in this process received wider recognition in the case of the Humboldt University in the centre of Berlin, where the Founding Dean, Wilhelm Krelle (Bonn), fired the old cadres and managed to hire a group of professors with high reputations. In the government's attempt to restore its earlier prestige, the Humboldt University was given preferential treatment at the expense of the Free University and Technical University in the west of Berlin.

German students are relatively old by international standards when they finish their diploma. With the six years from the beginning of their studies to the final exam they also study for a very long time. It can be expected that the recent agreement between the federal government and the *Bundesländer* to introduce the BA and the MA, as well, as final examinations will move the system in a more Anglo-Saxon direction. This can be interpreted as an international convergence process, which includes a strong component of European integration. The Socrates programme, following the Erasmus programme supporting the exchange of students and teachers, as well as other programmes funding the training and mobility of researchers, will further enhance this development. In Germany, as in other European countries, there is a clear need to improve graduate education in economics. Some initiatives, like the foundation of *Graduiertenkollegs* or the joint doctoral programme started by the University of Bonn with Louvain and the LSE several years ago, have covered this need.

The use of English as the lingua franca will support this process. It has already characterized the development in the last two decades. From 1963 to 1977 the *German Economic Review* published English translations of German papers and original contributions in English. When the journal had to terminate publication, like the *International Economic Papers* many years earlier, it did not cause much grief among economists. Meanwhile a new generation of promising young economists was submitting their papers directly to international journals. Also many German scholarly journals moved in the direction of publishing more, or exclusively, in English and partly changed their titles. One may deplore a bias in favour of English-speaking countries or a loss of national identity. However, this international convergence process is overall irresistible and necessary, provided that a plurality of methods and styles is retained. It can be expected that the current German system – where getting a professorship normally requires the writing of a '*Habilitation* thesis' (finished at the age of 40, until which time the candidates are still in a rather subordinate position), and where pressure on the individual to keep publishing largely ceases after appointment as a professor – cannot be sustained in the longer run.

Two themes have been dominating the theoretical literature as well as economic policy debates in the 1990s: German unification and European integration, topics which are closely interlinked. The revolutionary changes of 1989–90 in Central and Eastern Europe did not only pave the way to German unification but have also had a lasting impact on the speed and direction of the European integration process. In the wake of the economic and monetary union, which became effective on 1 July 1990, with its sudden and full internal and external liberalization process, the East German economy collapsed on a scale that even most pessimists had previously underestimated. Although the Kohl government cannot be blamed for the failures of the former socialist system (which, for example, resulted in the economically obsolete capital stock that the former GDR brought into united Germany, whereas the West German capital stock in 1948 had been remarkably modern), it clearly underestimated the costs of a successful restructuring of the East German economy, left wasteful subsidies in West Germany nearly untouched, over-borrowed and failed to build a consensus on how the bill for unification should be distributed. The Bundesbank, which faced a severe test of its anti-inflationary credibility in the German *Sonderkonjunktur* after unification, raised the key discount and Lombard rates to a peak of 8 per cent and 9.75 per cent respectively shortly after the Maastricht Treaty.

Although the more restrictive monetary policy was primarily intended to send warning signals to employers and unions to agree on less inflationary wage settlements, and to the German government to curb its spending, with the mark as the anchor in the European monetary system the Bundesbank's refusal to follow a more expansionary monetary policy and the priority to keep its anti-inflationary stance, contributed to the breakdown of the exchange rate mechanism in the two crises of September 1992 and summer 1993, which had also been caused by the failure of the EMS to allow for a timely upward realignment of the DM.

The Euro debate has affected German economists as much as the economists in other countries. The two hyperinflations following the two world wars, the relatively stronger emphasis on price-level stability among the German public resulting therefrom, and the success story of the DM may explain why, contrary to the political majority in the Bundestag and contrary to the economics profession in other European countries (as, for example, in Italy), the great majority of German economists have never been enthusiastic supporters of the Euro. The recent declaration (9 February 1998) of 155 German professors of economics, 'The Euro starts too early', compared to 58 economists signing the pro Euro-declaration last year, is an indicator for the current evaluation of the Euro prospects.

Notes

1 An earlier version of this chapter was presented at the invited paper session, 'Comparative study of the post-1945 development of economics in Europe', at the Twelfth Annual Congress of the European Economic Association in Toulouse, on 1 September 1997. For valuable comments on this draft I thank Heinz Rieter.

2 See the contributions in Coats (1997). For the analysis of the adjustment process and remaining differences between American and European economics and economists, see also Johnson (1973), Frey and Eichenberger (1992, 1993) and the contributions to the Kyklos-Symposium, 'Is there a European economics?' (Frey and Frey 1995).

3 For the Continental influence on the development of American economics, see also Craver and Leijonhufvud (1987).

4 See Heuß (1989) and, for an up-to-date assessment of (dis-)continuity in German economics in the 1930s and 1940s, the fine paper by Häuser (1998).

5 For a meticulous biographical portrait as well as a careful evaluation of Stackelberg's contributions to economic analysis, see the introductory essay of Möller to Stackelberg's *Collected Writings* (1992).

6 For recent and quite diverging views on the postwar growth process in West Germany, see Giersch *et al.* (1992), Carlin (1996) and Lindlar (1997).

7 The last meeting of the *Verein für Socialpolitik* was held in Dresden in January 1932; the last meeting of the Friedrich List Society – the other association of German-speaking economists, which dissolved itself in 1935 – took place in February 1933.

8 See in particular volumes 1-8 in the *Schriften des Vereins* and the report on capital shortage and unemployment in the social market economy from 26 February 1950 as an interesting example which, together with some other reports, are reprinted in Bombach *et al.* (1983).

9 At the end of 1997, with the Chief Economist Otmar Issing (as the only professor of the eight members in the Directorate) Helmut Hesse, Reimut Jochimsen, Hans-Jürgen Krupp and Olaf Sievert (that is, four out of nine presidents of the Central Banks in the federal states), the *Zentralbankrat* of the Bundesbank comprised five distinguished professors of economics.

10 For a detailed reflection on the reports, themes and controversies of the first twenty years, see Krelle (1984). The 1997-98 report with the title *Wachstum, Beschäftigung, Währungsunion – Orientierungen für die Zukunft* (Growth, Employment, Monetary Union – Orientation for the Future) was drafted by Herbert Hax (chairman and Professor of Business Finance and Investment at the University of Cologne), Jürgen B. Donges (Cologne, and former chairman of the Committee on Deregulation), Wolfgang Franz (Director of the Zentrum für Europäische Wirtschaftsforschung (ZEW) in Mannheim and labour-market expert); Rolf Peffekoven (Professor of Public Finance in Mainz) and Horst Siebert (President of the Kiel Institute of World Economics). The permanent research staff of the Council is located at the Federal Bureau of Statistics in Wiesbaden.

11 Schneider's *Introduction to Economic Theory* basically comprised three volumes – I, on National Accounting (1946); II, on Microeconomics (1949); and III, on Macroeconomics (1952) – all of them running to more than ten editions during his lifetime. In the mid-1960s a fourth volume on selected chapters on the history of economic theory was published by Mohr-Siebeck in Tübingen. Schneider was not the only propagator of Keynesianism in Germany. The second important textbook author was Andreas Paulsen, whose book *Neue Wirtschaftslehre* (New Economics, 1950) not only made the label of Keynesianism popular in Germany but also contributed to the dissemination of Keynesian economics among German students until the 1970s. On the research side, the pioneering monetary macroeconomic analysis of Carl Föhl, *Geldschöpfung und Wirtschaftskreislauf* (Creation of Money and Economic Circular Flow, 1937, 1955[2] Berlin: Duncker and Humblot), a remarkable PhD thesis from December 1935, influenced by Schumpeter and Keynes's *Treatise*, has to be mentioned. Although the book was highly praised by prominent economists, like Schumpeter and Schneider, and also favourably reviewed by H. W. Singer in the *Economic Journal* (48, 1938: 79-80), it was hardly noticed outside or even inside Germany. Föhl only made a very late academic career when in 1963, at the age of 62, he became Full Professor at the Free University of Berlin.

12 For further details, see Hagemann (1991).

13 See Enders (1996: 73). The data given in Dicke (1996: 77 and 83), which constitute an unbelievably high growth of the academic staff in the public sector devoted to economic research and teaching, by 146% from 3,300 in 1980 to 7,827 scientists in 1990, have to be treated with great caution. Naturally, the absolute figures are higher if *Fachhochschulen* are included. But an increase of professors (university professors)

from 973 (423) to 2,205 (885) in the 1980s is not only strongly at odds with reality but also with Dicke's own salary data.

14 Data source: *Bundesministerium für Bildung, Wissenschaft, Forschung und Technologie* (ed.) *Studenten an Hochschulen 1975 bis 1995*, Bonn.

15 See *Wissenschaftsrat* (1988) for these and the following data.

References

Bombach, G. *et al.* (1983) *Der Keynesianismus IV. Die beschäftigungspolitische Diskussion in der Wachstumsepoche der Bundesrepublik Deutschland*, Berlin-Heidelberg-New York: Springer.

Carlin, W. (1996), 'West German growth and institutions', in N. Crafts and G. Toniolo (eds) *Economic Growth in Europe since 1945*, Cambridge: Cambridge University Press, pp. 455–97.

Coats, A. W. (ed.)(1997), *The Post-1945 Internationalization of Economics*, Durham, NC: Duke University Press.

Craver, E. and Leijonhufvud, A. (1987) 'Economics in America: the Continental influence', in *History of Political Economy* 19: 173–82.

Dicke, H. (1996) 'Germany', in A. Kirman and M. Dahl (eds) *Economic Research in Europe*, Florence, pp. 73–85.

Enders, J. (1996) *Die wissenschaftlichen Mitarbeiter. Ausbildung, Beschäftigung und Karriere der Nachwuchswisssenschaftler und Mittelbauangehörigen an den Universitäten*, Frankfurt and New York: Campus.

Eucken, W. (1940) *Die Grundlagen der Nationalökonomie*, Jena: Gustav Fischer; English translation as *The Foundation of Economics*, Chicago: University of Chicago Press, 1951.

Frey, B. S. and Eichenberger, R. (1992) 'Economics and economists: a European perspective', *American Economic Review* 82: 216–20.

——(1993) 'American and European economics and economists', *Journal of Economic Perspectives* 7: 185–93.

Frey, B. S. and Frey, R. L. (1995) 'Is there a European Economics?' (A Symposium) *Kyklos* 48: 185–311.

Frey, B. S. and Pommerehne, W. W. (1988), 'The American domination among eminent economists', *Scientometrics* 14: 97–110.

Giersch, H., Paqué, K-H. and Schmieding, H. (1992) *The Fading Miracle: Four Decades of Market Economy in Germany*, Cambridge: Cambridge University Press.

Hagemann, H. (1991) 'Learned journals and the professionalization of economics: the German language area', *Economic Notes* 20: 33–57.

——(ed.) (1997) *Zur deutschsprachigen wirtschaftswissenschaftlichen Emigration nach 1933*, Marburg: Metropolis.

Hall, P. A. (ed.) (1989) *The Political Power of Economic Ideas: Keynesianism across Nations*, Princeton, NJ: Princeton University Press.

Häuser, K. (1998) 'Deutsche Nationalökonomie in der Diaspora: die dreißiger und vierziger Jahre bis Kriegsende' in K. Acham, K. W. Nörr, B. Schefold (eds) *Erkenntnisgewinne, Erkenntnisverluste. Kontinuitäten und Diskontinuitäten in den Wirtschafts-, Rechts- und Sozialwissenschaften zwischen den 20er und 50er Jahren*, Stuttgart: Franz Steiner, pp. 174–209.

Heuß, E. (1989) 'Die theoretische Nationalökonomie im deutschsprachigen Raum vor und nach 1945', in B. Schefold (ed.) *Studien zur Entwicklung der ökonomischen Theorie VIII, Schriften des Vereins für Socialpolitik*, vol. 115/VIII, Berlin: Duncker & Humblot, pp. 63–74.

Hutchison, T. W. (1979) 'Notes on the effects of economic ideas on policy: the example of the German social market economy', *Zeitschrift für die gesamte Staatswissenschaft* 135: 426–41.

Johnson, H. G. (1973) 'National styles in economic research. The United States, United Kingdom, Canada, and various European countries', *Daedalus* 102: 65–74.

Kirman, A. and Dahl, M. (1994) 'Economic research in Europe', *European Economic Review* 38: 505–22.

——(1996) *Economic Research in Europe*, Florence: European University Institute.

Krelle, W. (1984) '20 Jahre Sachverständigenrat: War es der Mühe wert?' *Journal of Institutional and Theoretical Economics* 140: 332–54.

Lindlar, L. (1997) *Das mißverstandene Wirtschaftswunder. Westdeutschland und die westeuropäische Nachkriegsprosperität.* Tübingen: Mohr-Siebeck.

Musgrave, R. A. (1996) 'Public finance and Finanzwissenschaft traditions compared', *Finanzarchiv* 53: 145–93.

——(1997) 'Crossing traditions', in H. Hagemann (ed.) *Zur deutschsprachigen wirtschaftswissenschaftlichen Emigration nach 1933*, Marburg: Metropolis, pp. 63–79.

Peacock, A. (1995) 'Professional "Gleichschaltung": a historical perspective', *Kyklos* 48: 267–71.

Rieter, H. and Schmolz, M. (1993) 'The ideas of German Ordoliberalism 1938–45: pointing the way to a new economic order', *The European Journal of the History of Economic Thought* 1: 87–114.

Samuelson, P. A. (1988) 'The passing of the guard in economics', *Eastern Economic Journal* 14: 319–29.

Schiller, K. (1962) Article, 'Wirtschaftspolitik', in *Handwörterbuch der Sozialwissenschaften*, Stuttgart-Tübingen-Göttingen, vol. 12, pp. 210–31.

Schneider, E. (1953) 'Der Streit um Keynes. Dichtung und Wahrheit in der neueren deutschen Keynes-Diskussion', *Jahrbücher für Nationalökonomie und Statistik*, 165: 89–122.

Stackelberg, H. v. (1992) *Gesammelte Wirtschaftswissenschaftliche Abhandlungen*, edited by N. Kloten and H. Möller, 2 vols, Regensburg: Transfer Verlag.

Wissenschaftsrat (1988) *Empfehlungen des Wissenschaftsrates zu den Perspektiven der Hochschulen in den 90er Jahren*, Cologne.

7   Economics in France

A manifold system

Christian Schmidt

The legacy of the past

Economics in France has some very specific traditions closely linked to the national institutions. Roughly speaking, the profession has been divided from the middle of the nineteenth century into two separate groups according to their educational background and their professional activity; namely, the professors of political economy (*professeurs d'économie politique*) and the economic engineers (*les ingénieurs économistes*). Whereas the professors are educated in law faculties mainly in law and humanities, the engineers have been trained in the French scientific schools (*les Grandes Ecoles*), primarily in mathematics and natural scientific matters. As the French system of universities is public and highly centralized, the first group completely dominates the faculty of economics. The engineers, on the other hand, are most often members of prestigious corps of civil servants (*ingénieurs des mines, ingénieurs des ponts et chaussées . . .*) and have a determining influence in the administrative decision-making process. Anyway, the relationship between the two groups has, up to now, remained occasional and relatively poor because of the narrow dimension of their intersection, in spite of some recent *rapprochements* which will be described later.

Two different traditions

In addition to an institutional segmentation such as this, the French community of economists has been split from its origin by a strong doctrinal opposition. On the one side are the *laissez-faire* supporters promptly labelled as liberals (*les libéraux*); on the other, there has been a more heterogeneous opposition grouping together the partisans of a socialism *à la Française* and/or national economic protection. Let us notice that a free market is not necessarily inconsistent with socialist ideals, as illustrated by Léon Walras's works, and that protectionism does not always lead to socialism, as exemplified by the writings of Paul Cauwes. Throughout all the nineteenth century and up to the end of World War II, the debate between the two camps was heated. Their opposition was institutionalized in societies, associations and journals. Thus, the liberals were organized around the powerful *Société d'Economie Politique*, created in 1847 and still active today, and controlled the well-known *Journal des Economistes* from 1841 to 1940. As for the opponents, they founded the *Société d'Economie Politique Nationale* in 1897 and, above all, the *Revue d'Economie Politique* in 1887 (Marco 1996), which is even now one of the main journals in the field.

It may seem strange to a foreign observer that the liberals largely dominate their opponents in a country such as France, where governmental intervention in the economy has been, since Colbert and *l'ancien régime*, a constant feature of political life. Such a discrepancy can be explained by a weak and relatively late professionalization of economists in France. Because the economists' expertise was, until recently, very under-utilized, the economic debate was relatively disconnected from actual practice. For example, the *Association Française des Economistes d'Entreprises*, grouping the economists who work in or for companies, was created only in 1975.

One can find liberals in the law faculties as well as among the economic engineers and the same is true for protectionists and – but on a more reduced scale – for socialists. Surprisingly, however, a greater number of professors sympathized with the protectionist doctrines while the economic engineers were more often liberal-orientated. Charles Gide, the founder of the *Revue d'Economie Politique*, provides an example of the first tendency. Jules Dupuit, known as a pioneer of utility theory and, more generally, one of the fathers of the public economy, was *Ingénieur des Ponts et Chaussées* and an active member of the very liberal *Société d'Economie Politique*.

The two phenomena must be explained separately. The professors of political economy in French universities were closely linked to public law because, at the origin in 1877, the recruitment for teaching economy in the law faculties was the same as for the teaching of public law (*concours d'agrégation de droit et d'économie politique*). Therefore political economy was understood from the viewpoint of the legislator and the public authorities. A special emphasis was initially given to public finance, taxation and related topics in the programmes. As for the economic engineers, their liberal orientation must be related to their connection to private companies, because of being fellows of the same *Grandes Ecoles* (*Ecole Polytechnique, Ecole Centrale, Ecole Nationale des Mines, Ecole Nationale des Ponts et Chaussées*). Indeed, in France nowadays, the majority of executives in big companies have been educated in the same prestigious schools. For this reason, the economic engineers even when they are civil servants, which is often the case, are prepared to share the views of free entrepreneurship. Moreover, while the professors considered economics from a political viewpoint, as a facet of the government's activities, the engineers were orientated towards economic calculation at a micro-level.

A third group must be mentioned which was at that time hardly considered as a group of economists. As early as 1883, the Paris Chamber of Commerce founded a special school for the education of professional managers, *HEC* (*Hautes Etudes Commerciales*). This school did not appoint full-time professors and the teaching programme was a mixture of lectures from professors in law faculties and narratives of managers' own experiences. But its influence remained relatively limited until the middle of the 1960s for two reasons. First-ly, there was nothing really original in the content of their economic programme. Second, top French managers were not educated in this school but came from the *Grandes Ecoles d'Ingénieurs*. Since the nineteenth century the major French companies have been primarily managed by engineers – a pecu-liarity which can explain several features of French industries. For example, French companies are traditionally successful in high technology, while French financial markets and banks are comparatively poorly competitive.

What is meant by economics?

The process of professional organization in the first half of the twentieth century coincides in France with a trend of national withdrawal. During this time Mar-shall's influence was virtually absent in France. As for Keynes, he is better known to historians for the *Economic Consequences of the Peace*, like Jacques Bainville (Bainville 1919),[1] or by some mathematicians like Emile Borel for his *Treatise on probability* (Borel 1924), than by academic economists for his eco-nomic writings, at least prior to *The General Theory*. The debates among French economists follow their own logic, largely disconnected from outside. A good example is provided by the discussion between Lescure and Aftalion about the economic cycle and the possibility of a crisis of a generalized over-produc-tion in the early twentieth century. This topic can be considered in retrospect as an anticipation of well-known debates in the Anglo-Saxon world around the business cycle. However, the French pose their own problem in their own terms. The language barrier is certainly a part of the explanation for such a situation. More profound factors are also to be taken into account, such as the law-orien-tated education of academics and the traditional role of the government and administration in the French economic system.

In France, political economy is neither derived from an economic theory gen-erated by a philosophical tradition as in England, nor from history at large, as in Germany in the same period. The failure of Cournot and Walras to be recog-nized by contemporary economists in their own country exemplifies the first point. The existence in the law faculties, and even in some *Grandes Ecoles*, such as the *Ecole Supérieure des Ponts et Chaussées*, of specific programmes in economic and social history, completely disconnected from the community of historians, are significant for the second point. The works of Emile Levasseur, who was Professor at the *Collège de France* at the beginning of the twentieth century gives a precise idea of this type of economic history *à la française*. Sceptical about the relevance of economic theory, and not really convinced that political economy is more than a special sub-set of an historical science, during the twentieth century the French economists built their own domain of investi-gation which was largely sheltered from foreign influence up to the middle of the twentieth century.

Evolution versus revolution

The institutional features previously described were not drastically modified after World War II but, rather, were progressively inflected stage by stage. In the end, however, the landscape has been profoundly changed. Let us start with the academics and the economic engineers. The division previously described still exists. Both have followed their own lines, but with different time sequences. Immediately after World War II, some of the economic engineers were organized into a new corps of civil servants who specialized in statistics and economic studies, named *les Administrateurs Civils de l'INSEE.*[2] *INSEE* (*Institut Nationale de la Statistique et des Etudes Economiques*) is the national institute which provides official statistical data on French economic activities. The academics became quite independent of the lawyers in the universities at the beginning of the 1970s. Finally, the schools of engineers (*les Grandes Ecoles*) have developed extensive teaching programmes in economics more recently, since the early 1980s. Two examples of this last stage are really significant. The *ECP* (*L'Ecole Centrale de Paris*) has organized a special option designed for economic engineers. Only two years ago, the well-known *Ecole Polytechnique* created a specialization labelled 'Applied Mathematics and Economics', which starts from the second year of the course. This new section is receiving 100 students each year, corresponding approximately to one third of the total number of students of the same level in the *Polytechnique*'s courses.

Careers

Many differences remain between the two groups, at least from an institutional point of view. Professors of economics in the universities are still recruited at a national level by means of a competitive examination (*le concours d'agrégation des sciences économiques*) after the PhD. Their courses are organized on a national basis by means of a centralized organization, the CNU (*Comités Nationaux Universitaires*). The professors of economics in universities are permanent civil servants and, in most cases, full-time professors.[3] Unfortunately, their social position, which is directly connected to their salaries, has continuously declined since 1945.

The situation is completely different for the professors of economics who teach in the *Grandes Ecoles d'Ingénieurs*. They are generally directly chosen by the board of the school. Furthermore, their link to the school is by a simple contract, and very few are full-time professors. At the *Ecole Polytechnique*, for example, among the twenty-five professors who belong to the Economics Department, only five are permanent and full-time officers. Such differences often generate divergent individual strategies which have repercussions on their intellectual work, most of them being closely linked to the process of policy-making through their administrative or private affiliations. Their wages are higher than those of the professors in universities, a factor which reinforces their difference in status and prestige.

In spite of those differences, some bridges have been built between the two populations, and their relationship has recently become closer. First of all, a connection exists at the level of their individual careers. Thus, a growing number of professors of economics in the universities have now been educated in the *Grandes Ecoles d'Ingénieurs* before going through the competitive examination (*concours d'agrégation*). They keep in touch with their school class-mates because of the very powerful fellowship that exists between them. On the other hand, some academics can be in charge of the departments of economics in one or other of the *Grandes Ecoles d'Ingénieurs*. This is the case for the ECP (*Ecole Centrale de Paris*), where an academic, Professor at the University of Paris I, is Head of the Economics Department. Such a position facilitates exchanges between engineers and academics, especially for the post-graduate programmes.

Research activities

Research Centres provide an especially welcome meeting point for the two groups. Indeed, the *Grandes Ecoles d'Ingénieurs* have their own Research Centres in Economics and Business. For example, the *Ecole Polytechnique* leads three big research institutes – namely, the *Laboratoire d'économétrie*, the *Centre de Recherche de Gestion* and, more recently, the *CREA* (*Centre de Recherches en épistémologie appliquée*).[4] Those Research Centres are obviously dominated by the engineers, but their connections with the academics are often very intricate. Under the impulse of the *CNRS* (*Centre National de la Recherche Scientifique*), created immediately after World War II, many researchers were administratively dependent on the *CNRS* as research directors, associates or assistants. In addition, these Centres have close contacts with several foreign universities through visiting researchers and joint programmes: for example, the *Laboratoire d'économétrie* of the *Ecole Polytechnique* is directly related to the University of Louvain-La-Neuve, the London School of Economics, the State University of California (Santa Barbara) and the State University of New York (Stony Brook).

However, the blend of the two populations is still more advanced than in some Research Centres either initiated a long time ago by the French *Commissariat au Plan*, or in recent years by a few academic institutes supported by the universities. For example, the *CEPREMAP* (*Centre d'Etudes Prospectives d'Economie Mathématique Appliquées à la Planification*) belongs to the first category. It results from the fusion in 1967 of two administrative centres dependent on the French Plan; namely, the *CEPREL* and the *CERMAP*. Chaired by a civil servant and directed by a university professor, the *CEPREMAP* has extended its domain to various fields of economic theory, especially in macro-economics. It groups together economic engineers from the *Grandes Ecoles* and academics from the major faculties of economics in Paris (University Paris I, Paris II, Paris IX and Paris X) and participates actively in the PhD programmes. The *Cremaq* (*Centre de Recherche en Economie Mathématique et Qualitative*) at Toulouse and the *GREQAM* (*Groupement de*

Recherche en Economie Quantitative d'Aix-Marseilles) at Aix-Marseilles exemplify the second category. Both mix academic and economic engineers in addition to full-time *CNRS* researchers. Their respective domains are very broad, with special attention to quantitative approaches, game theory and industrial economics.

The comparison between these two types of research institution reveals some differences. As previously mentioned, the *CEPREMAP*'s origin considerably precedes that of the academic research centres. For example, *GREQAM* was formed only in 1994, as an extension of the *Greque* (*Groupe de Recherche en Economie Quantitative et Econométrie*), which started in 1982. Furthermore, while the *Cepremap* is entirely located in Paris and works with Parisian researchers, the *Cremaq* and the *GREQAM* are exclusively provincial centres. Their creation, in the last ten years, resulted from a voluntary policy of decentralization around a small number of poles under the influence of the *CNRS* and the French Ministry of National Education.

One clear conclusion emerges from these separate trends: despite the institutional features which still divide academics and economic engineers in France, the intellectual gap between them has been significantly reduced during the period studied. Such an evolution has been facilitated by two major factors. Firstly, mathematical economics has progressively dominated the whole of economic theory, econometrics and almost all the applied economic studies, at least in academic circles. Mathematical works have now become a crucial necessity for French academic economists hoping to gain promotion. Furthermore, the most prestigious of our colleagues hoping for a Nobel Prize are mathematical economists like Jean-Jacques Laffont (Toulouse) or Jean-Michel Grandmont (*Ecole Polytechnique*). Second, the economic engineers are no longer self-made men in economics, but have received the benefit of a serious economic training. In other words, the original gap between the two economic programmes being taught has tended to lessen in recent years. At the intersection of these movements, a large part of the two populations can speak the same economic language.

The way towards internationalization

There is a temptation to understand this history from a nationalistic point of view as a definite victory of the economic engineers' camp over that of the academics. This interpretation is supported by some evidence: the only French Nobel Prize winner, Maurice Allais, as well as the latest Professor of Economic Analysis at the prestigious *Collège de France*, Edmond Malinvaud, were both educated at the *Ecole Polytechnique* and clearly belong to the category of economic engineers. Nevertheless, things are more complex than that. Allais and Malinvaud are not members of the same generation, and whereas Allais was primarily appointed as an *Ingénieur des Mines*, Malinvaud immediately became a professional economist. Furthermore, the Nobel Prize is an international distinction quite independent of the French debate of academics versus engineers, whereas the election of Edmond Malinvaud in 1987 to the *Collège de France* is a more significant indication of a change in the mentality of French economists since it proves that international recognition is now taken into account in the French national system of evaluation. Indeed, Malinvaud was a well-known civil servant in French economic administration, but his academic prestige was merely the consequence of his recognition outside France.

Let us compare this account with Gérard Debreu's situation thirty years before, when he was obliged to emigrate to the United States.[5] Both Malinvaud and Debreu had joined the Cowles Commission as young researchers during the 1950s (Arrow *et al.* 1991), but Malinvaud quickly came back to France as a civil servant, and Debreu became an American citizen. The comparison is not, however, entirely apt. A pupil of Allais, Debreu is a mathematical economist, but not an economic engineer, because he was educated at the *Ecole Normale Supérieure*, a very prestigious place for pure scientists which has nothing to do with engineering. Such a subtle sociological distinction has remained very significant in France up to now, because the *Ecole Normale Supérieure* educates pure mathematicians, whereas the *Ecole Polytechnique* is devoted to applying mathematics to engineering matters. While Malinvaud could easily find a job as a civil servant in France, Debreu as an academic mathematician encountered considerable difficulties in finding a position in the field of economics in his own country at that time. Anyway, mathematical economics has an old and vigorous tradition in France mainly due to the engineers (Zylberberg 1990), but Malinvaud's election also symbolizes a rising internationalization in French economic thought.

The necessity of a consistent formation in economic analysis for French civil servants primarily trained in mathematics must also be historically related to the French economic situation just after the war. The economic recovery was mainly due to the work of civil servants who brought together statistics to provide reliable data, and to a renewal of the economic approach mainly inspired by the ideas of Keynesian macroeconomics – a strange reversal *vis-à-vis* Keynes in France, when we remember the negative reaction of the majority of French economists to the *Economic Consequences of the Peace* (1919), as well as to the *Treatise on Money* (1930) (Arena *et al.* 1997). The most telling example of this change is provided by the publication in 1949 of *Esquisse d'une Théorie Générale de l'Equilibre Economique* by Claude Gruson, an *Inspecteur des Finances* educated at the *Ecole Polytechnique*. Gruson's book was the first outstanding original French interpretation of the *General Theory*.

The aim of institutions such as *INSEE* was to combine economic statistics derived from the engineers' expertise with the view of economics as a global system deduced from political economy. The *ENSAE* (*Ecole Nationale de la Statistique et de l'Administration Economique*) was created at the same time to ensure the training of the *INSEE* administrators. This new school was specifically devoted to the training of statistician-economists by means of an important programme of economic analysis. A few years later, a small team of researchers was organized by Claude Gruson in the French Ministry of Finance under the title *SEEF* (*Service des Etudes économiques et financières*). Civil servants, such as Simon Nora joined Gruson's team, and even some academics, like Jean Benard, who became Professor of Economics at the University of Paris I. Together they built the foundations of the French System of National Accounts (the national economic budgets) and generated the first applied econometric modelling exercise. This national accounting system has several national characteristics, such as an original distinction between the production and the product, but Gruson's group was connected to other groups working on the same topic in Europe, especially in Great Britain, around Richard Stone. Subsequently, Gruson became the general director of *INSEE* (from 1961 to 1967). In this way this current of thought has prepared the way for the internationalization of economics in France. Once again, the academics have moved closer to the economic engineers (and vice versa) at the same time as economics has become more open to foreign influences.

As for the business economists, their take-off has directly resulted from a closer relationship with the American business schools. At the beginning of the 1960s, the case-studies approach inspired by Harvard emerged from the teaching programmes of *HEC* (*Hautes Etudes Commerciales*) and other schools spawned by the various chambers of commerce. Later on, when the *FNEGE* (*Fondation Nationale pour l'Enseignement de la Gestion et des Entreprises*) was created, scholarships were granted to young students in order that they might study in the United States. Because many of them came back to France with American Master's or PhD degrees, the staff of *HEC*, which is now composed of more than 100 full-time professors, is basically built on the American model. Two departments strongly dominate this organization, namely Marketing and Finance, with a special emphasis on finance, which is obviously linked to economics. Anyway, the recognition of Management as an organized branch of economic knowledge in the French *Ecole de Commerce* has been directly correlated with its Americanization.

Does it mean that the distinctive French specificity is disappearing, to be progressively dissolved in the international standards of the profession? The reactions of French economists to the emergence of an international community are not so simple. One can always find some French economists at the heart of the international associations. As early as the 1930s a few French economic engineers were very active when the European Society of Econometrics was created. The same attitude was apparent when the IEA (International Economic Association) was founded in 1950. Its office is still located in Paris and its Secretary-General has been a French professor from the very beginning. Jean-Paul Fitoussi, who chairs the *OFCE* (*Observatoire Français de la Conjoncture Economique*), is now in charge, a small indication of the attraction of international institutions for French economists. The IEA was the starting point for the creation of the French National Association, the *AFSE* (*Association Française de Science Economique*) also in 1950. Its initial *raison d'être* was to participate as a national association in the IEA.[6] Once again, the same stance of the French community of economists *vis-à-vis* international institutions has recently been observed on the occasion of the creation of the ESHET (European Society for the History of Economic Thought) in 1996. Several French historians of economic thought were at the origin of the process, and up to now, among its various national components, the French are by far the most numerous members of the society. On the other hand, the temptation always exists to produce an alternative approach to economics and/or to isolate intellectual debate around national fashions. This characteristic of national separatism will be studied in the next part of this chapter. One can argue at this stage that participation in international organizations offers the French community of economists an additional opportunity to cultivate their difference.

Does a French specificity still exist in economics?

Despite the institutional conservatism, the general landscape of economics has been significantly transformed in France since 1950. New kinds of demarcations have successively appeared during this period.

The Moderns versus the Ancients: a hypothetical conflict

We have seen that, in spite of their differences, the most active members of the academic population have now joined those among the engineers who are the most theoretical. Let us note in this sense the recent bridge between the two populations via the increasing number of professors of economics in French universities primarily educated in the *Ecole Polytechnique* or the *Ecole Centrale*. Another sign is provided by the meeting of both groups in several associations, such as the *Association Française de Science Economique*. This does not mean that all the academics have followed this movement. On the contrary, a kind of discreet opposition is being quietly organized by the old-fashioned professors, often through alliances with the business establishment. An interesting index is provided by the speed with which the ratio of academics is rising in the election of the members of the old *Société d'Economie Politique*, around 75 per cent during the last five years. Another illustration is the recent renewal of a journal adhering to that line – *Les Chroniques de la SEDEIS* (*Société d'Etudes et de Documentation Economiques Industrielles et Sociales*) founded by Bertrand de Jouvenel after the war and reshaped by Albert Merlin in January 1996 and a new team, with the title of *Societal*. Several academics, professors in well-known universities such as Paris I and Paris IX, rejoined the board of *Societal* in November 1996.

According to the liberal tradition of economics of the *Société d'Economie Politique*, the group is spontaneously orientated to free trade and non-interventionist, but its real unity is less doctrinal than methodological. The group claims to be against the excess of mathematical abstraction in political economy and argues in favour of a more policy-orientated approach to economic problems. If there is no formal debate between this group and the researchers previously mentioned, a new line of opposition is to be drawn, which evokes an ancient literary controversy of the seventeenth century: on one side, the Ancients, who advocate traditional analysis of economics, mainly descriptive, institutional and closely related to law; on the other side, the Moderns, who develop more and more sophisticated techniques for understanding economics. Must it be considered a rearguard conflict? A positive answer is not quite satisfactory. Mathematical economics and econometrics have, in fact, dominated French economic thought. But doubts arise, notably among the statisticians and some economic engineers, right up to the *INSEE*, about the relevance of economic modelling on a large scale. In addition, the enlarging of the gap between the expected and the observed data in France during the last five years has generated scepticism about the relevance of some of the recent technical sophistications in the field.

The combination of all these observations has recently led French economists to a larger debate about the meaning and the scope of economics as a 'hard' or a 'soft' science.[7] Roughly speaking, French economists generally consider that economics is a very specific social science, quite apart from other social sciences, such as sociology or political science, for two main reasons: the possibility of sophisticated computations due to quantifications, and its closed relationship with rationality through decision-making assumptions. On the other hand, however, economics cannot be assimilated with a natural science in spite of the recent fashion for experimental economics. Economics generates a social order to be accepted by the agents. The position adopted by Malinvaud on the matter is very significant (Malinvaud 1996). For Malinvaud, and contrary to natural science, physics, chemistry and even biology, scientific discoveries do not exist in economics. Such a thesis looks like a provocation from a mathematical economist who argued lengthily in favour of rigorous standards in economics. This does not mean that Malinvaud changed his mind and moved over to the other camp, but rather that economics itself has degenerated into mimicking natural science. Thus, in an unexpected fashion Malinvaud's position opens the road to a kind of reconciliation between the two traditions.

Balanced cooperation or even peaceful coexistence cannot, however, be observed in every field. The case of industrial economics is an example of a different situation. By the mid-1970s, the time when public economics was a leading topic and a powerful incentive for French economists was over. Let us remember the transformation of the *CEPREMAP* during the 1970s. Alternative sources of inspiration were to be found. Industrial economics provided an interesting paradigm for theoretical and political reasons. This paradigm sounds new because there was no real French tradition in this field, except for Fayolle's works on labour organization in companies. Therefore various directions were opened up to develop a new paradigm. In 1977, a journal was created, *La Revue d'Economie Industrielle* (Marco 1996). The majority of its editorial board consisted of old-fashioned academics. The editorial lines which were defined in the first issue of the journal were based on three ambitions: interdisciplinarity, analytical eclecticism and orientation *à la française* in order to avoid an Anglo-Saxon domination. Someone even spoke at that time of a New French School of Industrial Economics, but beyond the rhetoric, this current was a remake of the insights of the old professors of political economy – old wine in new bottles.

A few years later, a quite different approach to industrial economics was developed in France, on the basis of rigorous analytical tools, mainly derived from game theory. Jean-Jacques Laffont, Jean Tirole and Jacques Cremer, among others, were the pioneers of what they called 'the new industrial economics' and all of them were partially educated in US universities. Such a reconstruction, mainly based on game theory, has actually no connection with the so-called New French School and is more inspired by an institutionalist approach. The seminal papers of these authors have been published in foreign journals. Still more significant, they prepared a special issue to be published in French in 1987, not in *La Revue d'Economie Industrielle*, but in the *Annales d'Economie et de Statistiques*, a journal which still belongs to the group of *INSEE*'s publications. The battle between the Ancients and the Moderns has never taken place. The gap between the two approaches is too large to allow an opportunity for debate. One must, however, underline an opposite strategy to promote the French flavour in economic analysis. Whereas the founders of *La Revue d'Economie Industrielle* aimed at a French alternative to the Anglo-Saxon current of industrial organization, the Moderns were plainly integrated in the international research community and they only tried to incorporate some original French views inspired by Cournot into this stream.

The recurrent temptation of a French alternative approach to economics

The heterodox temptation which periodically reappears in France is not always due to the old-fashioned professors of economy, as a pure restatement of the past. On the contrary, the school of regulation in the late 1970s and the economics of convention ten years later were led by young researchers perfectly aware of mathematical sophistication and modern techniques of economic analysis, as well as the dominant fashions in Anglo-Saxon countries. Moreover, many of them were closely related to well-known and dynamic centres, such as the *CEPREMAP* for the regulation, and the *CREA* for the conventions (at least at its beginning).

In the second half of the 1970s, a group of economists led by Michel Aglietta, Robert Boyer and André Lipietz elaborated a research programme as an alternative to neoclassical macro-economics (Boyer 1986). Its main idea can be summarized as follows. The cornerstone of the economic system is to be found in its long-run dynamics, which can be modelled as a socio-economic regulatory process. To market adjustments, the regulationists opposed the procedures of social organization, such as the 'Fordist' system of wage-earning. For the regulationists, wages are not only an income but the masterpiece of a system of social organization which regulates the evolution of the whole economy. Indeed, they focus the analysis on the accumulation of capital in an historical prospect in a Marxian spirit, but they deny the relevance of general laws to explain the observed tendencies of the dynamics. The French regulationists have tried to export their ideas to avoid being reduced to a Franco–French debate. But their attempts to convince some circles of radical Americans have remained globally unsuccessful, in spite of the individual prestige of some leaders, such as Boyer. Consequently, the school declined from the mid-1980s.

The domain of the 'economics of convention' is different. Its starting point was provided by the identification of a missing point in economic analysis; namely, the conventions implicitly or explicitly accepted by the economic agents during their transactions.[8] For the conventionists, such as Olivier Favereau or Laurent Thevenot, these conventions cannot be reduced to individual contracts as in standard micro-economics, but must be analysed in the framework of a common knowledge. The study of connected concepts, such as credibility, reputation and truthfulness, is to be developed from this conventionalist viewpoint. At first sight, similarities appear between the conventionalist approach and some extensions of the game theory programme. But it would be a mistake to combine the two kinds of analysis. Whereas the rationality of individual behaviour is the basic hypothesis of game theory, the economics of convention underlines the social dimensions of economic co-ordination based on accepted rules. Several applications of this conventionist economics have been explored in the fields of job markets and industrial organization. As with the regulationists, the French conventionalists devoted their energy to attracting foreign economists' attention with almost the same result.

Despite their differences, these two schools share some common features. Both programmes are based on two pillars: a criticism of the so-called 'standard economics' and a deliberate interdisciplinary approach to economic phenomena. The first pillar, more systematically developed by the conventionists, is the result of an exercise in reconstruction. The second pillar is an attempt to mix several economic ingredients with other scientific fields: history *à la Braudel* for the regulation school, institutionalist sociology for the conventional school. Strangely enough, the New French School of Industrial Economics also participated in the same spirit, although it does not offer a renewal of analytical tools. In all cases, this reflects a very old French tradition which can be checked whenever a new journal appears (see the *Revue Economique* in 1950 and the *Revue d'Economie Politique* in 1887).

The difficulty for these national currents in penetrating the international community of economists raises a real problem. The linguistic barriers of the past no longer operate with the regulationist and the conventionist approaches. Their leaders had the opportunity to express their views in books and papers published in English. Therefore the explanation must be found in another direction. Such strictly French schools of thought aim to reconsider the whole orthodox approach to economic phenomena. By contrast, their positive proposals are relatively limited and narrow because the core of their doctrine forms a curious mixture of critical statements and positive propositions. So their contents are not so drastic as some critical American movements of economics, such as the Radical School, and they do not provide analytical concepts sufficiently precise to counterbalance the mainstream arguments. A comparison between the treatment of the coordination problem by means of game theory, as against convention economics, illuminates the point.

The final outcome will be about the same in both cases. Some new economic ideas have to be captured in each of these schools of thought; but after a certain time the strongest part of their respective edifices tends to be integrated into the more conventional corpus. Is it a sign of their failure to represent a specific French current? Not necessarily, because what remains of all those attempts is some kind of revolution in terminology: a national originality to be studied, which offers an additional explanation of their isolation.

The unexpected effect of internationalization on French economics from 1945

What picture can be drawn of the community of French economists *vis-à-vis* the general trend in the internationalization of the profession? Its features are primarily highly contrasting and close to self-contradictory. To sum up, on the one hand many French economists were enthusiastic about the creation of various types of international association. Let us just recall their role at the very beginning of the International Economic Association (IEA), when they organized international meetings and willingly participated in congresses and symposia in the United States as well as in many other foreign countries. On the other hand, several French economists, among the most determined, have continually insisted on underlining their difference via the periodic emergence of autonomous schools of thought, such as the regulation theory around the mid-1970s, and the economics of convention since the end of the 1980s – a duality which can also be observed in international policy.

A preliminary explanation would be to consider that international life is viewed by French economists mainly as an arena in which to compete with the American intellectual domination. Such an interpretation is only partially relevant. Maurice Allais's publication of his famous article, '*Le comportement de l'homme rationnel devant le risque: critique de postulats de l'Ecole Américaine*', in *Econometrica* (1953), provides a good illustration of this behaviour. A similar strategy to support a different message was followed by Robert Boyer twenty-five years later in publishing papers in different American journals in order to promote his alternative approach of regulation theory to the standard macro-economics.

This explanation is not completely convincing. One can object that neither Allais nor Boyer succeeded in organizing international networks strong enough to counterbalance in their respective domains the American mainstream. Did they really believe they could reach this supposed target? Second, a more subtle direction has been explored in the past decade by native French economists educated in France who decided to live in the United States and to teach in American universities: people like Olivier Blanchard for macro-economics at MIT and Hervé Moulin for game theory at Duke University. While they were established in the United States, Blanchard and Moulin did not cut their French roots, as witness the fact that Blanchard was appointed in 1997 to the Council of Economic Advisers created in France by the Prime Minister, Lionel Jospin. As for Moulin, he regularly returns to French universities and participates in research programmes promoted by French centres. Therefore, it would be better in both cases to speak of a two-way relationship between French and American economic ideas.

Another explanation is much more satisfactory. Indeed, the general process of internationalization does not really spare the French economists through the normalization of the profession in line with American standards. Journals use the same reference procedures, the sessions of colloquia are organized according to similar patterns. More seriously, the learning programmes of economics in universities have grown progressively closer to American canons, but the French exception is elsewhere. As has been emphasized here, two different cultures of economics do exist in France, historically represented by the engineers and the professors of law. The standardization encouraged by internationalization offers a bridge which greatly contributes to an internal reconciliation between them. Such an unexpected impact does not mean that differences no longer exist among the two populations, and still less that both have accepted the American mainstream, but the process of internationalization provides a common language for the two camps. Such shared knowledge is used as a starting point for elaborating joint research programmes which curiously, as we have said, often deviate from the most orthodox American approaches.

Statistical annexes

The statistical data gathered from official sources contain some quantitative information about the evolution of the numbers of students and professors of economics and business in French universities during the period. Unfortunately, these data are not homogenous, either because the accounting systems were not the same from one period to another and/or because economics and business are sometimes mixed together and sometimes separate. In spite of such limitations, the different figures reflect useful aspects of information concerning this evolution.

Beyond the general progression of the whole during the period (numbers of students more than doubled between 1971 and 1996), two points must be noted.

Table 7.1 Number of students of economics and business, 1971–96

Academic years	No. of students enrolled
1971–72	48,200
1982–83	80,537
1983–84	87,449
1993–94	153,469
1994–95	139,740
1995–96	103.541

Table 7.2 Number of students of economics and business in major French universities*
1985–1993

University	1985	1986	1987	1988	1989	1990	1991	1992	1993
Université d'Aix-Marseille II	1,898	1,863	1,951	2,408	2,512	2,740	2,788	3,066	3,198
Université d'Aix-Marseille III	2,998	2,737	2,819	2,792	3,326	3,369	3,582	3,696	3,867
Université d'Orléans	726	755	885	955	1,169	3,139	2,200	3,386	2,655
Université de Bordeaux I	3,656	3,350	3,336	3,315	3,233	3,483	3,766	3,964	4,269
Université de Caen	2,262	2,402	2,373	2,666	2,800	3,182	3,315	3,460	3,595
Université de Clermont I	1,417	1,573	1,352	1,559	1,631	1,772	2,133	2,502	2,673
Université de Dijon	1,103	1,210	1,270	1,207	2,305	2,329	2,576	2,907	3,131
Université de Grenoble II	3,072	3,298	3,412	3,559	3,890	4,244	4,464	5,136	5,221
Université de Lille I	2,647	2,696	2,703	2,726	2,986	3,276	3,570	3,320	3,400
Université de Lyon II	1,976	1,905	2,169	2,514	2,389	3,008	3,059	3,209	3,135
Université de Lyon III	3,891	3,990	3,675	4,100	3,819	3,691	3,720	4,023	4,239
Université de Montpellier I	3,053	3,094	3,201	3,418	3,715	3,917	4,230	4,206	4,511
Université de Nancy II	2,170	2,270	2,263	2,453	2,872	3,140	3,436	3,690	3,817
Université de Nice	1,956	1,994	2,063	1,714	2,134	2,368	2,337	2,497	2,499
Université de Paris I	10,110	10,150	11,286	11,919	10,664	11,240	11,019	10,969	10,833
Université de Paris IX	4,294	4,322	4,718	4,528	5,330	5,059	5,620	5,616	5,602
Université de Paris X	4,864	5,141	5,475	5,908	6,251	6,249	5,691	6,089	6,083
Université de Paris XII	3,303	3,213	3,585	3,923	4,278	4,284	4,408	4,770	5,093
Université de Poitiers	1,898	1,973	1,992	2,196	2,591	3,041	3,550	3,538	3,811
Université de Reims	1,060	1,065	1,136	1,126	1,301	1,783	2,242	2,601	3,049
Université de Rennes I	2,120	2,237	2,453	2,523	2,641	3,083	3,378	3,616	3,672
Université de Toulouse I	5,738	5,559	5,448	5,703	5,908	5,989	6,205	6,412	6,469
Université de Tours	1,526	1,600	1,686	1,826	2,214	2,523	2,643	2,713	2,863
Total (all French universities)	89,724	70,383	73,238	77,026	81,948	88,899	91,923	97,378	99,678

Note
* By major universities, we mean universities where total students enrolled exceed 2,500

The first one is a strong acceleration between 1981–82 and 1982–83, which reflects a general expansion of the size of almost all departments due to the socialists taking power. In the opposite direction, a decline can be observed from 1994–95 which is mainly explained by demographic considerations. According to these data, the impact of the separation of business from economics on the total number of students, which was implemented in 1976, seems to have been negligible.

The data cover too short a period to enable us to evaluate the growth of economics and business departments in the universities. Among the seventy-seven registered universities, including overseas institutions, sixteen have only very recently opened teaching programmes in those fields. The total number of students enrolled in economics and business for all French universities has

Table 7.3 Number of graduate students in economics, 1960–94*

	DEUG (DEEG before 1975)	DEUST	Licence	Maîtrise 1977 Licence in 4 years	MSTMSG	DESS	DEA	Doctorate Cycle	Doctorat Etat	Total
1960										
1970	4,300			3,690						
1975	4,715				640					
1980	4,880		3,805	3,503		2,286	1,307	437	149	16,367
1981	5,020		3,822	4,118	1,165	2,440	1,255	577	108	18,505
1982	4,959		4,029	6,978		2,874	1,292	457	102	20,691
1983	5,293		3,849	7,363		1,509	1,234	504	82	19,834
1984	5,547		4,061	4,295		3,156	1,144	500	81	18,784
1985	5,655		4,030	4,688		3,543	1,110	417	81	19,524
1986	6,089		4,205	5,067		3,492	947	301	61	20,162
1987	6,076		4,346	5,482		4,154	1,062	337	95	21,552
1988	7,073		4,664	5,891		4,118	1,143	325	100	23,314
1989	7,282	279	5,248	6,991		4,765	1,557		275	26,397
1990	6,665	295	4,897	6,283		4,693	1,280		275	24,388
1991	8,151	292	5,624	7,269		5,508	1,603		300	28,747
1992	8,907	334	6,540	7,932		6,288	1,898		313	32,212
1993	9,810	310	7,840	9,229		7,114	2,062		396	36,761
1994	10,115	250	8,900	10,274	5,771	7,227	2,201		464	45,202

Note
* DEUG and DEUST correspond to BA, Licences and Maîtrises to MA, and Doctorats to PhD

Table 7.4 Agrégations

(a) Economics, 1964–95

Year	No. of Candidates	Passes	Posts Available
1964		24	25
1966	90	19	28
1968	97	26	30
1969	61	12	12
1970	75	25	25
1971	51	15	15
1973	112	30	30
1975	143	32	32
1976–77	133	25	25
1978–79	82	12	12
1980–81	86	12	12
1982–83	136	25	25
1984–85	65	20	20
1987–88	57	20	20
1989–90	85	25	25
1991–92	64	23	30
1993–94	91	30	30
1995–96	119	30	30

(b) Business, 1976–96

Year	No. of candidates	Passes	Posts available
1976–77	48	12	12
1979–80	65	16	16
1981–82	78	25	25
1983–84	41	16	20
1986–87	32	10	14
1988–89	40	13	20
1990–91	28	12	22
1992–93	41	14	30
1994–95	44	12	25
1996–97	83		25

increased from 95,564 in 1985 to 153,469 in 1993. Two additional observations can be made: the enormous concentration around Paris, with its thirteen universities and a total of almost 40,000 students, the emergence of three provincial poles – namely, Aix-Marseille, Toulouse and Lyon – each of them receiving between 6,000 and 7,000 students. Let us note the connection with the major centres of research (cf. the *CREMAQ* for Toulouse I, the *GREQAM* for Aix-Marseille II and III, and the *EHESS*).[9] Finally, some differences emerged from their respective organizations. Whereas economics is concentrated in only one university in Toulouse (Toulouse I), the Departments of Economics and Business are split between two universities in Lyon and in Marseille. Political reasons alone explain such local singularities. Anyway, this demonstrates that a degree of competition can be consistent with a centralized and public system.

A comparison of Table 7.2 with Table 7.3 shows the importance of the gap between the number of students registered in economics in French universities and the students who leave university as graduates in Economics. One must, however, be cautious about the results, because the data are not homogenous in both Tables: Table 7.2 concerns all the students following economics and business courses, Table 7.3 is only devoted to degrees in economics, and does not take business degrees into account. But the scale of the gap is so large that it underlines a major problem of the French system. While a progression can be observed at every level (BA, MA and PhD), the schedule of the progression varies from one to the other. The rate of growth accelerated during the period 1987 for undergraduates, but only after 1992 for postgraduates. This is a phenomenon to be linked to the rise in unemployment. Finally, the most spectacular explosion seems to concern the PhD. But this is mainly the consequence of a spurious effect. Indeed, the system of PhD changed many times during the period (*thèse de 3e cycle, thèse de doctorat d'Etat*) and therefore one can argue that the total number of PhDs in economics is much the same in 1994 as it was ten years before, and even smaller. The change has to be appreciated in terms of quality.

Table 7.4 is related to a characteristic of the French system. The normal course of events to become a full-time professor is to be successful at a competitive national examination (*agrégation*). Until 1976, no special examination existed for business, thus economics and business were mixed in a single examination. The creation of a proper examination for business explains the drastic reduction of the number of appointments in economics in 1978–79 and 1980–81. It must be observed, however, that after this adjustment period, the number of new appointments in economics returned to its average (between 20 and 30 per year). If now we put together the proposed appointments for economics and for business, the number in 1996 represents more than double that of 1964. There is an interesting difference between the situation in economics and that in business, for while the number of appointments is exactly the same as the number of successful candidates in the former, a discrepancy appears from 1983 to 1984 in the latter, which culminated in 1994–95. Such a gap can be explained by different considerations because the universities are not obliged to accept all the successful candidates. But another reason seems more realistic. Several successful candidates have probably preferred to use their position as an additional qualification to find a job in the private sector, rather than in the university system, for financial reasons.

Notes

1 Bainville's book, entitled *Les Conséquences Politiques de la Paix*, appeared in 1919, immediately after Keynes's, *Economic Consequences of the Peace*. On this question, see Arena *et al.* (1997).
2 A special school, the *ENSAE (Ecole Nationale de la Statistique et de l'Administra-*

tion Economique), directly connected to *INSEE*, has been created for the education of these economists.

3 Except for some universities where half of the teachers are not academics but professional people, as for example at the University of Dauphine in Paris.

4 The domain of *CREA* is larger than economics, but economics represents one of its most active research teams.

5 Debreu stayed at the Cowles Foundation first as an associate researcher, between 1950 and 1955, then as associate professor from 1955 to 1961, before becoming a professor at the University of California, Berkeley.

6 Some of the founders of the *AFSE*, such as Henri Guitton, asserted this humorous interpretation.

7 See A. d'Autume and J. Cartelier (eds) *Economics as a Science*, Aldershot: E. Elgar, 1996.

8 See *L'Economie des Conventions*, Special Issue *Revue Economique* 40(4) 1989.

9 *CREMAQ (Centre de Recherche économique, mathématique et qualitative)*; *GRE-QAM (Groupement de Recherche en économie quantitative d'Aix-Marseilles)*; *EHESS (Ecole des Hautes Etudes en Sciences Sociales)*.

References

Allais, M. (1953) 'Le comportement de l'homme rationnel devant le risque: critique des postulats et axiomes de l'Ecole Américaine', *Econometrica* 21(4): 503–46.

Annales d'Economie et de Statistiques 1 (1987).

Arena, R., Schmidt, C. and Gruson, C. (1998) 'Keynes before and after the *General Theory: theoretical contents of French economists' reactions*, in L. Pasinetti and B. Schefold (eds) *The Impact of Keynes on Twentieth Century Economics*, Cheltenham: E. Elgar.

Arrow, K., Debreu, G., Malinvaud, E. and Solow, R. (1991) *Cowles Fiftieth Anniversary*, New Haven, CT: Yale University Press.

Bainville, J. [1919] (1995) *Les Conséquences Politiques de la Paix*, Paris: Edition de l'Arsenal.

Borel, E. (1924) 'A propos d'un traité de probabilités', *Revue Philosophique* 8: 336–61.

Boyer, A. (1986) *La Théorie de la Régulation, une analyse critique*, Paris: La Découverte.

D'Autume, A. and Cartelier, J. (eds) (1996) *Economics as a Science*, Aldershot: E. Elgar.

Gruson, C. (1949), *Esquisse d'une théorie générale de l'équilibre économique*, Paris: PUF.

Keynes, J. M. (1919) *The Economic Consequences of the Peace*, London: Macmillan.

Malinvaud, E. (1996) 'Pourquoi les économistes ne font pas de découvertes', *Revue d'Economie Politique* 6: 929–42.

Marco, L. (ed.) (1996) *Les Revues d'Economie en France (1751–1994)*, Paris: L'Harmattan.

Revue Economique (1950) 1.

—— (1989) 'L'Economie des Conventions', 40(4).

Revue d'Economie Politique (1887) 1.

Zylberberg, A. (1990) *L'Economie Mathématique en France: 1870–1914*, Paris: Economica.

8 Europe and the post-1945 internationalization of political economy

The case of Italy

Pier Luigi Porta[1]

Italy and the European setting

This chapter provides an outline of some developments of teaching and research in political economy in Italy through the post-1945 years. The focus of attention is not confined to the academic institutions in themselves, although the protagonists of our story by and large belong to the university system.[2] The outline does not aim at comprehensiveness and completeness; rather, it aims – much as in the lines adopted in the internationalization project – at revisiting episodes or developments which appear of some significance in the process of internationalization and in contributing to explain the special characteristics of the process itself, as it has taken place in the postwar years. In this context close attention will be given to the European setting.

This present reconstruction of Italian economists and Italian economics during the post-1945 period will touch on several points under three main headings. As just hinted, it is a feature of the present contribution that it aims at an understanding of Italian economists and Italian economics within the *European context*. The ongoing discussion on European economics must be taken into account.[3]

In the second place it appears to be of special importance for Italy to understand the *role of economic studies and teaching* in economics within the wider context of the overall growth of the system of higher education in the country. In the present exposition, however, we shall only hint at an analysis of that kind, since it is presented, for example, in the *Hope* Supplement edited by A. W. Coats (Coats, ed., 1997). More particularly, the *Hope* Supplement provides comparative highlights on the issue, in both its general terms and with respect to the economic sciences in particular.[4]

Third, as a part of an analysis of the growth of economic studies and of the economic profession in the country with the European context in mind, the need must be emphasized for tackling adequately the *link between economic ideas and policy*. On this issue, the investigation turns on the evaluation of the inspiration and 'vision' of the different schools of thought and on their comparative effectiveness and impact.

A few preliminary remarks on each of the three points just mentioned can usefully open our discussion.

The European context

There are obvious and important differences between the developments of political economy in the different European countries. Europe is far from being a homogeneous entity. This is not meant to deny, however, that there are European traits on which it is worth dwelling briefly.

Frey and Eichenberger 1993: 185) point out three characteristics which seem to be important for a comparative description and analysis of European economics. In the first place, European economists have a special predilection for participating in local and national affairs. Second, economic research in Europe tends to be involved in practical issues. Third, in European higher education economics tends to absorb teaching efforts mainly at the undergraduate level. To outline these characteristics reflects comparative interests, and the authors show in particular how different, in these respects, Europe is from America.

The outlined characteristics would need to be explained in terms of what we may call the institutional history of political economy in the European countries in order to bring out more precisely the dividing lines of a European tradition from the rest of the world. Research on the issue is still in its formative stages, as the consciousness of a diversified but identifiable European style emerges from the new political realities and ambitions of present-day Europe. We take here the first two characteristics to be strictly linked together, and they are in fact treated as a unified point. The third characteristic emerges clearly from the Italian experience, and in what follows some hints on the developments of the Italian system of higher education are offered.

Political economy in teaching and research

One emerging conclusion from the internationalization project, referred to above, turns on the fact that internationalization through the post-1945 years should be distinguished and kept separate from a different, though related, process, affecting in various ways the post-1945 world, commonly termed 'Americanization'. In particular it is the *former* process, rather than the latter, which commands greater attention as the dominant phenomenon on the Italian scene. This, incidentally, highlights some considerable aspects of *continuity* with the preceding periods of the history of the country during which the international connections of the Italian economic profession had emerged and asserted themselves very strongly.[5] While Americanization in any particular context is meant to convey the idea of a causal link originating from external factors and from the environment, 'internationalization', as a term, happens to be neutral with respect to causes, and particularly to *external* causes: it merely indicates a process without further implications. The history of postwar economic thought and analysis in Italy appears to be one of continuing and intensifying internationalization in teaching and research.

It can be argued that the preservation of the term '*economia politica*' in Italy signals the peculiar significance of the *internal* factors in the development and in the internationalization of the discipline. The failure to introduce the Italian term *'economica'* (which would exactly correspond to 'economics' in English) into common parlance is a telling sign of the strength of autochthonous roots.[6] Incidentally, this is why in the context of this chapter, even in English, we retain the expression 'political economy' to indicate our discipline. Although this may sound slightly odd or, possibly, even misleading in English, it should be recalled that 'political economy' corresponds to *'economia politica'* as the basic term to describe the discipline in the current Italian usage.

One significant conclusion emerging from the internationalization project concerns the comparatively *limited scope for political economy* proper within the system of higher education in Italy.[7] It is suggested in this chapter that this phenomenon has had a direct effect on the trends in the *scientific* debates taking place in political economy within the academic profession and on their consequences for the debates on economic policy. There are probably also European traits of this particular process alongside the properly Italian ones. A relevant perspective in this connection could be and certainly is provided by the comparison of Italy within Europe on one side with the Anglo-Saxon world on the other. There is little doubt that this, as a long standing contrast, has certainly been revived and singularly reinforced by the particular atmosphere created after the late war by the Anglo-Saxon world emerging as the *de facto* winning force of the conflict. But – this is the point to be emphasized in the present context – the phenomenon is *not* to be described in terms of degrees of Americanization: it is something different and probably more complex.

The comparative underdevelopment of the role of political economy in the curricula of higher education in the Italian system gives rise to a curious imbalance between the part played by political economists in the worldwide arena of research on one side and their role within the home institutions hosting teaching and research in the discipline, particularly the universities, on the other side. Such a process has resulted from deep historical roots which can only be hinted at in this chapter; however, some analysis of them certainly is called for even within a paper like the present one which is not intended to stretch beyond the 1945 divide.

In so far as the drive to internationalization was becoming an important force in shaping *theoretical* positions and rhetoric instruments through the postwar period, it must be taken into account that the appeal of internationalization came to find an important source in the acute perception of the need for elevating political economy in Italian universities to a status comparable to that which the discipline was enjoying in the Anglo-Saxon world. The under-rating of political economy in the Italian system, among the educational qualifications of graduates, was for a long time so striking that it gave rise to a strong urge to update curricula, expand subjects and introduce greater specialization. This in turn gave rise to a whole set of processes which can best be described as 'internationalization': to a considerable extent, all that was built upon a generational rift among economists and implied a disavowal of the home tradition.

However, the switch from political economy to economics, so to speak, was never fully completed. Internationalization, seen from the Italian vantage-point, is basically to be conceived as a critical elaboration of the international literature rather than its absorption. The difference is that the critical elaboration, differently from sheer absorption, methodologically proceeds from a judgement founded on a pre-existing standpoint.

It will also be interesting to observe the results achieved through time of the efforts to internationalize the system and consider the present position of political economy *vis-à-vis* the other disciplines that are normally part of the higher education curricula world-wide.

Economic ideas and economic policy

It immediately appears to be necessary to face the question of the identity of the 'Italian School' more directly, and retrieve and re-interpret the seeds of the so-called 'Italian School of political economy'. The Italian School of political economy has been too often (and perhaps too lightly) accused of being lost in abstractions and almost entirely confined to the realm of pure theory. A long-overdue debate in re-appraisal is currently under way in Italy.[8] This, as a debate, is bound to have strong repercussions on the whole historical reconstruction of the postwar period in Italy. Contemporary historiography in Italy is still noisily crossing swords on the reappraisal of the Fascist period; but there is little doubt that the time is rapidly approaching when the postwar years and the whole business of the hopes betrayed and lost opportunities, especially in the post-1945 period, will be in the limelight. There are also very clear promises of an important cross-fertilization between the debate on Italy itself and the emerging scientific interests on European economics both in itself and *vis-à-vis* the American counterpart: on the whole a European dimension of some kind has always had a significant place in shaping and fostering economic ideas in the country.[9] The debate at present is bringing into sharper focus the question of the link between economic research and economic policy in the Italian context.

It is a running theme through the historiography on Italy that Italian history is largely a history of *cities*.[10] This idea was developed during the nineteenth century in a celebrated essay by Carlo Cattaneo on cities or civic communities through Italian history. More generally, the point has been elaborated and lies at the roots of fairly successful explanations on Italian economic development since the Middle Ages. Famous studies by Carlo M. Cipolla, for example, are an indispensable background to the currently popular analyses by Putnam and associates.[11] This phenomenon is also at the root of the North–South divide: for the 'civic traditions' have been lively and pervasive north of Rome, while the South did not experience the same sort of freedom from a centralized rule.

That the case of the city of Milan stands out in this conceptual context is common knowledge, and it is hoped that it is fully appreciated well beyond possible, though misleading, mental associations with recent political movements. It is certainly not by chance that one of the impressive achievements sponsored by the prestigious Institute for the Italian Encyclopaedia has been, since the end of World War II, the twenty-odd volumes of the history of the city of Milan, just recently updated and reprinted. More particularly, a primacy of Milan stands out all the more when we come to political economy. This is not only true of past centuries as historians of political economy know all too well. It should be noted – as an element equally affecting both teaching and research on the one side and economic analysis and policy on the other – that the particular developments taking place in Milan in the course of the twentieth century, as far as economic teaching and research are concerned, should be kept in the forefront. It might seem odd at first sight that the effort to put internationalization processes into proper focus should encourage the revisiting of local histories. In fact there is no clash nor contradiction: Milan has of course been prominent for the economic environment, the development of industry, banking and finance, the stock market. No wonder that Milan has been giving life to some of the leading institutions in higher economic education.[12]

This need to keep a close eye on what happens in Milan in order to understand the Italian experience is emphasized here throughout. It should be mentioned that emphasis on the role of individual cities through Italian history is at present increasingly spelt out in current historiography; more particularly the special characteristics of the municipality of Milan are being made the object of close scrutiny.[13]

The legacy of the Italian school

The first two of the points made by Frey and Eichenberger on the characteristics of European economics may be linked also with the specific training and the structure of the faculties in which economics is mainly taught. This is a field of research which is inextricably linked with the historical developments of a number of modern faculties – law and political sciences, for example; above all, it is linked with the rise and the consolidation of the faculties named until recently 'economics and business' (now renamed 'economics').

We shall briefly examine some of the features of the Italian case. It should be remembered that a number of such features probably parallel the experience of other European countries.

Political economy in higher education: the Italian experience

The establishment and the development in Italian universities of a kind of economic training which resembles the one that we have at present, had its origins during the latter half of the nineteenth century. Although the teaching of political economy largely took place in the law faculties at that time, a significant role came to be played by the emergence of the so-called '*Scuole superiori di commercio*'. In the curricula of the schools, accounting and business economics were largely dominant with emphasis on vocational training, which of course was a break with respect to the strictly academic atmosphere of the law faculties.

Historically there is a parallel here with other European experiences, especially with that of Germany.[14] A number of such institutions were founded, particularly in Venice, Bari and Genoa, and later in other cities such as Rome and Turin.

The *Scuole*, rather than the law faculties, are the real forefathers of the contemporary faculties of economics. Originally – that is, roughly speaking, at the beginning of the twentieth century – the *Scuole* were placed under the supervision of the Ministry of Agriculture, Industry and Commerce. A number of steps then led the *Scuole* to be incorporated into the universities of their respective towns. This set the stage for the *Scuole* to be turned into proper faculties within each university under the supervision of the Ministry of Education. This happened at a time (1925–35 approximately) when university curricula came to be subjected to a regime of increasingly rigid, centralized rules still largely in force. The consequence has been that the curricula of the *Scuole* largely dictated the style of training and the internal cultural environment of the future faculties of economics.

Turin provides a typical example. With a decree of 1906 the *Scuola superiore di studi applicati al commercio* was founded: the *Scuola* was the ancestor of the Faculty of Economics and Business, now Economics. At the same time the Law Faculty of Turin already hosted a well-known innovative *Laboratorio di economia politica,* founded by Salvatore Cognetti de Martiis by the end of the nineteenth century. The *Laboratorio* soon developed into an influential institution devoted to emphasize the fundamental role of political economy proper as a scientific discipline in higher education. It is interesting to observe that the *Laboratorio* was the parent stem of the present *Dipartimento di economia politica* of the University of Turin, which has little connection with the Faculty of Economics and is, to the present day, still closely attached to the Faculties of Law and of Political Sciences in the University of Turin. In sum: the *Laboratorio* has had little influence on the formative steps of the Economics Faculty. Its influence is confined to the non-economic faculties, where, on the other hand, the scope for political economy proper is bound to be limited. The same developments made it impossible for research into training and teaching of political economy to acquire a dominant position within the Faculties of *economia e commercio* themselves, precisely because their line of descent came from the *Scuole*, where, as just recalled, business studies and, more particularly, accounting had an established dominance.

This and similar developments explain the Italian peculiarity that, in spite of a generally strong school of *research* in political economy, the *teaching* of the discipline has been, since the start (and, incidentally, as we shall hint, it still is) confined to a relatively minor role even within the faculties of economics proper. The conclusion is that the teaching of political economy has generally taken its place as an *auxiliary discipline*, albeit an important one, with respect to other fields, notably jurisprudence, business studies and accounting, and, particularly at a later stage, political or social studies. We shall also see the implications of this in an evaluation of the present position of political economy.

The *Laboratorio* in Turin had an influence at the time – particularly through Luigi Einaudi, who had been a pupil of Cognetti – on the early stages of the Bocconi University, founded in Milan in 1902 on the initiative of a wealthy tradesman, Ferdinando Bocconi. That well-known institution was keen from the beginning to emphasize its difference from the *Scuole*. The very name of *Università* was indicative of a programme of studies, which, among other features, explicitly put political economy as a scientific discipline at centre stage: however, it is particularly interesting to observe that a thriving Italian school of economists was unable to seize the occasion and acquire a leading role even in that institution. A story in many ways parallel to Bocconi could be told about the Catholic University, which was founded, again in Milan, some years later, in 1921. The foundation in Italy of a Catholic University in *Milan*, rather than in Rome, had a sure connection with the fact that programmes in the field of political economy and the social sciences were dominant: the prevailing neoscholastic intellectual atmosphere and philosophy assigned an important place also to political economy within the social and political sciences. Giuseppe Toniolo, who had died in 1918 and had been perhaps the main advocate of the project of a Catholic University since the turn of the century, was himself a political economist.

It would be impossible to understand the present and recent developments of political economy in Italy without considering the fact that there has *not been a single example* within the Italian system where a real primacy of the study of political economy can be said to have been established. This observation suggests a significant interpretation of the development of political economy in Italy; namely, that Italian political economy did not suffer only from political events or from lack of continuity of any kind. An extraordinarily large research potential was unable (or unwilling) to acquire a correspondingly large place and audience in the curricula of higher education, compared to what was happening abroad, particularly in the Anglo-Saxon world. With time that limitation proved to fetter the development of an established tradition and also of the social recognition of the place and dignity of studies in political economy. An insufficient consolidation of the profession would, in turn, be bound to breed defensive attitudes. There are close parallels and inevitable interactions, which have been generally overlooked, between the formative processes of a discipline and the institutional environment within which those processes take place.

The reasons why the recent developments of Italian political economy could hardly be described as a process of 'Americanization' are not hard to find. It is not so much the fact that the example of North America was in fact superseded, in the hearts of many, by that of the Soviet Union or even of China. More importantly, in Italy *internal* factors or forces proved more significant than external ones. Xenofilia – and the drift to internationalization attached to it – has been, at least when it came to take the shape of Anglophilia, one way to reverse the situation described, or at least an attempt to do so.

The influence of the Italian tradition in postwar Italy

An Italian economist of the past generation, in a perceptive paper on economics and economists in postwar Italy, spoke of a 'loss of cultural identity' among Italian economists.[15] He added that the same has become true of Germany, an observation which appears to draw attention to *some* European dimension of an indeed real phenomenon of decline of the national traditions together with parallel generational rifts. That was a timely denunciation of an overinflated intellectual fashion. On the other hand, the overriding forces of postwar internationalization and Americanization, with their peculiar features, have at times somewhat amplified the difficulty of making subtle, but not unimportant, distinctions. With the advantage of hindsight it is possible today to evaluate the transformation and development of political economy in Italy in a more balanced way with particular reference to the relationship of present developments in the tradition of the Italian School.

In the Italian case, in particular, the prevailing opinion during the postwar years has generally been in favour of emphasizing a *negative* impact of the national tradition in the study of and research into political economy. That prevailing opinion has come of late to be even reinforced and presented in a rather more extreme form by explicit hints, in some of the more recent contributions, that the national tradition actually acted as a barrier to the international circulation of ideas: from quite diverse standpoints, the point has been argued by several authors, among whom, for example, are Cardini (1993), de Cecco (1989), Faucci (1995) and Zamagni (1994). This extreme form of the prevailing position has been challenged, for example, by Bocciarelli and Ciocca (1994) and Porta (1997a). The latter, among others, has argued that the Italian School has made significant contributions to the international circulation of ideas and cannot be indicted as being 'lost in mere abstractions', as it were. On the other hand, the Italian School's impact did not result in any leadership within the developing university research and curricula in the economic field: this is not merely an Italian characteristic, but a common feature in a number of European (Continental) experiences *vis-à-vis* the Anglo-Saxon world.

The interpretation of the effectiveness of the role of the Italian liberal tradition is currently at issue: on the one side we are confronted with the attempt to establish a *purely negative* and abstract role for the Italian tradition; on the other, on the contrary, there is the case for bringing into focus the *active role* of the school itself as a practical inspiration of politico-economic thinking and action and as an effective counterweight to the radical-utopian bias which notoriously abounds among Italian progressives. The debate has two aspects: the first is mainly theoretical, and concerns the circulation of economic ideas and, more particularly, the intellectual connections and openness of Italian scholars to the international circulation of ideas in political economy; the second mainly touches on the link between economic ideas and policy. Both aspects are relevant to the implementation of the present research project.

Perhaps the most prominent features in the current debate seem, at the moment, to concern the second of the above-mentioned aspects, although both of them are vital. It is easy to prophesy that we are here and now on the eve of increasingly important discussions on the reconstruction of the intellectual sources of the Italian debates on economic policy. It is certainly significant to understand how those debates, through the postwar years, marked the turning points and contributed to shape the identity of Italian political economy. This chapter has no ambition to present a fully fledged treatment of the issue. It will mainly be limited to giving some indication on lines of investigation which can possibly shed new light on the more recent developments of political economy in Italy.

Italian economists and economic policy

In the immediate postwar period there were two traits of economic policy in Italy that deserve to be mentioned, especially in view of the debate around them. The first trait concerns trade liberalization after the policy of control of the Fascist regime; the second is the preservation and strengthening of the state-controlled industrial system, by the IRI, established in 1933.

The idea of laissez-faire

At an early period during the war, in 1941, the internationally best-known and highly reputed Italian journal in political economy, the *Giornale degli economisti*, published a series of contributions which was then collected together in one volume the following year under the title *Reconstruction of the Economy after the War*.[16] The authors were well-known representatives of the Milanese intelligentsia: some of them had strong connections with Bocconi. Among them Giovanni Demaria, the editor of the *Giornale* from 1939 through to 1970, was the incumbent of the chair of Political Economy at Bocconi. Luigi Einaudi, in particular, had given a regular course in public finance for many years at Bocconi at least until 1925, when his collaboration was interrupted because of political dissension. Costantino Bresciani-Turroni held the chair of political economy at the Faculty of Law at the University of Milan, founded in 1924, although in the meantime he had been teaching abroad for a number of years. Gino Borgatta was also a professor at Bocconi.

The volume in question is a significant example of what some of the outstanding Italian economists at the time had to say on economic policy. It is interesting that the book itself is cropping up time and again in the current debate on the reappraisal of the role and teachings of the Italian tradition in political economy.[17] Perhaps the best example of what then could emerge from the Italian School on economic policy is provided by the essay by Giovanni Demaria, '*Il problema industriale italiano*', contained in the 1942 book. Demaria enjoyed credibility and an international reputation at that time; some of his works would be mentioned by Schumpeter (of whom he had been the first translator into Italian) in his *History* as examples of freedom of research in Italy in the inter-war years. Indeed Giovanni Demaria's essay on the industrial problem in Italy stands out for the strong indictment he directs at the commercial policy of the regime based, since the early 1930s, on autarchy. Demaria denounced the evils and the disadvantages of that policy, and his own explicit and courageous plea for a policy of international openness based on freedom of trade can be read, with hindsight, as a prophetic anticipation of what was in fact to happen.[18] Both for his academic standing and for the position taken at that stage, Demaria would later chair the works of the Economic Commission for the *Assemblea Costituente*, in charge of the drafting of a new Constitution for the first Italian Republic soon after the end of the war.[19]

What is more interesting in the present context is the development of Demaria's position and the way in which he could become, at that precise moment, the expression of a whole current of thought on economic policy inspired by the teachings of the Italian School. In that sense Demaria's position not only was at the time voicing the point of view of selected influential economic thinkers and actors, but was also expressing a powerful line of thought which had to be identified and taken into account in reconstructing the link of economic theory to policy in the postwar years. Demaria embodies a significant reincarnation of the political involvement which had always characterized the Italian school, and can be seen to be part of the intellectual experience of its main protagonists.

It is important at this point to recall two elements of the intellectual background to the story that would, in due course, lead to the full liberalization of exchange and trade of the postwar years. In the first place, there is a link between the Northern economists we have just mentioned, and the Bank of Italy. In the second place, we should reconsider the revisiting of the free-trade doctrine given by Demaria himself in 1942; the latter was a kind of shock to the regime and led to the suspension of the publication of the *Giornale degli economisti* until after the war.[20] Demaria's position on the 'new order' – an ever-living phrase subjected to the widest range of variance in meaning in Italian political thinking – happened to be the centre of vast reactions both at home and abroad. What is significant in our present context is the explicit appeal to the tradition of the Italian School of political economy that served as the basis for Demaria's argument. Moreover, the position thus expressed had been elaborated and prepared in conjunction with the Bank of Italy.[21] Thus the Bank of Italy and the Milanese professors combined their energies for the first time, as an early signal of postwar economic thinking, to revive and apply the teachings of a school of political economy – sometimes termed 'the Italian liberal tradition' – a school which is certainly far from being lost in abstractions. In line with the tradition of its founders – Pantaleoni, Pareto, De Viti, De Marco, Ricci, Fanno and others – the Italian School is actively at work and is producing a powerful ingredient in the development of latter-day Italian political economy.

The academic representatives in this story are fully aware of what is happening in economic theory at the international level. This can be well documented for the cases here at hand of the Milanese professors and of the Bank of Italy. Keynes and Beveridge, in particular, were widely read and commented upon in Italy in the course of that transition from *Corporativismo* to *Liberismo*. Beveridge appears to have commanded a good deal of sympathy. Keynes continued for quite a while to raise numerous eyebrows from all quarters. From the standpoint of the links of theory and policy in political economy, which we are discussing at this stage, it is almost self-evident that Keynes's theory of employment had little to say about the conditions of a country in the phase of reconstruction. This is, of course, a common trait with other European experiences.[22]

Dirigisme, *development and planning*

As we have mentioned above, for sixty-odd years starting from the late 1920s, there was a close continuity through Italian economic history in the system of state-controlled industries. Even at the present time the future of the country tends to look fairly uncertain in this respect. This peculiar feature of the Italian financial and industrial system has naturally given rise to a whole host of debates. Fortunately, we need not enter the maze of the historico-economic problem. What we propose to do is summarize here those lines of economic thinking on the issue which appear to be relevant for a reconstruction of latter-day Italian political economy in the light of the internationalization process.

Let us observe at the very start that the justification of the Italian system based on the *IRI*, the Institute for Industrial Reconstruction established in 1933, is the offspring of the teachings of Francesco Saverio Nitti (1868-1953), the great Italian economist and politician who had theorized and pleaded, since the turn of the century, for an active state role in certain sectors of the economy. Nittian socialism came later to be elaborated, developed and put in practice by the extraordinary personality of Alberto Beneduce, Nitti's follower and the real engineer of the *IRI* system.[23] We are thus in the presence of a typical product of Italian economic thinking, though falling outside the mainstream of the Italian School. Donato Menichella, the most outstanding civil servant among Bene-duce's men and later to become Governor of the Bank of Italy, explained the rationale of the above mentioned continuity to the Americans, in the person of Captain Andrew Kamarck, when the transition came to the postwar economy.[24]

From our present focus, the issue should be understood in conjunction with two other problems: the question of the unequal development of Southern and Northern Italy (*Meridionalismo*) and the idea of planning. This peculiar conjunction of issues seems to provide the meaningful distinction between prewar Nittianism and its postwar aftermath and development, and it is pithily brought out in the work and action of one of the outstanding personalities in Italian political economy through the post-1945 period, Pasquale Saraceno. Through Saraceno it is possible to trace not only the formative steps and development of postwar Nittianism, but, more significantly, to appreciate how far postwar Nittianism is, in fact, the product of a network of exchanges at the international level. We should really speak of exchanges, rather than influences, to bring out the internationalized character of Italian thinking in political economy.

By contrast with the epigones of the Italian liberal tradition, Saraceno conceives the technocratic design of a regulated capitalism. Regulated capitalism is still undoubtedly based on the market and the free-enterprise system; however, reconstruction initially and subsequently development are planned. The market system needs checks and corrections. The social question is faced directly. A whole series of episodes can be mentioned to summarize the different levels and widespread impact and influence of a reformist philosophy looming so largely through Italian political economy in the last fifty-odd years. Postwar Nittianism and its international connections are reflected in the activity of *Svimez*, the association for the development of Southern Italy established soon after the war, where a new educational programme was launched with strong international participation and innovative curriculum and where the famous Vanoni plan of 1954 was constructed and discussed.[25] From here the whole philosophy takes its inspiration from the positive effects of economic programmes on such issues as distribution and full employment, of private and social investment and consumption and finally on the welfare system. Ugo La Malfa's celebrated *Nota aggiuntiva* of 1962 is one of the best expressions – and, in a way, a summary view – of the reformist philosophy.

Svimez originated soon after the war from the joint action of Pasquale Saraceno and the socialist leader and political economist, Rodolfo Morandi. *Svimez* was soon involved in the promotion of intense exchanges with a number of foreign economists, among whom Paul Rosenstein-Rodan should be singled out. Also linked with the issues on which the activity at *Svimez* concentrated is the work of other economists in Italy, all of them with strong international connections. The early scientific activity of Paolo Sylos Labini touches on problems of income distribution, planning and technical progress. He soon went on to work on oligopoly and produced his famous book on oligopoly and technical progress. Similarly, parallel considerations apply to the scientific work of Giorgio Fuà, one of the leading economists in postwar Italy. Augusto Graziani belongs to a younger generation; his scientific activity has significantly touched the link between Italian theory and policy in many ways. These and other economists certainly deserve further study in order to bring out their international connections together with the characteristics of the schools to which they gave rise. It would be impossible to do justice to the subject within the limits of this chapter. Francesco Vito had promoted early research on market power at the Catholic University of Milan: his activity stimulated and inspired Siro Lombardini soon after the war and, later, some of the economists of the younger generation; for example, Beniamino Andreatta and Romano Prodi. In public finance the names of Cesare Cosciani and, more particularly, of Sergio Steve – who was associated with both of the lines of thought we have so far discussed – should be mentioned. On planning, private and social consumption, welfare and income distribution, the activity (strongly linked with *Svimez*) of Claudio Napoleoni and his group should be remembered. For many years in the post-1945 period Napoleoni's interpretations commanded the attention of the profession, through his intense teaching activity and numerous publications, including the periodical *La Rivista Trimestrale*, which reflected the intellectual activity of Napoleoni's group.

Italian political economy and the idea of Europe

Debates and interpretations on the development of the economy have been numerous and come from various quarters. This is not the place either to rehearse them or to attempt a bibliography.

During the 1960s and 1970s Italian economists were generally quite vociferous in debating the state of the economy and exchanging views. One may argue that the so-called age of increasing expectations actually made everyone much more talkative, and political economists were no exception. Of course, while this may contain more than a grain of truth, the whole story cannot be as simple as that. We propose to review here a few episodes which can help to explain the subsequent silence or general change of mood concerning the debate on policy issues and see how the idea of Europe worked its way through general opinion. Perhaps the story here, although it directly involves European sentiments, is rather special to Italy. We shall then bring our exposition to a close with some concluding remarks on the present position of political economy in academic institutions and, more generally, in economic research circles in the country.

In this section it seems proper to emphasize the stream of research that was stimulated and implemented through the action of agencies external to universities, although of course academic economists did play a considerable part in them. It goes beyond the limits of this chapter to attempt to map the research institutions that might be relevant for our subject.

We can, however, single out three major inspiring forces of the debate in the Italian context. They are the Bank of Italy, the trade unions and the Confederation of Industry. The Bank of Italy was the first of the three forces to inaugurate a coherent programme of research.[26] The Confederation of Industry will only be mentioned here. Through its scientific journal, the prestigious *Rivista di politica economica*, its newspapers, its research staff and activity, the Confederation's work has gained momentum, especially recently, and it is still perhaps too early to evaluate its impact.

The trade unions never achieved the status of a research unit as such. Nevertheless, their contribution needs to be mentioned here, as much of reformist thought came to find its identity in the name of the trade unions or under their rubric. 'Reformist' thought is a highly ambivalent and potentially explosive mixture, which covers the spectrum from La Malfa's incomes policy to the extreme pronouncements on the wage-rate as the independent variable of the system. Italian reformism is full of contradictory elements, which on the one side make for a strong moral and intellectual appeal, while at the same time do indeed almost pave the way to much of the slippery ground which, through recent years, fuelled some even of the most extreme and destructive purposes. Much more than any of the existing parties (including the Communist Party), Italy's trade unions for a time came to represent 'reformist' thought quite well in the above sense and in all of its varieties. Let us recall that for some time recently Italy was in grip of terrorism, and that an economist, Ezio Tarantelli, was identified with the 'reasonable' side of reformism, and became a target.[27]

Let us now turn briefly to the central Bank and its role in promoting research on the link between theory and policy while also fostering important international connections. The Bank of Italy – through the personalities of the successive governors, from Luigi Einaudi, to Donato Menichella, Guido Carli, Paolo Baffi, Carlo Azeglio Ciampi and Antonio Fazio, as well as through the activity of its officials and research staff – has been a privileged observatory on the link between theory and policy in the Italian context. The recent centenary of the foundation of the Bank has provided the occasion for extensive historical work in a special series printed by Laterza publishing house. Moreover, its international connections have always been significant. We have already mentioned above Paolo Baffi's well-known essay on the issue, which covers the immediate postwar years. Through Carli (1993) and Rey and Peluffo (1995) we can get more than a glimpse of what has been happening through the subsequent years, until the 1990s. Among the names of major consultants to the Bank to be singled out, let us recall the activity of Vera Lutz during the 1950s and Franco Modigliani, especially since the 1960s. Such issues as growth, dualism and income distribution were prominent, although of course short-run concerns were also present. For example, during the 1960s the Bank was one of the places where the theory of distribution came to be discussed and Modigliani's life-cycle theory of saving, investment and growth was compared with other approaches. For example, through the work of Luigi Pasinetti and other economists the Cambridge equation and more generally the message of the Cambridge School came to be very lively and influential in the country. In particular, the link between income distribution and saving, as established by the Cambridge School, came to play a role in many discussions, and a number of them took place at the Bank.[28] Further, and linked with it, the Bank produced one of the first econometric models of the Italian economy in the late 1960s. In the aftermath of that work the scientific output of the Bank's research unit greatly intensified, following plans inspired by Governor Guido Carli. Modigliani and his associates have repeatedly intervened with significant contributions, keeping Italian policy issues at the forefront. A number of those contributions are connected with the research activity of the Bank. The series of *Contributi alla ricerca economica*, published by the economic research unit of the Bank, has included a number of analyses of the Italian economy.

As mentioned earlier, it would be impossible to achieve completeness within the limits of the present chapter. What can be done here is to identify significant lines of debate which can provide a clue to the intellectual developments among Italian economists in the postwar period on issues of theory and policy.

Guido Carli (1993) argues that a decisive role has been played in the developing conception of economic policy by *external constraint*. For example, in the immediate postwar years it was the need to join the new international monetary institutions which stengthened the case for the introduction of the market economy after the years of corporativism.[29] As we have seen, Italian thinking on policy nevertheless continued to breed ideas of a regulated economy with different justifications. At present it is only through the need, and tendency towards enthusiasm, to cope with the requirements of the Maastricht Treaty that Italian thinking on economic policy has decidedly turned away from the lures of a regulated system, the origins of which are to be seen within the system of state-run industry and the concomitant legal status of the Central Bank, as established by the law of 1936.

After many years of fluctuation and indecision, the Italian intelligentsia has had to make a choice between two alternatives, both extreme in their way. Roughly speaking, the choice has been between a trade unionist philosophy and a Bank of Italy philosophy. In very simple and sketchy terms the history of postwar political economy in Italy could be woven by using these two threads alone. Their drifting apart coincides with the era of increasing expectations, revolutionary enthusiasm leading to violence and ultimately terrorism; their coming together, among other things, is the supporting pillar of the present Euro-enthusiasm. Not even in the late 1920s could the 'working classes' (wherever they can be traced now) be said to be as happy as they are today with a policy of low wages and strong currency (naturally such historical parallels need caution). This model of thinking could easily be shown to work historically even beyond the postwar period: in particular, the connection between the Bank of Italy and the northern professors (see above) has become, in a way, a leading thread in the development of Italian political economy especially through the postwar years. The latter fact also explains the ongoing reappraisal of the Italian School of political economy and allows us to cast the development of Italian political economy in a new light, especially with respect to an international perspective.

Reformist thought and reformist activities, as history sadly shows all too well, are often different things, and Italy is a case in point. To avoid here the necessary detour into the realm of ideology, let us close with some remarks on the Italian situation at present. Even if the more destructive elements of the typically Italian quest for largely unspecified 'reforms' and of the complaints about 'missed opportunities' have been tamed for a while, there is little cause for triumph. This has happened, alas, at the cost of embracing, under the pressure of the external constraint, an extreme philosophy which largely ignores the changing nature of the present problems connected with labour and employment. In this respect Italian political economy shares the fate common to many parts of the world in showing complete unawareness of the challenge. In particular, for example, we are confronted, in the immediate future, with a curious blend of mixed feelings toward financial capitalism which sounds *déjà vu*. For the time being, given the successes of financial capitalism, the young generations in particular keep assenting in the hope to achieve at least some gain.

Political economy in universities

We may here conclude our exposition by adding an observation on the present place of political economy in universities, with special attention to curricula in the degree courses. Much has changed and there certainly is a new widespread awareness of the need and significance of political economy in the background of graduates. On the other hand, almost paradoxically, political economy still remains basically an *auxiliary*, albeit significant, discipline to a number of curricula in economic, political, sociological and juridical studies.

The subject needs to be cast in an historical perspective,[30] as mentioned above. The two lines of development of economic curricula, along a legal-professional line and social-economics line (reflected in the early experience of the Bocconi and the Catholic universities respectively), continue to survive and to perpetuate within themselves the auxiliary role of political economy properly defined.

The conventional wisdom at present seems to be provided by the model curricula elaborated by the reform of the faculties of economics in the early 1990s, whereby political economy with a strongly applied bias is blended in many different ways especially with business, management and accounting subjects in order to produce a number of specialized professional profiles. The model was tested and launched initially by the Bocconi University of Milan, especially from the 1980s. The role of Milan in the country again seems exemplary. This induces the overemphasis on specialization while basic teaching and research suffer. In Britain, polytechnics have been transformed overnight into universities. But one could say that it is universities which increasingly look like polytechnics in the sense of too slavishly leaning on the vocational. Moreover, the marketing – rather than production – activities of professional profiles tend to take the lead and result into a fuzzy supermarket of 'culture'.

With these drawbacks in mind we can only hint here at the international character which is perhaps the dominant note of the present model of economic studies in Italy. Concerning the future, any treatment of the prospects will have to take account of a certain universal retrenchment in the general appeal for economic studies. This may well be a response to the fuzziness hinted above: in particular, as far as political economy proper is concerned, a lesson to be drawn is that the multiplication of the cocktails does not make the sale of the brandy any easier. Trying to fool people all the time is not a good strategy, as we all of course know. It is possible (in a simple view) that, given the present state of the supply, certain 'basic' demands of economic education have, alas, been satisfied and the marginal utility of the subject, despite its behavioural kinship (in principle) with the marginal utility of money, tends to be driven to abnormally low levels. On top of that there is an observation to be made which concerns political economists in particular, and that concerns the economists' tendency to oscillate between the 'imperial science' hubris, whereby everything in the world tends to be seen through economic spectacles on the one side, and scientific-technical overdevelopments of a discipline in search both of increasing specialization and scientific prestige, on the other. Unfortunately, economists, historically, fail to realize that the two routes are idiosyncratic and not synergic. Fostering overpretentious specialization is hardly friendly to the 'imperial science'. The boldest dreams of political economy are, for some time to come, once again doomed to be unfulfilled.

Notes

1 A first draft of this chapter was presented at the working party 'The post-1945 Development of Economics in Europe', December 20–22, International House, London, 1996. An acknowledgement is due to A. W. Coats for his active and stimulating contribution as the coordinator of the working party.
2 The analysis presented in this chapter is part of the research agenda on the internationalization of economics in the postwar years, a project promoted and coordinated by A. W. Coats. See in particular the *Hope* 1996 supplement volume (Coats 1997).
3 See in particular the *Kyklos* 1995 symposium 'Is there a European economics'; also Frey and Eichenberger (1993).
4 Although it is vital, and probably particularly so in the case of Italy, to recall the significance of the issue, we shall do so in a very cursory and summary way in the present context. On the point, the reader should consult the chapter on Italy in the *Hope* internationalization volume (Porta 1997b). On postgraduate studies in Italy, see Stirati and Cesaratto (1995).
5 See Coats (1997). The issue – internationalization vs. Americanization – as observed by Coats himself (Coats 1997: Introduction, p. 5) runs through the whole of the internationalization volume. Cf. also the editor's own remarks in the 'Conclusions' to the volume, ibid., pp. 395–400. On the specific impact of the issue in the Italian context, 'international forces [Coats observes] have been dominant intellectually both before and since 1945': cf. ibid., p. 5. See also Porta (1997b, esp. pp. 166–7).
6 Perhaps the most conspicuous attempt to that effect was made in the Italian translation, by Paolo Sylos Labini and Luigi Occhionero, of Schumpeter's *History of Economic Analysis*. Concerning the expression 'political economy' in current English usage, the reader should consult the discussion in Coats (1997: 347–51).
7 See Porta (1997b, esp. pp. 173–6).
8 See, for example, Bocciarelli and Ciocca (1994); Zamagni (1994); also Porta (1997a).
9 The issue is not pursued in this chapter. See, however, for example, Carli (1993), on which we shall comment later. In slightly more general terms, it might be said that much of the postwar history of political economy in Italy could be read in terms of a somewhat strained but ongoing relationship with a 'European' model, however defined, of how the economy works. This is not merely true either of the more recent years or of the present-day (1998) outburst of Euro-enthusiasm; it is either explicit or recognizable through a number of postwar contributions to Italian political economy.
10 See, for example, Putnam (1993, esp. ch. 5).
11 See Putnam (1993). Putnam's book has had a disproportionately wide readership recently, especially among economic and political historians both in Italy and internationally.
12 Acknowledging the weight of such and similar similar grounds, the Italian economist and European Commissioner Mario Monti suggested a few years ago that the seat of the Bank of Italy should be moved from Rome to Milan.
13 I have no ambition for a fully fledged treatment of the subject in this chapter. Among numerous recent contributions we shall have in mind and refer to some of the results of an ongoing project on economic research and teaching in Milan during this century, *La cultura economica a Milan nel secolo ventesimo,* sponsored by *Ciriec,* the Italian Centre for Research and Information on Public Economics. The *Ciriec* project includes contributions by a number of Italian economists and historians, such as Giuseppe Bognetti, Angelo Moioli, Gian Luigi Trezzi, Daniela Parisi, Claudio Pavese, Pier Luigi Porta, Pier Angelo Toninelli, Marianna Cavazza Rossi, Gian-

domenico Piluso, Claudia Rotondi and Gianluca Sartor. Among others, the works by De Luca (1997), Porta (1997a), Porta (1997b) and particularly *Ciriec* (1998) reflect the ongoing activity of the *Ciriec* group.

14 On the experience of the *Handelshochschulen*, see my contribution in *Ciriec* (1998, esp. pp. 179–85).

15 Bagiotti (1974: 5).

16 See AA.VV (1942).

17 Bocciarelli and Ciocca (1994), for example, reproduce the Demaria chapter from the book.

18 The issue need not detain us here, but it is interesting to notice that it is widely debated. The interested reader should see, for example, Checco and D'Andrea (1976); Rasi (1981); Barucci (1978, esp. pp. 186–96); and Saraceno (1969).

19 The work of the Demaria Commission, practically ignored for many years, seems now to be made the object of intense studies in progress.

20 That particular rehearsal of the free-trade position was offered on the occasion of a meeting on the *Ordine nuovo* taking place at the University of Pisa in May 1942. The episode is fully documented in Demaria (1951: 473–502). On the subsequent process of exchange liberalization, a recent perceptive reconstruction is given by Carli (1993: ch. 1).

21 On the significant involvement of the Bank of Italy, see Caracciolo (1992, esp. pp. 41–4).

22 See Paolo Baffi's thorough discussion of the exchanges and interaction with foreign economists at the Bank of Italy, ca. 1942–52, in his essay '*Via Nazionale e gli economisti stranieri, 1943–54*' (see Baffi 1990: 93–152). The international openness of Italian economists during the interwar period is discussed, with special refence to the case of the Bocconi University, by Romani (1997).

23 On Beneduce, see Bonelli (1984). Beneduce – whose family name curiously means something like 'Hail the Duce' – was able to implement the design of the *IRI* system taking advantage of a strong personal trust in Mussolini.

24 See Menichella (1944), also Saraceno (1975). It is interesting that the line of thinking under discussion appears to be less linked, compared to the line discussed in the preceding paragraph, to academic research as such. The analysis of the relationship of academic and extra-academic research, extremely important both to a sociology of the profession and to the history of economic analysis, goes beyond the scope of this chapter.

25 See Zamagni and Sanfilippo (1988).

26 See Baffi's essay on the Bank of Italy and foreign economists in Baffi (1990: 93–152).

27 Ezio Tarantelli was shot dead by the 'Red Brigades'.

28 See, for example Graziani (1981); Rey and Peluffo (1995). That the nature of these debates is a proof of the character of the process of internationalization taking place in postwar Italy is discussed in Coats (1997: 165–83).

29 Coats emphasizes the significance of corporativism. For a recent treatment, see Faucci (1995) on the case of corporativism and economic thought in Italy.

30 See in particular my contribution in *Ciriec* (1998: 163–92).

References

AA.VV. (1942) *Ricostruzione dell'economia nel dopoguerra*, Padua: Cedam. Essays by G. Borgatta, C. Bresciani-Turroni, G. Demaria, L. Einaudi, G. Lorenzoni, originally published in *Giornale degli economisti e annali di economica*, n.s., 1941.

Baffi, P. (1990) *Testimonianze e ricordi*, Milan: Scheiwiller.

Bagiotti, T. (1974) 'Economia ed economisti in Italia', in *Rendiconti del comitato veneto per il potenziamento degli studi economici e per la programmazione*, Treviso: Canova, vol. IX: 3–19; repr. in *Momento analitico e momento civile nell'esperienza dell'economista*, A. Agnati, A. Montesano and P. L. Porta (eds), Padua: Cedam, 1994, pp. 319–36.

Barca, F. (ed.) (1997) *Storia del capitalismo italiano dal dopoguerra a oggi*, Rome: Donzelli.

Barucci, P. (1978) *Ricostruzione, pianificazione, mezzogiorno. La politica economica in Italia dal 1943 al 1945*, Bologna: Mulino.

Bocciarelli, R. and Ciocca, P. L. (eds) (1994) *Scrittori italiani di economia*, Bari: Laterza.

Caracciolo, A. (1992) *La Banca d'Italia tra l'autarchia e la guerra*, Collana storica della Banca d'Italia, serie documenti, vol. IX, Bari: Laterza.

Carli, G. (1993) *Cinquant'anni di vita italiana*, in collab. with P. Peluffo, Bari: Laterza.

Checco, A. and D'Andrea, A. (1976) 'Piccola e media impresa nella crisi del fascismo: un dibattito degli anni 1941–42', *Studi storici*, pp. 96–110.

Ciocca, P. (1987) 'Integrazione, sviluppo, occasioni mancate, 1950–70', in *L'instabilità dell'economia. Prospettive di analisi storica*, Turin: Einaudi, pp. 213–60.

Ciriec (1998) *La cultura economica a Milan nel secolo XX*. Vol. I: *Gli anni 1890–1920* P. L. Porta (ed.), Milan: Angeli.

Coats, A. W. (ed.) (1997) *The Post-1945 Internationalization of Economics*, Annual Supplement to Vol. 28 of *History of Political Economy,* Durham and London: Duke University Press.

De Cecco, M. (1989) 'Keynes and Italian economics', in P. A. Hall (ed) *The Political Power of Economic Ideas*, Princeton, NJ: Princetown University Press, pp. 195–230.

De Luca, G. (ed.) (1997) *Pensare l'Italia nuova: la cultura economica milanese tra corporativismo e ricostruzione*, Milan: Angeli.

Demaria, G. (1941) 'Il *problema industriale italiano*', *Giornale degli economisti e annali di economia*, n.s.: 516–52. Repr. in AA.VV (1942) and in English in an essay by G.A. Tesoro, *The Bankruptcy of Fascist Economy through the Eyes of Italian Economists*, Washington, DC: Bureau of Latin American Research (1943) pp. 27f.

Demaria, G. (1951) *Problemi economici e sociali del dopoguerra, 1945–50*, ed. by Tullio Bagiotti, Milan: Malfasi.

Faucci, R. (1995) 'La cultura economica', in A. Del Boca, M. Legnani and M. G. Rossi (eds) *Il regime fascista*, Bari: Laterza, pp. 507–28.

Frey, B. S. and Eichenberger, R. (1993) 'American and European economics and economists', *Journal of Economic Perspectives* 7(4) (Fall): 185–93.

Frey, R. S. and Frey, R. L. (1995) 'Is there a European economics?' *Kyklos*, special issue, 48:4.

Fusco, A. M. (1997) '*Gli studi di economia in Italia: momenti di riflessione teorica, 1946–96*', *Economia italiana* 1(2): 107–68.

Gattei, G. (1995) '*La "cultura economica" del Ventennio (1923–1943)*', *Storia del pensiero economico* 29: 3–50.

Graziani, A. (1981) 'La teoria della distribuzione del reddito', in G. Lunghini (ed.) *Scelte politiche e teorie economiche in Italia*, Turin: Einaudi, pp. 285–340.

Hall, P.A. (ed.) (1989) *The Political Power of Economic Ideas: Keynesianism across Nations*, Princeton, NJ: Princeton University Press.

La Malfa, G. and Modigliani, F. (1987) 'Su alcuni aspetti della congiuntura e della politica monetaria in Italia', in *Reddito, interesse, inflazione*, Turin: Einaudi, pp. 301–48.

Menichella, D. (1944) 'Le origini dell'IRI e la sua azione nei confronti della situazione bancaria', typescript; now in Banca d'Italia *Donato Menichella: scritti e discorsi scelti, 1933-1966*, Rome, 1986.

Porta, P. L. (ed.) (1996) 'Milano nel primo novecento', *Economia pubblica* 36(2) suppl.

——(1997a) 'Milano e il pensiero economico. Aspetti della cultura della concorrenza e del mercato tra corporativismo e ricostruzione, 1935–50', *Rivista di storia economica*, 13:2 (August): 197-220. Also in G. De Luca (ed.) (1997) *Pensare d'Italia nuova*, Milan: Angeli, pp.111–36 (under the title 'Milan e il pensiero economico. Quale "fortuna" per il liberismo?').

——(1997b) 'Italian economics through the postwar years', in A. W. Coats (ed.) *The Post-1945 Internationalization of Economics*, Durham, NC, and London: Duke University Press, pp. 165–83.

Putnam, R.D. (1993) *Making Democracy Work: Civic Traditions in Modern Italy*, Princeton, NJ: Princeton University Press.

Rasi, G. (1981) 'La politica economica e i conti della nazione', in Annali dell'economia italiana, Milan: Ipsoa, vol. IX, 1, pp. 85ff.

Rey, G. and P. Peluffo (eds) (1995) *Dialogo tra un professore e la Banca d'Italia*, Firenze: Vallecchi.

Roggi, P. (1987) *Scelte politiche e teorie economiche in Italia nel quarantennio repubblicano*, Turin: Giappichelli.

Romani, M. A. (1997) 'Bocconi über alles. L'organizzazione della didattica e la ricerca (1914–45)', in AA.VV. *Storia di una libera università*, vol. II, 'L'Università Commerciale Luigi Bocconi dal 1915 al 1945', Milan: Egea.

Saraceno, P. (1969) *Ricostruzione e pianificazione*, introd. di P. Barucci, Bari: Laterza.

Saraceno, P. (1975) *Il sistema delle imprese a partecipazione statale nella esperienza italiana*, Milan: Giuffrè.

Steve, S. (1997) *Scritti vari*, Milan: F. Angeli.

Stirati, A. and Cesaratto, S. (1995) 'The Italian Ph.D. ten years on: educational, scientific and occupational outcomes', *Higher Education*, 30(1) (July): 37–61.

Zamagni, V. and Sanfilippo, M. (eds) (1988) *Nuovo meridionalismo e intervento straordinario: la Svimez dal 1946 al 1950*, Bologna: Mulino.

Zamagni, V. (1994) 'Did the economy contribute to the redefinition of the Italian identity after World War II?'. Contribution presented at the European Institute in Florence, October, typescript.

9   The advent of modern economics in Portugal

Carlos Bastien

This chapter aims at analysing the conditions and the process of modernization of economic ideas in Portugal after 1945. Firstly, we will describe the circumstances at the threshold of this period. To sum up, there was a clear backwardness and unfamiliarity with the economic theory produced in the main innovating centres in the world.

Second, we will focus on the period 1945–55, when the advent of modern economic growth in Portugal required a thorough renewal in the field of economic doctrines and theories. This process was associated with a reform of economic teaching and the advent of both research institutions and specialized reviews.

Third, we will consider the following decades, when the process of modernization of economic ideas was pushed further under the new encouraging environment; namely, the integration of Portugal in the wider world economy and international cultural life. However, implementation has been very slow. Only very recently has a true community of economists been set up.

Economic ideas in Portugal by 1945

Prior to 1945, Portugal was a small, backward and semi-peripherical national economy under an authoritarian regime set up by a *coup d'état* in 1926, which led to a corporative state that was institutionalized in 1933. The dominant strategy thought out by the new government was to maintain economic and social equilibria. The dominant social role was performed by an alliance of wealthy landowners, non-entrepreneurial industrialists and commercial bankers. They resisted both modernization and social and cultural change. Some ideologues, mainly engineers, thought out a strategy of economic growth but they were not supported either by society or by the political leadership.

The economic policy implemented in the 1930s was clearly conditional upon the above-mentioned goal of social and political stability. Budget equilibrium, monetary stability, autarky, but mainly the setting up of the so-called 'industrial conditioning' were to become important components in a complex corporative apparatus aiming at controlling the whole of economic and social life. Such a policy was basically a voluntarist attitude relying on no refined economic theory.

Throughout the 1930s, in spite of some efforts to create a corporative economic doctrine, economic discourse continued to be poor, non-specialized and non-theoretical. Politicians, jurists, engineers and journalists, mostly self-taught and with no specific competence, were its main interpreters.

At that time there was no social group that could be viewed as professional economists; research units in the field were almost absent, scientific reviews or any other periodical publications on economic issues were rare. The *Instituto Superior de Ciências Económicas e Financeiras – ISCEF* (Higher Institute of Economic and Financial Sciences), of Lisbon, founded in 1911, was the only school at university level dedicated to economic sciences, though high-level studies of political economy were undertaken in traditional law schools.

Knowledge and debates on economic theory were rather poor. Theoretical innovations that had arisen since the end of the nineteenth century were almost unknown. This is the case with the so-called 'marginalist revolution'. In fact, if names such as K. Menger, A. Marshall or V. Pareto were incidentally quoted, most of their works remained unnoticed. Generations of economists that would adopt critical or divergent views of the so-called 'first neoclassical synthesis' – namely, institutionalists, Marxists and Schumpeterians – were also mostly ignored.

The teaching of economic theory in the *ISCEF*, as the responsibility of professors with juridical training, was dominated by what could be considered a naive institutionalism. It had neither the sociological emphasis nor the critical views inherent in Veblenian institutionalism. It was a mere description of the institutional and legal aspects of economic life, as the main textbooks of this period show (Marques 1934; Netto 1936; Guedes 1944–46). Economic theory was then considered to be a subject of cultural interest but of little or no instrumental value (Pereira 1935).

During this period José J. Teixeira Ribeiro, a professor of political economy at the University of Coimbra from 1937 onward, was the main exception to this generalization. As his PhD dissertation shows, he was aware of the theories of monopoly and even of monopolistic competition (Ribeiro 1934). He dared to implement an eclectic teaching – in spite of the limits imposed by the ruling culturally obscurantist regime – where both the prevailing and the less influential schools of economic thought deserved to be mentioned. Costa Leite was another exception. His study of the theory of economic crisis revealed his awareness of the most important contributions of Cambridge's economists (Leite 1933).

After 1933–34, the corporative doctrine was definitely the most influential one. Its primacy led to attempts to create something like an indigenous Portuguese corporative economic theory that would legitimate that doctrine as well as guiding state economic interventionism. In fact it turned out to be a rough version of the Italian corporative economic theory.

The outcome of all this was rather perverse. The hoped-for original consistent theory did not emerge and meanwhile the various theoretical conceptions produced abroad were either undervalued or introduced only after great delay.

The beginning of a new epoch

By 1945, almost all over the world, a new economic, social and cultural epoch arose. Portugal was not an exception. The immediate post-World War II period turned out to be pivotal in Portuguese society.

In spite of the persistence of clear signs of backwardness, a process of industrialization and economic modernization took off in the beginning of the 1950s. Social structures were reshaped as the industrial bourgeoisie strengthened its position within the ruling social coalition.

In spite of its apparent stability, the political regime also underwent some changes. The appearance of stronger anti-fascist movements, both of liberal or Marxist inspiration; the emergence of lobbies inside the regime apparatus; and popular protest were responsible. After a short period of international isolation, internal political disturbance and some uncertainty as far as its survival was concerned, the so-called *Estado Novo* (New State) was able to retain and even develop its corporative apparatus after all.

However, the new international environment, the partial revival of the social background of the regime, political pressure and the new economic ideas, all had important consequences. The purely conservative strategy of social equilibria implemented since the 1930s was significantly complemented with a strategy of industrialization supported by new forms of economic regulation, under protectionist policies. By the beginning of the 1960s a new strategy of internationalization was taking place. It was interrupted in 1974–75 when a revolution overthrew the *Estado Novo* and tried to implement a socialist society. After that brief period the previous strategy of internationalization re-emerged, being heavily confirmed when Portugal became a full EEC member in 1986.

The cultural scene, as well, experienced some changes at the end of World War II in spite of the persistence of traditionalist doctrine and of the restrictions generated by the obscurantist cultural policy of the *Estado Novo*. These changes took place mainly outside official circles. The import of new scientific knowledge and the strengthening of some of the existing artistic, philosophical and scientific ideas, contributed to a renewed rationalism, an increasing value given to the idea of progress and an underlining of the civilizing and instrumental role of science.

Those changes were also experienced in the specific field of economic ideas. Popular and cultivated opinion, as well as democratic opposition forces and even a developmentalist group inside the ruling coalition, demonstrated a major concern for economic issues and were aware of Portuguese backwardness.

Common sense began to reject the idea that Portugal was inevitably a poor country because of the scarcity of its natural resources. In the following years, as the relationship with the other European societies was intensified, claims for better standards of living, closer to the levels of other Western economies, emerged.

Several economists – namely, those who were committed to support political opposition movements – made severe attacks on the uneven distribution of income and wealth and on the conservative nature of the effective economic strategy and they put forward pro-development views which demanded the transformation of the country's basic economic and political structures. This process would include the dismantling of the corporative economic apparatus, the nationalization of big industry and banks, the implementation of agrarian reform, and also a change of political structures in favour of democracy.

Even those committed to the regime felt that, in a period of political uncertainty, this was a unique opportunity and they tried to force their pro-growth views. Ferreira Dias and Araújo Correia, both engineers, were the most representative. They were committed to the regime but they did not actually form a group. Nevertheless, they shared some common views: namely, a cautious mistrust of the efficiency of the corporative apparatus but also a belief in an authoritarian, strong, interventionist state. Actually, they thought that to catch up successfully the state should reorganize and concentrate most of the industrial branches by administrative means (Dias 1945). It should also be directly responsible for the infrastructures needed to make the best economic use of the rivers, in order to modernize the agricultural sector and, even more important, to obtain a source of energy to foster industrialization. In their opinion, long-term planning should be an important regulating mechanism in this process (Correia 1952).

Their immediate success was limited, but their projects proved to be quite relevant to the economic modernization actually experienced by Portugal in the following decades. Even the quite conservative corporative official doctrine would show a clear sensitivity to the ideas of industrialization, economic planning and economic growth. At the beginning of the 1970s technocratic views would take over this trend (Martins 1970).

Theoretical innovations[1]

The sub-field of economic theories was also experiencing important changes as a reaction to the emergence of paradigms other than corporative economics.

Corporative economics

Despite the survival of the *Estado Novo* in the critical postwar environment its corporative economic apparatus was not significantly strengthened. Corporations would continue to be substituted during the next decade by a dense network of public agencies responsible for an extended degree of economic regulation. Actually, they were more efficient in control than in coordination between sectors.

The apparent failure to set up an effective corporative economy and the new international post-World War II environment, proved to have far-reaching consequences. The defeat of the fascist states and the consequent contempt for the corporative ideal led to the discredit of its doctrine and to a temporary collapse in the effort to introduce corporative theoretical innovations. However, as the *Estado Novo* managed to survive, a new period, the so-called 'new corporative take-off' (Cardoso 1949: 8–9), emerged.

Some economists tried then to reimpose the corporative doctrine and theory and this injected a touch of Portuguese originality into the international intellectual scene in economics.

The theorizing adopted in the first half of the 1950s aimed at integrating some new topics and concepts into the prevailing corporative doctrine, many of which were imported from other theoretical, doctrinal schools. The initial theoretical concerns to concentrate the efforts of the corporative economists of the first period – namely, the definition of *Homo corporativus*, the determination of the corporative price and of the corporative wage – were extended to three new items: efficiency and equilibrium of the corporative firm, economic planning and the theory of economic systems.

The first of these efforts led to the most curious results. The attempt was to determine, in a Marshallian style, the equilibrium conditions of the firm in a corporative system by comparing the hypothetical equilibrium of the same firm in the context of a capitalist system. The main conclusion of this counter-factual exercise was that, under a corporative system both a higher level of employment and a stronger growth dynamics would be achieved (Nunes 1952; Silva 1953).

As a theoretical topic, economic planning was ignored by corporative economists before 1950. The advent of this instrument of economic regulation in several Western European mixed economies after World War II generated some interest in the subject. In the long run, discussions on the theme would lead to the introduction of modern techniques of economic planning. However, in the short run, the point was to justify the compatibility of an economic plan (by then considered a typical instrument of the socialist economies and so to be despised) with its use as an instrument in the context of the corporative structure.

It was accepted that 'we are not supposed to expect that common welfare will come automatically' and that 'the corporative economy will only realize its aim fully – common welfare – through a planned intervention implemented by the corporations in cooperation with the state' (Pereira 1953: 50). This would imply the institutionalization of a complex hierarchical structure of corporative councils.

In this period, as far as the theory of economic systems is concerned, the crucial change was the abandonment of the idea that the corporative system should be a third way between capitalism and socialism. Consequently the efforts to build up a corporative economics fade out. The adoption of the theory of economic systems that W. Eucken set out in 1939, implied that from then on corporative economies would be considered simply as a particular mix of market and centrally planned economies – as in any other existing economies – and so falling under general economic laws (Moura 1950).

Stubbornly, however, some jurists went on insisting that 'the main features of a corporative economy separate it from any other system' (Martinez 1960: 35). Even in the 1970s, when the *Estado Novo* was undergoing its final crisis, there were still attempts to reassert the corporative ideal and to prove that the corporative system could lead to economic modernization (Pires 1973; Xavier 1973).

Neoclassical economics

Along with the abandonment of the above-mentioned project to create a corporative economics, at the end of the 1940s there was an opportunity to import the almost unknown neoclassical economics. This school of economic thought would prove to be an important device to legitimate the institutionalization of the liberal capitalist order after the eventual collapse of the *Estado Novo* in the aftermath of World War II. Meanwhile, that new theoretical body could still be useful to legitimate several important political and economic ideas of the *Estado Novo*. This was the case with such topics as economic agents' harmony, monetary stability, balanced budget, economic inequality and so on.

In these circumstances, and considering that academic institutions were heavily dependent on the political leadership, there was a fundamental precondition for a successful introduction of the new school: it had to be 'purified' from the liberal political prescriptions with which it had usually been associated.

The first step towards the acceptance of this new school was to demonstrate its scientific nature. It was important to isolate it from important trends in the economic literature of the epoch, both in terms of methodology and concepts. However, any doctrinal discussion of the economic systems or on guidelines of economic policy was completely unacceptable to the majority of the academic staff. It was only acceptable as positive economics, 'looking only for facts and its laws . . . prescribing nothing, neither normative, nor imperative' (Barbosa 1943: 236) in order to avoid any pollution, either from doctrinal values or from political demands.

The neoclassical paradigm was transmitted through university textbooks deviating little from the international standard. Some particularities were the result of specific conditions – namely, the late introduction of the theory in Portugal. As far as consumer theory is concerned, some textbooks published in the 1940s failed to make clear the distinction between the first versions of the marginalist analysis, based on cardinal utility and the more refined versions based on the indifference curves and ordinal utility formulated by Pareto and later by Hicks. In any case, the concern in analysis is apparent at a logical level underlying the merely formal nature of that type of analysis; namely, when noting that 'indifference curves are quite vague, imprecise concepts that can be accepted at a logical level but [they] are absolutely useless for practical purposes' (Barbosa 1950, vol. 1: 122).

Production theory was also diffused according to the conventional international presentation. It is worth emphasizing that this part of the theory had the most significant immediate impact in studies of applied economics; namely, in the appraisal of the efficiency of some industrial sectors.

Market theory fitted this pattern. Textbooks in the 1940s included detailed references to perfect competition, to unilateral and bilateral monopolistic and oligopolistic markets. Their originality, if any, lay in emphasizing that perfect competition markets had a mere didactic value, but certainly not prescriptive value (Barbosa 1950, vol. 2: 461), and in introducing the distinction between what were called 'theoretical prices' and 'real prices', in order to justify state intervention with prices (Barbosa 1950, vol. 2: 544).

On the whole, these topics were discussed in a rather dogmatic way. The marginalist analysis was said to be superior because it was 'appealing to gather all the elements inherent to value, while previous theories were aware of the fact that it depended on utility, scarcity or labour but could not combine these factors' (Ulrich 1948: 40). The realism of such a construction was never discussed, neither how to measure utility nor the validity of the law of diminishing returns, just to mention two of the weakest aspects of the theory.

During the following decades, neoclassical economics remained basically an academic subject, having hardly any impact on economic policy. The law of increasing returns was incidentally quoted to support the industrial policy which favoured concentration. The virtues of competition were also incidentally recalled – namely, whenever some industrialist felt he was being hurt by the application of the 'industrial conditioning' legislation.

In the last twenty years neoclassical economics has gained credibility in the context of the so-called second crisis of economic theory and the advent of the liberal wave of the 1980s. Only then were some practical implications of the theory felt and general economic equilibrium theory received significant scholarly attention.

Keynesian economics

Any appraisal of the meaning of the Keynesian revolution in Portugal during the 1940s must take account of how small and backward Portugal was. It had not yet experienced a take-off and so its monetary and financial markets were very small and inefficient. Economic cycles were basically determined by the impact of external forces and by agricultural cycles. Unemployment was still hidden by the important role of the traditional structures of agriculture.

The impact of Keynesianism was also minimized by political and cultural factors. The theoretical discussion and analytical progress that took place in Cambridge during the 'high theory years', which led to *The General Theory*, were unknown to the large majority of Portuguese economists. Though he never read Keynes, Salazar, the chief leader of the *Estado Novo*, who had been Professor of Political Economy and Public Finance at the University of Coimbra, thought Keynesianism was 'a disease' (Nunes 1986: 59). This fact is not insignificant once one realizes the above-mentioned rigid dependence of the university on the political leadership. Above all, the strong economic intervention by the state under the *Estado Novo* had been well established long before and had its own forms of legitimation in corporative doctrine. So Keynesian ideas were not very appealing, especially as they minimized the importance of and even contradicted, the rigid monetary and budgetary orthodoxy which was a leitmotiv of *Estado Novo* propaganda.

It was no suprise that those mainly responsible for the introduction and diffusion of Keynesian ideas were economists in political opposition to the regime;

some of them were expelled from the university. They thought the new paradigm could be used to legitimate their opposition to Salazar's economic and cultural policy. Abstracts of *The General Theory* were published (Abreu 1948; Pinto 1952), Keynes's innovations in economic analysis were underlined; and the similarities and differences between Marx's and Keynes's ideas were discussed (Sousa 1950). Some of those papers dared to demonstrate the irrationality of specific aspects of Portuguese economic policy from a Keynesian point of view (Abreu 1949; Leal and Falcão 1952).

Later, Keynesianism would be accepted by the *Estado Novo* economists, at least in its pure, formal character. As it was no longer feasible to ignore the theoretical innovations, they disseminated an interpretation of the paradigm that would legitimate the corporative system and the economic policy implemented under it. They mentioned that 'the possibility of a third system . . . had been already theoretically accepted by distinguished economists, namely J. M. Keynes', and that 'that system cannot be other than the corporative system' (Veiga 1944: 214–15). For instance, regarding economic policy, they wrote that 'some Keynesian doctrines, which were not ignored, were consistent with some attitudes reflected in the Portuguese laws and administration' (Oliveira 1947: 147).

In the 1950s, the Keynesian revolution was introduced into the universities. From then on, Keynesian economics became dominant at that level and at last influenced the political discourse. Textbooks introduced the main concepts of the new theory included in the so-called neoclassical-Keynesian synthesis based on the IS-LM model. In the mid-1950s PhD dissertations show a clear influence of Keynesian theory (Beleza 1955; Nunes 1956; Pinto 1956).

In the 1960s the most important textbooks used in the teaching of economic theory reveal a powerful influence by Keynesian ideas (Moura 1964 and 1969a). Important interpretations of the Portuguese process of economic growth were also influenced by that paradigm (Moura 1969b). The most prominent men of the *Estado Novo*, both on the political and economic scene, became sensitive to the new economic conceptions. Araújo Correia, mentioned earlier, tried to support his developmentalist ideas using Keynesian concepts. The Second Development Plan, elaborated in 1958, was based on a Harrod-Domar type mathematical economic growth model. After 1955, even the Minister of Finance's discourse integrated concepts and a Keynesian lexicon, though the classical financial orthodoxy inherent to Salazar's governments persisted.

Portugal was also touched by the second crisis of economic theory and by some divergent and critical views that emerged in that context. However, the neoclassical-Keynesian synthesis remained the main school of economic theory taught in the universities.

With respect to economic policy, matters were different. After a brief period of dominance of socialist economics in the mid-1970s, monetarist economics became the mainstream in the 1980s and in the first half of the 1990s.

Marxist economics[2]

Marxism was another school of economic thought in Portugal during this period. It was not entirely new to Portuguese culture, for its presence was apparent during the nineteenth century. However, it was not until the 1930s that a first generation of Marxist intellectuals appeared. Their action would not be felt until the war period.

The spread of Marxist ideas was the consequence of its prestige as an ideal, of the strengthening of the workers' movement and of Communist forces during wartime. By then, some Marxist economists emerged, most of them non-academic. They introduced and discussed several topics relating to Portugal, such as imperialism, workers' immiseration, underdevelopment and agrarian reform.

This doctrinal intervention, sometimes propagandistic, was accompanied by several theoretical developments. Among these, the subjective theory of value, predominant in the academy, was criticized and its limitations were underlined, while the superiority of the Marxist theory of labour-value was emphasized (Castro 1948). An under-consumptionist interpretation of Portuguese capitalism (Castro 1949) was a lasting interpretative matrix among Portuguese Marxists and the broad trends of the agricultural sector were described (Castro 1945). Attempts were made to test the validity of the theoretical law of pauperization under Portuguese economic conditions (Alarcão 1948). However, as mentioned earlier, the most important and lasting theoretical efforts of these economists were dedicated to the criticism of Keynesianism.

During the 1950s, in Portugal as elsewhere, Marxism retreated, in respect of both its political and practical attitudes, as well as its theoretical elaboration and diffusion. However, after the mid-1960s it once again became appealing to Portuguese intellectuals, following a similar trend in Western Europe. This was to have positive effects on economic thought.

Abstract theoretical topics, such as the historical forms of the capitalist mode of production and the theory of economic crisis, attracted the attention of these authors and there were some written elaborations. However, many other economic topics that were central in international Marxist discussions were generally ignored in Portugal. Controversial themes, such as the evolution of the world economy, the division of labour inside the factory and the functioning of the socialist economies, were mostly absent.

Meanwhile, after the mid-1960s, relatively numerous writings appeared dealing with particular aspects of Portuguese capitalism. The most important theoretical reference was the theory of state monopoly capitalism according to the interpretation of the French Communist Party and of the Academy of Science of the USSR. However, the urgency of political intervention resulted in most of these texts in a short-term approach and a critical descriptive character. Alvaro Cunhal's book on the agrarian question (Cunhal 1966), but chiefly his report on the Portuguese situation (Cunhal 1964), are important exceptions. He tried to analyse Portuguese capitalism by means of a broad, systematic approach.

The military *coup* of 25 April 1974 toppled the forty-eight-year-old fascist dic-

tatorship. It changed many features of the political, economic and cultural landscape and – this is now the main point for us – it opened up the doors to the wider
spread and influence of Marxism. Since then Marxist ideals have echoed power-
fully in the academy, because Marxist intellectuals, previously forbidden to speak
out, were now integrated as scholars and investigators in some universities.

Armando Castro, who had just been authorized to lecture at the university,
published the first academic textbook on Marxist political economy ever written
in Portugal (Castro 1983). At the same time, the presentation of several PhD dissertations on subjects such as inflation, economic crises, economic policy and
the history of economic thought, just to mention a few, were a significant proof
of the impact of this paradigm of economic thought in the academy.

Cooperativism, Schumpeterianism and structuralism

Portuguese intellectuals were aware of other schools of economic thought, but
their influence was minor. One was the so-called 'social economics', especially
its cooperativist approach. It had had a certain tradition in Portugal since the
nineteenth century, as in some other Catholic countries and re-emerged as a project to reorganize both the economy and the society in the aftermath of World
War II and again in the 1970s, when the collapse of the *Estado Novo* made the
reformulation of the Portuguese economic structures an acute issue.

According to its supporters, 'the feasible socialism to be implemented now,
(is not yet) pure socialism but a pre-socialism' (Sérgio 1947: 17–18). It would
rely temporarily on a large public sector, which would be a device to assure the
way to a generalized cooperative system.

The defence of this system was basically ethical – 'to transform the economy
through moral principles' (Sérgio 1985: 65) – but there were, incidentally,
attempts to show the economic rationality of the system and, consequently, a
generalized cooperative system was feasible. These efforts were rather inconclusive, and for analytical purposes their authors had to call on neoclassical
micro-economics (Barros 1978).

The so-called 'basic needs approach' constituted another version of social economics during the 1970s, designing an economic policy in accordance with the
values of democratic socialism (Rijckeghem and Barreiros 1979). Its most striking result was a medium-term plan for 1977–80 drawn up by the state planning
department. Though it was never implemented, it embodied a set of specific
goals in relation to the basic needs of the population.

Schumpeterian economics was also incidentally acknowledged during the
1950s, especially in the context of business-cycle discussions (Sousa 1950).
However, Schumpeterian views on the theory of economic development and on
the entrepreneur were ignored. The scarcity of Portuguese entrepreneurs, the
important role of state interventionism and the survival of models of political
authoritarianism to explain the entrepreneurial function, help to account for the
irrelevance of Schumpeter's ideas.

In respect to structuralism, the situation was somewhat different. The implementation of a pro-growth strategy demanded that the analysis of the economic structures be transformed. This called for an appropriate set of empirical and theoretic concepts. By 1954, a first result of the efforts to 'study the economic structure of the Portuguese mainland . . . just the structure and not a general study on the Portuguese economy' (Moura *et al.* 1954: 22) was published. New analytical tools such as input-output analysis then began to be used in studies of applied economics (Moura *et al.* 1954; Tintner and Murteira 1959).

Structuralist economics, influenced by some French and ECLA economists – in particular, Raul Prebisch – continued to be discussed during the following two decades. Its main contribution, as an instrument of legitimation of pro-growth attitudes, was to characterize Portuguese backwardness in a very clear and thorough way (Pereira 1954).

However, political constraints compelled the academic versions of structuralism to focus on technical aspects; namely, on economic planning techniques. It was purified of some relevant critical views adopted by those Latin-American authors; that is, in what concerns the definition of the social basis of the development process and foreign economic policy.

The spread of research and educational apparatus

Just as economic ideas have changed and been modernized, the apparatus specialized in the production and dissemination of those ideas underwent important transformations after the mid-1940s. One result was the advent of the profession of economist during the 1960s.

Scientific research apparatus

The first research units to be created had a direct relationship with the above-mentioned attempt to think out an original Portuguese corporative economics. The *Centro de Estudos Corporativos* (*Centre of Corporative Studies*), at the Law Faculty of the University of Coimbra, was founded in 1941 and was active till 1945. It appears to typify the first period of efforts to formulate that theory.

The *Gabinete de Estudos Corporativos* (*Corporative Research Bureau*), created in 1950 in the *Instituto Superior de Ciências Económicas e Financeiras* (*ISCEF*), is the result of the initiative of the intellectual leaders of the 'second corporative take-off', most of them professors of that Institute. As this project failed, in 1961 this *Gabinete* turned to sociology, becoming the very first research centre in the subject.

On the other hand, that same Institute had a strong tradition in the teaching of pure mathematics, but not of mathematics applied to economics. As noted above, until the 1940s the Portuguese tradition in economics was dominated by institutionalism and by corporative economics, both of which were adverse to mathematical formalism. However, that situation started to change in 1938 when the *Centro de Estudos de Matemática Aplicada à Economia* – (*CEMAE*)

(Research Centre of Mathematics Applied to Economics), also in the *ISCEF* – began its research activities. This Centre, in spite of its short existence, played a crucial role in the evolution of economics in Portugal. It gathered together some of the most brilliant Portuguese mathematicians – for example, Bento J. Caraça, its founder – and through its research programmes during the 1940s introduced mathematical economics and econometrics.

The first PhD dissertations on economics using quantitative methods extensively were major results of *CEMAE*'s activity (Freire 1945; Costa 1947; Rodrigues 1947). Preliminary efforts to calculate Portuguese national income were also initiated. Unfortunately, the government expelled Caraça and all his main collaborators from the university and closed down the *CEMAE* in 1946, for political reasons.

Sometime after that purge a new research unit, the *Centro de Estudos de Estatística Económica* (Economic Statistics Studies Centre) was created to replace the *CEMAE*. It was to have an important role in preparing *ISCEF* professors in econometrics. Until 1964, when it ended its activity, it had enjoyed collaboration from visiting professors, such as Erich Schneider, Gerhard Tintner, Edmond Malinvaud and René Roy.

The *Gabinete de Investigação Económica* (Economic Research Bureau) was active between 1958 and 1969. It was also a research unit of the *ISCEF* essentially devoted to implementing studies of economic theory, especially the modern theory of economic growth.

Further significant improvements on economics research in the context of university institutions would only come after 1974. By then, the large expansion of the university institutions was accompanied by the spread of specialized research units and of PhD dissertations more and more conforming to international standards, as far as both their contents and the use of formal models was concerned.

In 1945, apart from the university, the *Centro de Estudos Económicos* (Economic Studies Centre) was founded, also by official initiative, in connection with the Central Statistical Office. It was supposed to produce economic studies – especially, quantitative research using data produced by that centre – to illuminate state economic interventionism. However, it never had a full-time team of researchers. Its main activity was the production of a journal: *Revista do Centro de Estudos Económicos*.

Up to the 1960s there was very little recognition of the importance of applied economic studies in political decision-making. It was only in this decade that some ministries began to organize their own research departments and units, especially in industrial economics. In 1962 a central planning department was established and was responsible in the 1970s for the production of the first macroeconomic models for the Portuguese economy.

Some other institutions, other than universities and public administration, implemented studies on applied economics within their economic research centres. For example, the *Secção de Estudos Económicos* (Economic Studies Department), created by the *Associação Industrial Portuguesa* (Portuguese Industrial Association) in 1947, followed by the *Gabinete de Estudos de Economia Aplicada*

(Applied Economics Studies Bureau); and the *Centro de Economia e Finanças* (Economics and Financial Studies Bureau) of the *Fundação Gulbenkian* (Gulbenkian Foundation), which existed between 1965 and 1971, deserve to be mentioned. However, the most important of them all was the *Gabinete de Estudos do Banco de Portugal* (Study Bureau of the Bank of Portugal), which since 1975 has also been producing important studies, especially on Portuguese economy.

The small number of PhD dissertations presented at the *ISCEF* – thirty between 1931 and 1980 – many of which were undertaken outside of these centres, constitutes a modest scientific output especially in pure investigation. Until very recently, the small group of professors teaching economics in the Portuguese universities, their involvment in public life and in private business, the limited size of the centres and of their financial resources, the non-professionalization of their members, the small number of grants awarded for economic research (see Appendix – Table 9.1), and the political criteria applied to the selection of teachers and researchers during the *Estado Novo* period combine to explain that state of affairs.

The fragmentation of the discipline was not felt until the 1980s, as well as a relative explosion in the number of doctors in economics. Many of them obtained their degree in universities abroad.

The appearance of academic economic journals is another sign of progress in scientific research. Most of them were published by the above-mentioned research centres. Until 1945 *Economia e Finanças*, published in the *ISCEF* from 1931 to 1973, was the only one available. In 1945 the above-mentioned *Revista do Centro de Estudos Económicos* joined it until 1958. The *Revista de Economia* came out under the initiative of a group of economists previously gathered in *CEMAE* from 1948 to 1964. In 1952 the Faculty of Law of the University of Coimbra started publishing the *Boletim de Ciências Económicas*. The *ISCEF* also published the *Revista do Gabinete de Estudos Corporativos*, between 1950 and 1961, and *Análise Económica* between 1956 and 1969.

Recently, other scientific journals have been published under a pattern closer to international standards, with respect to both their contents and the use of formal models. The most relevant ones are *Economia*, edited by the *Universidade Católica Portuguesa* (Portuguese Catholic University) since 1977, *Estudos de Economia*, published by the *ISCEF* since 1980 and *Notas Económicas*, published by the *Faculdade de Economia* of the *Universidade de Coimbra* (Faculty of Economics of the University of Coimbra) since 1993.

In spite of this progress, the semi-peripherical character of Portuguese culture and the language barrier explain the persistent limited external impact of the economic research carried out in the country. After 1950 the most important papers published in the *Revista de Economia*, sometimes with abstracts in English and French, were mentioned in international economic bibliographies, especially in *Documentation Economique* and some well-known economists and economic historians – namely, Ragnar Frisch, Celso Furtado and Albert Silbert – published some papers in that review. During the 1950s, the future Nobel Prize winners Jan Tinbergen and John Hicks, among other well-known

European economists, came to lecture at the *ISCEF* and published some of their lectures in *Economia e Finanças*. However, these events did not significantly change the degree of isolation.

During the 1990s there have been some positive signs. Actually, as a recent study using database Social Scisearch of the Institute for Scientific Information (Mata 1995) shows that a closer integration into the international scientific community is being achieved (see Appendix, Tables 9.2 and 9.3).

The teaching of economic ideas

The introduction and diffusion of modern economic theory took place basically in state institutions; namely universities and research centres. In the nineteenth century it usually took place in a law faculty, but in the twentieth century the teaching of economics spread to all schools of commerce, in accordance with what happened in other countries of Continental Europe. The subject thereby achieved a higher status and was more fully integrated in the university. So, by 1945 economics was an ancillary subject, an auxiliary discipline to the engineering and juridical components in the curricula of the Faculties of Engineering at the *Universidade do Porto* (University of Oporto) and the *Universidade Técnica de Lisboa* (Technical University of Lisbon); at the Faculties of Law at the universities of Coimbra and Lisbon; and also at the above-mentioned *ISCEF* at the *Universidade Técnica de Lisboa*, the only university-level school dedicated exclusively to economic sciences.

There, students were intended to master mathematics, economic geography, economic history, international policy, law, accounting, chemistry and commercial techniques. In its curricula only one discipline dealt specifically with economic theory. A genuine course on economics was not started until the reform of 1949, a decisive contribution to the progress of economic knowledge. Many subjects on commercial techniques and technology were omitted, while many others were introduced into new disciplines. Economic theory was a major subject in four disciplines; the study of financial sciences spread into three syllabi; the traditional course in economic history began to include the history of economic doctrines; new specialized areas were introduced, such as the economics of transportation and the economics of the firm. Mathematics and statistics teaching was further strengthened and econometrics was one of the disciplines in the curriculum, while in the teaching of economic theory (from the beginning of the 1950s based on the the the neoclassical-Keynesian synthesis) mathematical formulation became increasingly apparent. At the same time the teaching of economics and related areas came under the responsibility of economists rather than jurists, as it had previously been. Some teaching texts published during the 1950s and the 1960s, on microeconomics (Barbosa 1950), on macroeconomics (Pinto 1952), on growth theory (Nunes 1964–65) and on econometrics (Murteira 1957) illustrate that new state of affairs.

In the following years these curricula and teaching methods were modified in several reforms – for example, in 1972, when new disciplines of quantitative methods (such as operational research and computing) and new basic economic courses (like international economics and national accounting techniques) – were introduced.

In these years new faculties of economics were created, most of them adopting the curricula of the *ISCEF*. The creation of economics faculties in state universities in Oporto in 1953, in Coimbra in 1972, in Lisbon, at the *Universidade Nova de Lisboa* (New University of Lisbon) in 1977, in Evora in 1981 and in Braga in 1995, were the main examples of this process. The *ISCEF* and the *Universidade Nova de Lisboa* were the first to introduce postgraduate courses in economics in 1981.

There is no strong tradition of private high schools and universities in Portugal but, during the 1980s, several degrees in economics were created in these institutions. However, scientific research in those private schools has been almost non-existent and the quality of the teaching is inferior to that in the state faculties. The academic degree at the *Universidade Católica Portuguesa*, created in 1972, is the only exception.

As far as the scientific curricula are concerned there are some relevant differences among the existing academic degrees. Some, following the example of the *ISCEF*, have a tradition of eclecticism and openness to different cultural and theoretical areas, in spite of the teaching being supported by the neoclassical-Keynesian synthesis. It is worth noticing that the reform of 1949 was justified by A. Pinto Barbosa, its main author, as the result of the acknowledgement of the works of Keynes, of the journal *Econometrica*, of the works of the *Institut de Science Economique Appliquée* – ISEA (Institute of Applied Economics) in Paris under the direction of F. Perroux and the *Theory of Games* by J. von Neuman and O. Morgenstern (Barbosa 1984: 159–60).

In 1957, important but diversified international scientific journals were regularly received at the *ISCEF*. *The American Economic Review*, *Econometrica*, *Economic Journal*, *Oxford Economic Papers*, *Economie Appliquée*, *Revue d'Economie Politique*, *Rivista Internazionale di Scienze Sociale* and *El Trimestre Economico* were probably the best known out of the twenty-eight titles available. The *ISCEF*'s library and the research unit of the Banco de Portugal were receiving the most important books, including the main textbooks, published in the well-known production centres of economic ideas.

However, the professors of that Institute continued the tradition of producing their own teaching texts and textbooks. Usually, bibliographical references in those textbooks showed much eclecticism and included references to paradigms other than the dominant one. Significantly, *Economics* by P. Samuelson, the reference that was certainly a major instrument in the achievement of uniformity of the teaching of economics in the Western world, was never recommended to students as *the* fundamental textbook before the 1980s.

Other mechanisms of the internationalization of economic teaching have been also commonly used – however, again only significantly in the 1980s. The coming of foreign visiting professors and the sending of assistant teachers to prepare their PhD dissertations at foreign universities have been the most important of those mechanisms. Until recently, this type of linkage was basically with France and England. In the last decade it has become more geographically diffused, with other European countries (as a result of Portugal's full integration in the EEC since 1986) and the USA rising in importance.

So, the *ISCEF* and most of the other faculties of economics in Portugal have for several decades conformed to the 'acceptance of heterodoxy' described by W. Baumol as a basic feature of the teaching of economics in Europe (Baumol 1995). However, the faculties of economics of the *Universidade Nova de Lisboa* and, to a lesser extent, of the *Universidade Católica Portuguesa*, adopted the American pattern *ab initio*. Many visiting professors have come from universities in the USA, and an important percentage of their own professors have gained their PhD degree in those universities. Most bibliographic references in research texts and textbooks are to North American mainstream economic literature. Theoretical heterodoxy has been given little attention. During the 1980s, Robert J. Barro's *Macroeconomics* became the fundamental textbook used in the teaching of macroeconomics. This demonstrates the influence of the North American theoretical fashion; for example, in rational expectations theory and monetarist views.

The making of the profession of economist

The emergence and increasing recognition of economists as a social and professional group were important consequences of the process described here, both in the research and the teaching of economics. However, before 1945, as well as during the two following decades, the productivity of the educational system remained very low. The absolute and relative number of students graduating in economics was quite small and, surprisingly, decreased during the 1950s. Their number only rose significantly after 1969. By 1981, the last year for which information is available, there were 470 new graduates, a total approximately eighteen times greater than in 1955 (see Appendix, Table 9.4).

The small scale of the educational and research systems meant that a limited number of economists was involved. As mentioned before, research activities were basically performed by the few professors of the universities. Until 1974 there were hardly any professional researchers. At the same time, secondary schools had no economic themes in their curricula, with the sole exception of commercial schools, where the teaching of economics was elementary. However, the scene has changed since then, as economists have been hired to teach at grammar schools as specific economic curricula were introduced.

Even so, the small number of economists during these decades did not prevent them from gaining increasing social visibility in Portuguese society. In 1955, for the first time, an economist graduating from the *ISCEF* joined a cabinet of the *Estado Novo* as Minister of Finance (and some state secretaries and top officials were also economists). Public institutions started to recognize the necessity of hiring economic experts and the number of economists working in public administration rose significantly in the 1960s concurrently with the widening dimensions and increasing complexity of the Portuguese public sector. Since then, it has become common to look for expert advisers in matters of economy and finance (such as the Commission on Fiscal Reform at the end of the 1950s). The strengthening of Portugal's integration into the world economy – that is, when it became a member of several international economic institutions (OEEC in 1948, EPU in 1950, EFTA in 1959, the IMF and the World Bank in 1961, GATT in 1962) – and the need to use a technical, specialized language to participate in their activities reinforced that trend.

Economists began to be in great demand in the 1960s in the private sector, in banks and in industrial firms integrated in economic groups set up after World War II. The *Companhia União Fabril*, the head of an economic group installed in banking and in the chemical branch, had a leading role in the practice of hiring economists along with the traditional technical staff of engineers, jurists and accountants. However, a study produced in the mid-1960s showed that only 6 per cent of the industrialists heading the largest manufacturing enterprises had a degree in economics (Makler 1969: 143). By 1989, the last year for which information is available, that proportion had risen to 9 per cent (Silva 1989: 37).

Before the war, the 'commercialists' – the traditional name for economists – were represented by a not very influential trade union at national level. During the war and in the disturbed postwar years, economists, as a group, demonstrated some social dynamism. Scientific associations, such as the short-lived *Sociedade de Ciências Económicas* (Economic Science Society) or even associations for political intervention (like the *Comissão de Economistas do Movimento de Unidade Democrática* (Economists' Committee of the United Democratic Movement) were created, in 1941 and 1949 respectively. By then, the professional trade union became more active, setting up training courses and publishing a bulletin. The efforts to promote their profession went further, once that union fought to become a professional organization, like the other traditional intellectual professions, such as lawyers and physicians. The government would never allow it, arguing that most economists were wage-earners and so lacked the social status of those professions.

The *Associação Portuguesa de Economistas – APEC* (Portuguese Economists' Association) was one, among other professional organizations, to emerge later, in 1976. At the beginning of the 1990s it had more than 3,500 members. Their national meetings have become increasingly publicized.

The increase in the number of specialized publications and the appearance, in 1954, in the daily newspapers – namely, in the *Diário de Lisboa* – of specific pages devoted to economic affairs were also important contributions to the economists' identification as a professional group in the postwar years. A similar importance may certainly be attributed to the organization of the congresses of economists, which gathered together a significant number of academic and non-academic professionals. The first took place in Angola in 1955; the second, the most important one, took place in Lisbon in 1957. Debates focused basically on economic policy; presentations of results of economic research were rare. Especially after 1957 it was clear that economists and no longer engineers, were the authors of the most sophisticated developmental strategies, inverting the traditional trends of the early decades of the twentieth century.

Since the 1980s the presence of economists has increased further. A specialized press on economic matters has emerged as well as a large quantity of economic information on newspapers and on TV stations. This has helped to raise the demand for economists and their public reputation as a professional group.

The increasing dependence of politics upon economic discourse has strengthened the social influence of economists. The growing involvement of economists – mainly professors – in public affairs to legitimize the conflicting strategic views in Portuguese society is internal to the present working of the political system.

Concluding remarks

It is clear from the above that Portugal experienced, after 1945, a process of modernization of economics parallel to modern economic growth and to the concomitant internationalization of the economy, first in the 1960s but, above all, in the 1980s. As far as economic theory and doctrines are concerned, modernization meant the minimizing of indigenous original approaches (mainly corporative economics) and the adoption of the same patterns of economic discourse as existed abroad. The impact of these patterns was never homogeneous. Ideas were introduced and diffused after some transformation according to the cultural and strategic particularities of Portuguese society during the last half century.

The educational apparatus was conditioned by political and social conceptions of a voluntarist, elitist character. The late expansion of the faculties of economics, the small number of graduates and the absence of the teaching of economics at the intermediate level of education, are an apparent outcome of those conditionings, not to mention the very recent introduction of postgraduate education and the spread of the PhD in economics.

The research apparatus underwent three phases of evolution. Until 1945 it was either absent or short-lived; in the next three and a half decades, there was a slow expansion of those organizations; since the 1980s they have grown in number, and their international contacts have become more regular. As a result, only in this period has a true scientific community been installed, thanks also to the cultural and political freedom brought about in 1974, when the crude, sectarian system of cooption of professors was dismantled.

Formal and informal networks of Portuguese researchers have been created only very recently. However, the level of mutual citation among them remains very low and most of their work is still ignored by the international scientific community. The habit of producing their scientific results in the English language is a still more recent development.

In association with the spread of modern economics, economists have emerged as a social group since the 1960s. Two main reasons may account for this. Firstly, modern economic growth, which raised the demand for their expertise both in the public as well as in the private sector was again apparent after 1960. Second, there was the conscious development of an active strategy of self-promotion.

Modernization and the internationalization of economics, as well as the social arrival of economists, was slow and in many respects late. This was inevitable as modern economic growth in Portugal dates only from the 1950s and the relatively successful process of catching up did not prevent Portugal from remaining a semi-peripherical economy and society. In spite of that, there was a parallel process of successful convergence in economics, with no diverging periods.

Appendix

Table 9.1 Grants for scientific research*[†]

Year	Total	Economics
1940	90	0
1941	91	0
1942	100	0
1943	94	0
1944	84	0
1945	102	0
1946	122	0
1947	118	7
1948	122	8
1949	96	8
1950	121	8
1951	116	9
1952	125	10
1953	149	3
1954	138	5

Source: *Anuário Estatístico*

Notes
* Public sector only.
† Statistics do not include data for the period after 1954.

Table 9.2 Economic scientific publications by authors in Portuguese organizations*[†]

Year	Publications
1980	1
1981	3
1982	1
1983	0
1984	0
1985	0

Table 9.2 cont.

Year	Publications
1986	6
1987	5
1988	4
1989	6
1990	6
1991	5
1992	10
1993	14
1994	12

Source: Mata (1995)

Notes
* Publications in reviews included in Social Scisearch only.
† Papers only. Small notes and other publications not included.

Table 9.3 Economic scientific publications in Western Europe, 1980–94*

Country	Publications	No. of publications per head of population
Austria	870	111.5
Belgium	1,633	165.0
Denmark	899	176.3
Finland	808	161.6
France	2,942	51.6
Germany	1,502	18.7
Greece	247	24.7
Ireland	1,223	349.4
Italy	2,195	38.4
Luxembourg	157	392.5
Netherlands	2,373	158.2
Norway	624	145.1
Portugal	89	8.4
Spain	445	11.4
Sweden	1,321	157.3
Switzerland	1,215	189.3
UK	21,925	382.0

Source: Mata (1995)

Note
* Publications in reviews included in Social Scisearch only.

Table 9.4 Graduates in higher schools and universities*[†]

Year	Total	Economics and business administration	Economics and business administration (%)	'Modern economics'[†]	'Modern economics' (%)
1940	1,060	109	10.3	•	•
1941	1,123	22	2	•	•
1942	989	•	•	•	•
1943	1,143	59	5.2	•	•
1944	1,219	47	3.9	•	•
1945	1,214	62	5.1	•	•
1946	1,293	63	4.9	•	•
1947	1,281	71	5.5	•	•
1948	1,407	53	3.8	•	•
1949	1,270	95	7.5	0	0
1950	1,369	107	7.8	0	0
1951	1,337	91	6.8	0	0
1952	1,451	80	5.5	0	0
1953	1,406	53	3.8	0	0
1954	1,299	56	4.3	4	0.3
1955	1,959	55	2.8	26	1.3
1956	1,975	46	2.3	•	•
1957	2,095	43	2.1	23	1.1
1958	2,237	65	2.9	•	•
1959	2,199	64	2.9	32	1.5
1960	2,263	75	3.3	•	•
1961	2,063	67	3.2	36	1.7
1962	1,994	73	3.7	•	•
1963	2,278	77	3.4	58	2.5
1964	2,164	72	3.3	•	•
1965	2,704	100	3.7	77	2.8
1966	2,542	120	4.7	•	•
1967	2,959	101	3.4	73	2.5
1968	2,782	150	5.4	•	•
1969	2,406	156	6.5	114	4.7
1970	3,321	202	6.1	135	4.1
1971	3,068	227	7.4	166	5.4
1972	3,082	271	8.8	159	5.2
1973	3,613	512	14.2	244	6.8
1974	6,414	569	8.9	261	4.1
1975	4,339	1,007	23.2	388	8.9
1976	9,676	1,255	13	635	6.6
1977	9,723	759	7.8	418	4.3
1978	12,624	1,042	8.3	554	4.4
1979	10,551	480	4.5	224	2.1
1980	10,101	997	9.9	415	4.1
1981	10,942	1,162	10.6	470	4.2

Source: *Anuário Estatístico* and *Estatística da Educação*

Notes
* Official statistics do not include specific data for the period after 1981.
† 'Modern economics' refers to graduates in economics after the curricula which were introduced ir 1949.
• Information not available or without significance.

Notes

1 For detailed bibliographical references covering the period 1945–54, see Bastien (1989), where systematic analysis on this subject is provided.
2 For a comprehensive analysis and bibliographical references to Marxist economics, see Bastien (1993).

References

Abreu, L. S. (1948) 'Algumas notas sobre as teorias de Keynes', *Revista de Economia*, 1, 3.
——(1949) 'Política fiscal e Keynesianismo', *Revista de Economia*, 2, 1.
Alarcão, J. (1948) 'Estimativa do nível de vida da população operária portuguesa', *Revista de Economia*, 1, 1.
Barbosa, A. M. P. (1943) 'A economia do ponto de vista positivo e do ponto de vista teleológico', *Economia e Finanças*, 11.
——(1950) *Economia I*, 2 vols, Lisbon, mimeographed.
——(1984) 'A reabilitação do quantitativo na Economia', *Boletim de Ciências Económicas*, 27.
Barros, H. (1978) 'A doutrina cooperativa e as ciências sociais', *Estudos em homenagem ao Prof. Doutor J. J. Texeira Ribeiro*, Coimbra.
Bastien, C. (1989) 'Para a história das ideias económicas no Portugal comtemporâneo: a crise dos anos 1945–1954', Unpublished PhD thesis, Universidade Técnica de Lisboa.
——(1993) 'Marxism, labour movement and culture in Portugal', *Estudos de Economia*, 13, 2.
Baumol, W. J. (1995) 'What's different about European economics?' *Kyklos* 48.
Beleza, J. P. (1955) *Teoria do Juro – a controvérsia Keynesiana*, Coimbra.
Castro, A. (1945) *Alguns aspectos da agricultura nacional*, Coimbra.
——(1948) 'Origem e destino da teoria subjectiva do valor', *Revista de Economia,* 1, 3.
——(1949) 'A indústria nacional e a expansão do mercado interno', *Indústria Portuguesa*, 252.
——(1983) *Lições de Economia*, Lisbon.
Cardoso, J. P. (1949) *Uma escola corporativa portuguesa*, Lisbon.
Correia, J. D. A. (1952) *Elementos de planificação económica*, Lisbon.
Costa, A. M. S. (1947) *Sobre alguns problemas da teoria das cadeias de mercado*, Lisbon.
Cunhal, A. (1964) *Rumo à Vitória* (place of publication not indicated).
——(1966) *A questão agrária em Portugal*, Rio de Janeiro.
Dias, J. F. (1945) *Linha de rumo*, Lisbon.
Freire, J. R. (1945) *Estudos de demografia portuguesa*, Lisbon.
Guedes, A. M. (1944–46) 'Notas para um curso de Economia Política', *Economia e Finanças*, 12–14.
Leal, A. C. and Falcão, J. M. S. (1952) 'Sobre a observação estatística das finanças públicas', *Revista de Economia*, 5, 4.
Leite, J. P. C. (1933) *Ensaio sobre a teoria das crises económicas*, Coimbra.
Makler, H. M. (1969) *A 'elite' industrial portuguesa*, Lisbon.
Marques, H. (1934) *Economia Política*, Coimbra.
Martinez, P. S. (1960) *Sentido económico do corporativismo,* Lisbon.
Martins, R. (1970) *Caminho de país novo*, Lisbon.
Mata, J. (1995) 'A investigação em economia em Portugal: 1980-1994', *Economia*, 19, 2.

Moura F. P. (1950) 'Reformas de estrutura (introdução a um estudo de economia)', *Revista do Gabinete de Estudos Corporativos* 1.

——(1964) *Lições de Economia*, Lisbon.

——(1969a) *Análise económica da conjuntura*, Lisbon.

——(1969b) *Por onde vai a Economia Portuguesa?* Lisbon.

Moura, F. P., Pinto, L. M. Teixeira and Nunes, M. J. (1954) 'Estrutura da economia portuguesa', *Revista do Centro de Estudos Económicos*, 14.

Murteira, B. (1957) *Econometria. I curso. Apontamentos baseados nas lições do Prof. Bento Murteira, proferidas no ano lectivo de 1955/56*, Lisbon, mimeographed.

Netto, A. L. (1936) *Elementos de Economia Política*, Lisbon.

Nunes, A. S. (1952) 'Crise social e reforma da empresa', *Revista do Gabinete de Estudos Corporativos*, 10–11.

Nunes, M. J. (1964–65) *Economia III, notas para estudo*, Lisbon, mimeographed.

——(1956) *Rendimento Nacional e Equilíbrio Orçamental*, Lisbon.

——(1986) 'Algumas notas sobre o Keynesianismo em Portugal', in E. S. Ferreira and J. L. Cardoso (eds) *O cinquentenário da Teoria Geral de Keynes*, Lisbon.

Oliveira, A. A. (1947) *Portugal perante as tendências da economia mundial*, Lisbon.

Pereira, A. G. (1935) 'As novas exigências da economia política', *Economia e Finanças*, 3.

Pereira, A. R. (1954) 'Portugal e o quadro das estruturas económicas subdesenvolvidas', *Revista de Economia*, 7, 1.

Pereira, R. S. (1953) 'Perspectivas da planificação económica', *Revista do Gabinete de Estudos Corporativos*, 13.

Pinto, L. M. T. (1952) 'Algumas notas sobre o equilibrio Keynesiano', *Economia e Finanças*, 20.

——(1956) *Alguns aspectos da teoria do crescimento*, Lisbon.

Pires, F. L. (1973) 'O Estado pós-corporativo', *Revista da Corporação dos Transportes e Turismo*, 2.

Ribeiro, J. J. T. (1934) *Teoria económica dos monopólios*, Coimbra: Coimbra Editora.

Rijckeghem, W. and Barreiros, L. (1979) *Employment and Basic Needs in Portugal*, Geneva.

Rodrigues, O. M. (1947) *O problema dos orçamentos familiares*, Lisbon.

Sérgio, A. (1947) *Alocução aos socialistas*, Lisbon.

——(1985) *Sobre o sistema cooperativista*, Lisbon.

Silva, F. G. (1953) 'A evolução da empresa – III', *Indústria Portuguesa*, 306.

Silva, M. (1989) *Empresários e gestores da indústria em Portugal*, vol. 1, Lisbon, mimeographed.

Sousa, A. (1950) 'O Keynesianismo e as suas directrizes', in E. Roll, *História do Pensamento Económico,* vol. 2, Lisbon.

Tintner, G. and Murteira, B. (1959) 'Um modelo "input–output" simplificado para a economia portuguesa', *Economia e Finanças*, 27, 1.

Ulrich, R. E. (1948) *Economia Política (circulação)*, Lisbon.

Veiga, A. J. M. (1944) *A economia corporativa e o problema dos preços*, Lisbon.

Xavier, A. P. (1973) *Economia de mercado e justiça social*, Lisbon.

10 The development of economic studies and research in Spain (1939–95)

An overview[1]

Salvador Almenar

A complete analysis of the most recent developments in economics in various European countries requires a broad vision, a merging of approaches traditionally isolated in separate special fields, such as the history of economic analysis, the study of the international transfer of knowledge, the sociology of research (professionalization, organization), the examination of the policy-making process, among others. An extensive literature (e.g. Eagly 1968; Albertone and Masoero 1994; Colander and Coats 1989; Hall 1989; Coats 1987, 1994, 1997) has posited the suitability of treating internal and external factors as complementary in the explanation of scientific development. This chapter forms part of this approach.

Previous studies on the contemporary history of Spanish economic thought do not abound. Most of them are monographic studies by individual economists, but there are few general or sector overviews (Gallotti 1958; Velarde 1974, 1990 and 1993). I have tried to formulate a general interpretation with the aid of varied information, generally quantitative but hitherto scattered or not available, on essential aspects of the process (teaching, research, spread of economic ideas, specialization patterns, internationalization and so on).

The chapter is divided into two parts preceded by a brief introduction, in accordance with the academic criterion, although they coincide broadly with the fundamental stages of the peculiar political and cultural history of Spain in the last sixty years. The first part, devoted to the period between the end of the Civil War (1939) and the transformation of education and research in the 1970s, deals with the process of forming a scientific community and the settling of the principal styles together with theoretical and doctrinal orientations. The second part, which studies the last two decades, analyses the changes in teaching and research that have meant a rapid – though still limited – process of internationalization. As a background to both periods, there are two cultural environments and two different political systems, from the Franco regime (1939–75) to democratic normality from 1977–78 onwards.

A silver age of Spanish economics, 1923–39

The nineteenth century produced a heavy intellectual dependence of Spanish economists on French 'optimistic' economic literature, which ended up by sterilizing, to a large extent, the process of institutionalization of economics in the universities.

During the first third of the twentieth century the study of economics in Spain was limited to the subjects of political economy and public finance in the law faculties of twelve public universities. Other aspects of economics were taught in colleges of commerce (then considered to be non-university professional studies), in agricultural and industrial engineering courses, and in the combined studies of economics and law at the Deusto centre in Bilbao. The first faculty of economics was founded in 1943, after the Civil War (1936–39).

Between twenty and twenty-five teachers, half of whom were professors, covered the teaching requirements of economics. The professors were government employees with tenure for life. According to my estimate, in 1936 over 80 per cent of the professors of economics, or members of the three research institutes, had specialized in economics at foreign universities, mainly German ones, thanks to the public grants distributed by the Committee for Extension of Studies.[2]

The organization of the scientific communities was hierarchical, in 'schools' imitating the German ones. The school directed by Professor Antonio Flores de Lemus (1876–1941) was the hegemonic group, and its scientific production was characterized by a not anti-marginalist historicism, the use of statistical instruments (correlation) in the exploration of hypotheses, and priority in research applied to the Spanish economy. Flores received training in Tübingen and Berlin with W. Lexis, A. Wagner and L. Bortkkiewicz. This triangle illustrates a conception that accepts the utilization of some marginalist theories but with subordination to the historic, institutional and statistical analysis (Velarde 1961, 1990). The works of Flores's disciples embrace a spectrum that goes from the strictest new historicism ('realistic school') to the econometrics based on marginalist models. However, the Flores School did not favour the diffusion in Spain of the marginalist and neoclassical economics during the first third of the twentieth century.

As well as Flores, other small groups or personalities developed (J. M. Zumalacárregui, A. Bernis, L. Olariaga, G. Bernácer, R. Perpiñá, O. Fernández) all of them with a high level of knowledge of the principal contributions of foreign economic literature, with slight but appreciable repercussion of their work abroad. In the 1930s there were three Spanish members in the Econometric Society (Flores de Lemus, Fernández Baños who presented some papers in the European section, and J. Vandellós). Altogether they made an extraordinary effort of academic professionalization, as true pioneers. Both the *Review of National Economy* (1919–35) and *Spanish Economy* (1933–36) were mixed journals (academic and business, both in Spanish), and there were very few publications on economic subjects. The university professors held high social prestige. Several professors of economics were advisers to the government, ministers of finance and financial directors.

The forming of a scientific community, 1939–75

The academic consequences of the dictatorship

The consolidation of General Francisco Franco's dictatorship (1939–75) after the Spanish Civil War altered the cultural environment in general and, in particular, the development of economics as a field of scientific activity, as it reduced the academic power of the Flores de Lemus 'school' (many of its members were removed from their posts or exiled) and because it radically reorientated the previous scientific policy by abolishing the Committee for Extension of Studies, but public institutes of education and research and the first academic journals were created.

Two sub-periods can be distinguished. During the first (1943/44–1956/59), both the academic studies and the profession of economist were founded and consolidated, in a highly regulated academic milieu (Montoro 1981) and a cultural environment of isolation, while the Spanish economy experienced low growth rates and the predominance of agriculture. In the second sub-period (1956/59–1973/75) there was a relaxation of the most isolationist cultural and economic aspects of the Franco regime, and with the general process of high economic growth and industrialization there was a notable expansion in economics courses, in centres (faculties) and lecturers, and some changes in scientific production. Let us look at the most important facts.

Degree courses in economics[3]

The most important initial process was the creation and development of the first Faculty of Political and Economic Sciences in Madrid. In the syllabus for the economic sciences section, established by the government, the teaching of economics (economic theory, econometrics, economic history, economic structure, economic policy, public finance and taxation systems) represented the main emphasis (Table 10.1), with a presence of law, accountancy and business

Table 10.1 Subjects in syllabuses (percentage of class time devoted to subjects) and professors by chairs

Subjects	1944 syllabus	1953 syllabus	Professors in economics faculties, 1974
Economic theory	17.5	12.0	11.9
Economic history	9.8	5.0	8.3
Applied economics	24.6	25.0	27.8
Mathematics, statistics & econometrics	16.5	17.5	12.9
Accounting	4.9	7.5	6.5
Business administration	2.9	10.0	9.2
Politics and sociology	8.3	7.5	7.5
Law	15.5	15.0	15.8

Sources: Tabulated from *Decreto 7 julio 1944 (Plan de estudios 1944)*;
Decreto 11 agosto 1953 (Plan de estudios 1953); and MEC (1974)

administration. The guidelines (the syllabuses of 1944 and 1953) determined the training of economists until 1973, and at the same time the long-term orientation of the specialist fields of the scientific community (Table 10.1, last column).

The decay of the first economic research institutes from 1945 was determined by the creation of the faculty, and the scientific community of economists was concentrated almost exclusively in the University of Madrid, and after 1955 in the faculties of Bilbao and Barcelona; moreover, ten more faculties were created by 1974. The growth of centres was a consequence of the demand for studies. In the period 1943–73 the number of students multiplied by twenty (from about 1,000 students to more than 20,000), while the total number of lecturers in all economic subjects multiplied by ten (from about fifty to about 500).

The training of a scientific community

The first scientific community after the Civil War was formed by about twenty or thirty professors and lecturers in political economy in the faculties of law, and in higher schools of industrial and agricultural engineering (Naharro 1950). Most of them had legal training but with postgraduate studies abroad.

The new regime created the Institute of Political Studies and the Sancho de Moncada Economics Institute. The former organized postgraduate courses from 1941 to 1943, which were replaced by Higher Economics Studies (1943 and 1944) given by H. F. von Stackelberg. It also contributed to the spread of foreign economic literature through a succession of journals such as the *Revista de Economía Política* (Journal of Political Economy, 1945–82). The Sancho de Moncada Economics Institute was the publisher of the journal *Anales de Economía* (Annals of Economics, 1941–75) and a collection of books by Spanish economists up to 1948. The transfer of some members of both institutions to the professorships of the new faculty (and the death of Stackelberg in 1946) caused both to languish from 1947 onwards. There was a high degree of identity between the directors of the Sancho de Moncada and those of a rhetorically corporative official government body (the National Economic Council, where the first estimations of the national accounts were made).

The academic career system was regulated in minute detail. Doctoral studies abroad were stopped until practically the 1960s (in an isolationist context) and, except for the first years, consisted almost exclusively in the reading of a doctoral thesis.

The system of access to non-permanent teaching posts depended on the discretional criteria of the professor, while the competitive exams for selection to professorships still valued certain teaching and rhetorical skills in relation to merits previously acquired (publications). It was a hierarchical system in which 'loyalty' could prevail over 'merit'. The scientific community developed according to a dual scheme depending on the specialized subject and on the methodological styles of the 'schools', at times closed but resulting in a high degree of doctrinal pluralism.

During the academic expansion of the 1960s the universities resorted to very young lecturers in the process of training, so that in 1974 it is estimated that only 30 per cent of lecturers and collaborators were doctors (see distribution by groups of categories in Table 10.2).

Structure of scientific communication

The flows of scientific communication were completely asymmetrical. The input flow of economic ideas from abroad was re-established with difficulty after the Civil War due to restrictions on the import of books and journals, but functioned more fully after 1945 (with the exception of those publications which contained criticism of the regime or diffused Marxist, socialist or other ideas). On the other hand, Spanish authors did not publish in foreign journals and the foreign projection of Spanish journals was negligible until the 1970s.

Scientific production was concentrated, in the period 1940–59, particularly in three leading Spanish journals with academic format: *Anales de Economía* (Annals of Economics, 1941–75), *Moneda y Crédito* (Money and Credit, 1942–) and *Revista de Economía Política* (Journal of Political Economy, 1945–82), with contents of a general nature, while other journals such as the *Boletín de Estudios Económicos* (Bulletin of Economic Studies, 1946–), *De Economía* (On Economics, 1948–77), and the *Revista de Derecho Financiero y Hacienda Pública* (Journal of Financial Law and Public Finance, 1951–) were more specialized in content.

The journals were published entirely in Spanish, and the contributions by foreign economists were above all translations of papers already published. But they paid close attention to the currents of economic thought abroad, as can be appreciated through the reviews of books. In *Anales de Economía*, 67 per cent of the books reviewed were by foreign authors in the period 1941–62, and this became 94 per cent in 1963–67, which has been considered the abandonment of the 'autarchical' economic thought model (Velarde 1971). My estimate for the journal *Moneda y Crédito* reveals, on the other hand, an increase in reviews of books in Spanish (and of translations into Spanish of original books in English) (Table 10.3).

Table 10.2 Professors and teachers in economics (percentage of distribution by groups)

	1963	1974
1 Professors and associates/lecturers (with tenure)	28.2	12.4
2 Assistants/lecturers (without tenure)		
2.1 Doctors	15.8	16.1
2.2 Graduates	52.2	36.8
3 Teaching assistants		34.8
4 Special	3.8	

Sources: *INE* (1966), *INE* (1976).

Table 10.3 Language of books reviewed (percentage in *Moneda y Crédito*)

	1941–51	1959–61
English	52.6	25.7
French	15.7	12.5
Italian	2.4	4.6
German	3.1	3.9
Other		3.2
Spanish	20.1	31.8
Spanish trans. from English	4.1	10.4
Spanish trans. from French	0.0	5.0
Spanish trans. from Italian	0.7	1.1
Spanish trans. from German	0.3	1.8
Total of books reviewed	(293)	(280)

Source: Tabulated by author from indexes

The two most important publishers until 1960 were the Sancho de Moncada Institute which put out a collection of books by Spanish economists, and Aguilar Publishers, directed by Professor Manuel de Torres, which published a special collection of books with a Keynesian orientation and which were dominant in translations from books in English (Table 10.4). Also other publishers (*Revista de Derecho Privado, Revista de Occidente* and the Mexican *Fondo de Cultura Económica*) constituted windows on the outside world, with very little delay after the appearance of the originals.

In the 1960s and 1970s new specialized journals appeared, such as *Información Comercial Española* (Spanish Commercial Information, 1959–) and *Hacienda Pública Española* (Spanish Public Finance, 1971–), or general ones such as *Revista Española de Economía* (Spanish Economic Review, 1971–) with monographic sections that included many translated articles. The publishing scene was completely transformed. The earlier publishing houses

Table 10.4 Books on economics by original language, Aguilar Press (percentage)

Original Language	1949	1963
English	69.4	51.9
German	5.6	3.8
French	2.8	5.1
Swedish	8.3	3.8
Danish	5.6	2.5
Italian	2.8	5.1
Spanish	5.6	27.8
Total published books	(36)	(79)

Source: Tabulated by author from the accumulative catalogues

disappeared and others arose (Tecnos, Gredos, Labor, Oikos-Tau, Ariel, Alianza) with mainly translated books.

The textbooks used in teaching were mostly by Spanish authors in the period 1943–59. From the 1960s onwards internationally successful texts were introduced (Lipsey, Samuelson, Henderson and Quant, Ackley, Matthews).

The development of professional economists

The economists produced by the faculties up to 1973 found no special employment difficulties, joining private firms and the public administration as advisers in three bodies of civil servants: as commercial experts, state economists and in the financial inspectorate. From 1961 onwards, as a consequence of the process of economic expansion and industrialization, the demand for economists by private firms grew much more rapidly. In 1974 the occupational structure of economists in Barcelona was as follows: 74 per cent employed in firms, 13 per cent freelance, 7.5 per cent in teaching (at all levels) and 7.1 per cent in the public administration (*Colegio de Economistas de Cataluña* 1976).

This trend generated a growing tension between the demand for graduates in business administration and the training given in the faculties (more orientated towards macroeconomic advisers), which the government attempted to solve with the 1973 syllabus reform.

Analytical orientations and political influence of economic thought

The most important trends in economic thought were conditioned in general by the specialized subjects of the lecturers, although the main activity of nearly all the academic economists of the period was applied analysis of the Spanish economy. There were few original contributions to theory, and unlike in Italy or Portugal, there were not even any attempts, beyond mere initial propaganda, to develop or apply economic analysis in a 'falangist' or corporativist direction. On the other hand, there was a constant effort to establish and consolidate a basic set of analytical instruments and evaluation criteria which were already common in other countries, and to apply them or adapt them to the conditions of the Spanish economy.

Marginalist and neoclassical economics[4]

The most important transformation of the postwar period was the new attention paid to economic theory, as a consequence of the loss of influence of the moderate historicist tendency of the Flores de Lemus School and the influence of H. von Stackelberg as the teacher in Madrid of a group of Spanish economists at the Political Studies Institute. However, the lack of tradition and the cultural isolation caused the original theoretical work of Spanish economists to be generally unimportant until the 1970s, taking the form of diffusion in textbooks.

In this task of consolidation we should mention the influence of J. M. Zumalacárregui (1879–1956), one of the first Spanish marginalist economists, in the teaching of his two important pupils J. Castañeda and M. de Torres. Later he published an essay on Pareto in 1949 and specialized in transport economics, giving some doctorate courses in the new faculty in Madrid.

Stackelberg's stay in Madrid from 1943 to 1946 acted as a catalyst, because it helped to complete the advanced training of the Political Studies Institute group of economists (Vergara, Ullastres, Alvarez, Paredes, Castañeda and Piera) who helped him in the new revised edition of his *Grundzüge* and its translation into Spanish (Stackelberg 1946a). Stackelberg himself contributed with some publications to Spanish journals, among them a vigorous criticism of the Keynesian revolution (Stackelberg 1946b; Harmes-Liedtke 1992; Velarde 1996).

The main contribution on microeconomics was that of José Castañeda (1900–87). His doctoral thesis, presented in 1936, was not published until 1945; it is an econometric study of the demand for tobacco in Spain, similar to the work of H. Schultz on sugar. In the area of teaching he was influential for many years (1945–68) both as lecturer in microeconomics and indirectly through his book *Lessons in Economic Theory* (first published in 1946). Despite Stackelberg's enormous influence, the *Lessons* are in the Walrasian tradition, with notable traces of Pareto, Amoroso and Hicks. His doctoral course (in the 1940s) on Higher Economic Analysis was based on *Value and Capital*.

The standpoint of Valentín A. Alvarez (1891–1982) is closer to Marshall's partial equilibrium. As well as writing an *Introduction to Political Economy* (published in 1944), he devoted some articles to the analysis of market morphology, and to the development of an analytical instrument that he called the 'market indicator', which is the quotient between the derivatives of the functions of demand and supply (Sánchez 1991: 133–55).

Luís Olariaga (1885–1976) was a second focus of the spread of neoclassical economic theory, situating himself defensively against the Keynesian literature of the 1940s and 1950s. In numerous articles in the journal *Moneda y Crédito* and in his book *Money* (published in 1947–54) he incorporates the monetary theses of traditional English literature (Robertson, the Keynes of the *Treatise*, Sayers and so on) and the new critique by Albert Hahn of Keynes's *General Theory*.

It must be added that Olariaga's defensive position found outstanding support in the arguments of the so-called Freibourg School (Röpke, Eucken).[5] This neo-liberal resurgence in the 1940s and 1950s, in which the principal economists with the best theoretical preparation participate, can be interpreted as a resistance to the 'autarchical' economic and political culture propounded by the Franco regime and consisting of heavy intervention in quantities and prices.

Until the 1960s the publication of microeconomic theory by Spanish authors was rare. The exceptions are J. Castañeda, V. A. Alvarez, M. Paredes, E. Chacón, F. Bermejo, G. Pérez de Armiñan and J. M. de la Torre, who devoted more attention to the theory of imperfect markets. Translations of recent contributions to the theory of demand, welfare economics and other subjects were regularly published. But this low productivity may be a consequence of the lack of tradition, as a witness of the time remarked, because 'we studied Keynes before

Marshall' (Beltrán 1981: 15). The perception of a foreign intellectual climate unfavourable to the logic of the market also had an influence.

From Keynesianism to macroeconomics[6]

The initial diffusion of the *General Theory* was delayed by the Civil War (1936–39). The reception of Keynesian ideas (in a broad sense) was more important in terms of the theory of economic policy and constituted one of the most abundant specialized subjects in Spanish economic literature until the mid-1950s.

The academic world viewed with suspicion Germán Bernácer's (1883–65) contributions on monetary theory and cycle theory in the 1920s and 1930s. He was considered an outsider. Denis H. Robertson (1940) claimed for Bernácer the merit of anticipating many ideas of the *General Theory*. Robertson's favourable judgement and the fact that Bernácer was partly critical of some of Keynes's positions in his last book encouraged the publication of a number of his articles in foreign journals, constituting a unique case of the 'internationalization' of Spanish economic literature.[7]

The principal works of Manuel de Torres (1903–60) published after 1940 represent contributions to, or applications of, Keynesian literature. The *General Theory of the Multiplier* (published in 1943), is a review of the question and an attempt at a dynamic synthesis in a similar direction to Samuelson's multiplier–accelerator relation. The remaining works are situated on the plane of the relations between Keynesian economic policy and theory, from the theoretical influence of the Danish economist J. Pedersen and of the German E. Schneider: the *Theory of Social Policy* (published in 1949) and *Theory and Practice of Economic Policy* (published in 1955), and most of the volume *Judgement on Current Spanish Economic Policy* (published in 1956). Keynesian theory is the basis for introducing 'rationality' into economic policy in a technocratic view, so that his work has a critical significance with regard to the government's unsystematic economic policy, even though Torres was ideologically sympathetic to the Franco regime. To this should be added his important initiative and coordination in 1945 of the preparation of the first National Accounts of Spain as an instrument of analysis and the quantitative basis of economic policy (Schwartz 1977).

The economist Joan Sardá (1910–95), trained at the LSE in the 1930s, was one of the focal points for the direct diffusion of the *General Theory*, whose ideas he considered compatible with Lerner's contributions to the theory of control and welfare, and in part with some critiques of planning by the Freibourg School of economists.

The first contributions by E. de Figueroa (1911–82) are in the forefront of the diffusion of the first Keynesian literature, such as his doctoral thesis on economic policy and business cycles (published in 1948), and the extensive *Theories of Economic Cycles* (published in 1947). In the 1950s and 1960s he adapted Keynesian and Kaleckian guidelines to explain the workings of the Spanish economy with regard to the relative scarcity of 'capital' and the existence of 'structural' inflation.

There was also a broad treatment of Keynesian policy (especially of the ideas of W. Beveridge, who gave some lectures in Madrid in 1946), and scrutiny of the political and economic processes of stabilization through taxation and monetary policy in Great Britain and the United States.

In the early 1950s there was an interesting debate in the journal *De Economía* on the 'possible application to Spain of the General Theory', among young economists trained in the new faculty as disciples of M. de Torres. In 1951 Enrique Fuentes Quintana (b. 1924) presented a review of the matter heavily influenced by the work of L. Klein on the Keynesian revolution, and by the structural analysis of the Spanish economy by R. Perpiñá Grau. All participants in the debate acknowledged the importance of Keynes's contribution on the crisis theory, but the subsequent debate focused the employment problem in Spain as a consequence of the 'lack of capital' or underdevelopment. Shortly afterwards this group initiated a public proposal of economic reforms in the volume *Notes on Spanish Economic Policy* (published in 1954), propounding a progressive taxation reform, budgetary control, the liberalization of the degree of industrial and financial monopoly, or the opening up of the Spanish economy abroad. This group agreed with M. de Torres on important points. For all of them, Keynesianism became an argument for criticizing, 'rationalizing' and reforming the government's unsystematic and interventionist economic policy.

The coordinated action of various ideas developed by some Spanish Keynesian economists found a favourable opportunity in the period 1957–59, inspiring the 'Stabilization Plan' of 1959, which would have enormous importance in the subsequent development of the economy and politics of Spain.

But the Keynesian academic literature turned progressively into macroeconomic literature in the mid-1950s, and this transformation, which also implied a certain distancing of academics from the initial political implications of Keynesian theory, also coincided with a generation change in the teaching of economics and with the arrival of some economists with postgraduate study abroad. It is almost symbolic to identify this process of renovation with J. R. Lasuén, R. Trías Fargas and L. A. Rojo.

The pages of economic journals devoted space to the new theories of the cycles, but above all there was a persistent and more substantial reception of the theories of economic growth and development that lasted until the 1970s, in a favourable context with the process of Spain's economic growth from 1960 onwards. Previously, José R. Lasuén (b. 1932) had specialized in theory and policy of regional development, an aspect of great importance in a country with notable economic and territorial disparities. Also, he had published some of the first studies on Keynesian economic growth models.

Luís A. Rojo (b. 1934) with *Keynes and Current Macroeconomic Thought* (published in 1965), gave an updated overview of the macroeconomic literature subsequent to the neoclassical synthesis. During the 1960s Rojo also introduced the IS–LM standardized macroeconomic model in an open economy as a basic instrument in the teaching of macroeconomics. But immediately he became one of the first Spanish economists to spark the debate between monetarists and

Keynesians, with an implicit message on the empirical properties of economics. Indeed, this 'cooling' of Keynesianism occurred parallel to a rebirth of attention to the methodological position of K. Popper and M. Friedman around the group that collaborated with Rojo both in the Department of Economic Theory (University of Madrid) and in the Bank of Spain Studies Service.[8] Rojo set out a synthesis of the new orientations in a systematic volume entitled *Income, Prices and Balance of Payments* (published in 1974), which, by its orientation, marks the end of Keynesian macroeconomics in Spain.

Unlike the fate of microeconomic theory, where theoretical incursions by Spanish authors were rare, in the case of monetary, employment and income theory, there was, from 1940 to 1970, a constant stream of contributions by Spanish economists, with a certain preference for the political and economic derivations of the macroeconomic analysis.

Applied analysis: institutionalism, structuralism and economic history[9]

The most important group of subjects in economic literature of the whole period 1940–75 is applied analysis of the Spanish economy. Most of these empirical studies are the work of lecturers devoted to the teaching of 'economic structure', 'economic policy', 'public finance and taxation systems' or 'economic history'.

Some of the first studies were influenced by the interpretations of A. Flores de Lemus, R. Perpiñá Grau and M. de Torres, made before the Civil War. The three authors had highlighted the strategic importance of the foreign sector in the internal inter-sector equilibrium, notwithstanding the lack of openness of the Spanish economy. This perspective was projected in the first studies by E. Fuentes Quintana or J. Velarde in the 1950s and 1960s. Subsequently, Fuentes' work would be a fusion of the historical tradition and the Keynesian theory of public finance.

The first applied economic studies by a team refer to the indirect estimates of National Income directed by M. de Torres from 1945, and the standardized elaboration of the National Accounts also organized by Torres in 1958 (Schwartz 1977). We should also highlight the first efforts to construct the first input-output tables for the Spanish economy (published in 1958), which were prepared with the help of the Italian expert Vera Cao Pinna. The teams working on these two studies had several economists and statisticians in common.

Structural analysis was one of the directions most often taken by Spanish economists. The initial studies by José L. Sampedro (b. 1917) deal with the spatial location of economic activity, or the disparity of development processes, the problems of European economic integration and the possibilities of Spain's integration (in several studies published in 1959–60). But his most influential works are the essay 'The economic forces of our time' (published in 1967, and translated into six languages) and the textbook *Economic Structure* (published in 1969, in collaboration with R. Martínez Cortiña (Beiras *et al.* 1987).

With a similar specialization of disciplines, R. Tamames (b. 1933) produced a number of works devoted to the study of the Spanish economy from a triple perspective: structural (relationships between sectors), historical and institutional. These works are teaching materials, such as his *Economic Structure of Spain*, republished innumerable times since 1960.

However, neo-institutionalism in Spain is associated more with certain specialists in the analysis of Spanish economic policy, such as F. Estapé (b. 1923), who, between the 1940s and 1960s also made several studies of the works of Schumpeter, Galbraith and Veblen. The main contributions to economic history also go back to the merging of the German institutionalist tradition (L. Valdeavellano, R. Carande) with the approach of the French journal *Annales, Economies, Sociétés* by J. Vicens Vives, F. Ruiz Martín, G. Anes and J. Nadal; and with the contribution of the Marxist influence (P. Vilar, M. Dobb) by way of J. Fontana.

The real influence of Marxism was negligible until the late 1960s (except in the field of economic history), partly because it was prohibited until the 1960s. Some applied economic studies in the 1960s were inspired by the Latin-American or French contributions on the 'terms of trade' and 'unequal development'. In the 1970s, theory was notably influenced by P. Sraffa (and the discussion on Marx's theory of exploitation), M. Kalecki and post-Keynesian macroeconomic literature.

Political influence of economists on the Franco regime

Economists had no influence over the policy-making process until the late 1950s. The proportion of economists in the Franco governments was also minimal until the 1960s (Miguel 1975). From 1939 to 1957 the political structure of the totalitarian state, with corporativist forms and the personal exercise of power by General Franco, favoured the influence of experts and politicians with the academic training of lawyers and engineers, as well as outsiders converted into economists, fundamentally in two institutions, the National Institute for Industry and the National Economic Council. The economic literature of the engineers was aimed, generally, at the maximization of production, costs and prices being of secondary importance, and this was the basis of the economic policy of autarchy (Velasco 1984; Catalán 1995). One of the outsiders with the most influence (on Franco himself) was Higinio Paris, a doctor of medicine who had acquired notions of economics in Berlin with E. Wageman (in 1938), and who distinguished himself by defending an activism of demand similar to 'vulgar' inflationist Keynesianism, with the introduction of numerous direct controls (González 1976).

This policy of autarchy was the subject of severe criticism from academic economists such as the Keynesian M. de Torres and his disciples (Fuentes Quintana, Velarde, Varela, Figueroa and others). They advocated true coordination of taxation, money and foreign policies. Torres adapted some ideas from Tinbergen and from Dutch planning, and proposed an agency to coordinate investments.

The 'engineering mentality' of the postwar period finally lost its influence in 1957 with the beginning of Franco's 'technocratic' governments when economists were taken on as advisers (belonging to the new bodies of economist civil servants) and even as ministers (A. Ullastres, M. Navarro Rubio). Faced with an extreme situation of the exhaustion of foreign currency reserves, there was coordinated action by economists in key advisory posts (academic economists and experts such as Joan Sardá, M. Varela, E. Fuentes Quintana, J. L. Sampedro) and others, such as politicians, plus the support of foreign economists of the international agencies (IMF, OEEC). The joint action was a Stabilization Plan in the Keynesian mould to combat inflation, promote internal liberalization, an opening up to external investment and trade, and the start of reforms in several spheres. Despite resistance to its formulation and development the Plan had a lasting impact on the Spanish economy, and it is considered a turning point in the economic history of twentieth-century Spain (Anderson 1970; Ros Hombravella 1975; González 1979; Preston 1990). This isolated Keynesian influence is a peculiar case of the process formulated by Hirschman (1989).[10]

In 1962 a technical commission from the World Bank invited by the Spanish government drew up an extensive report to explore the possibilities of economic development in Spain. One sector of the academic economists who had collaborated in the preparation of the Stabilization Plan of 1959 expressed its agreements and disagreements with the foreign experts' report. Finally, the government (influenced by the Minister L. López Rodó, Professor of Administrative Law) adopted and capitalized politically the French model of indicative planning, inspired by P. Massé.

In the preparation of the three Development Plans (1964–67, 1968–71, 1972–75) practically all the expert economists of the administration participated (González 1979), consolidating certain policy-making practices in a similar way to those of other European countries. But given the undemocratic nature of the Franco regime, the experience had the effect of concentrating economists in government bodies devoted to calculation, analysis and proposal (Planning Commission, National Statistical Institute, Studies Service of the Bank of Spain among others).

This partial adaptation was also facilitated by the process of professional socialization of some Spanish experts into international agencies. After the admission of Spain into the OEEC and IMF in 1958, the few Spanish economists who remained in training with the OECD or the IMF were civil servants from the advisory bodies (Commercial Experts and State Economists or from the Studies Service of the Bank of Spain). Some of them remained in their posts for a long time (J. Muns, C. Lluch), but the majority returned to Spain. Professor J. Muns, previously economist and executive director at the IMF, has emphasized that the flow of Spanish economists to the IMF has represented only a small proportion relative to the potential opportunities, either in programmes, courses or seminars (in total thirty-one for the period 1960–82), or as part of IMF personnel (fewer than five from 1960 to 1968, around 10–15 from 1969 to 1982) (Muns 1986: 224–6, 261–6, 433–6). I know of no specific study on Spanish economists in the OEEC or OECD.

The beginning of internationalization, 1975–95

The era of economists

Since 1975 Spanish universities have experienced an explosive growth in the number of students of economics. During the 1970s there was a substantial change in the environment of economic studies, the academic organization of the teachers and the training system and there were new networks of scientific communication and, at a professional level, a rapid 'penetration' of economists into Spanish society in areas hitherto reserved for other professions. The most important organizational changes for academic economists took place between 1983 and 1993. Finally, throughout this period, starting with the change in the political system (from dictatorship to democracy between 1975 and 1978), there occurred the greatest leap forward in the influence of economists in Spain's political life.

These transformations have led me to head this section, somewhat facetiously, with words similar to those used by Burke to define the eighteenth century and to the title of a book published in 1966 by D. R. Fusfeld, *The Age of the Economist*, characterizing what for him were 'our times'.

Reforms in study plans and the explosion of demand

In 1970 the General Law on Education reformed university studies. The old Higher Schools of Commerce were abolished, and a three-year diploma course in 'business studies' was created, to be taught at 'university schools'. In 1973 another syllabus or plan was started, which divided the teaching of economics into two different degrees, one in 'economic sciences' and another in 'business studies', to be taught jointly in 'faculties of economics and business studies'. The economic sciences course was formally organized into two cycles (of three and two years).

The most important changes from the curricular structure of the '1953 syllabus' introduced by the new economic sciences syllabus in 1973 were a slight reduction in the number of law subjects and the appearance of specialized branches in the second cycle, determined by the universities themselves. The heterogeneity of the titles of the specialized subjects, as pointed out by Gutiérrez and Velasco (1982) was, in fact, nominal. In practice, the number of class hours devoted to economic subjects was not appreciably affected by the 1973 'economic sciences' syllabus in comparison with that of 1953.

The total number of students of economics and business studies multiplied by 6.2 in the period 1973–94 (from 25,000 students in 1973 to 160,000 in 1994), and in the new business studies diploma courses it multiplied by 8.5 from 1974 to 1994 (from 11,300 to 96,100).[11]

The increase in demand for studies was met by the growth in absolute terms of public spending on universities (Almenar 1989) which, in the case of economics, went into financing more teachers, new centres (faculties, schools), and – secondarily – on research. Only at the end of the period did private colleges and universities begin to have some importance in the teaching of economics. The number of faculties (or authorized centres) rose from twelve in 1974 to fifty in 1991.

In 1983, the Law on Reform of the Universities (LRU) established the universities' academic and budgetary (expenditure) autonomy from the central or regional governments. It reformed the grading system of lecturers, the access to posts, enhanced the organization of the department as the research unit (as against the traditional role of the professorship), and transformed the system for the doctorate. At the same time the lecturers' salary system was reformed, for the first time introducing incentives to research.

The transformation of the scientific community

The increased demand for economic and business studies, the steady increase in public financing of universities, and the content of the study plans determined – once again – the volume and composition of the scientific community.

GROWTH

The number of lecturers in economics also grew steadily, though at a slightly slower rate than that of students. My estimate (hindered by the lack of homogeneity in categories of lecturers and types of university centres during the period under study) allows me to affirm that the total number of lecturers and teaching assistants of all categories devoted to the teaching of economics (economic analysis, applied economics and economic history) rose from 500 in 1974 in the faculties to 2,560 in 1991 (but now including the teachers of these subjects in both faculties and university schools).

ACADEMIC CAREERS – STRUCTURE AND PROMOTION

The process of expansion has been accompanied by a transformation in the composition of the categories of lecturers. Altogether three stages can be distinguished. During the period 1970–83 there appeared many different categories of teachers on temporary contracts, who were required to teach classes. During the period 1984–92 the system of categories of lecturers with tenure (civil servants) was simplified to four types. Two were for teachers in faculties: university professor (*CU*: *catedrático de universidad*), associate lecturer (*TU*: *titular de universidad*) – and two others for teaching in schools – professors of university schools (*CEU*: *catedráticos de escuelas universitarias*, academically equivalent to TUs), and lecturers without a doctorate (*TEU*: *titulares de escuela universitaria*). In this same period a high proportion of lecturers on contract between 1970 and 1983 obtained tenure, after fulfilling the academic conditions (doctorate, publications and suchlike) and competitive selection exams convened by the universities.[12] For example, the number of economics professors multiplied by 4.8 from 1974 to 1992, from 59 to 285 (see Table 10.5). In the period 1987–92 alone (for which homogeneous data are available) the number of doctor lecturers with tenure (*CU, TU, CEU*) rose from 600 to 848, but the *TEU* group expanded much more, from 145 to 319 (see Table 10.5). The area of applied economics expanded somewhat more rapidly. Finally, from 1988 there was again a fast increase in the number of lecturers on contract (*asociados*), especially in the area of applied economics, so that in 1991 the *asociados* represented 45 per cent of all teachers. In relative terms the segment of collaborators in training has stagnated (*Consejo de Universidades* 1991).

The scale and speed of the process implied a reduction in 'competition' for lectureships with tenure as a joint consequence of the abundance of posts on offer, and a new system of selection by universities which, in practice, favoured the candidates from the university itself. The information available allows us to affirm that the new system reduced the geographical mobility of lecturers and

Table 10.5 Professors and lecturers with tenure by areas of knowledge and status

Area of knowledge	CU	TU	CEU	TEU	Total
1974					
Total	59				
1987					
Economic analysis foundations	45	88	5	29	167
Applied economics	113	242	20	97	472
Economic history & institutions	25	42	20	19	106
Total	183	372	45	145	745
1992					
Economic analysis foundations	65	110	4	66	245
Applied economics	180	326	32	218	756
Economic history & institutions	40	70	21	35	166
Total	285	506	57	319	1,167
1987–1992 (% growth)					
Economic analysis foundations	44	25	−20	128	47
Applied economics	59	35	60	125	60
Economic history & institutions	60	67	5	84	57
Total	56	36	27	120	57

Sources: MEC (1974), *Consejo de Universidades* (1988) and *Anuário El País* (1993)

Abbreviations: *CU* – professors (chair); *TU* and *CEU* – lecturers (post-PhD); *TEU* – lecturers in business schools (without PhD)

real competition for posts (see the discussion on mobility or 'inbreeding' in *Consejo de Universidades* 1991: section 3.5).

DOCTORATE

Doctoral studies until 1985 (with exceptions) were centred on the preparation and presentation of a doctoral thesis, the quality of which was assessed by a commission of five members. As well as this official scoring, the academic community established an 'invisible' valuation of the thesis by its results (papers or books), by the prestige of the director of the thesis, and so on.

The evolution of doctoral theses on economics and business administration can be divided into two periods (1976–84 and 1985–94). During the first period there was moderate growth, while in the second there was accelerated expansion due to an extraordinary increase in the number of theses on business administration and bordering fields. The most reliable estimate for theses on economics and business (series UNE53EE in Figure 10.1, now excluding theses in other faculties) shows a profile of expansion, though at a slower rate.

The distribution of theses by fields of specialization (Table 10.6) corresponds in the medium term to the distribution of the new teaching posts. These data support a simple observation from experience: practically only those who had expectations of obtaining a lectureship with tenure did a doctoral thesis. The Table also reveals that one of the novelties of the years 1976–84 compared with the previous period was the development of a very important group of research studies in economic theory and econometrics, and the coexistence of the two styles of approaching applied economics. Firstly, studies continued with the descriptive, historicist and institutionalist perspective of applied economics as had been done in the 1950s and 1960s (on economic policy, public finance, industrial economics and other general, sector and regional studies). The second style applied to other studies, where applied economics was conceived as an empirical testing of theoretical models using econometric tools.

In the period 1985–94, theses on economic theory, economic activity, econometrics and public finance and fiscal policy declined proportionately but they increased in absolute terms. Applied economics of the second type was consolidated, through studies of sectors, of international economics (associated with European integration), and of industrial economics and technical change (see Table 10.6).

In general, the lack of teaching for the doctorate was substituted by a self-teaching effort, and in part by master's or doctorate studies in foreign universities. My personal estimate indicates that between 1970 and 1980 the proportion of lecturers of economics with tenure (professors and assistants/lecturers) who had done postgraduate studies abroad did not exceed 20 per cent. This situation evolved rapidly from 1980 to 1995 with the help of a system of study grants and visits to prestigious foreign universities. Nowadays that proportion has increased, but above all it has diversified from the areas of economic theory and econometrics towards applied economics. This transfor-

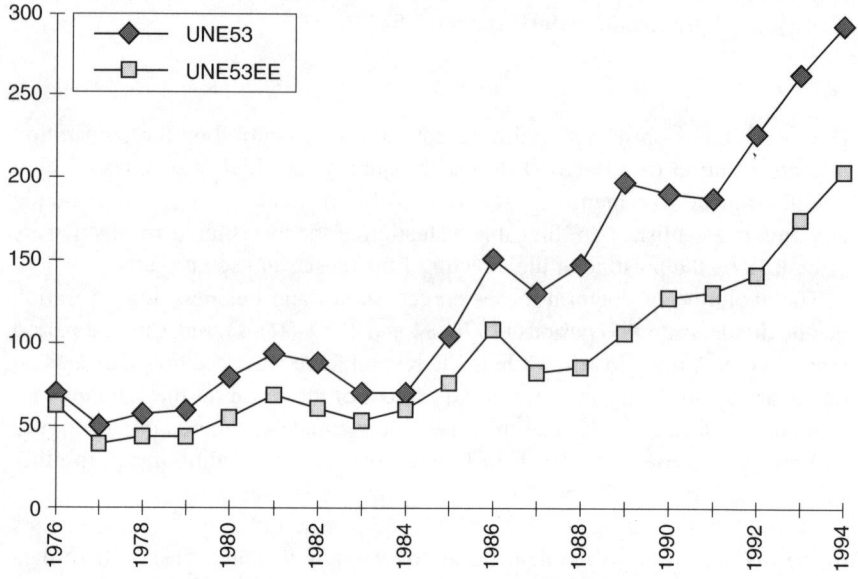

Figure 10.1 Doctoral theses on economics and business administration, 1976–94

Source: Teseo online database, Madrid: *Ministerio de Educación y Cultura*;
        search and tabulation by author

Note
UNE53: doctoral theses with the Unesco field code 53 ('Economic Sciences'); UNE53EE: doctoral theses with the Unesco field code 53 and presented in the economics and business administration faculties.

mation in training is one of the most important factors in explaining the recent rapid progress of the internationalization of economics in Spain. Most of the doctors trained abroad returned to Spanish universities importing international lines of research, forms of academic conduct and personal links.

At the same time, a new third cycle of studies has been regulated since 1986, in two parts. A two-year doctoral programme formally imitates the system in British or American universities, as well as the doctoral thesis itself. A certain 'market' in competitive doctorates has arisen as well as quality rankings, but competition has also encouraged cooperative solutions: joint doctorates, such as the Quantitative Economics Doctorate organized by the universities of Alicante, Bielefeld, Copenhagen, Lisbon and Vienna, or the international doctorate in economic analysis of the Autonomous University of Barcelona, integrated into the European Network for Training in Economic Research.

ACADEMIC CAREERS – COMPETITION AND INTERNATIONALIZATION

The law of 1970 grouped the lecturers of several related subjects (professorships) into 'departments', but the centre of organization of teaching and

Table 10.6 Doctoral theses on economics in Spain by fields, 1976–94[1]

Unesco fields in JEL[2] order	Distribution (%)		Annual averages		
	1976–84	1985–94	1976–84	1985–94	Growth
General economics	4.3	4.0	3.0	7.6	153.3
Economic theory	19.5	11.9	13.8	22.6	64.0
Economic history[3]	3.0	2.3	2.1	4.4	108.4
Economic systems	1.9	1.0	1.3	1.9	42.5
Economic activity	7.9	7.7	5.6	14.6	162.8
Econometrics	7.4	6.6	5.2	12.5	139.4
Public finance and fiscal policy	5.5	5.1	3.9	9.8	152.0
International economics	4.6	7.2	3.2	13.7	325.2
Business administration	17.2	24.0	12.1	45.7	277.3
Accounting	6.5	8.9	4.6	17.0	273.2
Industrial organization and policy	5.7	6.3	4.0	12.0	200.0
Economics of technological change	3.5	4.0	2.4	7.7	215.0
Sectoral studies	22.0	18.3	15.6	34.8	123.7
Total[4]	(635)	(1,905)	70.6	190.5	170.0

Source: Teseo online database, Madrid: *Ministerio de Educación y Cultura*;
      search and tabulation by author

Notes
1 In the Teseo database each thesis is indexed into one or more basic Unesco fields with six digits. The table represents the distribution of references (occurrences) by general Unesco fields (three digits) in percentage concerning the total of the published articles by period. Although the addition of the references percentages is over 100%, its distribution is an indicator of the specialization pattern. The comparison of the specialization patterns along the two periods does not require a previous standardization.
2 *Journal of Economic Literature*
3 Theses on 'Economic history' (Unesco 550606) only in the economics and business administration faculties.
4 Figures in parentheses represent the total number of doctoral theses on 'Economic sciences' (Unesco 53 field) by period.

allocation of resources was the faculty. The 1983 reform grouped economics lecturers into three 'areas of knowledge': 'economic analysis foundations' (economic theory, econometrics); 'economic history and institutions'; and 'applied economics' (statistics, economic structure, public finance, international economics, political economy). The departments now group the teachers of one or two areas of knowledge in each university, and are in charge of teaching the doctorate and coordinating research. Only in the largest universities are there two departments per area of knowledge.

Since 1985 the academic career patterns have changed substantially for teachers of economics in Spain. One of the 'symbolic' changes was the introduction of salary incentives for publishing works of quality (in journals with impact, and with anonymous referees). But there are still great differences among the 'areas of knowledge' mentioned and among the different departments of the universities. In an important unpublished study, J. García and F. Pérez (1998) have posited the existence of three types of departments in the fields of economics and business studies, which I have reformulated (accepting conceptual suggestions by Hirschman and Schumpeter).

1   *Traditional model* Prevalence of internal doctoral training, the hierarchical system, research has no priority, greater dedication to teaching work. Recruits lecturers trained by the department itself, where loyalty to the boss predominates over merit and the scientific result is not innovative.
2   *Renovated traditional model* As model (1) but with more attention to external training (PhD, master's, periods abroad), research activity, congresses, publications, etc. But there still prevails a mixed system of selection and promotion: voice, merit and loyalty.
3   *Competitive model* Fundamentally imitates foreign university departments considered the best, which clashes with the regulation of the public universities (civil servants). Merits in competition are valued (doctorate in foreign universities, publishing in international journals of prestige, work in other universities). García and Pérez (1998) studied seven Spanish centres that can be considered 'competitive' (with a total of 300 lecturers, assistants or researchers).[13] In these departments the lecturers will have taken their doctorates in foreign universities: 42.9 per cent in the United States (Minnesota, Chicago), 7.8 per cent in the United Kingdom (LSE, Oxford), 38.2 per cent in Spain, and 10.8 per cent in other European universities.

The teachers and researchers of the competitive centres have specialized in the different fields and lines of economic analysis that constitute the 'basic nucleus' of economic theory, sometimes a long way from the conventional studies of applied economics. The lines of specialization indicated by García and Pérez (1998) are confirmed by my calculations on the economic literature published by Spanish authors in foreign journals. The reproduction of the model is almost automatic in academic terms. The 'senior' lecturers impart doctoral programmes in their specialized subjects and generate new specialists. They all publish their work in English. But the model has its limits in the rigid structure of teaching posts with tenure, although around these competitive departments a 'job market' has formed to favour the mobility of the younger lecturers.

There are departments that are evolving rapidly from the traditional model to the renovated model, and others from the renovated to the competitive. The general trend towards internationalization does exist but is diverse in the different areas and universities.

Economists in the employment market

During the period 1974–95 the evolution of the employment market gave rise to a very high unemployment rate overall, and especially in youth unemployment.

The growth of demand for economics and business studies reflects employment expectations above the average for university graduates.

The most important feature of the period is the break with the model of the professional economist consolidated in the previous period. The existing 'stock' of graduates in economics and business studies multiplied ten times, from about 10,000 in 1974 to 100,000 in 1993 (Guillén 1989; García and Pérez 1998). On the one hand, the public administration's demand for economists only grew significantly in inspection or management of public finance (in the 1980s), but economists have also occupied middle-rank posts in the general administration. Nor did business increase its demand for economists at the extraordinary rate at which the universities produced graduates. The result was threefold: economists are employed first in unskilled posts and, in time, are promoted within the firm (or public administration or other institution). On the other hand, the unemployment rate among economists has risen notably (according to the indicators provided by the professional associations). And thirdly, there is an important difference between the expectations of economics students and their professional practice.

The 'success' of economists in politics

In this period economists played an extraordinarily large part in Spanish society, above all through their political influence in three fields of activity: (1) as technical experts; (2) as ideologists; (3) as politicians. Their influence (at times interwoven) stands out, particularly, at three decisive moments: firstly, at the transition to democracy (1976–78); second, during the implementation of the policy of economic adjustment and recovery (1982–85); third, on Spain's entry into the EEC (1985–86) (Fuentes Quintana 1993).

The general hypothesis is that economists have had a great influence on the policy-making process particularly because, in the development of Spanish democracy, they were in the front line of politics, long before Franco's death. It seems to me a plausible hypothesis that this was a process of substitution of political elites required by a change in the political system and in the international context of Spanish society. Perhaps the conversion of expert economists into politicians could be seen as a paradox given the loss of social prestige of the macroeconomists after the crisis of 'Keynesianism', but in Spain that loss of prestige was confused with the failure of the last 'development plans' and the end of Franco's dictatorship.

During the transition there was a movement of 'experts' from the advisory corps, study services and the teaching staff of universities into active politics (government, parliament, party executives, unions). These were economists familiar with foreign economic literature, and with international organizations (OECD, IMF, the World Bank), universities and so on. The qualifications of the ministers of finance of the dictatorship and in democracy evolved in this direction. From 1939 to 1975 only 10–15 per cent of Franco's ministers of finance were economics graduates or had similar qualifications. In the period 1975–96 the proportion was 67 per cent, most of them expert economists or university teachers with professional experience in international agencies. From 1982 to 1995 all the ministers of finance and governors of the Bank of Spain were expert or academic economists, some of them with important contributions to economic literature.

One important consequence of the influence of this heterogeneous group of economists was an economic policy plan called the 'agreements of the Moncloa'. These were agreements among the principal political parties to stabilize prices and wages, introduce reforms in public revenues and expenditure, and make possible economic stability to facilitate a peaceful political transition. The economic theories that made the concordance possible were not identical. But perhaps there was analytical accord on the existence of a wages–prices–exchange-rate spiral (following either Friedman–Modigliani or Tobin–Kalecki–Sylos–Labini), and a prior political agreement driven by the fear of social instability as an environment adverse to peaceful transition to democracy (the memory of the Spanish Civil War, or the failure of democracy in Chile).[14]

The economic crisis inherited from the 1970s was aggravated by the second rise in oil prices. The Socialist Party (PSOE) won the elections in 1982 with an expansionist programme, but the previous failure of the first 'Mitterrand experiment' was perceived rapidly by a government which contained numerous expert and academic economists both at ministerial and intermediate levels (deputy ministers, directors-general). In this period, the initial political discourse (based on the search for equity) was reconverted into another politico-economic discourse in which the goal of economic growth (based on efficiency and competitiveness) was presented as a necessary precondition for equity. The 'adjustment' was the necessary step to growth.

The Spanish team negotiating entry into the EEC was made up of a notable set of expert economists and political economists, the line between them not being clear. Membership in the EEC has reinforced the economic content of political discourse to the present day, in the form of an 'external' imperative of 'convergence'.

The gradual internationalization of Spanish economic literature

The institutional and sociological changes in the profession of academic economist analysed above can be synthesized as follows:

1   Extraordinary growth in the number of teachers, which has even enabled the formation of critical masses of researchers in specialized subjects. Despite the dimensions reached, the development of scientific associations and periodical meetings of specialists is still on a small scale.[15]

2   New academic organization into 'areas of knowledge' and university departments which, in practice, can develop in three ways: as hierarchical departments (traditional model); as competitive departments (competitive model); and mixed departments. The principle of 'merit' and valuation of published research work is progressing notably as against the principle of loyalty or time served.

3   The initial training of researchers has evolved from a doctorate almost
     exclusively orientated to the preparation of a doctoral thesis, towards a new
     third-cycle of prior studies in formal imitation of some foreign universities.
     Moreover, a growing number of teachers have taken their doctorate or spent
     periods 'visiting' abroad, which has constituted one of the main factors in
     the internationalization of a part of Spanish economic literature.

As well as these institutional and sociological changes, two other 'external' factors must now be studied: the scientific communication networks and the
financing of research. These conditions of the development of the scientific
community and its environment help us to understand the most important features of Spanish economic literature, the changes experienced in recent decades,
and its links with the predominant currents of foreign economic thought.

The networks of scientific communication in economics

The flows of scientific communication continue to be asymmetrical. However,
the greatest transformation has occurred in the last fifteen years, in which a part
(proportionately small, but growing) of Spanish economic literature has started
to be published in international journals.

Throughout this second period, which began in the mid-1970s, the collections
of books on economics gradually transformed their function. Until the mid-
1980s the specialized series that continued to exist (Ariel, Oikos Tau, Alianza
and the Mexican *Fondo de Cultura Económica*) and others that sprang up then
(Vicens Vives, Pirámide, A. Bosch) contained a growing proportion of books by
Spanish authors, although most of the volumes were translations. The proportion of Spanish authors was higher in other collections with public or
institutional financial support. In recent years the publishing system has been
completely transformed (by concentration and by multinational publishers and
for other reasons), and the bulk of work published in economics is textbooks
with a high volume of production.

Nearly all the first general economic journals, created in the postwar years and
belonging to public bodies, disappeared in the 1970s and early 1980s,[16] while
other specialist journals belonging to other bodies of the public administration[17]
were consolidated as 'academic' publications (because of the authors' profession,
though the publishers were not academic). The space left by the journals that disappeared was disputed, shared or substituted by new ones, such as *Cuadernos de
Economía* (Economic Notebooks, 1973–) and *Investigaciones Económicas*
(Economic Research, 1976–). Throughout the 1970s the *Revista Española de
Economía* (Spanish Economic Review, 1971–) was a forum of scientific debate
and a platform for the diffusion of the currents of foreign economic literature,
while in the 1990s it has been profoundly transformed – into a journal with
greater specialization in economic theory and econometrics.[18] But the latter and
the older *Moneda y Crédito* or *Investigaciones Económicas* have re-orientated

their style and organization (with academic editors and 'referee', preference for subjects, and the use of English, depending on how the original is written).

In the field of applied economics *Papeles de Economía Española* (Spanish Economic Papers, 1979–) and the more recent *Revista de Economía Aplicada* (Applied Economics Review, 1993–) have been outstanding, in addition to the specialized journals already mentioned. The *Revista de Historia Económica* (Economic History Review, 1983–) and the *Revista de Historia Industrial* (Industrial History Review, 1992–) should also be mentioned.

The political development of the regional autonomous governments has made possible the publication of other academic or quasi-academic economic journals, mostly on applied economics, with regional scope. The proliferation of journals has widened the differences of consideration and academic prestige between publications with a system of recognized editors and anonymous referees, and the journals that do not yet have such a system.

The 'working papers' formula has been spreading in Spain as habitual scientific documentation since the late 1970s. In the course of the 1980s many departments, faculties or institutes of economics came to publish them regularly, and in English (the 'competitive' departments, while the 'traditional' ones habitually publish in Spanish).

The medium of research

At the start of the 1970s a dual process of consolidation of economic research began to take place. On the one hand, the regular (not sporadic) process of academic 'reproduction', of transmission of the specialization in lines of research from the 'masters' to the 'disciples', was favoured by the existence of a sufficient number of teaching posts. On the other hand, an accelerated process of internationalization in training and the adoption of behaviour patterns of American or British universities (imitation of the theoretical fields and the quantitative methods of research, external evaluation and scientific competitiveness). One of the most important features of this transition period was the setting up of scientific groups with stable research projects with the stimulus of non-university institutions, especially in the field of applied economics (FIES Foundation, INI Foundation, Bank of Spain Studies Service, Institute of Taxation Studies, as well as the Studies Services of the Banco de Bilbao, Banco Urquijo and others).

In the last fifteen years the most important factors of change have been the regularity of grants for study abroad (pre- and post-doctorate) and the diversification of the financial support for economic research. University autonomy now enables departments and institutes to contract studies or reports. This has stimulated numerous applied economics projects habitually requested by public institutions (although they are heterogeneous, they consolidate lines in research with a stronger interaction than existed before between the theoretical models and the quantitative methods). At the same time there has been an increase in direct public assistance for economic research and in the number of projects (although the average grant per project has decreased and the grants have depreciated in real terms) (see Figure 10.2).

Subsequently the organizational support for research has been diversified with the creation of several institutes in some universities, in the national research body (*CSIC – Consejo Superior de Investigaciones Científicas*) and in some regions (the Public Economics Institute in Bilbao, *Instituto Valenciano de Investigaciones Económicas* in Valencia, *FEDEA* in Madrid).

Economic literature in the 1970s: groups, schools, styles and fashions

It is important to remember that the 1970s were especially turbulent years in Spain: the decade saw the crisis of Keynesian macroeconomics, the microeconomic re-founding of macroeconomics, the development of general equilibrium, but also the rebirth of neo-Ricardian or Marxist post-Keynesian economics. This turbulence was perceived in the Spanish academic community as a period of theoretical change, but also of social changes, because it coincided with the period immediately before and after the 'political transition' to democracy. This section attempts to highlight the existence of some more dynamic *groups*, although the organization of research was still generally individualistic.

The main currents of economic thought in Spain in the late 1960s and early 1970s had changed quite a lot from the preceding period. In the economic literature published in Spain at that time there was a growing presence of contributions to economic theory and econometrics. In the area of macroeconom-

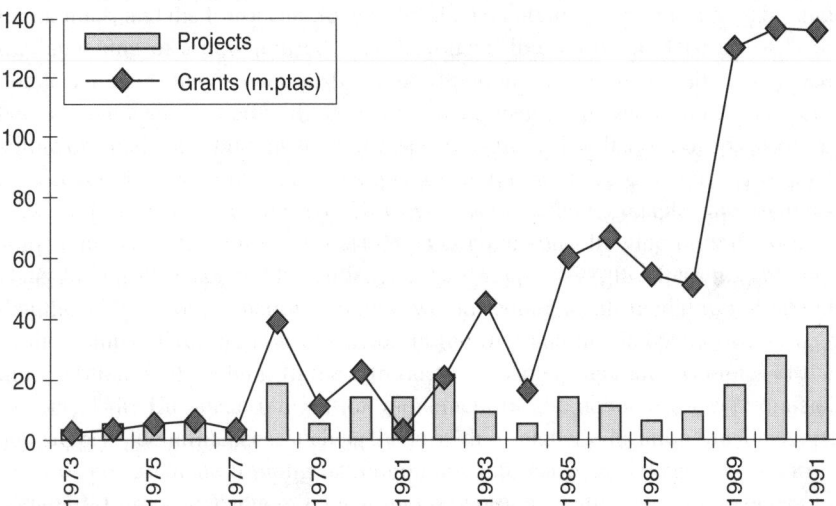

Figure 10.2 Public grants to economic research, 1973–91

Sources: CICYT (1983); Urrutia (1993: 44)

Note
Grants in current money (millions of pesetas).

ics (money theory, econometrics and cycles), a group was consolidated with a relatively high concentration of researchers in Madrid, around L. A. Rojo in the *Universidad Complutense* and in the the the Bank of Spain Studies Service. As well as this orientation, specialist lines were developed in microeconomics, welfare economics, and general equilibrium in the Autonomous University of Barcelona or in Bilbao, as a consequence, firstly, of the 'link' with the outside world, and second, of the return of some Spanish economists with studies abroad or with the support of those who already held teaching posts in American or British universities (A. Mas Colell, J. Silvestre, X. Calsamiglia, S. Barberá, A. Zabalza). We should also emphasize the impetus of econometric studies in Spain (partly on the basis of existing groups, J. L. Raymond, A. Espasa, A. Maravall, A. Pulido, Terceiro, E. Uriel), with a renewed theoretical and experimental base, time series, dynamic multi-equational models and various applied studies.[19]

At the same time, from the 1970s there was appreciable reception of a critical orientation on two fronts – particularly (1) Sraffa's work and its derivations (critique of the neoclassical theory of capital, rebirth of Ricardian and Marxist economics); (2) the critical approach by A. Leijonhufvud and R. Clower to the neoclassical–Keynesian synthesis, the 'recovery' of M. Kalecki, and the reconstruction of post-Keynesian economics (among them Robinson, Kahn, Eichner, Kregel). These orientations influenced theoretical work in the University of Valencia, and the Autonomous Universities of Madrid and Barcelona, with bilateral relations with some Italian economists from Cambridge. Two groups were formed on the history of economic thought (P. Schwartz, E. Lluch).

In applied economics, in the 1970s several lines of work developed in the form of 'schools' differentiated by approach and technique. The first of these focused on a historical study of the most important factors conditioning Spain's 'economic structure' (the 'brakes' imposed on development by the oligopolistic banking structure; the effects of a long economic isolation on competitiveness and so on). These were small groups that would undergo a notable expansion. One initially focused in Madrid around J. Velarde (J. L. García Delgado, Santiago Roldán, Juan Muñoz, Angel Serrano, as well as A. Viñas) and another around F. Estapé in Barcelona (E. Lluch, J. Ros). Furthermore, two economic history groups in the universities of Barcelona and Valencia expanded around J. Nadal and J. Fontana. Both 'styles' would be imitated throughout Spain in other departments of economic structure, economic policy and economic history, until the 1980s.

The second line was renewed attention to the regional economy (R. Cuadrado, E. Lluch), sectorial analysis of the Spanish regions and their relative development, which would have an extraordinary expansion in the 1980s with the consolidation of the political autonomy of the regions.

The third line is an institutionalist orientation for the study of the environment and effects of economic policy (J. Ros, L. Gamir), and fourthly, a perspective of quantitative studies to test models on various aspects such as industrial structure (INI Foundation under the direction of J. Segura) and the macroeconomic situation (Bank of Spain, FIES Foundation under E. Fuentes Quintana) that possessed a specific infrastructure of material means, together with which – despite the heterogeneity – should be counted the economic history group coordinated by G. Tortella (who introduced the orientation of the 'new economic history').

This incomplete descriptive review of the most active groups of the 1970s permits an anticipated conclusion: Spanish economic literature was characterized by a substantial *pluralism* which was, in appearance, greater than that expressed in the principal British and American journals. From the period 1977–82 onwards, Spanish scientific literature began to modify its patterns. The critique of mainstream theory was followed with amazing rapidity by an imitation of the new theoretical currents that reconstructed neoclassical theory. In the 1980s the traditional lines of research into applied economics were steeply reduced in importance (the first and third of those mentioned, except for studies in economic history, strictly speaking). In their place has emerged a new style of applied economics studies characterized by the use of formal theoretical models (generally similar to those used in other countries) and econometric instruments for testing hypotheses. Two symbolic examples of this transition are the manuals by Martínez Serrano *et al.* (1982) and García Delgado (1993).

The fields of analysis and specific styles corresponding to the old disciplinary divisions of the chairs and the 'schools' have become blurred to the point of disappearing in many cases. The reduction of pluralism in the sphere of analysis and the internationalization of Spanish scientific production in economics are two sides of the same coin. This is a complex evolution in which some methodological traditions and the incentive of social influence through criticism (in an authoritarian political environment) have given way to other, more limited motivations such as the search for prestige and academic and economic rewards.

Changes in and internationalization of scientific production, 1978–95

I know of no previous quantitative studies of Spanish scientific production in economics for the period studied, except those collected in international databases. I have complemented these studies with some first bibliometrical estimates for the literature published in Spain (Almenar 1996), whose conclusions can be synthesized as follows.

Firstly, the first analysis refers to the scientific production of five Spanish journals of general economics, for the period 1978–93, shown in Table 10.7. The distribution of the articles published by fields of specialization permits comparison with the occupational structure of the teaching staff due to their teaching obligations. The comparison between the two reveals that the structure of scientific production is similar, not identical, to the general occupational pattern of the lecturers, which seems to confirm the hypothesis, already tested when commenting on the thematic distribution of doctoral theses, that the occupational structure of the universities' teaching staff strongly conditioned the scientific production and its distribution by subjects. This affirmation does not imply a determinist judgement, as within a generic specialization researchers have enjoyed various degrees of freedom in the choice of orientations and approaches.

Second, in order to study the evolution of the specialization pattern I have analysed three sub-periods in accordance with the results of Table 10.7. From the sub-period 1978–79 to the end of the third sub-period 1990-93, the most important trend was a *relative* decrease of production in general economics (from 36.2 to 22.1 per cent) and a spectacular increase in quantitative and econometric methods (from 12.1 to 43.9 per cent). Given the nature of the ISOC database we cannot infer an increase in econometric theory as such; however, we can do so in the mathematical and econometric tools used in studies on pure and applied economics. Other trends are the decrease in studies of growth and development (from 16.1 to 9.2 per cent) and greater attention to the industrial economy (from 7.0 to 16.6 per cent), to the job market and to the international economy. These variations indicate similar trends to those observed in doctoral theses (in Table 10.6), although a discrepancy on trends of econometrics exists. The most important point is that the specialization pattern of Spanish economists is coming closer to that of their foreign colleagues.

Third, the study by J. Urrutia (1993) reflects valuable comparative information on the evolution of scientific production in economics in various countries, prepared by the Institute for Scientific Information (ISI), as shown in Table 10.8. Two solid conclusions can be deduced: the growth of 'internationalized' Spanish economic literature is very steep (compared to other countries) because it started at a very low level. As a consequence of the steeper relative growth, the proportion of Spanish economic literature on the whole has also increased.

Table 10.7 Spanish literature on economics: articles in five journals, 1978–93*

	1978–79	1980–89	1990–93
General fields		%	
0 General Economics, theory, history, ec. systems	36.2	32.0	22.1
1 Economic growth, development, fluctuations	16.1	8.8	9.2
2 Quantitative economic methods and data	12.1	18.9	43.9
3 Financial and monetary institutions, fiscal policy	18.6	16.2	22.1
4 International economics	4.5	9.8	9.8
5 Business administration, marketing, accounting	5.5	12.1	11.0
6 Industrial organization	7.0	20.5	16.6
7 Agriculture & livestock, natural resources	7.0	6.2	3.4
8 Labour, population	5.0	13.7	9.8
9 Welfare programmes, consumer ecs, urban ecs	5.5	12.4	6.1
Total articles (1,442)[†]	(199)	(917)	(326)

Source: ISOC database in CD-ROM, Madrid: *Consejo Superior de Investigaciones Científicas (CSIC)* and Micronet (October 1995); search and tabulation by author

Notes
* This table has been composed from published articles in five Spanish economics journals during the period 1978–94: *Revista de Economía Política*, Madrid, 1978–83; *Moneda y Crédito*, Madrid, 1978–94; *Cuadernos de Economía*, Barcelona, 1978–93, *Investigaciones Económicas*, Madrid, 1981–93; and *Revista Española de Economía*, Madrid, 1978–92. On distribution, see note * in Table 10.6.
† Figures in parentheses represent the total number of published articles by period.

Table 10.8 International literature on economics: articles published in journals, 1972–92

	Annual average			Growth (%)	
	1972–80	1981–85	1986–92	1972–80/ 1981–85	1981–85/ 1986–92
Spain	5.3	16.6	25.6	211.3	54.0
France	99.8	137.2	141.7	37.5	3.3
Italy	86.2	116.4	86.7	35.0	–25.5
United Kingdom	843.3	962.6	1,017.4	14.1	5.7
USA	2,951.7	3,772.6	4,321.1	27.8	14.5
Total econ	7,448.4	8,591.0	8,727.1	15.3	1.6

Source: Tabulated from Urrutia (1993) and International Scientific Information (ISI)

Fourth, the Spanish scientific literature published in international journals can be considered an indicator of the internationalization of Spanish economists. Using two databases (Econ-Lit and SSCI), the results shown in Table 10.9 are not conclusive, because there are disparities between the two. However, common aspects appear:

1 The initial specialization pattern of the 'competitive' Spanish economist is in economic theory, in subjects in progress (general equilibrium, microeconomics, game theory, social choice, among others), and more recently also in areas of econometrics and applied economics with reference to the Spanish and European economy.

2 A substantial part of 'Spanish' economic literature (the country of residence of the author/s) published in internationally registered journals corresponds exclusively to one or more Spanish authors. A quarter, at least, corresponds to foreign visiting professors in Spain.

3 A preliminary observation reveals that the pattern of quotations (authorities) of Spanish economists is similar to that of other economists for each specialization, with a slight bias towards quotation of self or of the group to which the author belongs.

Fifth, a contrast between the specialization patterns of Spanish literature published inside and outside Spain suggests an apparent contradiction with regard to the greater relative importance of economic theory in the publications abroad. In fact this is a sub-sector of scientific production which (due to the competitiveness of its authors in relation to editors preferences) is published directly in international journals.

Sixth, another, less powerful indicator of internationalization is the use of textbooks by foreign economists in the teaching of economics. In the 1980s the predominance of texts by foreign authors was practically total at all levels in Spanish faculties; the earlier pluralism of the 1970s disappeared with a general return to Anglo-American orthodoxy (Samuelson or Lipsey in the 'introduction', Ferguson or Quirk in microeconomics, Branson or Dornbusch–Fisher in macroeconomics, and so on). In the 1990s the amplitude of the market has favoured the publication of numerous textbooks and exercise books by Spanish teachers, and some have been quite successful in the 'introductory' course. But at higher levels the predominance of British and American authors is almost complete, although it has begun to diminish very recently.

Internationalization, disparities and basic consensus

The internationalization process has been perceived by the scientific community, in general, as positive, as a factor of modernization that broke with the isolation and relative backwardness of Spanish economic literature. The diffusion of Spanish contributions on economics in the international journals is more recent and proportionately less than in other fields (physics, medicine, biology, astronomy). These disciplinary differences possess historic and economic roots, there seems to exist a high correlation between the international diffusion of scientific literature and the financial effort in R&D for the various fields of research (Pestaña 1993).

The important change that took place in Spanish economic literature since 1975 has not provoked overall reflections or debates among the several theoretical or economic policy focuses. The discussions have been limited to the specialized field or to the concrete problems, in a similar form as in the development of 'normal science'. However, it is possible to detect several hidden visions of the best courses for economic research.

Table 10.9 Spanish literature on economics: articles in foreign journals*

Database Distribution by fields	EconLit 1987–95	SSCI 1989–94
	%	
0 General economics, theory, history, ec. systems	31.0	48.1
1 Economic growth, development, fluctuations	6.9	9.1
2 Quantitative economic methods & data	10.3	18.8
3 Monetary & fiscal theory and institutions	14.0	8.8
4 International economics	9.5	6.6
5 Business administration, marketing, accounting	7.8	8.8
6 Industrial organization, technical change	13.4	7.1
7 Agriculture, natural resources	5.8	3.7
8 Labour, population	6.5	6.0
9 Welfare programmes, consumer ecs, urban ecs	7.1	8.3
Total articles[†]	(464)	(351)

Sources: American Economic Association, *EconLit Database on CD-ROM*, 1995; and Institute for Scientific Information (ISI), *Social Sciences Citation Index* CD-ROM, Philadelphia, PA, 1995 – search and tabulation by author

Notes
* On distribution, see note * in Table 10.6.
† Figures in parentheses represent the total number of published articles by period.

Some groups propose the full integration of Spanish economists in the wider tendencies of economic science (Barberá 1991: 88–9), although implicitly this is identified with the mainstream in North America. This position is characteristic of a set of brilliant economists, pioneers of internationalization since the beginning of the 1970s, with strong ties with American universities (one group especially, with Minnesota), specialized in branches of general equilibrium, social choice and game theory, who uphold the importance of pure economic theory such as the 'construction of a conceptual coherent world', with independence from their 'applications' (Urrutia 1993: 47).

A second sector, much more numerous and heterogeneous, also considers internationalization necessary (in the process of postgraduate specialization, in the models and methods utilized, in journals in order for papers to be published) but conserving as a priority analysis of Spanish or European economic problems. Although the discrepancy among both groups is latent, the differential element is the emphasis on the relevance of the problems studied and the convenience of attaining practical conclusions or applications.

Lastly, the absence of fundamental debate among academic economists on economic policy could be interpreted as the manifestation of a basic consensus on the fundamental problems of the Spanish economy, and on the general framework in which the several programmes of economic policy should be laid out (the goals and convergence process to Economic and Monetary European Union). (On political consensus, see Coats 1997a).

The process of the reduction of doctrinal pluralism has played an important part in the formation of that basic consensus (which does not exclude its diversity), parallel with the internationalization of economic research in Spain, and with the conversion of numerous professional economists partly from the new political elite starting from the transition. This triple process is similar to that analysed for Latin America by Veronica Montecinos (1997).

Summary and conclusions

The interpretative framework used begins with the analysis of the teaching of economics because, except at the start of the period or very recently, the institutes of economic research have not played an important role. As there exists a homogeneous public organization for careers in teaching, the syllabuses have conditioned the structure of specializations of Spanish academic economists. But this disciplinary structure was not deterministic.

During the Franco years training for the doctorate was closed to the outside world, but the contributions of Spanish economists can be understood as the fruit of the blending of external influences of an innovative nature (Stackelberg, Keynesianism) and the renewed continuity of the moderate historicist, structuralist and institutionalist approach consolidated in the period prior to the Spanish Civil War. The new networks of scientific communication facilitated contact with international ideological and theoretical orientations. The persistence of isolation strengthened the definition of differentiated 'styles' or 'schools'. The fundamental results were the consolidation of a scientific community characterized by a high degree of pluralism of discipline, methodology and technique, as well as a persistent and cumulative gain in the knowledge of Spanish economic reality, and a political and economic influence limited by the nature of the political regime.

From the 1970s onwards, the growth of the academic community has taken place parallel to organizational changes which tend to reduce the separation between the old disciplines to create wider areas, and since the period of turbulence in the 1970s, a greater openness to the outside world in pre- or post-doctorate training. The general expansion of the methods and techniques of econometric analysis, and the consolidation of a central neoclassical current in the 1980s, coincided with an exhaustion of the lines of research associated with the most traditional 'styles' or the heterodox currents arising in the 1970s. Economists played an important part in the substitution of political elites in the new democratic system, and their influence has broadened and diversified.

A dual process of homogenization and internationalization of Spanish economic literature has taken place, and at the same time a diversification among the different departments and university groups both by theoretical orientations or priorities and by the predominance of some criteria of academic assessment (merit, quality and so on). The relative reduction in the scale of general economics studies has led to a specialized expansion of research into applied economics using models and techniques that are internationally common. Unlike in the previous stage, the Spanish networks of scientific communication have lost importance as a vehicle for transmission of foreign influence, and the research institutes (independent of the universities but staffed by lecturers) have gained importance as a medium for the new theoretical and applied research. Despite the progress in the internationalization of economic literature in subjects in expansion (such as general equilibrium, social choice, game theory, macroeconometrics or applied studies of the job market, economic and monetary European integration), the number of 'internationalized' Spanish economists is still very small.

Notes

1 In preparing this chapter I have had the stimulus and the valuable and patient help of Professor A. W. Coats, as well as comments from other colleagues in the preparatory meetings in Lisbon and London, and in the Economic History Seminar of Valencia University. Thanks to the kindness of Professor E. Fuentes Quintana (FIES Foundation, Madrid) I have been able to consult unpublished material from the projected book on economics and Spanish economists (Fuentes (ed.) 1998). Obviously, none of them is responsible for the errors that the chapter may contain.

2 Since the late nineteenth century the idea of 'Europeanizing Spain' through culture had spread in some intellectual circles, and a practical means was postgraduate study at universities in Germany, France and Italy. The *Junta para la Ampliación de Estudios* (1907–36) was an agency that distributed government grants for studying abroad.

3 The principal preceding analyses are by Torres (1958) and Roper (1969).

4 This section owes much to the unpublished paper by J. Segura (1998).

5 The journal *Moneda y Crédito* spread the work of Eucken, Röpke and the 'Ordo' group. The Ignacio Villalonga Foundation published Mises, Hazlitt, Röpke and Erhard in the 1950s. The *Revista de Occidente* (directed by the group from the Political Studies Institute: Alvarez, Vergara, Paredes) published Hayek, Eucken and Röpke, but also Boulding, Moulton and the Keynesian bible *The New Economics*, edited by S. Harris.

6 For a more complete exposition, see Almenar (1983 and 1998).

7 There is an abundance of literature claiming Bernácer's originality. Three books stand out: J. Savall (1975), G. Ruiz (1982) and J. Villacís (1993). An alternative interpretation is in Almenar (1998).

8 The Studies Service of the Bank of Spain was created in 1930, as an internal department of research and assessment of current economic activity and rate of exchange. After 1939 there was less activity, until the appointment of Professor Joan Sardá as director (1957–65). Sardá modernized their functions in accordance with experience acquired in the National Bank of Venezuela (and the relations with the IMF). After the nationalization of the Bank of Spain in 1960, the Studies Service extended their activities to monetary and financial theory, history and policy, consolidating it as the principal centre for advice on monetary policy. Professor L. A. Rojo, former director of the Studies Service (1971–88), has been the Governor of the Bank of Spain since 1992.

9 This section has benefited from the information in the article by J. Velarde (1967).

10 Hirschman suggests that the international spread of Keynesian policies was channelled by means of the influence of the United States as a new power after World War II. The expert Americans who administered the Marshall Plan, and the new international organizations, played a very important part. To Hirschman there seems to exist a parallel between English hegemony in the nineteenth century and the extension of free trade, and North American hegemony in the twentieth century and the spread of Keynesianism. Spanish international isolation, mitigated by bilateral defence agreements with the United States from 1953, represents a unique case, because Keynesianism did not penetrate economic policy until the 1959 'Stabilization Plan'. The formulation and development of the Plan counted among its advisers some IMF economists, and Spanish Keynesian economists, which seems to confirm the Hirschman thesis, but with two differences: Keynesian policy was used for the first time in Spain to cool the economy; and it was applied later to other European countries.

11 Official statistics indicate the number of students by centres. My own estimate of the internal distribution is that at the start of the 1980s the students of 'economic sciences' represented 40%, whereas in 1995 they constituted 30% of the total number of students in faculties of economics and business studies.

12 From 1984 related subjects in economics were grouped into three 'areas of knowledge': economic analysis foundations; applied economics; and economic history and institutions. There are also other areas, of business administration and economics, of finance and accountancy.

13 *Centro de Estudios Monetarios y Financieros del Banco de España* (Madrid), *Universitat Pompeu Fabra* (Barcelona), *Universidad Carlos III* (Madrid), *Universidad Autónoma de Barcelona* and *Instituto de Análisis Económico, Universidad Complutense de Madrid, Universidad del País Vasco, Universidad de Alicante.*

14 There is extensive literature on the 'political transition', less so on its economic aspects. See Rodríguez (1989), Fuentes Quintana (1993), Lluch (1996), and the brilliant monograph by Trullén (1993); in English, Preston (1990: 144–9), Bermeo and García-Durán (1994).

15 There was no scientific association of Spanish economists until 1996. The Spanish Association of Regional Science and the Economic History Association could be mentioned. Periodical meetings are held for industrial economy (Madrid), public economy (Bilbao) and economic analysis (Barcelona), as well as regular meetings on

health economics, education, and the Spanish economy.
16 *Anales de Economía* (1941–75), *De Economía* (1948–77), *Revista de Economía Política* (1945–83).
17 The following should be noted: *Hacienda Pública Española, Información Comercial Española, Economía Industrial, Pensamiento Iberoamericano, Boletín Económico del Banco de España.*
18 The diffusion of foreign economic literature has continued – above all, with monographic numbers of *Cuadernos Económicos de ICE* (1977–).
19 It is necessary to highlight the importance of the fact that numerous academic economists and highly qualified technical staff of the administration who were involved in the preparation of the Third Development Plan (1972–75) were responsible for impetus in the work on quantitative economics, statistics and econometrics. At this period several research and consulting firms started up – under the direction of academic economists – whose importance should not be underestimated.

References

Albertone, M. and Masoero, A. (eds) (1994) *Political Economy and National Realities*, Turin: Fondazione Luigi Einaadi.
Almenar, S. (1983) 'Keynesianos en España, 1936–1953', *Debats* (Valencia) 6: 103–8.
——(1989) 'Las aportaciones presupuestarias del Estado y de las administraciones públicas', in *La Financiación de la Enseñanza Superior*, Madrid: *Consejo de Universidades.*
——(1996) 'The international process of economics: the case of Spain (1930–1990): a first quantitative approach', Paper presented at the Annual European Conference on the History of Economics, Lisbon (February).
——(1998) 'Difusión e influencia del keynesianismo en España', forthcoming in E. Fuentes Quintana (ed.) *Economía y economistas españoles*, Madrid.
Anderson, C. W. (1970) *The Political Economy of Modern Spain: Policy-making in an Authoritarian System*, Madison, WI London: University of Wisconsin Press.
Anuario El País (1993) Madrid: Ediciones El País.
Barberá, S. (1991) 'El pensament econòmic als anys noranta: permanència i canvi', *Revista Econòmica de Catalunya* 17: 85–9.
Beiras, X. M. *et al.* (1987) *Homenaje al profesor Sampedro. Ciclo de conferencias*, Madrid: Fundación Banco Exterior.
Beltrán, L. (1981) 'El estudio de la economía en España', *Moneda y Crédito* 157: 3–18.
Bermeo, N. and García-Durán, J. (1994) 'Spain: dual transition implemented by two parties', in S. Haggard and S. B. Webb (eds) *Voting for Reform. Democracy, Political Liberalization, and Economic Adjustment*, New York: World Bank and Oxford University Press.
Catalán, J. (1995) *La economía española y la segunda guerra mundial*, Barcelona: Ariel.
CICYT (Comisión Asesora de Investigación Científica y Técnica) (1983) Proyectos de investigación (1965-1982), Madrid: Ministerio de Educación y Ciencia.
Coats, A. W. (1987) 'Economics as an academic discipline and profession since the 1880s: some Anglo-American impressions', *Quaderni di storia dell'economia politica* 5, 1–2: 3–35.
——(1994) *The Sociology and Professionalization of Economics: British and American Essays*, vol. II, London and New York: Routledge.
——(1997a) 'The internationalization of economic policy reform: some recent literature', in A. W. Coats (ed.) *The Post-1945 Internationalization of Economics*, Durham, NC and London, Duke University Press, pp 337–54.
——(ed.) (1997b) *The Post-1945 Internationalization of Economics*, Durham, NC and London: Duke University Press.

Colander, D. C. and Coats, A. W. (eds) (1989) *The Spread of Economic Ideas*, Cambridge: Cambridge University Press.
Colegio de Economistas de Cataluña (1976) *El economista en Cataluña*, Barcelona.
Consejo de Universidades (1988) *Anuario de estadística universitaria 1988. Documento avance*, Madrid: *Consejo de Universidades*.
——(1991) *Pleno (Sesión 17–18 de diciembre 1991). Anexo Documental. Datos de profesorado*, Madrid: *Consejo de Universidades*, mimeo.
Eagly, R. V. (ed.) (1968) *Events, Ideology and Economic Theory: The Determinants of Progress in the Development of Economic Analysis*, Detroit: Wayne State University Press.
Fuentes Quintana, E. (1993) 'Tres decenios largos de la economía española en perspectiva', in J. L. García Delgado (ed.) *España, Economía*, Madrid: Espasa Calpe, pp. 1–140.
——(ed.) (1998) *Economía y economistas españoles*, Madrid, forthcoming.
Gallotti, R. (1958) 'La literatura económica contemporánea en España', *Moneda y Crédito* 67: 29–51.
García, J. and Pérez, F. (1998) 'La enseñanza de la Economía en España: formación analítica y conocimiento experimental', in E. Fuentes Quintana (ed.) *Economia y economistas españoles*, Madrid.
García Delgado, J. L. (ed.) (1993) *España, Economía* (first edition 1988), Madrid: Espasa Calpe.
González, M. J. (1976) 'Neomercatilismo en Madrid. Dos economistas de la postguerra', *Información Comercial Española* 517: 125–43.
——(1979) *La economía política del franquismo* (1940–1970). *Dirigismo, mercado y planificación*, Madrid: Tecnos.
Guillén, M. F. (1989) *La profesión de economista. El auge de economistas, ejecutivos y empresarios en España*, Barcelona: Ariel.
Gutiérrez, A. and Velasco, C. (1982) 'La situación actual de los estudios universitarios de economía y ciencias empresariales', *Información Comercial Española* 589: 25–32.
Harmes-Liedtke, U. (1992) 'Heinrich von Stackelberg y la economía nacional española', in J. L. García Delgado (ed.) *Economía española, cultura y sociedad. Homenaje a Juan Velarde Fuertes ofrecido por la Universidad Complutense*, Madrid: Eudema, vol. II, pp. 553–71.
Hall, P. A. (ed.) (1989) *The Political Power of Economic Ideas: Keynesianism across Nations*, Princeton, NJ: Princeton University Press.
Hirschman, A. O. (1989) 'How the Keynesian Revolution was exported from the United States, and other comments', in P. A. Hall (ed.) *The Political Power of Economic Ideas*, Princeton, NJ: Princeton University Press, pp 347–59.
INE (*Instituto Nacional de Estadística*) (1966) *Estadística de la enseñanza superior en España (Cursos 1960–61, 1963–64)*, Madrid: *INE*.
——(1976) *Estadística de la enseñanza en España (Curso 1974–75)*, Madrid: *INE*.
Lluch, E. (1996) 'Transición económica y transición política 1978–1980', in J. Tusell and A. Soto (eds) *Historia de la transición 1975–1986*, Madrid: Alianza, pp. 252–63
Martínez Serrano, J. A., *et al.* (1982) *Economía española: 1960–1980. Crecimiento y cambio estructural*, Madrid: H. Blume.
MEC (*Ministerio de Educación y Ciencia*) (1974) *Catedráticos de Universidad. Escalafón de catedráticos*, Madrid: MEC.
Miguel, A. de (1975) *Sociología del franquismo. Análisis ideológico de los Ministros del Régimen*, Madrid: Euros.
Montecinos, V. (1997) 'Economists in political and policy elites in Latin America', in A. W. Coats (ed.) *The Post-1945 Internationalization of Economics*, Durham, NC and London: Duke University Press.
Montoro, R. (1981) *La Universidad en la España de Franco (1939–1970). Un análisis sociológico*, Madrid: *Centro de Investigaciones Sociológicas*.

Muns, J. (1986) *Historia de las relaciones entre España y el Fondo Monetario Internacional 1958–1982. Veinticinco años de economía española*, Madrid: Alianza.

Naharro Mora, J. M. (1950) 'Organización actual de los estudios de economía en España', *Revista de Economía Política* 2, 1: 86–91.

Pestaña, A. (1993) 'Un modelo bibliométrico para el estudio de la actividad científica. Aplicación a España y otros países ribereños del Mediterráneo', *Política Científica* 35: 47–51.

Preston, P. (1990) 'Spain', in A. Graham and A. Seldon (eds) *Government and Economies in the Postwar World: Economic Policies and Comparative Performance, 1945–85*, London: Routledge, pp. 125–53.

Robertson, D. H. (1940) 'A Spanish contribution to the theory of fluctuations', *Economica* n.s. 7, 25: 50–65.

Rodríguez, J. (1989) 'El periodo de la transición política desde la perspectiva del análisis económico', in J. F. Tezanos *et al.* (eds) *La transición democrática española*, Madrid: Sistema.

Roper, J. F. H. (1969) *L'enseignement des Sciences Economiques au niveau universitaire*, Paris: Conseil de l'Europe and A. Colin.

Ros Hombravella, J. (ed.) (1975) *Trece economistas españoles ante la economía española*, Barcelona: Oikos-Tau.

Sánchez, A. (1991) *Valentín Andrés Alvarez. Un economista del 27*, Zaragoza: *Universidad de Zaragoza*.

Schwartz, P. (ed.) (1977) El producto nacional de España en el siglo XX, Madrid: *Instituto de Estudios Fiscales*.

Segura, J. (1998) 'Una nota sobre la historia de la introducción y asimilación del análisis microeconómico moderno en España', in E. Fuentes Quintana (ed.) *Economía y economistas*, Madrid.

Stackelberg, H. F. von (1946a) *Principios de teoría económica*, Madrid: *Instituto de Estudios Políticos*.

——(1946b) 'Interés y dinero (Discusión de algunas teorías monetarias)', *Anales de Economía* 6, 23: 221–39.

Torres, M. de (1958) 'Informe sobre la enseñanza en España', in C. W. Guillebaud (ed.) *Las ciencias sociales en la enseñanza superior. Ciencias Económicas*, Madrid: Unesco–CSIC, pp. 151–7.

Trullén i Thomas, J. (1993) *Fundamentos económicos de la transición política española. La política económica de los Acuerdos de la Moncloa*, Madrid: *Ministerio de Trabajo y Seguridad Social*.

Urrutia, J. (1993) 'La investigación española en Economía', *Política Científica* 36: 41-7.

Velarde Fuertes, J. (1961) *Flores de Lemus ante la economía española*, Madrid: *Instituto de Estudios Políticos*.

——(1967) 'Les tendences actuelles de la recherche économique en Espagne', *Social Science. Information sur les Sciences Sociales* 6, 2–3: 247–61.

——(1971) 'Final y principio de época para Anales de Economía', *Anales de Economía* 3rd series, 1: 3–8.

——(1974) *Introducción a la historia del pensamiento económico español en el siglo XX*, Madrid: *Editora Nacional*.

——(1990) *Economistas españoles contemporáneos: primeros maestros*, Madrid: Espasa Calpe.

——(1993) 'La base ideológica de la realidad económica española', in J. L. García Delgado (ed.) *España, Economía*, Madrid: Espasa Calpe, pp. 1253–300.

——(1996) 'Stackelberg and his role in the change in Spanish economic policy', *Journal of Economic Studies* 23(5–6): 128–40.

Velasco Murviedro, C. (1984) 'El ingenierismo como directriz de la política económica durante la autarquía (1936–1951)', *Información Comercial Española* 606: 97–106.

11 Institutional constraints and the internationalization of economics

The case of Greece[1]

Michalis Psalidopoulos

In the mid-1950s, Unesco undertook the task of investigating the state of the social sciences in a number of its member states, with the aim of showing ways of possible improvement in the relationship between scientific research and economic growth in those countries. The report on Greece, written by Professor Pierre de Bie, of the University of Leuven, Belgium, is a document written with caution and care.

The author devoted much space in this analysis to sociology, but economic science also came under his thorough investigation. He concluded that the condition of teaching and research in economics was in general satisfactory. On the other hand, taking into account developments in economics internationally and the need for accelerated economic growth in the country, he thought economics in Greece was still 'insufficient' in helping the country to cope with its economic problems (de Bie 1956–57: 42). Even if there is no direct link between Unesco's report and reforms undertaken in Greek higher economic education in the late 1950s/early 1960s, one should not underestimate its importance: it paved the way for a slow but irreversible transformation of Greek economics into the internationally more or less uniform modern economics of today.

The purpose of this chapter is to tell the story of the internationalization[2] of economics in the postwar period in Greece. It will be argued (1) that because of national peculiarities this process was delayed until the mid-1970s and got under way only after the fall of the military dictatorship in 1974. In this sense economics in Greece is still in a process of transition towards full Americanization; and (2) that the close links between academic life and the sphere of politics are a central issue in understanding past resistances to the adoption of a new, and more up-to-date economic discourse in Greek economics.

As we shall see, the first half of the post-1945 era was characterized by the dominance of economists who had started their careers in the interwar years. This generation obtained its postgraduate degrees mainly in Greece itself, and those of its members who went abroad to study, went to Germany and, to a smaller degree, to France. These economists came to retirement age shortly before or during the military dictatorship (1967–74). After the fall of the *junta*, a new generation of economists conquered Greek academia. The vast majority of these economists had followed postgraduate studies in the United Kingdom and the United States and were therefore familiar with a mathematical approach to economic problems and quantitative methods in economic research.

The argument will unfold in the following manner. In the first section we will see how the old generation came to gain a stronghold over Greek economics. Then we move to trace developments in the institutional reproduction of economic knowledge in the country. We then turn to the broader scientific community of economists in Greece, to journals, research centres and schools of thought. We finally offer a brief assessment as a conclusion.

The Pre-World War II background

In order to understand the delayed adoption of international standards in economic education in Greece, one has to go back to the interwar years, when economics as a science made considerable progress in the country and a single individual, Professor Andreas Andreades,[3] helped a number of distinguished young scholars to occupy university chairs. This process was of great importance since they greatly influenced economic discourse in Greece until the late 1960s/early 1970s.

Andreas Andreades, Professor of Public Finance, was an eclectic liberal economist who, as a senior academic, was appointed to all selection committees responsible for filling university positions at the time. It is therefore worth noting his opinion on what was to be done with economics in Greece.

Andreades believed that both the classical and neoclassical schools as well as the German historical school were products of certain political and philosophical ideas which sprang out of concrete historical and economic facts. These theories were therefore valid for a limited time and for certain countries sharing the same characteristics. 'The Greek scientist should not belong exclusively in any one [of these schools]. He should inquire how far this teaching could be applied in his country' (Andreades 1927: 237).

Andreades thought that after a period of intense historical research and debate among different schools of thought there could follow a phase of more theoretical work and of efforts to establish an economic theory suitable to the needs of the Greek economy.[4] It is precisely for this reason that he helped various economists of very different world views and theoretical viewpoints to advance their civil/academic careers. The most influential of his protégés proved to be the following:

1   Professor Xenophon Zolotas (University of Athens), a liberal who can be considered as the most important of Andreades's choices. Zolotas was active in his university chair from 1928 to 1967. He was also Governor of the Central Bank, the Bank of Greece, between 1955 and 1967 and 1974 and 1981. Furthermore, he became Prime Minister in the National Unity government of 1990.

2   Professor Demosthenes Stephanides (University of Thessaloniki/University of Athens), a historicist with national socialist tendencies, active from 1928 to 1965.
3   Professor Kyriakos Varvaressos (University of Athens), a state socialist, active from 1923 to 1955. He was also Deputy Governor of the Bank of Greece in the 1930s, its Governor in exile 1940 to 1944, and a Deputy Prime Minister in 1945. After his early retirement he lived in the USA and worked as a World Bank expert.
4   Professor Demetrios Kalitsounakis (Athens Graduate School for Economics and Business), a social democrat, active from 1925 to 1960.

Zolotas and Kalitsounakis were the editors of the two interwar scientific economic journals, the Review (*Epitheorisis Koinonikis ke Dimosias Oikonomikes*, Review of Social and Public Economics) and the Archive (*Archion Economikon ke Koinonikon Epistimon*, Archive of Economics and Social Sciences) respectively.

Whereas the Archive defined economics in a broader social sciences setting, and its editor espoused interventionism, the Review placed emphasis only on economics and public finance and the bulk of the contributions therein mostly followed the then prevailing neoclassical paradigm.

Seven out of the many contributors to the Review who already had a PhD submitted monographs in the late 1930s to the University of Athens to become '*ifigites*' (readers).[5] Here Zolotas and Varvaressos assumed the role played by Andreades a decade earlier. In the 1940s and 1950s these readers in economics at the University of Athens proceeded to occupy existing or newly created chairs at other Greek universities. Andreades's dream had somehow been fulfilled. Greek economists had multiplied in numbers; economic monographs and articles were being published in growing numbers; and all schools of thought, with Marxism existing but outside academia, flourished.

The world economic depression led to Greece's default in 1932 and to a *de facto* acceptance of interventionism by liberal and interventionist economists alike.[6] Whereas in the 1920s debates and controversies centred on a sound monetary policy and the limits to social policy, now the argument was about the proper functions of government in order to restore and maintain economic prosperity. Whereas liberal economists tried to work out a theory which could incorporate interventionism, interventionists, happy with their success in policy, did not try to formulate a coherent theory of their own. When Keynesian economics became known, its framework of analysis was rejected by both these schools of thought.[7]

Institutional framework and facts

Academic life did not change much during the twenty-five years after World War II. Out of thirty-three economists who came to occupy a university post from the 1920s to the late 1960s, twenty had done their PhDs in Greece, nine in

Germany, four in France, two in the UK, one in the USA and one in Switzerland. Four professors held two PhDs, from Athens and elsewhere; twenty-two out of the thirty-three had done an '*ifigessia*': sixteen at the Law School in Athens, four in Thessaloniki and two at the Athens Graduate School for Economics and Business. Three out of the thirty-three professors had obtained their positions in the 1920s, three in the 1930s, thirteen in the 1940s, ten in the 1950s and only four in the 1960s. (Psalidopoulos 1997a).

The University system remained very closely modelled on the German example, as it had also been in the past. From the academic year 1955–56 onward the minimum time required to obtain a first degree ('*ptichion*'), was expanded from three to four years of study. Moreover, the qualification for getting a university chair remained until 1982 very low: according to the law, only a PhD and one publication were needed. Any new position was filled through a majority vote of the members of the specific faculty. The voting body usually followed the recommendation of a select committee consisting of those three members of the faculty who were more closely associated with the subjects connected with the new position. The Ministry of Education was obliged to appoint the person elected. Lecturing needs were frequently covered by assistants, with or without a PhD,[8] specialists having successfully completed an *ifigessia* and by the existing ordinary professors themselves.

One should mention in this connection the fact that postgraduate training in economics in the country was completely absent. PhD candidates were encouraged to travel abroad, or, if they preferred, to write a thesis in Greece. In the latter case they only had to follow their supervisor's courses, which were not institutionally required by the university for the degree.

From the nineteenth century economics in Greece had been situated in law schools, not in philosophy departments. The Law School of the University of Athens awarded a first degree (*ptichion*) in economics to law students who sat for an extra year of study after their first degree, in order to complete additional courses in economics and public law successfully.

The Law School of the University of Thessaloniki has awarded a first degree in economics since 1953. Here too at least half of the courses required were in law.

A third institution devoted solely to economics and business studies was the Graduate School for Economics and Business Studies, founded in 1920. Here too, courses in law and various non-economics courses represented more than 50 per cent of total degree requirements. It was in this school, however, that accounting and business administration were first introduced as academic disciplines. The school awarded an economics or business degree according to the option students chose. Needless to say, most students chose the business degree and sought employment in the private sector.

Other universities offered courses, but not a degree in economics, including Panteios Graduate School for Political Science (modelled after the Paris *Ecole des Sciences Politiques*) from 1933, as well as the Higher School of Industrial Studies, a semi-public school for professional education, which later became the Graduate School of Industrial Studies in Piraeus.

The practical outcome of this situation was that the economics profession hardly existed. Most economics graduates preferred a career as a lawyer than as an economist, the demand side for which rarely came from the public sector.

Consolidation of power

During the interwar years, the effort to create commercial schools in secondary education, where graduates of the Athens Graduate School of Economics and Business Studies would teach, was halted in 1938, when professional education was defeated by a law that reconfirmed the classical ideal of a general, broad education for all. Commercial schools declined in importance, and economics as a discipline remained in the embrace of law.

In 1957 a new Graduate School for Industrial Studies was established in Thessaloniki, and in 1960 the Industrial Graduate School in Piraeus was called into life, but the curricula of studies, despite carrying some innovative elements, remained orientated to law.

Ordinary professors of economics became very influential in the postwar period and formed a circle that was not easy to penetrate. On the one hand they helped their assistants or young economists to do PhDs in Greece, but, preoccupied as most of them were with consulting posts in government, they did little for university reform: in fact they resisted it. It was, in any case, difficult in post-Civil War Greece, and beyond, to implement reforms in the educational system that would curtail the power of a distinct group of the academic elite, such as the economists.

It is worth noting in this connection that the economics professors in Thessaloniki taught not only courses in subjects in which they were specialists, but also other courses as diverse as economic geography and accounting, or financial law and history of economic thought. Instead of pushing for new appointments, when the Industrial School in Thessaloniki came into life most professors of the Law Faculty held joint appointments at both universities, instead of letting the new university elect its own staff. It is clear that this situation was very difficult to sustain in times of accelerating student numbers. Students found themselves in huge auditoriums listening to the 'expert', with no practical chance to pose questions or enter an argument. The student movement of the 1960s, united under the slogan '15 per cent for Education' (meaning the percentage of the budget that ought to be devoted to education instead of the then slim existing 3.5 per cent) pressed for changes. These eventually came about, but later.

The Greek Society for Economic Sciences

The postwar community of economists in Greece was initially very small. When in 1951 – and following the suggestion of American economists affiliated with the American Mission for Aid to Greece – the Greek Society for Economic Science was founded, it consisted of only about twenty-five members. Membership was limited only to those holding a postgraduate degree in economics, and the society therefore remained a closed club of prominent members. However, the pressure to attract higher civil servants into the Society led to the adoption of the status of 'affiliated' member. In 1962 the total number of members grew to 123 – sixty-seven ordinary and fifty-six affiliated. The role of the Society in the development of economics in Greece remains to be evaluated. There were no annual meetings, and the Society organized big conferences every three years: for example on 'The economic development of Greece' (1960); on 'The association between Greece and the EEC' (1963); on 'The balance of payments' (1966); on 'The organization of the economy' (1969); and, the last one, on 'Commercial shipping in Greece' (1972). Its most prominent members were university professors, some of whom personally translated important foreign books into Greek (see Appendix), and led frequent discussion sessions on current economic problems, followed by dinner. Every young economist interested in pursuing a career in government or academia had to be accepted by this circle if he wanted to gain a reputation as an economist.

When the old guard of economists retired and the dictatorship broke down, in 1974, the Society fell into oblivion. Lately it has been reactivated, and the future will tell if it is going to replicate the glorious days of the past and embrace all Greek economists or not.

Curricula of studies and increments of change

In the meantime, at the universities – despite marginal changes – little was done in terms of reforming the curriculum of studies. A few examples help to clarify this point:

- The teaching of development economics as a separate area of knowledge and research started around 1965. The first chair in this subject was inaugurated in 1964 at the Graduate School in Piraeus. One might have expected that, with economic development being the goal of all Greek governments, special attention would have been given to the field sooner.
- Econometrics was first introduced around 1971.
- The academic unit in operation was the year, which meant thirty weeks of teaching plus exams.

A typical programme of study at the Athens Graduate School[9] in 1956 consisted of the following economics courses (the other courses were in law, and other related subjects).

1st year = 2 hours per week	Demand, supply, market equilibrium, price formation of factors of production.
2 hours per week	Economic history.
2nd year = 1 hour per week	Theory of money, economic fluctuations, international exchanges.
3 hours per week	Agricultural, industrial, social, monetary and credit policy.

3rd year =	2 hours per week	Internal/external commercial policy, policy against economic fluctuations.
	3 hours per week	History of economic thought.
	4 hours per week	Public finance and financial law.

By 1967 the situation had changed as follows:

1st year =	2 hours per week	Market equilibrium, consumer and producer equilibrium.
2nd year =	3 hours per week	Microeconomic theory.
	3 hours per week	Agricultural and commercial policy.
3rd year =	3 hours per week	Labour economics.
	2 hours per week	Macroeconomic theory.
4th year =	4 hours per week	Employment and income theory, and theory of money.
	2 hours per week	Economic development and planning.

These two snapshots reveal that elements of micro- and macroeconomic theory were introduced in the curricula of study in the late 1950s/early 1960s. The first chairs devoted to the subject of modern economic theory bore the title 'Economic Analysis', and were created not at the respective departments of the law schools, but at the Graduate Schools for Industrial Studies in Piraeus in 1962 and Thessaloniki in 1969. In 1968, G. Koutsoumaris, a University of Chicago PhD, newly elected professor at the Athens Graduate School of Economics and Business, presented a new textbook, entitled Economic Analysis, totally different from the ones previously available in Greek. In the same year D. Karagiorgas, an LSE PhD, Associate Professor at Panteios Graduate School, presented two modern textbooks on public finance and fiscal policy.

It should be noted that textbooks still play a major role in university education in Greece. They are considered 'bibles of truth' regarding an area of study, and students preparing for exams learn their 'truths' by heart.

To sum up, academic economics in Greece remained descriptive and antiquarian until the mid-1960s, compared to what was happening in the rest of the world, the main reason for this being the practical standstill in electing new economists at a time of rapid changes in economic education internationally. Of course these changes were closely followed by Greek professors and found their way into lectures of '*ifigites*', or even the professors themselves, provided they were not too technical in character. However, during that period, Greek economics lacked on the one hand the philosophical depth and background of a moral science and, on the other, remained faithful to the German encyclopaedism of the historicist tradition. The image of the 'good economist' which was most widely propagated and accepted at this time was that of a wise, well-read person, an authority whose recommendations on economic policy were always sound and never extreme. Yet steps towards a new era had been taken.

Winds of change

Economic policy in Greece faced many problems in the post-world war period. Because of political turmoil and the Civil War, recovery was long delayed, government finances deteriorated and inflation was high. The successful devaluation of the currency in 1953 and its stabilization at a parity of 30 drs to US$1, as well as a trade liberalization, were the preconditions of fast growth rates after the late 1950s, with 6 per cent annual increases in GNP, up to the mid-1970s. Monetary stability was proclaimed the first and foremost target of economic policy, and it was hoped that the problem of widespread unemployment (12.1 per cent in 1960) would be overcome in the future through increased private investment. X. Zolotas, Professor at the University of Athens and Governor of the Central Bank, was the most outspoken supporter of this view.

The neglect of the unemployment issue plus the problem of the political system, which was oppressive and hostile to reforms, attracted criticism from a younger generation of scholars. The most prominent of these was Professor A. Papandreou, who, after a successful career at the universities of Harvard, Minnesota and California at Berkeley in the 1950s, came as a consultant to the Greek government and raised money from Greek as well as US sources to found a Centre for Economic Research in 1961, which was renamed the Centre for Planning and Economic Research (KEPE) in 1964. The Centre invited many American and British economists to conduct research and give seminars to its young staff.[10] These scientists brought into Greece mathematical techniques, a policy-orientated economic analysis, and a Keynesianism, typical of the time, of the neoclassical synthesis variety. The Centre sponsored scholarships for its staff. About twenty-five scholarships were awarded between 1963 and 1965 to young economists, who went mainly to the UK. One group of five preferred the University of Manchester and took PhDs in economic planning. Others went to the United States, where the universities of Rochester, North Carolina/Raleigh, and Wayne State attracted small groups of candidates.[11] Papandreou also brought with him some Greek economists working in US universities, who, with one exception (the aforementioned G. Koutsoumaris) and despite their credentials, were not offered university positions in Greece.

The Central Bank, the Bank of Greece, encouraged economists working in its Department of Economic Research to follow postgraduate studies abroad as well. Its policy allowed each individual economist to choose a scientific field and a university completely freely, keeping only in mind the broad needs of the service and the development process in the country. Many economists of this group chose Yale University, which offered a special PhD course in international foreign economic administration.

Both KEPE and the Central Bank used a salaries policy as an incentive to attract bright young economists. Even though they belonged to the public sector, these institutions were freed from salaries regulations valid for all government officials and could offer better financial perspectives to their employees. There was therefore a large supply of candidates throughout the 1960s and 1970s aiming at becoming KEPE/Central Bank economists.

In the late 1960s there were many MAs[12] and PhDs from the UK (most notably the University of London) and the USA who were familiar with the then mainstream ideas and techniques in economics, thinking of themselves as bearers of a new spirit, eager to enter prestigious university positions but unable to do so. Among this group of people many sought a career elsewhere and went abroad again – for good.

The military dictatorship proved to be a catalyst for the internationalization process in a twofold sense. Firstly, and in order to strengthen its ideological influence, it enforced an opening of the university system, thus helping some economists of this generation to become academics. The old generation of economists was in retirement, anyhow.

Second, because of the emphasis placed by the military on economic development, a need grew for economist specialists capable of analysing problems and issues in the context of the country's structural change. This led to a shift in the students' choices. The ratio of students preferring an economics rather than a business degree went from 1:6 in 1966 to 2:5 in 1974 (Psalidopoulos 1997a). In the wake of an educational reform pushed through by the military, separate departments of economics and politics were created within the law schools from the academic year 1970–71 onward. This began the gradual diminishing of the importance of law courses for an economics degree.

After the fall of the dictatorship and in the wake of the cleansing of the public sector of anti-democratic elements, many of these young economists were dismissed from their positions, but the stream of events had changed.[13] It is ironic that, in spite of the widespread anti-American sentiment in Greek public life after the fall of the *junta*, because of US support of the Colonels no one questioned the beginning of the domination of American textbooks in student reading lists. To top these developments, many scientists who had been dismissed from their posts by the *junta* returned either to their old jobs, or from abroad.

The role of foreign economic advisers and agencies

After World War II, with the Truman Doctrine (1947), Greece had become subject to intensive American foreign policy interest and one is tempted to assume that foreign, especially American, economists would have disseminated American economics in Greece and influenced economic thinking in the country. British economists were also active as members of the United Nations Relief and Rehabilitation Administration in Greece, or as consultants to the British Embassy in Athens before and after 1947. International organizations such as the FAO commissioned surveys of Greek agriculture, and in general, specialists of all kinds were interacting with their Greek counterparts, especially in the first post-1945 decade. After all, it was during this decade especially that American interest in foreign economic development as a collateral to diplomacy became evident (Simpson 1987: 641).

However, there is no evidence that this multiple Greek–US/British interaction led Greek economists to major changes in attitude towards analysing economic policy problems. To start with, American-trained economists during that period had been taught according to the administrative tradition of Roosevelt's New Deal (Nelson 1987: 52–4) and were therefore no diehard supporters of *laissez-faire*. Economists in the British civil service were also accustomed to planning for war and its aftermath, even though not in a collectivist sense. The situation of the Greek economy in the immediate postwar years – with hyperinflation, an infrastructure destroyed by occupation, the private sector unable to provide basic needs and the government involved in a civil war – motivated many economists to offer advice on how to restore economic welfare. Agreement was anyhow unanimous on basics: balancing the budget; seeking currency stabilization through sound monetary policy; relieving the poor; liberalizing the economy. There were, of course, differences in method, extent and timing as regards different measures; harsh political battles were fought over them, but differences in the style of economics played no major part therein.

After the end of the Civil War, American interest in the Greek economy declined as interest in Korea grew. The Fulbright Foundation gave scholarships to young Greek economists and civil servants to study economics, among other disciplines, in the United States. It also encouraged American scholars to visit and conduct research in Greece, but little use was made by American economists of this opportunity and any possible influences these visits exerted were marginal.

On the contrary, when in the late 1950s the Greek government sought foreign help to carry through the first five-year plan, it officially invited Professor Pasquale Saraceno, of the University of Rome, to assist. The reasons for this choice were the desire of the government to avoid showing continual reliance on US help for internal political reasons and the similarity of Greek underdevelopment at the time with economic conditions in Southern Italy that the Italian expert had long studied.

In the 1960s the Ford Foundation played a significant part in the development of economics in Greece. It sponsored the creation and financing of the first activities of the Centre for Planning and Economic Research (referred to in detail above). When the military dictatorship took over and despite the close links between official American policy and the Colonels, the Ford Foundation came to sponsor artists and intellectuals in opposition in order for them to pursue activities and research that would not otherwise have been possible. This activity, hotly debated in Greek public life after the fall of the dictatorship as fake interest by the 'ugly American', benefited economics in the sense that the Ford Foundation financed translations of seminal articles on economics that were distributed in classes taught by Professor I. Pesmazoglou, an Athens/Cambridge PhD, shortly before the latter was expelled from the former university and exiled by the *junta*. These articles were circulated among students for many years, and closed the gap of illiteracy prevailing among Greek economics students at that time.

In all, foreign economic advice had little to offer for the modernization of Greek economics. In an open and outward-looking country, with intellectuals eager to learn from foreign counterparts, this would not be necessary anyhow. It was, finally, the institutional constraints described above – the tight control of the professional elite over new appointments – that delayed the internationalization of economics in Greece, and not the possible missing of the necessary international advice to catch the boat of emerging modern economics.

Schools of thought: journals and arguments

The economic development of the country was the most important issue for Greek economists in the post-1945 era. The more appropriate strategy to remove obstacles and set accelerated growth in motion was the task of articles, books and pamphlets, even if they dealt with technical questions. Intertwined with economic development was the question of Greece's association with the EEC in 1962. In the early 1960s, as well as in the late 1970s, shortly before full Greek membership of the European Community, clear-cut debates took place on whether Greece would sustain high rates of growth and its political independence, if allied with the EEC. In general, three camps or schools of thought can be identified concerning these issues: they were liberal-dirigiste, structuralist-interventionist and Marxist.

The liberal camp considered economic development as an inevitable process, if the institutional framework of the Greek economy were adjusted to principles governed by the logic of the market. Reliance on foreign technical and financial assistance for this camp was important in the development process because of the lack of native capital which could be used in the servicing of large investment projects. Even if there were a high price to pay in terms of profit repatriation for foreign investment in the country, foreign capital was welcome.

However, Greek liberals always kept in the back of their minds the idea of strong government action in the economy, if needed. This notion was based on their postgraduate training in interwar Germany, and also on the fact that economic liberalism in Greece was a doctrine imported into the country from France, not Britain (Psalidopoulos 1989). French liberalism was, in Schumpeter's term, a 'political liberalism' (Schumpeter 1954: 394), and Greek liberals did not dogmatically object to interventionism, if the outcome were to reward the right-wing party in power. Greek liberals, facing as they did the economic misery of the country after the Great Depression, had developed a broad sense of social policy to adopt whatever government action was necessary, if the financial means to implement it existed.

As expected, this liberal camp espoused Greece's association with and, later, full membership in the EEC, minimizing in various degrees the possible negative effects of the gradual loss of protection of Greek industry and the right to autonomous economic action in future circumstances.[14] A major figure in this camp was Professor Zolotas, who, besides his other appointments, was editor-in-chief of the most prominent postwar economics journal, the 'Review' (*Epitheorisis Oikonomikon ke Politikon Epistimon – Review of Economic and Social Sciences*). The Review ceased publication because of the dictatorship, but in the meantime it distinguished itself as a forum for scientific contributions, not necessarily committed throughout on the lines described above.

Actually, there were two distinct phases of editorial policy and contributors: one that lasted from 1944 to the mid-1950s, and a second from then until 1967. In the first phase, and especially in the first years of publication, papers in the Review tended to share the then prevailing vision of 'full employment in a free society', were critical of mainstream economics, and were sometimes even 'socialist'. In the second phase, which coincided with the editor's tenure as Governor of the Central Bank, the pages of the journal got shorter, the articles were written by young MAs and PhDs, some of them working at the Central Bank, who used mathematics as part of their discourse, being technical in approach.

The structuralist-interventionist group identified Greece not as a less developed European country, but rather as a Third World one, finding itself in a vicious circle of political dependence on the Great Powers and, necessarily, of economic underdevelopment. What was needed by these economists was strong government action in all fields of social life. The vision was somehow voluntaristic in nature. It foresaw that if administrative reforms, especially in human capital, were to be implemented, then a huge developmental potential would reveal itself and Greece would create an industrial sector (then hardly existing) that would upgrade the economy, transforming it to a 'European' one. External economic relations in this scenario became crucial, and this camp espoused the findings of R. Prebish's Economic Commission for Latin America, that the terms of trade between rich and poor countries favoured the former. Democratic planning on a large scale, it was claimed, could make the vision of a modern industrialized Greece a reality.

An important advocate of this camp in academia was Professor A. Angelopoulos,[15] editor of the monthly *New Economy* (*Nea Oikonomia*). Andreas Papandreou as a Centre Union politician in the 1960s was close to these ideas. *New Economy* was a pluralist, scholarly journal. Here, too, two phases of editorial policy can be distinguished. One, up to 1958–59, was more pro-Third World, and planning successes in existing socialism were praised. The second was characterized by the inclusion on the editorial board of many young economists who had completed or were completing postgraduate studies in the UK. Even if the tone was critical of government policies – for example, as far as concessions to foreign capital were concerned – the fact is that *New Economy* adopted a very distinct approach to Greek economic problems.[16] The EEC question proves the point. *New Economy* advocated association sometime, but under other economic conditions; that is in a time when the Greek economy would be better able to compete on an equal basis with the industrialized European nations.

The Marxist camp bore the prestigious heritage of the National Liberation Movement which, during the German occupation, had nourished a whole generation with the idea that Greek underdevelopment was due to the political dependence of Greece on foreign countries. In the early postwar period D. Batsis showed in a persuasive way that there were enough financial sources and technical skills in Greece to build up heavy industry, provided that there was the political will to tame the bourgeois class that opposed the project (Batsis 1947).[17]

After the Communist defeat in the Greek Civil War, the Marxist camp found it difficult to discover means of expression. *Modern Issues* (*Synchrona Themata*) was a Marxist review of letters and social sciences. Economic contributions therein applauded economic successes in existing socialism and were critical of all aspects of government policy in Greece. Association with the EEC was like throwing the Greek economy into the lion's den, as the leader of the legal party of the left put it (Iliou 1962:278). Consequently, given the political assumptions about the role of the EEC in the bipolar era against the Soviet camp, Greek Marxists were, until the 1970s, vehemently opposed to Greece's association with the EEC.

This survey cannot, of course, do justice to all the details of Greek economics. Technical treatises, theoretical contributions and scholarly papers appeared not only in the above-mentioned journals, but in others as well, such as Professor Kalitsounakis's *Archive* (until 1970), and *Studies* (*Spoudai*), the journal of the Graduate School of Industrial Studies in Piraeus.

On the eve of the internationalization of economics in Greece all schools of economic thought still existed. It was the way of putting arguments forward that was to be changed in the future, either for big issues like Greek economic development, or minor ones.

Keynesianism

Having mentioned above the salient features of various schools of economics in postwar Greece, we turn now to Keynesianism, the novel achievement in economics in the twentieth century.

In seeking to explain if and why Keynesian ideas acquired influence or not in some countries in the post-World War II period, Peter Hall emphasized the explanatory power of four interrelated factors (Hall 1989: 376–89):

1   the orientation of the governing party;
2   the structure of the state, and state–society relations;
3   the nature of political discourse in the country under investigation; and
4   events that shaped political developments in that country after 1945.

Basing his findings on those of a series of comparative studies, Hall concluded that Keynesian concepts of demand management spread more slowly where the economics profession was small and where the university system was hierarchical and dominated by professors deeply committed to economic doctrines attacked by

Keynesian economic philosophy. These findings are verified by the Greek experience, as we have shown extensively elsewhere (Psalidopoulos 1996).

Keynes had been very well known in Greece from the interwar years, both as a monetary theorist and as an authority on international policy issues. His *Tract on Monetary Reform* and *The End of Laissez-faire* had been translated into Greek, his proposals for a managed currency discussed, and his objection to anti-deflationist policies as a way out of economic depression approved by Greek interventionists. However, and because of the absence of a British tradition in economic thought in Greece, his work was not comprehended as, at first, a continuation of, and then, a break from Marshallian economics.

When the *General Theory* came out, it was, as in other places in the world, received negatively by Greek liberal and interventionist economists alike. Keynes's attack on savings as a potential source of economic instability was unacceptable for X. Zolotas. Other liberal academics disapproved of the new jargon introduced, the framework of analysis and the hypotheses put forward by Keynes. The dissonance of Greek interventionists with the *General Theory* was explicitly articulated after 1945. The polarized political climate between conservatives and the Communist-led National Resistance Movement, as well as the Civil War, made economists like D. Kalitsounakis and A. Angelopoulos reject Keynesianism on the ground that it espoused an interventionism of a very special kind that would preserve the basic features of the free enterprise economy.

This rejection of the *General Theory* did not change in substance when Keynesianism established itself in the 1950s and 1960s as the main economic paradigm, mainly in British and US academia. Professorial authority in Greece meant, as we saw, that younger scientists had to be very cautious, should they arrive at different conclusions from those of their teachers, as the contributions in the special issue of Professor Zolotas's Review to commemorate Keynes's death confirm. We conclude, therefore, that the rigid academic environment in the country and the absence of a generation change at the universities led to the new gospel of modern economics not being praised by a Greek academic until after the fall of the dictatorship (Krimpas 1975).[18]

Turning now to the orientation of the governing party towards certain economic ideas – Hall's most important factor (Hall 1989: 376) – we find that subsequent governments in the 1950s and 1960s, despite their paternalistic attitudes towards the working poor, did not approach economic policy issues with a Keynesian framework. The most prominent politician on economic issues of the right wing ERE Party in the 1950s and 1960s and the New Democracy Party in the 1970s was Panagis Papaligouras, an efficient, widely read intellectual, who defined the economic policy of the governments he served as 'realist liberalism' (Psalidopoulos 1997b: 27). For Papaligouras, nineteenth-century liberalism lacked a moral dimension and ignored social policy, whereas twentieth-century liberalism, the 'realist' one he espoused, was a system where the administration intervened wherever the government felt it appropriate in order to weaken socially unacceptable circumstances for the poorest strata of society and the unemployed. The limits to such action were set by government revenue and productivity increases in the economy. Papaligouras had a high esteem for Keynes as an economist, but objected to effective demand manipulation because of peculiar problems facing the Greek economy: a scarcity of capital, the need to promote savings, balance of payments restrictions and the need to maintain price stability. The official doctrine of sound monetary policy pronounced by Professor Zolotas and monitored by the Central Bank was responsible for high rates of growth in the 1950s and 1960s, and would be endangered if deficit spending was to be introduced for achieving full employment. The opposing political party, the Centre Union, on the other hand, with the son of its leader, Andreas Papandreou, as its main speaker, was committed in the early 1960s to a different agenda; namely, structural reforms. With all due respect to Keynes, his theories were still regarded by the Centre Union as irrelevant for countries like Greece.

The internationalization process eventually brought Keynesian economics to the forefront of a wider audience of students, scholars and professionals. Every holder of an MA or a PhD degree from an Anglo-Saxon university became to some extent familiar with Keynesian economics and the economics of Keynes.

However, the Greek politicians' overall philosophy did not change much regarding Keynesianism. After all, the 1970s and 1980s were characterized by high inflation, unemployment and low growth rates, which were not identifiable by the mainstream Keynesian interpretation of the day. Economic policy-makers watched GNP growth rates in Greece fall from 6.6 per cent in the 1960s, to 5.6 per cent in the 1970s and 1.8 per cent in the 1980s, with rates in industrial output falling from 9.8 per cent, to 6.4 per cent and 0.5 per cent respectively. The inflation rate averaged 16.2 per cent per year between 1983 and 1995. Industrial decline led in the 1980s to the overtaking of 'ailing' firms by the government in order for unemployment to be kept to a minimum. Government expenditure rose from 30 per cent of GNP in the 1970s to 50 per cent in the late 1980s, whereas government investment fell from 6.7 per cent of GNP in 1970, to 5.6 per cent in 1980 and 5.3 per cent in 1989 (Bank of Greece 1989). The old guard of liberal policy-makers and academics like Papaligouras and Zolotas could do no more to counteract these developments other than lead the country to full European Union membership.[19]

It is ironic that during the 1980s , the decade of right-wing hegemony across most of the West, with Margaret Thatcher's and Ronald Reagan's governments applauding monetarism and supply-side economics, in Greece, Andreas Papandreou and his Socialist Party (PASOK) were trying to lead Greece in 'the third way', as he put it, something in between capitalism and communism. Keynes's theory, developed to remove deficiencies of the capitalist system, could not be his favourite, as every member of his party knew.

Papandreou's party was strongly influenced by dependency theory, which was put forward as a means of explaining particularly Latin American underdevelopment and was popularized by P. Sweezy's *Monthly Review* magazine. All prominent PASOK economic policy officials were committed to lines of economic management set up by Papandreou himself in his numerous publications. Eventually the rhetoric of a transition to socialism was abandoned for the sake of an economic administration that tried to counteract a poor economic perfor-mance and worsening economic indicators with a variety of *ad hoc* measures. It is therefore, in our view, misleading to suggest, just because demand and mon-etary management techniques as instruments of government policy exist, that Greece experimented with a 'Keynesian economic policy' at times when there were austerity programmes (more especially between 1985 and 1987).

Our final conclusion, therefore, is that political peculiarities, a rigid academic environment and an orientation of the governing parties towards other economic paradigms contributed to an unfriendly reception of Keynesianism as a school of thought in Greece, and that Greek technocrats, despite their familiarity with Keynesianism, have not approached the country's macroeconomic instabilities in J. M. Keynes's terms.

Assessment of the post-1975 era

During the period 1975–95 higher education in Greece has been transformed from an elite to a mass system. In 1982 a new university law specified require-ments for university positions,[20] and in the same decade three new departments offering degrees in economics were established at the universities of Crete, of Patras and of the Aegean.

The 1980s saw the economics departments separate completely from political science, and in the wake of the 1982 reform the government financed the trans-formation of the universities from elite schools to mass universities. The generous government support also provoked an explosion in the number of appointments. According to an estimate, approximately 300 academic econo-mists exist in Greece today.

In a final act of reform, in 1989, all existing graduate schools were renamed as universities and new departments giving highly specialized first degrees were introduced.

This enormous expansion, after decades of institutional constraints on seeking academic positions, changed the landscape of economic education in Greece completely. Within a short time the curricula of studies were changed to reflect the new situation. The internationalization of economics had come to Greece.

The known classification between economists in different schools of thought applies in Greece as well, but the respective discourse has also changed. All schools of thought are represented at the universities in varying degrees.[21]

This chapter has dealt with the internationalization of economics in Greece primarily as a story of generation change, this change brought a clear shift in economics in Greece. In 1975, at the Graduate School of Economics and Busi-ness only two full-time professors were serving. In 1991, the Department of Economics of the Economic University of Athens (the former Graduate School's successor) consisted of a staff of twenty, eleven of whom held a PhD from a US university, seven from a UK university, one from Germany and one from Greece. This does not, however, mean that economic analysis has completely lost some of its national elements. Many economists still publish only in Greek;

wide-scale postgraduate studies do not exist, and neither do Greek scientific journals, with the notable exception of *Studies* (*Spoudai*).

The internationalization of postwar economics in Greece meant, primarily, the coming of age of the UK–American-trained economist. The surviving close links between academia and party politics and the complete reliance on public sources for research pose very interesting problems in relation to the internationalization of economics in Greece, the significance of which goes beyond the scope of this chapter.

Notes

1 Ideas expressed in this chapter were presented at the 1993 History of Economics Society conference in Philadelphia, at the 1995 European Conference on the History of Economics in Lisbon and at the 1996 meeting of the study group on the postwar internationalization of economics headed by Bob Coats in London. I benefited greatly from comments received by Bob Coats and other conference participants, but remain responsible for errors or omissions. This article draws heavily on Psalidopoulos (1997a).

2 Following Coats (1997: 395–6), we define 'internationalization' as the process of homogenization of curricula of studies on a world scale, based on Anglo-Saxon textbooks and mathematic modelling of economic problems. Americanization then indicates the transplantation of the US model in graduate training throughout the world. See the fascinating articles in Coats (1997).

3 It is worth noting that Andreades, who died in 1935, is the only Greek economist referred to in 'The New Palgrave'.

4 It is therefore clear that despite his liberalism, Andreades was on this issue closer to Schmoller than Menger.

5 Like the German *Habilitation*, *Ifigessia* consisted of an original theoretical monograph defended before the professorial body.

6 On economic developments in Greece in the interwar years and beyond, see Freris (1986).

7 On Keynesian economics, see below. For a history of economic thought in interwar Greece, see Psalidopoulos (1989). It is perhaps worth noting that according to this source, out of thirty-six of the most eminent economists working as bankers, journalists and civil servants and taking part in these debates, twenty-five had a PhD from a German university and eleven from a French one.

8 The assistant to a university chair held a *ptichion* and was supposed to prepare a thesis. The assistant with a PhD was named *epimelitis* ('monitor' of the chair) and waited for the professor's permission to start working on an '*ifigessia*'. Both positions were introduced in the late 1950s and early 1960s. It is worth noting in this connection that the Graduate School for Economics and Business awarded between 1928 and 1991 sixty-two PhDs, an average of just one per year. Seventeen PhDs were awarded between 1928 and 1944, twenty-seven between 1945 and 1974 and eighteen between 1974 and 1991 (Psalidopoulos 1997a).

9 See the respective yearbooks of the school for the years 1955–56 (36–7) and 1967–68 (52–5), respectively.

10 Names include among others: G. C. Archibald, Kenneth Arrow, George Break, Martin Bronfenbrenner, Robert Eisner, Howard Ellis, Milton Friedman, Arthur Goldberger, Robert Gordon, Peter O. Steiner, Daniel Suits, Ralph Turvey, Benjamin Ward and Pan A. Yotopoulos.

11 Some of these early KEPE economists returned eventually to Greece and some of them came to hold academic appointments in the 1970s.

12 To illustrate the political power of pressure groups in Greece, it must be noted that the pressure of the lobby of MA holders in Greece succeeded for some time in the 1970s in having this degree recognized as equal to a PhD, as far as promotions in the civil service were concerned.

13 At the Athens Graduate School three out of five full-time professors had to go, leaving behind a huge gap in teaching needs.

14 Space does not allow the breakdown of this camp into its many sub-groups. Mention must, however, be made of Professor Stephanides's reactionary views based on socio-biology. Stephanides rejected Greek association with the EEC because of the subordination he expected to take place of the 'weak' Greeks to the 'fittest' Germans.

15 Angelopoulos was Professor of Public Finance at the University of Athens between 1938 and 1946. He was expelled from the university because of his active participation in the national resistance movement during the war. In 1960 he was re-elected Professor of Applied Economics at Panteios Graduate School.

16 See Ioannides *et al.* (1994) for an in-depth content analysis of *New Economy*.

17 Sometime later Batsis was accused of spying for the illegal Communist Party, found guilty in an unfair trial and executed.

18 One notable exception was the Reader in Economics at the University of Athens, G. Katephores, an enthusiastic supporter of Keynes's doctrine since 1938, who died at a young age in 1943, leaving Keynes without a defender in Greek academic circles.

19 In the 1980s some Greek liberals abandoned this liberal–dirigiste tradition and sought in M. Friedman, F. Hayek and Thatcherism an alternative. However as the 1990–93 period has shown, when the New Democracy Party was in power, they exercised little influence in economic policy despite some of them holding political offices.

20 This law was later modified but its main characteristics still prevail. Four categories of university staff exist: full professor, associate professor, assistant professor and lecturer. The law requires, *inter alia*, in detail numbers of publications, years of postgraduate teaching and years elapsed since a candidate's PhD for eligibility to compete for a university opening.

21 It should be noted in this context that the Minister of Education is still obliged to appoint the person elected by a majority vote of the specific department. This has led to the 'tyranny of the majority' in certain situations and to some departments being considered by public opinion as 'right wing' and others as 'left wing'.

References

General

Andreades, A. (1927) 'Griechenland', in H. Mayer, *Die Wirtschaftstheorie der Gegenwart,* Vienna: Springer, pp. 236–46.

Bank of Greece (1989) *Long-term Statistical Series of the Greek Economy*, Athens.

Batsis, D. (1947) *Heavy Industry in Greece*, Athens (in Greek).

Coats, A. W. (ed.) (1997) 'The post-1945 internationalization of economics', *History of Political Economy*, Annual Supplement to vol. 28.

de Bie, P. (1956–7) 'The social sciences in Greece', *Spoudai* 7:1–2, 25–42 (in Greek).

Freris, A. F. (1986) *The Greek Economy in the Twentieth Century*, London: Croom Helm.

Hall, P. (1989) *The Political Power of Economic Ideas*, Princeton, NJ: Princeton University Press.

Iliou, I. (1962) *The Truth about the Common Market*, Athens (in Greek).

Ioannides, S., Kalogirou, G. and Lyberaki, A. 1994. 'The quest for development in the journal *New Economy*', *Greek Society in the First Postwar Era,* Athens: Foundation S. Karagiorgas (in Greek).

Krimpas, G. (1975) *Keynes's General Theory*, Athens: Papazissis.

Nelson, Robert H. (1987) 'The economics profession and the making of public policy', *Journal of Economic Literature* xxv: 49–91.

Psalidopoulos, M. (1989) *The Crisis of 1929 and the Greek Economists: A Contribution to the History of Economic Thought in Interwar Greece*, Athens: Foundation of the Commercial Bank of Greece for Research and Education (in Greek).

——(1996) 'Keynesianism across nations: the case of Greece', *European Journal for the History of Economic Thought* 3(3): 449–62.

——(1997a) 'Economic science in Greece, 1944–67: from national peculiarities to the Anglo-Saxon paradigm', Unpublished paper (in Greek).

——(ed.) (1997b) *Panagis Papaligouras: Speeches, Articles*, Athens: Eolos (in Greek).

Schumpeter, J. (1954) *History of Economic Analysis*, London: Allen and Unwin.

Simpson, James R. (1976) 'The origin of the United States' academic interest in foreign economic development', *Economic Development and Cultural Change* 24: 633–44.

List of books on economics translated into Greek, 1950–75

(1955) J. R. Hicks, *Social Framework, An Introduction to Economics*.

(1955) J. M. Keynes, *The General Theory of Employment, Interest and Money*.

(1967) E. Roll, *A History of Economic Thought*.

(1968) P. A. Samuelson, *Economics*.

(1969) S. Kuznets, *Modern Economic Growth: Rate, Structure and Spread*.

(1969) A. Brown, *An Introduction to World Economy*.

(1970) A. H. Hansen, *A Guide to Keynes*.

(1970) F. S. Brooman, *Macroeconomics*.

(1970) J. Robinson, *Economic Philosophy*.

(1971) G. Myrdal, *The Political Element in the Development of Economic Theory*.

(1972) C. P. Kindleberger, *International Economics*.

(1972) P. A. Baran and P. M. Sweezy, *Monopoly Capital*.

(1972) J. A. Schumpeter, *Capitalism, Socialism and Democracy*.

(1972) H. Richardson, *Regional Economics*.

(1972) A. Stonier and D. Hague, *A Textbook of Economic Theory*.

(1973) C. E. Ferguson, *Microeconomics*.

(1973) J. Pen, *Modern Economics*.

(1974) C. M. Cipolla, *The Economic History of World Population*.

(1974) P. Lewis, *An Introduction to Mathematical Economics*.

(1975) W. J. Baumol, *Economic Dynamics: An Introduction*.

(1975) E. Mandel, *Late Capitalism*.

(1975) R. G. Lipsey, *An Introduction to Positive Economics*.

(1975) G. Ackley, *Macroeconomic Theory*.

12 Concluding reflections

A. W. Bob Coats

Taken together, the ten country studies in this volume provide a wealth of new information and insight into the post-World War II evolution of economics in Western Europe,[1] both as an academic discipline and a policy science. This broad, comparative research area has hitherto been entirely neglected by historians of economics and by other scholars, and the present study is designed to open up this extensive territory and to encourage the production of more systematic comparative research.

For obvious reasons, no attempt will be made here to summarize the individual studies,[2] which amply reveal the diversity of national circumstances and experiences. Instead, attention will be focused on certain common features, themes and trends that reveal the underlying pattern of ideas and events. It is hoped that others will be inspired to investigate the Western European countries excluded from this project, and to examine comparable developments in other regions of the world.

This concluding chapter is organized on topical lines, as follows:

1   the historical context and the modernization of European economics;
2   tentative intra-European East–West comparisons;
3   economists and policy-making in the European institutions;
4   professionalization, public recognition and internationalization; and
5   is there a European economics?

The historical context and the modernization of European economics

The main general features and trends in the post-1945 development of economics in Western Europe include, firstly, a vast expansion in the number of qualified economists (however defined), and a dramatic growth of academic and other facilities for advanced training in the field (such as provided by universities, research institutes, philanthropic foundations, government departments, international organizations, central banks, private businesses, and so on).

Second, there has been a significant narrowing of the academic curriculum, including the relative decline of the European law school tradition of political economy and the squeezing out of such cognate subjects as politics, sociology, history and philosophy. This is part of a seemingly irresistible trend towards ever-greater specialization and division of labour within the discipline, based on a standardized intermediate-level foundation of macro- and microeconomics.

Third, this trend has been accompanied (and in some cases preceded) by the increasing mathematization of economic ideas, models and theories, and by the emphasis on quantification (for example, in the rise of econometrics) and the employment of sophisticated statistical methods.

To some critics, the undeniable gains in precision, logic and technique have been achieved at the expense of the economist's general education and intellectual flexibility and, more specifically, his or her ability to contribute to policy-making and other forms of service to society.

Fourth, within the academic community there has been a growing professionalization; for instance, in the enhanced importance attached to formal credentials, publications in refereed national or international journals and membership in (and the receipt of honours from) national and international scholarly and scientific organizations.

Fifth, as noted at the outset, the extent and timing of these developments have varied considerably as between the various European countries – for example, in the adoption of ideas and practices derived from American graduate schools. How far a general process of Americanization has been at work in European economics is a more controversial matter (see below, p. 252).

Sixth, at the risk of oversimplification, the countries featured in the project can be subdivided into three groups, according to the degree of modernization of their economics, both academic and professional (including non-academic), achieved by the 1990s.[3]

> Group 1: the Netherlands, Sweden, the United Kingdom, Belgium and Germany.
>
> All five drew upon strong prewar doctrinal and disciplinary developments – with Belgium the weakest of the group. Belgium and the UK were late in modernizing after World War II, and so too was Germany, for obvious reasons.
>
> Group 2: Italy, France.
>
> These are intermediate cases, both with strong pre- and postwar intellectual traditions (in the French *Ecoles*, and in Italy the doctrine of economic liberalism). However, both were only partly modernized, as shown by the survival of the French law school tradition of political economy and the weakness of advanced training in Italy.
>
> Group 3: Spain, Portugal, Greece.
>
> These are the most interesting cases, in view of their generally backward prewar and early postwar condition. Of the three, Greece was the last to modern-

ize its economics, but all were held back by the incomplete economic, social and political development of the national economy and society. Even so, the pre-modern state corporatist system provided an institutional framework within which modern industrialism (Fordism) developed in Southern Europe, evolving into a corporate–liberal synthesis as each country's economy, polity and society became more closely involved in the international system.[4]

Seventh, generally speaking, economists tend to avoid close examination of the non-economic aspects of the process of historical change,[5] largely because these matters are so much less amenable to mathematical modelling and statistical measurement. Yet they recognize that the economic and social system does not exist in a vacuum.[6] Within any of the countries in our sample, and as between the three groups, it is clear that the economists' work is directly affected by differences in the prevailing societal beliefs, norms and ways of doing things. The significance of socio-cultural development, institutions, rules and regulations within an economic system derives from their role in socializing patterns of behaviour. Socio-economic laws and regulations change over time and are derived from historically specific conditions. In a manner somewhat akin to ideology, the culture provides criteria by which to evaluate the formulation and implementation of economic and social policy. Explanations in terms of 'interests' are unsatisfactory, if only because 'interests' are frequently ill defined, conflict with one another and to some extent cancel one another out.[7]

Eighth, general social and cultural attitudes towards intellectuals, professionals and experts have directly affected the development of economics in Western Europe, although no comparative study of these matters has been attempted in this volume. In some countries economists and other social scientists are still regarded as a strange new breed, to be treated much as natural scientists and technologists. This, it may be hazarded, has been less true of the countries listed in Group 1 than of those in Groups 2 and 3, for in traditional humanistic cultures the educational system has generally been less well equipped to provide the necessary resources and training facilities for social scientists. Those who do obtain the requisite qualifications may have found that their rewards, roles and status are inferior to those of personnel trained in more traditional subjects. This is one reason why the experience of study in the USA or in the UK has made a disproportionate impact on the development of an indigenous (that is, national or Europe-wide) economics profession.[8]

Tentative intra-European East–West comparisons

A fascinating contrasting perspective on the development of economics in Western Europe since 1945 has recently been provided in the large-scale research study of *Economic Thought in Communist and Post-Communist Europe,* organized by Hans-Jurgen Wagener.[9] In this project attention was focused on 'the theory of the economic system and its mechanism'; that is, on 'the cognitive prehistory of transformation and the first years of its proper history', rather than on the 'understanding of practical policy measures and evaluating them in the light of the theories discussed'.[10] In this context, Wagener explains, the Eastern economist's task was the essentially practical one of 'bringing his professional competence in line with the ideological doctrine prescribed, of keeping *à jour* with all the vacillations of party politics, and finally, of contributing his share to the long-term evolution of a more rational economic system'.[11]

How far this involved restrictions on intellectual and professional freedom depended on the national regime under which the economists worked and, to a lesser extent, on its evolution over time. The most restrictive was the GDR, whereas the Polish and Hungarian regimes were much more flexible. Economic thinking was not static, for there was a considerable feedback between economic ideas and system development. Unlike their Western counterparts, the Eastern economists were obliged to start with an imposed, transnational model, albeit one that could be (and was) modified intellectually (that is, 'reformed') under changing historical circumstances and political exigencies.[12] There were great differences in the extent to which economists in the various countries were familiar with, or had access to, Western economic ideas.[13] When asked about their indebtedness to particular schools of thought, the Hungarian economists gave priority to Keynesianism, followed by institutionalism, neoclassical economics, monetarism, Marxism, and the work of Janos Kornai, probably the most widely respected East European economist. Austrian economics received a single mention. Among Czech economists the votes went mainly to Keynes and the neoclassicists, followed by institutionalism and monetarism. There were single acknowledgements to Marx, the Austrians, and the West German ordo-liberalist school. GDR economists were primarily self-referential, being insulated from outside ideas, whereas Russian respondents stated that they had no knowledge of other schools.[14]

Economists and policy making in the European institutions

The chapters in this volume have, admittedly, added comparatively little to our knowledge of the interrelationships between economic ideas and policies, or the economists' roles in policy-making, either at the national or the European level.[15] These are complex matters, on which there is unfortunately a serious dearth of detailed knowledge and research, so that generalization is hazardous. Nevertheless, there is a large literature on the nature of policy-making in the European Community institutions, organizations that have provided an enormous range and variety of new employment opportunities for economists and other specialists. This literature provides some useful general insights into the European policy-making process, and indications of the economist's role in it.

Students of postwar European economic integration generally acknowledge the primacy of political over economic forces driving the sequence of events. From the Marshall Plan onwards, major economic and institutional innovations were undertaken with a view to their contribution to eventual political unification, whether or not in the form of federal government. But it would be quite wrong to argue, as some observers have done, that the rise of new economic, political and social institutions took place at the expense of the nation states. On the contrary, while some of these states were close to disintegration in the early postwar years, they have subsequently been integral to the Europeanizing process. Actions by strong and intransigent leaders such as Charles de Gaulle and Margaret Thatcher, to cite two extreme examples, effectively checked the European movement, albeit only temporarily. More typically, as in the case of fiscal harmonization, it appears that

> almost all of the key moves (as well as crucial non-moves) . . . were made by national governments . . . at no time during the VAT episode did it appear that the [European] Commission was able to make any national government do anything that it did not want to do. . . .[Thus] the policy process in this VAT case was marked by the almost complete absence of the exertion of power in the traditional sense.
>
> (Puchala 1993: 256)

The European institutions are involved in a tremendous variety of activities, and there is 'no single neat pattern of policy making applicable to all case studies and to all policy areas' (Webb 1977: 28). To emphasize the importance of national governments in some instances:

> is not to deflate the importance of the Commission, but rather to place it in proper perspective. . . . [During the fiscal harmonization episode] the Commission mapped the technical terrain, injected ideas, socialized and mobilized experts, orchestrated positions, intermittently pushed and prodded governments (rather gently for the most part) and policed the system during the post-decisional phase. But policy decisions were clearly the prerogative of the national governments. The policy process stalled when governments failed to act, and it moved when they acted.[16]

'The European Community is a unique political system with an institutional structure displaying both 'intergovernmental' and 'supranational' traits. . . . None of the other Western European organizations can match the Community's authority because of its legal order, institutional capacity and policy reach' (Laffan 1992: 67, 70). Nevertheless, given the political weakness of its central institutions, much of the Commission's work necessarily proceeds by negotiation rather than by authoritarian control. Unlike the ministries in national governments, whose sphere of responsibility is clearly defined in principle (if not necessarily in practice), the nature of the game in the European context is unusually ambiguous, for the functioning of the Community policy process does not depend on the allocation of clearly defined tasks to particular institutions. The Commission and the Council of Ministers play 'different roles at different times as each issue presents a variety of management problems' (Wallace 1983: 65).

Economists tend, like political scientists, to favour functionalist explanations of policy-making and to emphasize the 'rationality' of the policy process; but comprehensive policy-making models are less helpful in studying Community policy-making than in national governments, because the Community's operations are weak in generating political choices. There is a continuing tension between the centrifugal forces of the Community and the centripetal forces of national governments. The latter are primarily interested in achieving short-term gains which can immediately be demonstrated to constituents at home, whereas the Commission 'can stand back from the politics of bargaining and . . . underpin the debate with detailed analysis' of the issues, as in regional policy (Wallace 1983: 160).

According to a well-known Whitehall dictum, 'economists should be on tap, but not on top', and this seems to be roughly true, *mutatis mutandis*, of their role in the European institutions. However strenuously economists have endeavoured to convert political difficulties into technical issues, it is politics that has ultimately mattered. In major policy areas like agricultural, budgetary and regional policies, the economists' preference for market solutions has never carried the crucial weight in European policy formation. On the other hand, in monetary policy, which has become increasingly important in recent years, the situation has usually been very different. As Rosenthal has argued: 'By the very reason of its technicality, economic and financial policy, on both national and international levels, falls automatically within the domain of a small highly trained group of experts in each country', not all of whom have of course been professional economists. As a result, there emerged 'an elaborate structure of highly technical committees and groups that inevitably involved a certain amount of overlapping membership' (Rosenthal 1975: 118–19).

Several commentators on the European movement have emphasized the inadequacies of the economists' intellectual apparatus, which ignores or takes insufficient account of many issues that figure prominently in national governments' agendas. Both the economists' theory of economic integration and their traditional theory of international trade 'are very misleading because both basically ignore the reality of mixed economies where state intervention is not limited to border controls or macroeconomic policy'.[17] As noted earlier, economists tend to exaggerate the rationality of the policy process.[18] In practice, national elites and transnational networks of policy-makers have acquired significant influence, while innumerable small groups, informal committees and lobbyists[19] contribute inputs of various kinds to policy discussions.[20] Indeed, the overall situation is so varied and complex that it is virtually impossible to isolate and evaluate the economists' role.

Professionalization, public recognition and internationalization

As one shrewd observer has remarked, 'an industrializing society is a professionalizing society' (Goode 1960: 902), and the studies in this volume provide substantial, albeit limited, evidence of the professionalization of economics in Western Europe since World War II, even in regions of late industrialization. Indeed, the variable pace and extent of industrialization helps to account for the differing pace and extent of professionalization in different countries. Unfortunately, there has been no systematic comparative research on this subject, for most of the existing literature has been focused primarily on the UK and the USA.

This is not the place to embark on a detailed analysis of the concept of professionalism, one of the more elusive in the social scientist's vocabulary. Any acceptable definition must have both static and dynamic elements – that is, it must combine a list of characteristics or 'traits', which differentiate the professionals from the laymen, with an account of the methods by which this differentiation has been achieved and sustained. Any profession has both an internal and an external dimension: that is, its members must be subjectively aware of themselves as professionals, and be recognized as such by those who use their services, and by the public at large. Recognition must be based on the possession of degrees, diplomas and qualifications which are not readily accessible to laymen, and it usually takes the form of specialized appointments, above average remuneration, delegation of responsibility or authority, and social esteem.[21]

There is abundant evidence of significant developments in both the internal and the external dimensions of the professionalization of economics in Western Europe, despite the absence of legal or other formal controls over qualifications and entry: for example, the dramatic, almost universal expansion of advanced training in economics, coupled with growing recognition of the importance of academic qualifications; the increasing specialization, technical content and narrowing scope of the discipline (e.g. *vis-à-vis* other social sciences, history, law and public administration); the formation of (usually non-exclusive) specialist societies and associations; the emergence of a network of publications catering to technically qualified economists and interested laymen; the increasingly international character of this literature; and the rising demand for economic expertise in a wide range of governmental and political positions, and private and public institutions, including international organizations. Indeed, the opportunities for economists to work for longer or shorter periods in the European institutions (or, for example, the OECD) demonstrate that their credentials have been acceptable internationally. Moreover, they have contributed to the rise of professional standards at home. Such links may have been especially important in the later modernizing European countries.

Is there a European economics?

This question has aroused considerable scholarly and professional interest during the past decade, ever since the publication of two controversial articles in the *European Economic Review* by Richard Portes, 'Economics in Europe' (1987), and Serge-Christophe Kolm, 'Economics in Europe and in the United States' (1988). This exchange was a prelude to a substantial symposium on the question, 'Is there a European economics?' in *Kyklos* (1995), edited by Bruno S. and René L. Frey, with contributions by fifteen European and American economists.

It seems appropriate to conclude this volume with a brief commentary on these publications, which contain many stimulating and provocative observations on economics in the two regions, although in fact they have a less direct bearing on our subject than might appear at first sight.

There are three basic differences between the Portes/Kolm/*Kyklos* discussions and the present volume:

1   This volume is essentially historical, whereas the recent discussions have focused on the state of economics in the late 1980s and early 1990s;
2   The country studies in this volume are based on systematic research, whereas the *Kyklos* symposium, in particular, consists of a series of (admittedly often fascinating) comments, conjectures, comparisons and impressions based on personal experiences. In no case, as several of the symposiasts acknowledge, are they derived from serious empirical, especially quantitative, research.
3   The Portes/Kolm/*Kyklos* contributions are particularly concerned with the question, how far has European economics become Americanized, or is becoming more so? This is only a secondary concern for the authors of the country studies.

According to Portes, 'It is perfectly reasonable to ask whether there is now any economics outside of, and independent of, the USA' (Portes 1987: 1330). American predominance in the discipline, he argues, is evident in, for example: the preponderance of recent American Nobel Prize winners; the location of major journals; the number of distinguished American economists; and the fact that 'most of the innovative ideas and developments in economics during the past forty years originated in the USA' (ibid., p. 1332). In order to bring European economics closer to American standards he recommended drastic changes in the training of European economists, an increase in the size of university departments, increased labour mobility, higher salaries and greater competition within the profession.

In his reply Kolm questioned Portes's statistics on the comparative productivity of European and American economists, and launched into an outspoken attack on the narrowness, over-specialization, trivialization and sheer intellectual ignorance evident in much American economics literature. Many, probably most, American economists needed a much broader knowledge of the social sciences, ethics, history, philosophy and so on, in order to produce good applied economics and sound policy advice (Kolm 1988, *passim*). The adoption of Portes's recommendations would, according to Kolm, involve the imposition of a destructive American 'abysmal unculture' on the European system (ibid., p. 209).

It is easy to understand why this exchange, despite (or perhaps because of?) its extremism and polarization, inspired the editors of the *Kyklos* symposium.[22] Any brief summary of that substantial document must necessarily involve oversimplification; nevertheless, the major themes were that, by contrast with European economics, American economics is characterized by:

1   greater proneness to fashion and intolerance of heterodox ideas;
2   greater homogeneity across economics departments, at least in research-orientated universities;
3   more highly developed graduate education programmes;
4   greater emphasis on technique and less emphasis on applied theory;
5   less hierarchical organization of departments, with individuals free to pursue independent research at a much earlier stage;
6   more competitive labour markets and higher mobility;
7   less involvement in public policy debates; and
8   lower status of academics in society.[23]

Of course such sweeping generalizations cannot take adequate account of the variety of institutions and professional conditions in either continent. Admittedly, the American Economic Association's Commission on Graduate Education in Economics revealed the remarkable degree of homogeneity in the core courses taught in the USA (cf. points 2–4 in the preceding list), but such courses do not, by themselves, characterize the entire department in which they are taught, let alone the entire profession. Yet more of the symposiasts' remarks focused on the academic features of the American situation (whether or not they approved of Americanization), and paid comparatively little attention to the non-economic dimensions (points 7 and 8 above).[24]

The country studies published herein provide considerable indications of the spread of American ideas, techniques and educational practices in European universities, and undoubtedly many European economists welcome this trend as an integral part of the modernization and internationalization of their discipline, even though it is widely held that American graduate programmes unduly emphasize abstract theory, mathematization and advanced quantitative methods. These are undoubtedly important, but they are not the whole of economics. The Americanization of core elements in European economists' training does not entail the disappearance of a distinctive European economics, either now or in the future. The sheer scale and resources, not to mention the quality, of American economics since World War II makes it inconceivable that any country's economics can be fully 'independent' of American influence. Nevertheless, European economics is still remarkably diverse, not least because in each country it is embedded in a distinctive social, political and cultural context. Economics is not a universal science, at least in its totality, despite the illusion widely held by many (usually American) academic economists. And this is especially true when we consider applied economics and the economists' role in public policy.[25]

Notes

1 In the original plan of this project papers from Hungary and Poland were promised, but did not materialize. For comments on the work of Hans-Jurgen Wagener and his associates on Eastern Europe, see *infra*, p. 247.
2 A brief, highly selective review of the country studies is provided *supra*, p. 12 onward.

3 The first four items listed above at the beginning of this section can be taken to constitute the main features of modernized economics.
4 This is persuasively argued in Holman (1996, especially pp.16–18, 27–9, 66–7).
5 In surveys of national differences in economists' attitudes towards specific theoretical
and economic policy issues the 'culture' tends to be treated, if at all, as a residual
explanatory variable. For example,

> a major cause for dissension [among economists] are the differences in views between the
> economists in the five countries surveyed, attributable to the differences in culture and
> history as well as to the current economic and political conditions. Economists have had var-
> ying experiences with respect to the economic policies practiced in their countries, and there-
> fore have different points of reference.
>
> (Frey *et al*, 1984: 994)

As far as I am aware, there have been no systematic comparative studies of public attitudes towards economics as a discipline and/or profession comparable to those undertaken with respect to science. See, for example, Topf (1993).
6 The rest of the paragraph is based on Plaschke (1994, especially pp.116, 122). He provides an illuminating account of the differences in the French and German national
cultures, and their effects on the early postwar European movement (ibid., pp.
126–40).
7 For discussion of this point, see Coats (1997: 340–1).
8 The British case is unusual, for despite the country's distinguished contribution to the
development of economic thought (science), the culture of higher education did not
facilitate the advance of modern professional economics. See, for example, the initially slow growth in the number of economists in government since World War II.
Coats (1981: chaps 1 and 2). Hall (1989: *passim*) provides a variety of examples of the
cultural and other resistances to the spread of Keynesian ideas in Europe.
9 Wagener (1998). The countries covered are Russia, Hungary, Czechoslovakia, East
Germany (GDR), Poland and Yugoslavia.
10 Ibid., p.6.
11 Ibid., p.2.
12 Marxist economists might well claim that the so-called modernization of Western economics involved an increasing convergence towards the predominant form of liberal-
capitalist market ideology. They would, of course, completely reject the widely held
Western academic claim that economics is a positive, ideologically neutral science.
13 Education was on orthodox lines in all the countries, and young students encountered
other schools of thought only in courses on the history of economics or the political
economy of capitalism. Some of the Hungarian and Polish economists in Wagener's
sample had studied in the USA and were hostile to ideological indoctrination. They
pressed for curricular reform, but with very little success. (Wagener 1998: 20). It was
said that a citation in a Western economic journal was considered dangerous for an
East German economist, but regarded as an honour in Hungary (Wagener 1997: 184).
14 Ibid., p. 172.
15 The country studies provide numerous examples of prominent policy positions occupied by economists.
16 Puchala (1977) *loc.cit*. As noted earlier (p. 004), it is often the economic and technical
issues that dominate the actual negotiations.
17 Tsoukalis (1993: 78). See also ibid., pp. 28, 80, 93–4, 229–30. For further criticism of
orthodox economic analysis, see the various contributions to Baldassari and Mundell
(1993) by James Meade, p.21; Robert Mundell, p.86; and Richard Eckhaus, p.86.
18 Webb (1977: 9): the functionalist approach is congenial to economists: 'because it
emphasizes rationality and assigns considerable weight to experts. Issues are suppos-
edly divisible into technical and political categories, and some scholars divide bureau-
crats likewise. Economists like to think of themselves as apolitical.'

19 Unlike the situation in national governments, the Commission's staff cultivate relations with special interests. Functional legitimacy linked to expertise is vital, whereas democratic representation and legitimacy are not (Andersen and Eliassen (1993: 43).

20   'High politics and major initiatives like monetary union or common foreign policy may be reserved for meetings of national leaders but a great deal of everyday policy, unspectacular in itself but cumulatively of great importance, comes out of the Commission's directorates and their consultations with European interest groups and individual departments within national governments.'

Keating (1993: 381)

21 For extensive discussion and analysis of the development of the economics profession, see essays 21–3 in Coats (1993: 395–473).
22 It is clear from the first footnote in Kolm's article that the *European Economic Review's* editor was embarrassed by its tone and content, for he publicly expressed doubts as to whether it should be printed. The *Review* refused to publish further discussions of this general topic.
23 Adapted from Backhouse (1999).
24 In practice the symposiasts were probably more familiar with the elite economics departments in the USA, rather than with less prestigious institutions. (However, the force of this argument is reduced to the extent that the curricula and criteria of success are uniform.)
25 Some of the *Kyklos* symposiasts contended that European economists were faced with more challenging problems than their American counterparts, such as the processes of integration, European Union enlargement, European monetary unification, public sector retrenchment, privatizations, the transition of former socialist economies and the problems of small open economies. The intimate relations between economics and politics might also be mentioned. Indeed, it is not inconceivable that European economics will in future have considerable influence on American economics.

References

Andersen, Svein S. and Elaissen, Kjell A. (eds) (l993) 'Complex policy-making: lobbying the EC', in S. S. Andersen and K. A. Elaissen, *Making Policy in Europe. The Europeification of National Policy Making*, London: Sage, pp.35–53.
Backhouse, Roger E. (1999) 'Economics in mid-Atlantic: British Economics, 1945–95', in this volume.
Baldassari, Mario and Mundell, Robert (eds) (1993) *Building the New Europe*, vol. 1, *The Single Market and Monetary Unification*, London: Macmillan, St Martin's Press.
Coats, A. W. (ed.) (1981) *Economists in Government: An International Comparative Study*, Durham, NC: Duke University Press.
——(1993) *The Sociology and Professionalization of Economics: British and American Economic Essays*, vol. II, London: Routledge.
——(ed.) (1997) *The Post-1945 Internationalization of Economics*, Durham, NC: Duke University Press.
Eckhaus, R. (1993) 'Some lessons from developed economies for South and East Europe', in M. Baldassari and R. Mundell (eds), *Building the New Europe*, vol. 1, London: Macmillan, St. Martin's Press, pp. 143–67.
Frey, B. S. and Frey, R. L. (eds) (1995) 'Is there a European economics?' *Kyklos* 48: 185–311.
Frey, Bruno S., Pommerehne, Werner W., Schneider, Friedrich and Gilbert, Guy (1984) 'Consensus and dissension among economists: an empirical enquiry', *American Economic Review* 74 (5): 986–94.
Goode, W. T. (l960) 'Encroachment, charlatanism and the emerging profession: psychology, sociology, medicine', *American Sociological Review* 25: 902–14.

Hall, Peter (1989) *The Political Power of Economic Ideas: Keynesianism across Nations*, Princeton, NJ: Princeton University Press.

Holman, Otto (1996) *Integrating Southern Europe: EC Expansion and the Transnationalization of Spain*, London: Routledge.

Keating, Michael (1993) *The Politics of Modern Europe: The State and Political Authority in the Major Democracies*, Cheltenham, UK: Edward Elgar.

Kolm, Serge-Christophe (1988) 'Economics in Europe and in the United States', *European Economic Review* 31: 207–12.

Krauss, M. B. (ed.) (1993) *The Economics of Integration*, London: Allen and Unwin.

Laffan, Brigid (1992) *Integration and Cooperation in Europe*, London: Routledge.

Meade, James (1993) 'The building of the new Europe: national diversity versus continental uniformity', in M. Baldassari and R. Mundell (eds), *Building the New Europe*, vol. 1, London: Macmillan, St Martin's Press, pp. 19–70.

Mundell, Robert (1993) 'Monetary policies for the new Europe', in M. Baldassari and R. Mundell, *Building the New Europe*, vol. 1, London: Macmillan, St Martin's Press, pp. 71–88.

Plaschke, H. (1994) 'National economic cultures and economic integration', in S. Zetterholm (ed.), *National Cultures and Economic Integration*, Oxford and Providence, RI: Berg, pp. 113–43.

Portes, Richard (1987) 'Economics in Europe', *European Economic Review* 31: 1329–40.

Puchala, D. J. (1983) 'Worm cans and worth taxes: fiscal harmonization and the European policy process', in H. Wallace, W. W. Wallace and C. Webb (eds), *Policy-making in the European Communities*, London: Wiley, 237–64.

Rhodes, R. A. W., Bache, Ian and George, Stephen (1996) 'Policy networks and policymaking in the European Union: a critical appraisal', in Lisbet Hooghe (ed.) *Cohesion Policy and European Integration: Building Multi-level Government*, Oxford: Oxford University Press.

Rosenthal, Glenda G. (1975) *The Men Behind the Decisions: Cases in European Policymaking*, Lexington, MA: D. C. Heath.

Topf, Richard (1993) 'Advice to governments – some theoretical and practical problems', in B. Guy Peters and Anthony Barker (eds) *Advising Western European Governments. Inquiries, Expertise, and Public Policy*, Edinburgh: Edinburgh University Press, pp.182–98.

Tsoukalis, Loukas (1993) *The New European Economy: The Politics and Economics of Integration*, Oxford: Oxford University Press.

Wagener, H-J. (1997) 'Second thoughts? Economics and economists under socialism', *Kyklos* 50:165–87.

——(ed.) (1998) *Economic Thought in Communist and Post-Communist Europe*, London: Routledge.

Wallace, Helen, Wallace, William W. and Webb, Carole (eds) (1983) *Policy-making in the European Communities*, London: Wiley.

Wallace, H. (1983) 'National bulls in the china shop: the role of national governments in community policy making', in H. Wallace, W. W. Wallace and C. Webb (eds), *Policy-making in the European Communities*, London: Wiley, pp. 33–68.

——(1983) 'The establishment of the Regional Development Fund: common policy or pork barrel?' in H. Wallace, W. W. Wallace and C. Webb (eds), *Policy-making in the European Communities*, London: Wiley, pp. 137–64.

Webb, Carole (1983) 'Introduction: variations on a theoretical theme', in H. Wallace, W. W. Wallace and C. Webb (eds), *Policy-making in the European Communities*, London: Wiley, pp. 1–31.

Zetterholm, Staffan (ed.) (1994) *National Cultures and Economic Integration*, Oxford and Providence, RI: Berg.

Index